The Challenge of Cultural Heritage and Identity for Inclusive and Open Societies

INTERKULTURELLE PÄDAGOGIK
UND POSTKOLONIALE THEORIE

Herausgegeben von / Edited by
Heike Niedrig und / and Louis Henri Seukwa

BAND 10

PETER LANG

Louis Henri Seukwa / Elina Marmer /
Cornelia Sylla (eds.)

The Challenge of Cultural Heritage and Identity for Inclusive and Open Societies

Young People's Perspectives from European and Asian Countries

PETER LANG

Bibliographic Information published by the Deutsche Nationalbibliothek
The Deutsche Nationalbibliothek lists this publication in the Deutsche Nationalbibliografie; detailed bibliographic data is available in the internet at http://dnb.d-nb.de.

Library of Congress Cataloging-in-Publication Data
A CIP catalog record for this book has been applied for at the Library of Congress.

Funded by the EU Horizon 2020 Framework Programme
for Research and Innovation

ISSN 1867-626X
ISBN 978-3-631-86446-3 (Print)
E-ISBN 978-3-631-87242-0 (E-PDF)
E-ISBN 978-3-631-87243-7 (EPUB)
DOI 10.3726/b19410

Peter Lang – Berlin · Bruxelles · Lausanne · New York · Oxford

This publication has been peer reviewed.

www.peterlang.com

Table of contents

(by Louis Henri Seukwa)

Introduction

Choir of the marginalized (very quietly, only heard in the background as a slight murmur):
I want a place where I can feel comfortable.
A place where I can do something with others.
Where I can get inspired by what the others do,
I want that place and what is happening there to be inspiring.
I want it to be a place where we can hang out together. And suddenly someone has an idea and says: Let's do it.
I would like - very specifically - to be satisfied with the people who surround us there.
I want there to be a lot of free space and material to create this place always new and temporarily and differently.

Haschemi, Meyer & Rotter, 2017, in: Kulturelle Bildung im Kontext Asyl. Ein Dossier. Berlin (Cultural Education in the Context of Asylum. Translated by authors)

Background

A common conception of European identity is that it is constructed around values like liberty, democracy, international integration, and human rights. These values, however, appear to be threatened by recent political developments. Neo-nationalist movements are on the rise in almost all European countries and beyond. According to Bergmann (2020), who thoroughly analysed this phenomenon, in the post-war era, and especially after 1989, there seemed to be no ideological space for overt nationalism and nativism until these dramatically emerged more recently:

> *Three decades on, however, we now know that the story was not to be that rosy or that simple. The promise of 1989, of ever-increasing and globally spreading liberal democracy, did not materialize. Despite the multicultural and integrationist response to devastations of the two world wars, nationalism was still always an undercurrent in the post-war years, though perhaps mostly dormant at first.* (ibid.: 6)

The spread of new information technology has led to globalisation and further polarisation of cultural discourses. Social media platforms make all kinds of information available to almost everybody without clearly distinguishing factual from nonfactual, or scientific evidence-based realities from so-called fake news (manipulative fabrications created to raise fear or hatred, among other reasons). This makes political participation seemingly more accessible but at the same time more difficult to fully comprehend. Populist parties all over the world offer simplistic answers to perceived problems, creating the need for mainstream parties to "follow suit in the wake of the populists" (ibid.: 14), which leads to the general erosion of democratic values in politics.

From a postcolonial perspective, the very construct of Europe as being based on human rights and international integration has been fundamentally questioned. Theorists like Césaire (1955) and Fanon (1961) argued that, historically, notions of liberal and democratic Europe have been deeply intertwined with colonialism, racism and discrimination. Rommelspacher (2002: 175) terms the contradiction between Europe's democratic ideals and its exclusivist and discriminatory reality the "European dilemma". The liberal nation-state was never conceived to integrate all members of society into its concept of égalité. For instance, the French Declaration of the Rights of Man, written in the 18th century, was specifically created for white men; at the same time, the Code Noir regulated the treatment of enslaved and free Black people, as well as Jewish people.[1] Europe was still the coloniser of large parts of the world at the time of the Universal Declaration of Human Rights in 1948, and European democracy has always been rooted in nationalistic concepts as much as it is tied to the idea of nation states and borders. Even today, Europe is a major contributor to the production of global structural inequality, and its migration politics are "de facto in contradiction to the ethical consensuses formulated by the Universal Declaration of Human Rights or even EU Charter of Fundamental Rights" (Seukwa, 2018). From this point of view, current developments are far less surprising. They are just a new configuration of a historical tradition characterised by the self-referential narrative of Europe as having universal cultures and values. Fanon denounced this tradition when he wrote:

> *Leave this Europe where they are never done talking of Man, yet murder men everywhere they find them, at the corner of every one of their own streets, in all the corners of the globe. For centuries, Europe has stopped the progress of other men and enslaved them to its own*

---

1 Le Code Noir ou recueil des reglements rendus jusqu'a present (Paris: Prault, 1767) [1980 reprd. by the Societé d'Histoire de la Guadeloupe]. Translated by John Garrigus:https://web.archive.org/web/20150619233008/https://directory.vancouver.wsu.edu/sites/directory.vancouver.wsu.edu/files/inserted_files/webintern02/code%20noir.pdf.

designs and glory; for centuries, in the name of a so-called "spiritual adventure", it has suffocated almost all of humanity. (Fanon, 1961: 371)

One common feature of nationalistic discourses and narratives across the European continent and beyond is the appropriation of "culture" for purposes of division and exclusion. An illustrative example of this is the current debate on separatism in France, which began in mid-2020; for this purpose, the government officially launched a campaign against so-called 'Islamo-leftism'. This term, used by the Ministry of Higher Education and Research, refers to an imagined conspiracy against France fomented from within by traitors to the nation. The identified traitors named by the French President Emmanuel Macron in a speech on 2nd October 2020 are academics, *"children of the Republic, sometimes from elsewhere, children or grandchildren of citizens today of immigrant origin from the Maghreb, from sub-Saharan Africa, revisiting their identity through a post-colonial or anti-colonial discourse"* (Macron, 2020). The philosopher Nadia Yala Kisukidi analysed this statement as follows:

> *Attacks against postcolonial and decolonial studies are open attacks on academics who are perceived as exogenous elements of the nation and whose work is concerned with dismantling or analysing the forms of inequality and domination that structure contemporary postcolonial France. They are clearly labelled as enemies not even from within but from without (Maghreb, sub-Saharan Africa), despite their belonging to the republic, to whom France, victim of its generosity, would have attributed too much space by leaving the doors of republican meritocracy wide open.* (Yala Kisukidi, 2021)

Such heated debates about nation and identity assign specific importance to "culture", and have accorded the word with a whole new meaning. In the aftermath of World War Two and the Nazi regime, racism based on assumed biological hierarchies became increasingly discredited. This type of racism was gradually replaced by the concept of inherent group "culture" and the assumption of insurmountable "cultural differences" between groups. This turn to the irrevocability of cultural differences is a form of neo-racism that Balibar (2004) and Hall (1994) call "racism without races". Old and new narratives of cultural difference are booming worldwide. Dominant political actors in many countries strive to establish the "culture" of the respective dominant group (conceptualised as ethnic, religious or both) as essentially the national and, hence, the normative culture. This leads to demanding assimilation from those who are conceived to be "culturally different" – migrant communities, marginalised religious and lingual groups, etc. Understanding of what actually constitutes "culture" can be diffuse in such a context, but it is assumed to be inherited, rather homogenous, unchangeable, and profoundly important for social cohesion and peaceful coexistence within the borders of a nation state. In reality, however, full assimilation is not even an option for many racialised minorities, who are perceived as different as long as they are visible. This pressure on marginalised groups often leads to their re- and self-ethnicisation, and to the revival of traditionalist and sometimes exclusionist identities (Ha, 2000). These trends reflect struggles for cultural interpretation and legitimisation and, thanks to the social and political tensions they foster, endanger social cohesion in several countries. Yet there is also another, parallel trend: in-between spaces are being appropriated by young people who refuse to be reduced to a fixed traditionalist and exclusionist cultural identity. Instead, they seek allies across 'cultural' groups to create new hybridities and innovative cultural productions, which appear, perhaps unintentionally, to be a form of resistance to monolithic and exclusionist perceptions of culture (Harris, 2009). In these "third spaces" (Bhabha, 1994), cultural identities can be formed and reformed, giving "rise to something different, something new and unrecognizable, a new area of negotiation of meaning and representation" (211).

It is in this context that the transnational cooperative research project 'Cultural Heritage and Identities of Europe's Future' (CHIEF) identified the need to enhance cultural literacy among young people to give them a more inclusive understanding of culture. The CHIEF project studied different forms of youth cultural education in different countries with the aim of analysing how and why perceptions of cultural identity are developed by young people in Europe and beyond.

Therefore, a consortium of nine international research teams was created, made up of three 'old' EU countries – UK, Spain and Germany; three 'new' ones – Slovakia, Croatia and Latvia; and three countries outside the EU or Europe – Georgia, India and Turkey. This consortium was set up to conduct a transnational collaborative research project as part of the Frame of European Commission's Horizon 2020 Programme. The CHIEF project lasted for 42 months, from May 2018 to October 2021, and was executed by 10 international partner institutions:

- Aston University, United Kingdom, project lead
- Culture Coventry, United Kingdom
- Daugavpils Universitate, Latvia
- Institut Drustvenih Znanosti Ivo Pilar, Croatia
- Caucasus Research Resource Centers, Georgia
- Mimar Sinan Fine Arts University, Turkey
- Universidad Pompeu Fabra, Spain
- Univerzita Komenskeho V Bratislave, Slovakia
- The Savitribai Phule Pune University, India
- Hochschule Fuer Angewandte Wissenschaften HAW Hamburg, Germany

In all nine countries, a re-nationalisation shift can be observed, albeit on different levels. The UK, one of the 'old' EU countries at the time when the project proposal was drafted, is harvesting the most serious of consequences by, in 2021, becoming the first country to leave the European Union. In the Catalan region of Spain, where the Spanish research was carried out and where separatism and nationalism are historically rooted in the left, the drive for political independence from Madrid led to a major political crisis in 2017. The right-wing extremist party AfD has been represented in the German *Bundestag* (Federal Parliament) since 2017, as well as in all 16 *Länder* governments, and has a tight grip on the mainstream discourse formation in the country. A similar trend can be observed in Eastern European countries. Slovakia's current PM (in April 2021) is widely considered a right-wing hardliner. In Croatia, the mainstream conservative party has adopted the discourses of the extreme right to some extent, while the rising radicalisation of young people has been observed in the context of football hooliganism. In Latvia, nationalistic citizenship and language politics aiming at marginalisation, especially of Russian speakers, are turning a historically multicultural and multilingual country into a de jure monolingual state. Such ethnonationalism has been commonly observed across almost all post-USSR countries.

Our aforementioned approaches to conceptualise nationalistic trends are centred on Europe; however, we are not dealing with a purely European phenomenon, as the situation with our non-European project partners looks similarly grim. Far-right narratives have been able to gain mainstream legitimacy in post-Soviet Georgia; they are not openly condemned by the ruling party and are supported by the Georgian Orthodox Church. Meanwhile, in the aftermath of the 2016 coup d'état attempt, a nationalistic Islamist regime is being consolidated in Turkey, with a no-tolerance policy towards the opposition. Finally, the government of India, a classical example of a pluralistic and diverse nation, is redefining Hindu nationalism and encouraging the violent exclusion of Muslims in the form of a 2020 citizenship law.

Though their political and historical contexts might differ, each country involved in the research project is clearly experiencing a rise in nationalism and populism, a rightward shift in mainstream discourses, and increasing exclusionist rhetoric and actions aimed at marginalised groups. These tensions tend to be constructed around ethnicity, religion, language and, inevitably, 'culture'.

Key concepts, research objectives and methodology

Untangling the various meanings of 'culture' and the constructs of 'cultural identity' and 'cultural heritage', which are implicitly and/or explicitly used by the dominant as well as counter-discourses, is crucial to making sense of the recent developments described above. Therefore, a theoretical discussion on the various definitions of "culture" is the starting point for our conceptual framework.

Culture

Based on the definition by Verdery (1999: 34), we see culture as a performative concept. Culture can thus be everything that people define as such, every action that is led by values or ideas considered meaningful by an individual. Moreover, we argue that broadly-applied "traditional" ethnological and anthropological concepts of "culture" are deeply rooted in colonial discourses on European/Western superiority and serve to segregate and hierarchise groups, be it in terms of ethnicity, race, religion, ability, gender, or any other category. Appropriated in different national and political contexts, such concepts legitimise ethnocentrism and ideas of nationalist superiority. We present a postcolonial critique of these concepts, along with notions of culture, identity and heritage as being fluid, interconnected and continuous. In our view, postcolonial as well as post-structuralist approaches to culture (which became prominent through the emergence of Cultural Studies) are better suited as a base for the development of more inclusive concepts of cultural education. A more inclusive understanding of identification processes can empower young people to resist nationalistic trends and the accompanying dehumanisation of and discrimination against all those who are considered to deviate from dominant "cultural" norms.

Concepts of culture – relevant dimensions

In a very broad and basic definition, culture can be seen as everything created by humans. Therefore, culture is often understood in opposite to nature, this being one of the binaries on which so-called Western conceptions of culture are often based. However, as Mbembe (2015) argues, especially in the view of the ongoing environmental destruction and rapid climate change, there is an urgent need to recognise that human history is entangled with multiple other entities and species, and therefore "the dualistic partitions of […] nature from culture can no longer hold" (n.p.).

The culture-nature dualism is complemented with other binaries, such as *civilized* vs. *primitive*, *modern* vs. *traditional*, and *high* vs. *mass* culture. In fact, the initial purpose of ethnology and anthropology – disciplines that study culture(s) – was to classify groups of people considered inherently culturally distinct. "Anthropology emerged from the colonial expansion of Europe" (Lewis, 1973); cultural binaries (re)produced a certain hierarchy in favour of the Western anthropologist, who would most likely associate her or himself with the "civilized", "modern" and "high" culture.

These binary and mutually exclusive concepts of culture have been refuted by post-structuralist approaches, which understand culture not as a stable and fixed entity but rather as open and fluid, always in motion – an ever-unfolding process. Such approaches suggested that assumptions about "pure and uncontaminated" cultures needed to be questioned as well (Chattopadhyay, 2017).

With his notion of *hybridity*, Homi Bhabha brought a postcolonial perspective to post-structuralist concepts (Bhabha, 1994). In Bhabha's view, culture is characterised by its mixedness and interconnectedness; he dismantled the concept of cultural hierarchy, as established by European colonisers, that legitimised colonialism as *mission civilisatrice*. Taking this concept further, Appiah (2018) lays out what he calls a "more cosmopolitan picture in which every element of culture – from philosophy or cuisine to the style of bodily movements – is separable in principle from all the others" (ibid.: 207). Here, "all cultural practises and objects [are] mobile; they like to spread; and almost all are themselves creations of intermixture" (ibid.: 208). Culture can thus be understood as a melting pot with new, transformative elements constantly added; we can fashion our own cultural identities by mixing those elements that the world offers us. Viewed as a dynamic process of transformation, cultural identity offers subjects more agency to shape themselves than a "straight jacket of national identity" (Chattopadhyay, 2017).

This melting pot can be further conceptualised by the vision of *radical diversity* (Perko and Czollek, 2020), which aims at absolutely equal recognition of multiple and radically diverse identities. It calls for resisting the integration paradigm of *dominance culture* (and national identity), which is based on othering and produces exclusion and discrimination (Rommelspacher, 1995).

Cultural identity

We use the term cultural identity to describe individual and group-based representations of, and references to, certain *cultural heritage*, historical discourse, and social differences.

Hall introduces the term *cultural identification* as a process that is not arbitrary but *constructed on the back of a recognition of some common origin or shared characteristics with another person or group, or with an ideal, and with the natural closure of solidarity and allegiance established on this foundation.* (Hall, 1996: 2)

Identification, understood as a process of the construction of subjectivity and identity, is thus historicised and situated in particular contexts (ibid.):

Identities are never unified and, in late modern times, increasingly fragmented and fractured; never singular but multiply constructed across different, often intersecting and antagonistic, discourses, practices and positions. They are subject to a radical historicization and are constantly in the process of change and transformation. (ibid.: 4)

The discursive processes of cultural identification were examined by Dannenbeck (2002) in his study of German youth with a so-called *migration background* – or what we would rather call *migrantized* (El-Tayeb, 2015: 15)[2] youth – by making the interview process itself the subject of analysis. Dannenbeck looked on the interview as a space of an ongoing struggle for meaning, constant shifts in (cultural) positions, and as interactive cultural identity-work engaged in by all parties involved, including the interviewer. He suggests that the type of *identity crisis* commonly attributed to these particular youth could just as well be produced by the essentialist framework of the researchers themselves, by the way they posed their questions and reacted at young people's answers (Dannenbeck, 2002).

Culture and power

In Bauman's (1999: 98) view, culture is a social praxis of structuring the world in order to create a stable frame of reference for human actions. Despite being a product of active construction, the social order produced by culture seems solid to the point that it can orient people (Kron and Reddig, 2011: 452). Though it can enable human action, culture also has the limitation of strongly determining the ways in which people see and operate in the world. Bauman, therefore, sees culture as ambivalent, having both an enabling and a limiting effect (ibid.: 453). Due to unequal power relations, not everyone gets to change their position in the social order; therefore, culture and power are interlinked (ibid.: 455).

Power and its role in defining culture and constructing cultural identities is central to poststructuralist and postcolonial thought. For instance, Cultural Studies focuses on studying "the politics of those who claim dominant culture"

2 Considering "children and grandchildren of migrants of color as second and third generation migrants and not first or second generation citizens" is what El-Tayeb (2015: 15) defines as migrantisation.

(Spivak, 2000: 14). This highlights the value of researching everyday or ordinary culture, but also questions the social demarcation between *high* and *mass/popular* culture. For bell hooks, it is "the *popular* culture where the pedagogy is" because of popular culture's global impact on how people learn about race, gender or class and the politics of difference (hooks, 1997). Social inequality, power and violence, especially *symbolic violence*, are central to the work of Bourdieu and Passeron (1977). They argue that symbolic violence is transmitted through culture, i.e. through the symbolic dimensions of social life like worldviews and mainstream discourses, and that educational institutions play a key role in maintaining domination.

Cultural divisions run along multiple lines. For instance, notions of *high* culture serve to secure cultural spaces for the elites in a society (Bourdieu, 2010), regarding the culture of the rest as *popular/mass* culture and hence as less distinct or worthy by default. Notions of *dominant national culture* are meant to define national identity and belonging in opposition to the culture of the Other, which is considered less developed, less modern, less democratic, etc. The ideas behind *dominance culture* – so-called Germanness, Britishness, or Europeanness – combine elements of both *high* and *popular* cultures. Beyond conceptions of taste and aesthetics, they also include customs, traditions, values and manners. While *high* culture determines the division of class, *national/regional* culture often uses ideas of race (and ethnicity) to assign belonging and non-belonging. In both hierarchies and at their intersection, the effects of inclusion or exclusion reach far beyond the symbolic cultural sphere; they have real-life consequences for people's rights, wellbeing and even lives. For instance, the discrimination against those labelled as *culturally different:* Cinti and Roma, African descendants, Jews and Muslims, etc. It is this kind of discrimination that led to an inhumane European refugee policy. Every day people are dying at European boarders, every day mostly African refugees die in the Mediterranean Sea trying to reach them but not being saved.

The song "Non siamo pesci" by the young Nigerian-Italian singer Chris Obehi, who survived the dangerous clandestine sea journey,[3] is a contemporary example of cultural production in third spaces (Bhabha, 1994) as a form of resistance against dehumanisation: his message is "we are not fish, we are humans". "Non siamo pesci" also became the name of a political activist initiative[4] denouncing

---

3 https://www.dw.com/en/nigerian-music-sensation-chris-obehi-in-palermo/av-55420016

4 https://www.repubblica.it/cronaca/2019/01/28/news/migranti-217694568/

the Italian and EU migration policies that led to the frequent deaths of migrants at sea (Sow et al., 2016). *Hybridisation* is evident by the fact that Obehi "created something different, something new" (Bhabha, 1994: 211) from tradition, when he first became famous beyond his new hometown, Palermo, for his interpretations of traditional Sicilian songs.

Tradition

Tradition is another of the cultural concepts that can have multiple ambivalent meanings. In its most conservative sense, tradition means something that needs to be preserved as is, in order to remember and honour ancestors, learn from their alleged wisdom, and follow a laid-out path. This understanding of tradition seems to be universal but is evaluated differently according to hegemonic cultural standards: to respect and practice the traditions of a *dominance culture* is seen as a desirable part of a cultural canon, while similar practices are evaluated as 'backward' when it comes to marginalised cultural expressions. To begin with, traditions are not always created by ancestors but are sometimes invented as such (Hobsbawm, 1983). Another issue with traditions is that, even if they were created by ancestors, these ancestors were not necessarily always wise and honourable; the circumstances would have been very different from today and may no longer seem relevant. In this case traditions may be re-interpreted as something for people to use to study the past, re-examine and learn from. Alternatively, they may be adjusted, developed, or, in some cases, dropped altogether:

> *Identities [...] relate to the invention of tradition as much as to tradition itself, which they oblige us to read not as an endless reiteration but as 'the changing same': not the so-called return to roots but a coming-to-terms-with our 'routes'.* (Hall, 1996: 3–4)

In coming to terms with one's 'routes', there is also an emerging need to re-examine the meaning of cultural heritage.

Cultural heritage

This term can be defined as the significance a certain group assigns to certain aspects of *culture*, i.e. material or intangible heritage, practices, sites, or values. These artefacts may be attributed with an "authentic sense of past" (Rowlands, 2002).

What is categorised as cultural heritage is preserved, respected, and usually positively connoted, but may represent rather conservative historical positions that take a backward-looking approach to remembrance (Seukwa, 2021). It comes as no surprise that, from the postcolonial perspective, such an idealised and glorified construct of heritage is viewed with suspicion.

First of all, cultural heritage is always a result of power relations reproduced within and between particular groups. Second, people, groups and nations inherit cultural expressions from previous generations and are thus intertwined with all kinds of history: the dark chapters of the European past, centuries of colonialism and racism, brutality and exclusion, exploitation and annihilation have certainly impacted what has been culturally inherited and by whom. Though these facts are known and indisputable, there is a certain nostalgia for and glorification of European heritage that tends to veil the epistemic and cultural violence exerted over the colonised, marginalised and excluded, while also proclaiming the superiority of the white western "civilization".

Yet history and remembrance are constitutive of identification processes. Whose history is remembered and how? Which values are being passed on to the next generation?

The uncritical glorification of cultural heritage turns out to be rather a challenge for an inclusive and plural society; a postcolonial rereading of the concept (Seukwa, 2021) is needed in order to better represent the plurality and different perspectives of all its members. Going even further, cultural heritage should not be something young people are taught to passively preserve and adore. Rather, they should be empowered to become makers of cultural heritage themselves.

Cultural education and literacy

In line with this paradigm, Auma (2018) uses Bishop's analogy of *mirrors and windows* (1990) to suggest that young people's cultural education functions like a *mirror* by reflecting "their own lives and experiences as part of the larger human experience" (Auma, 2018: 74). As a *mirror*, cultural education can be a means of self-affirmation, but, at the same time, it should also be a *window* that exposes young people to all kinds of diversity. She stresses, that cultural education has to critically approach "social hierarchies and traditions of exclusions associated with art and culture" as well as address "discrimination and barriers to access" (ibid.: 74).

The CHIEF project aims to reimagine cultural education and literacy based on a culture of dialogue and mutual respect, and to create inclusive notions of cultural heritage and identity by focusing on the production and transmission of cultural knowledge in different educational settings (formal, non-formal, and informal). Non-formal and informal settings, which are often overlooked in educational policy, are considered here as especially crucial factors in the development of cultural literacy among young people.

Based on UNESCO's definition of cultural literacy as a social practice that "thrives when a state of connectedness – or nexus – of social relations among individuals, households, communities and social institutions is forged, nurtured and sustained" (Benavot, 2015: 284), this concept is not just seen as a technical matter (acquisition of skills and knowledge). It is also a social practice embedded in different forms of cultural expression that involve individual as well as collective cultural identities (Egloff and Seukwa, 2013).

Literacy is thus rooted in the context of activity, and its practices are connected to the social structures that shape and contextualise them. Its practices are 'situated' (Seukwa, 2007a), and while some situations are linked to the formal procedures or expectations of social institutions (such as the workplace, school and public authorities) and are relatively routine processes, others are governed more by more informal expectations and requirements of the private sphere (such as the home or peer groups).

A wider perspective on literacy is thus favoured here, one that takes into account the whole range of areas in which people act in society. This approach essentially seeks *to explain how individuals make use of literacy*, highlighting its significance for individuals at a specific place and time, under specific circumstances and in specific arenas. This perspective is based on the following assumptions: (1) Literacy is best understood as a set of social practices; these can be inferred from events, which are mediated by written texts. (2) There are different literacies associated with different domains of life. (3) Literacy practices are patterned by social institutions and power relationships, and some literacies become more dominant, visible and influential than others. (4) Literacy practices are purposeful and embedded in broader social goals and cultural practices. (5) Literacy is historically situated. (6) Literacy practices change, and new ones are frequently acquired through processes of informal learning and sense-making (cf. Seukwa, 2010; Barton et al., 2000).

Cultural literacy, in this context, is defined as "the competence to understand ('read') cultural references, enabling active cultural participation in society" (CHIEF project proposal: 11).

Formal, non-formal, and informal education

In order to grasp the whole spectrum of educational practices that lead to specific types of cultural literacy, it is not enough just to analyse schools. Although schools are certainly important factors in young people's education, the impact of families, peer groups, NGOs, museums, cinema, TV, and especially the internet, but also many other social spaces, on young people's acquisition of cultural literacy cannot be ignored.

According to a UNESCO classification (UNESCO Guidelines for the Recognition, Validation and Accreditation of the Outcomes of Non-formal and Informal Learning: 8), learning takes place on three different levels of formalisation: formal, non-formal and informal learning. Each of these stages is characterised by the settings in which it takes place, the presence or absence of structured curricula, and the level of acknowledgement by national authorities.

Formal education thus takes place mostly in state-certified institutions (schools), usually follows the pattern of teachers instructing learners, and follows a certain curriculum.

Non-formal education can be structured similarly but is often more fluid. It is mostly organised by non-governmental organisations. Qualifications gained in non-formal education can be (but are not necessarily) recognised by official authorities.

Informal learning is the name given to any form of learning that is not organised by any institution and does not lead to recognised certificates or qualification.

One issue with this system is that it artificially separates different forms of learning and attaches them to certain settings. In practice, the distinction is not usually as clear-cut. Informal learning can take place in formal settings, formal learning in non-formal settings, etc. As one interviewee put it:

> *I learn through the school but the school does not teach me. The school is only a mediator as it introduces me to friends. So, I am introduced to some other people in my friendship circle […] Culture is thus those differences, different things, and also, I think I acquire culture with my accompanying research.* (Tim, male, student, semi-urban school, Turkey, Chapter 1)

This segmentation of learning does not reflect the empirical observation that all three forms of learning frequently interact with each other. Learning might even be most effective when all three forms come together, such as when the content taught in schools is directly related to everyday experience.

CHIEF research, however, uses UNESCO's categorisation to identify and classify the different settings in which young people acquire their cultural knowledge and skills. First, teams analytically separated the three different types of settings and then organised research results to gain a full picture of how the three relate to each other and what role each setting plays in the development of cultural literacy among young people. In accordance with this analytical separation, each chapter in this book focuses primarily on one of the three categories, but they all take into account the relationship between the different education types.

In relation to their respective settings, the authors focussed on following research aspects and themes:

In **formal educational settings** (schools), the research perspective was on the relationship and interdependence between formal concepts of culture, pedagogical approaches, and the experiences of young people as they interact within the institutional framework of schools.

In **non-formal educational organisations** like sport, dance, film or music clubs, as well as political, environmental or religious organisations that offer content and activities for young people, the research aimed to identify bottom-up practices of learning, if and how they challenge official top-down concepts of cultural education, and how membership of certain communities is negotiated. A main focus was on the communication of differences and inclusion.

Research in **informal settings**, such as among self-organised youth that regularly meet to share various creative activities (sports, music, activism), wanted to present young people's own perceptions of culture and heritage-in-the-making, concepts that are significant to them. This research aimed to show how young people driven by their own specific motivations claim and/or utilise space to express their cultural identities.[5]

Methodology

This research project is in line with a recent paradigm shift in the social sciences, which emphasises uncovering or unravelling (hidden) power structures, avoids biological and deficit-oriented perspectives or categorisations of social structures (Seukwa, 2007b: 192; Pfaff, 2016: 82), and analyses meanings produced in social practice as well as the context in which they are embedded (Albright and Luke, 2008; Aitchison and Alidou, 2008; Barton and Hamilton, 1998; Barton et al., 2000; Gebre et al., 2009; Olson and Torrance, 2001; Street, 1999; UNESCO, 2006). The project therefore follows reconstructive and ethnographic approaches to investigate practices, their contexts, the production of meaning, and the significance for the education and cultural participation of young people. Researchers in this project aim not only to describe barriers and opportunities but also to critically

5 For the respective research questions please see each corresponding Part (I formal, II non-formal and III informal) of this book.

analyse power relations as represented in discourses, institutional mechanisms, and social interactions in general (Pfaff, 2016: 83).

Following Barton et al. (2000), there has been an assumption that literacy should be regarded as a set of practices often acquired in informal settings, specifically developed for different circumstances, and shaped by power relations as represented in social institutions (some being more visible than others, historically situated, and therefore subject to change). This led to a flexible multidisciplinary research design. Flexibility is especially essential for studying non-formal and informal settings, since these settings can be difficult to explore. Due to the fact that these settings rely on voluntary participation, the groups are likely to change over time. Democratic/participatory structures can also lead to abrupt changes in content or responsibilities, which makes research in these settings challenging, but all the more interesting: the processual character can itself be significant in opening up opportunities for the cultural participation of young people and for the acquisition of cultural literacy.

Based on the theoretical framework mentioned above, the construction of social space through practice (and the restrictions and barriers that come with this) were analysed via ethnographic methods, participant observation, and in-depth semi-structured interviews. The foci of data collection and analysis were informed by the historical context of each setting, and by recent political and social developments.

Research method

Research findings included in this volume have been obtained using qualitative research methods[6] such as interviews, participant observations and ethnographies. The exact methods of site selection, participant recruitment, data collection and data analysis differed according to the type of setting (formal, non-formal or informal), and therefore will be separately introduced in each corresponding Part of this book.

Structure of the book and summary of the outcomes

This book presents a selection of CHIEF's findings based on research reports from eight of the nine participating countries. The book is divided into three Parts, following the logic of educational settings: Part I presents findings obtained

6 Quantitative methods in the form of the survey were also applied in the context of the CHIEF project. However, these findings were not included in the present volume.

from research in schools (formal education), Part II is dedicated to cultural education at non-formal sites including interest clubs and youth organisations, while Part III is concerned with informal settings such as youth groups. In each Part, specific research methods and key questions are introduced, followed by the chapters with contributions from different countries.

The first Part, which covers formal education, presents research obtained from three different schools in Turkey, India, Slovakia and Germany as well as two schools in the UK. These schools are located in urban, semi-urban and rural areas, and the findings are supplemented by insights gained from related curricula research. All authors highlight the differences between the schools, in terms of socio-economic as well as cultural resources, and the impact these disparities have on young people's cultural literacy and participation. In Chapter 1, the Turkish contribution discusses how individual schools actively create their own cultural offers based on given resources and young people's demands, often despite the state curricula, which prescribe a rather nationalistic conservative education. In Chapter 2, the authors examine how schools in India foster plurality in some ways, while also perpetuating a cultural hegemony; institutional and ideological inclusivity coexists with forms of exclusion. It is argued that marginalised groups feel included in the context of normative cultural festivities, but, at the same time, their own cultural practices are not equally recognised. The focus of Chapter 3 is on the patriotic educational discourses and lack of conceptualisation of cultural diversity in formal education in the Slovakian context, where there is discrimination against Roma students in terms of access, segregation, language, recognition and representation. This chapter includes a reflection on the fact that researchers and educators from marginalised communities need to be involved in this kind of research. The British contribution in Chapter 4 shows how institutionalised multiculturalism falls short due to its fixation with satisfying different religious needs, while students' cultural identities are considered deficient according to dominant cultural norms. Finally, Chapter 5 analyses how young German students forge their identities depending on whether the dominant concepts of "German culture" grant them belonging or position them as the ethno-natio-cultural Other.

Contributions in Part II discuss findings from field work in Slovakian, Georgian, German and Indian clubs or organisations that offer content and activities to young people. The focuses of these organisations range from religion and spirituality, civics, politics, dance, music and film to photography, martial arts and the environment. In each country two sites with inherently different approaches to culture have been selected. All case studies reflect on the relationship between the "local" and the "global" and between "history" and "recent inventions/creativity". The Slovakian and Georgian chapters (Chapters 6 and 7) challenge the idea of "tradition", exploring how young people perceive recently invented practice as tradition that needs to be preserved. The connection between different conceptions of culture and different perspectives on regional history in Slovakia is explored by contrasting young people's takes on "tradition" and "diversity" in a neo-pagan organisation and an educational NGO that teaches young people about discrimination and inclusion. Chapter 7 discusses variations within concepts of "traditional" and/or "ethno-national" culture in Georgia, as these could be found in an elitist dance company and in a grassroots association that researches and practices specific martial arts techniques. The German (Chapter 8) and Indian (Chapter 9) case studies focus more on social hierarchies in general and how they are represented in youth culture, as well as how non-formal educational organisations are structured with regards to participation and communication. In Chapter 8, an analysis of German youth culture exposes underlying paradigms of classism, racism, and other forms of discrimination. The chapter contrasts one youth group that focuses on political education and one that incorporates political and social criticism into performing arts, paying particular attention to their styles of communication and their takes on diversity and identity. In the last chapter of this section (Chapter 9), the influence of social differences in India is shown by presenting the differences and commonalities of a film club, which offers educational opportunities and empowering young people within their community, and an art project that provides creative space to young people. Members of the latter organisation had mostly had previous contact with the international arts scene due to their privileged upbringing.

In Part III, authors from Germany, Croatia, Turkey and Spain introduce informal youth spaces of cultural education; researchers observed antifascist boxers and political rappers, squatters, a women's choir and hip-hop street dancers. The two German cases present political youth groups, discussing how discrimination and stigmatisation structure young participants' cultural practices, as well as informing their use of alternative cultural knowledge archives to forge their cultural identities (Chapter 10). The young Zagreb squatters in Chapter 11 also belong to a kind of marginalised (and even stigmatised) social group, the study of which, as the Croatian case argues, helps to reveal a lack of cultural norms based on inclusivity or solidarity in the dominant society. In the case of the Nightingales in Chapter 12, a pious Muslim women's choir, which performs for women only, faces stigmatisation from both sides: the secular Turkish society as well as the conservative, religious one. The chapter analyses how these young women navigate between conservative political stances and feminism to forge their own cultural identities without compromising their membership in the pious middle class. Finally, the street dancers in Barcelona (Chapter 13) re-define youth and subculture as 'set against adult-centred and authority-guided spaces.' Historically, street dance culture is based on hybrid cultural identities and empowerment of the marginalised. The chapter analyses aspects such as the intergenerational transfer of cultural knowledge and horizontal informal learning, while also touching on issues of street (un)safety and the harassment by the authorities faced by the street dancers.

This short summary vividly demonstrates the broad representation of locations, settings, spaces, orientations, ideologies and beliefs, as well as the diversity of the young individuals covered by this volume. However, we are aware that these can only be temporary glimpses into complex realities, and are additionally limited by the individual perceptions of the observing and interpreting researchers. These chapters invite readers to dive into the kaleidoscopic plurality of youth identities, cultures and heritages within and across sites, cities and countries. Readers will come upon some common patterns of how obstacles are poised on young people's identification. Such obstacles may be caused by local limitations, expectations and assumptions, but also by structural barriers, which arise from the confinement of what cultural identifications and expressions should be or do according to normative frameworks.

The volume aims to highlight how young people who desire to live in more inclusive ways are challenging those limitations and barriers. This is our contribution to ongoing the deconstruction and dismantlement of these barriers. We also hope to provide new (and old) inspirations for the desire to develop an open society commonly shared by the authors of this volume.

References

Aitchison, J. and Hassana, A., 2008. Sub-Saharan Africa the Development and State of Art of Adult Learning. Nairobi: UNESCO.

Albright, J. and Allan, L. (Eds.), 2008. Pierre Bourdieu and Literacy Education. New York: Routledge.

Appiah, A., 2018. The Lies That Bind. Rethinking Identity, Creed, Country, Color, Class, Culture. New York, NY: Liveright Publishing Corporation.

Auma, M. M., 2018. Kulturelle Bildung in pluralen Gesellschaften. Diversität von Anfang an! Diskriminierungskritik von Anfang an! In: A. Schütze and J. Maedler (Eds.), Weiße Flecken: Diskurse und Gedanken über Diskriminierung, Diversität und Inklusion in der Kulturellen Bildung. Kopaed.

Balibar, É., 2004. We, the People of Europe? Reflections on Transnational Citizenship. Journal of International Affairs. Translated by James Swenson. Princeton and Oxford: Princeton University Press.

Barton, D. and Hamilton, M., 1998. Local Literacies. Reading and Writing in one Community. London and New York: Routledge.

Barton, D., Hamilton, M. and Ivanič, R., 2000. Situated Literacies. Theorising Reading and Writing in Context. London: Routledge.

Bauman, Z., 1999. Culture as Praxis. New Edition. London, Thousand Oaks, New Delhi.

Bauman, Z. and Beilharz, P., 2002. The Journey Never Ends. Zygmunt Bauman talks with Peter Beilharz. In: Beilharz, P. (Eds.), Zygmunt Bauman, Vol. I. London. Thousand Oaks, New Delhi: 27–37.

Benavot, A., 2015. Literacy in the 21st century: Towards a dynamic nexus of social relations. International Review of Education 61(3): 273–294.

Bergmann, E., 2020. Neo-Nationalism – The Rise of Nativist Populism. Cham: Springer Nature Switzerland.

Bhabha, H. K., 1994. The Location of Culture. London: Routledge.

Bishop, R. S., 1990. Mirrors, Windows, and Sliding Glass Doors. Perspectives: Choosing and Using Books for the Classroom, 6(3), ix–xi.

Bourdieu, P. and Passeron, J. C., 1977. Reproduction in Education, Society and Culture. London and Beverly Hills: Sage Publications.

Bourdieu, P., 2010 (1984). Distinction. A Social Critique of the Judgement of Taste. London: Routledge.

Césaire, A., 1955. Discours sur le colonialisme. Paris: Présence Africaine.

Chattopadhyay, S., 2017. Homi Bhabha and the Concept of Cultural Hybridity. Postcolonial Literature, Lecture 14. National Program of Technology Enhanced Learning.

Dannenbeck, C., 2002. Selbst- und Fremdzuschreibungen als Aspekte kultureller Identitätsarbeit. Weinheim: Leske + Budrich.

Egloff, B. and Seukwa, L. H., 2013. Brauchen wir eine neue Definition des Analphabetismus?. Vierteljahresschrift für Heilpädagogik und ihre Nachbargebiete, [S.l.]: 344–350, sep. 2013. ISSN 0017-9655. https://www.reinhardt-journals.de/index.php/vhn/article/view/5380. (Accessed on May 22, 2021).

El-Tayeb, F., 2015. Anders Europäisch: Rassismus, Identität und Widerstand im vereinten Europa. Münster: Unrast.

Fanon, F., 1961. Les damnés de la terre. Paris: Éditions Maspero.Gebre, A. H., Rogers, A., Street, B. and Openjuru, G., 2009. Everyday Literacies in

Africa: Ethnographic Studies of Literacy and Numeracy Practices in Ethiopia. Kampala: Fountain Publishers.

Ha, K. N., 2000. Ethnizität, Differenz und Hybridität in der Migration: Eine postkoloniale Perspektive. PROKIA. Zeitschrift f. kritische Sozialwissenschaft, 120 (30): 377–397.

Hall, S., 1994. Rassismus und kulturelle Identität. Ausgewählte Schriften 2, Argument Verlag GmbH, Glashüttenstraße- Hamburg. ISBN 978-3-88619-226-7.

Hall, S., 1996. Who Needs Identity? In: Hall, S. and du Gay, P. (Eds.), Questions of Cultural Identity. London: Sage.

Harris, A., 2009. Shifting the Boundaries of Cultural Spaces: Young People and Everyday Multiculturalism. Social Identities, 15(2): 187–205, DOI: 10.1080/13504630902778602.

Haschemi, G. A., Meyer, V., and Rotter, P. V., 2017. Ein Empowermentmärchen – Chorisch. In: Kulturprojekte Berlin GmbH (Eds.), Kulturelle Bildung im Kontext Asyl. Ein Dossier. (Cultural Education in the context of asylum), Berlin: 33–36.

Hobsbawm, E., 1983. Introduction: Inventing Traditions. In E. Hobsbawm, E. and T. Ranger, T. (Eds.), The Invention of Traditions: 1–14. Cambridge: Cambridge University Press: 1–14

hooks, b., 1997. Cultural Criticism and Transformation. https://www.youtube.com/watch?v=zQUuHFKP-9s (Assessed on 15 December 2020).

Kron, T. and Reddig, M., 2011. Zygmunt Bauman: Die ambivalente Verfassung moderner und postmoderner Kultur. In: Moebius, S. and Quadflieg, D. (Eds.), Kultur. Theorien der Gegenwart (Culture. Contemporary Theories): Wiesbaden: Springer VS: 452–466.

Lewis, D., 1973. Anthropology and Colonialism. Current Anthropology, 14(5): 581–602.

Macron, E., 2020. Discours du Président de la République sur le thème de la lutte contre les séparatismes 2 octobre 2020 – Seul le prononcé fait foi. English version https://www.diplomatie.gouv.fr/en/coming-to-france/france-facts/secularism-and-religious-freedom-in-france-63815/article/fight-against-separatism-the-republic-in-action-speech-by-emmanuel-macron (Accessed on March 8, 2021).

Mbembe A., 2015. Decolonizing knowledge and the question of the archive. http://wiser.wits.ac.za/system/files/Achille%20Mbembe%20-%20Decolonizing%20Knowledge%20and%20the%20Question%20of%20the%20Archive.pdf (Accessed on December 15, 2020).

Olson, D. R. and Torrance, N., 2001. The Making of Literate Societies. Oxford: Wiley-Blackwell.

Perko, G. and Czollek, L. C., 2020. Ein Manifest zur konkreten Utopie Radical Diversity. In: Perko, G. (Ed.), Social Justice und Radical Diversity. Weinheim: Beltz Juventa: 91–96.

Pfaff, N., 2016. Kultur in Perspektiven auf Differenz – eine Einführung. In: M. Hummrich, N. Pfaff, İ. Dirim and C. Freitag (Eds.), Kulturen der Bildung. Kritische Perspektiven auf erziehungswissenschaftliche Verhältnisbestimmungen, Wiesbaden: Springer VS: 79–92.

Rommelspacher, B., 1995. Dominanzkultur. Berlin: Orlanda.

Rommelspacher, B., 2002. Anerkennung und Ausgrenzung. Deutschland als multikulturelle Gesellschaft. Frankfurt am Main: Campus Verlag.

Seukwa, L. H., 2007a. Soziokontextualität von Kompetenz und Bildungsprozesse in transnationalen Räumen. Der Habitus der Überlebenskunst. In Diskurs Kindheits- und Jugendforschung 2 (2007) 3, S. 295–309

Seukwa, L. H., 2007b. The Ingrained Art of Survival: The Nexus between Competence and Migration as Reflected in Refugee Biographies. Rüdiger Köppe.

Seukwa, L. H., 2010. Literacy as a Social Practice in West Africa. Application for the funding Program Point Sud; ZIAF, Frankfurt/Main.

Seukwa, L. H., 2018. Umbruch und Bewältigung: Die „Europäischen Werte" angesichts der Flüchtlingsfrage. Talk on 26.09. in Cologne, Germany. https://cms1.carinet.de/shared_data/forms_layout/efbvke/441704_Thesen_zum_Vortrag_Prof__Seukwa__docx_.pdf (Accessed on November 24, 2020).

Seukwa, L. H. 2021. Die Hauptkirche St. Michaelis: Eine postkoloniale Relektüre des Gedenkens im Michel. Goethe Institute. https://www.re-mapping.eu/de/erinnerungsorte/hauptkirche-st-michaelis (Accessed on January 15, 2022)

Sow, P., Marmer, E., and Scheffran, J., 2016. En route to Hell: Dreams of Adventure and Traumatic Experiences Among West African "Boat People" to Europe. In: Mannik, L. (Ed.), Migration by Boat: Discourses of Trauma, Exclusion and Survival. Oxford, New York: Berghahn: 235–252.

Spivak, G. C., 2000. Deconstruction and Cultural Studies: Arguments for a Deconstructive Cultural Studies, Deconstructions: 14–43.

Street, B. V., 1999. Social Literacies: Critical Approaches to Literacy in Development, Ethnography and Education. London and New York: Routledge.

UNESCO, 2006. Education for All Global Monitoring Report – 2005. UNESCO Publishing.

Verdery, K., 1999. The Political Lives of Dead Bodies. New York: Columbia University Press.

Winter, R., 2011. Stuart Hall: Die Erfindung der Cultural Studies. In: Moebius, S. and Quadflieg, D. (Eds.), Kultur. Theorien der Gegenwart (Culture. Contemporary Theories). Wiesbaden: Springer VS: 469–480.

Yala Kisukidi, N., 2021. Islamo-gauchisme: le pouvoir s'en prend aux espaces de production libre du savoir, désignés comme cibles. https://qg.media/2021/02/23/a-travers-laccusation-dislamo-gauchisme-le-pouvoir-sen-prend-aux-espaces-de-production-libre-du-savoir-designes-comme-cibles-par-nadia-yala-kisukidi/ (Accessed on March 8, 2021).

Part I Cultural literacy in formal education

This part presents and discusses findings on cultural literacy practices in schools, one of the main institutional settings in which young people acquire resources and develop their cultural literacy skills. The qualitative research in schools aimed to explore practices for the provision of cultural literacy: sources of cultural knowledge, learning experiences, young people's cultural participation, and issues of cultural identity and diversity.

Research questions

The empirical studies in all partner countries were designed to answer the following research questions:

- How do teachers perceive 'European/national cultural heritage', 'cultural identity' and 'cultural diversity'?
- How do teachers communicate these concepts to their pupils and, in particular, facilitate cultural competence and participation?
- How do young people see 'European/national cultural heritage', 'cultural identity' and 'cultural diversity'?
- How do young people describe their experiences of becoming familiar with the concepts of 'European/national cultural heritage', 'cultural identity' and 'cultural diversity'?
- How do they engage with these concepts in practice in formal education and outside school?

Method

To answer these questions, some 60 students aged 14–19 and 10–12 teachers of subjects somehow related to cultural education (history, languages, geography, art, civics, religion, etc.) from three secondary schools in each country participated in semi-structured in-depth interviews about their school experiences, notions of culture and cultural heritage, cultural identity and participation. This was complemented by a set of country-specific questions. The three schools were located in urban, semi-urban and rural environments, and were characterised by different degrees of economic development, as well as varying in terms of diversity, levels of migration, and cultural infrastructure.

Interview questionnaires for teachers and young people were developed for all countries, with country-specific questions developed by each partner team. These questionnaires were translated into national languages; in India, the study participants were able to choose one of several languages offered. In Slovakia, however, minority students could not be included because the interviews were not conducted in the languages they were fluent in; exclusion and fear of repression may also have played a role in this.

As schools operate using their own systems and structures, it was often impossible to recruit students (and, in some cases, teachers) directly. Often, the headteachers or other representatives of school management recruited interviewees, and the research team members sometimes observed that particularly active, interested and engaged students and teachers had been selected. Thus, the schools had an influence on how they wished to present themselves, which certainly affected the collected data.

All interviews were audio-recorded and then transcribed. After each interview, the researchers' general observations on the interview setting and process, the participant's openness, level of involvement and interest were recorded in the participant notes, which also contained basic socio-economic data. This data varied slightly according to each national context. Both interview transcripts and participant notes were coded using NVivo software. The coding and analysis processes in all countries followed the grounded theory approach (Charmaz, 1996). Personal information about the interviewees, including gender, parents' occupation (in case of students), citizenship and languages spoken, was used for interpretation when deemed appropriate. The findings were analysed and discussed in view of CHIEF's aim to advocate for a more inclusive interpretation of European cultural heritage as a site of the production, translation and exchange of heterogeneous cultural knowledge.

(by Yıldırım Şentürk and Ayşe Berna Uçarol)

Chapter 1 Schools as a package of cultural participation for youth raised with digital technology in Turkey

Abstract: This chapter argues that common social categories previously used in Turkey to characterise young people (such as secular/modern versus conservative/pious) are insufficient to fully understand today's cultural practices and identities of youth in Turkey, even though they are still crucial and controversial subjects of public interest. The chapter explores the cultural practices and learning experiences of young people in Turkey based on our qualitative field research, which we conducted in three public high schools. The chapter examines how each school presents a specific 'package of cultural participation' through a flexible combination of the curriculum, teachers' re-interpretation of the curriculum, extra-curricular courses and activities, student clubs, the schools' facilities, etc. Although today's young people have different expectations and objectives depending on their social backgrounds, they also have greater opportunity to interact with different people, social groups, organisations and places through the use of new digital communication platforms and information technologies. These platforms are instrumental in young people's pursuits to improve themselves through their interests and aspirations. This chapter approaches youth culture in Turkey as a dynamic field of practices shaped by various human and non-human actors interacting in educational settings.

Keywords: youth, formal education, cultural participation, digital technology, Turkey

Introduction

Educational policies have presented a significant field of tension and contradiction over a long period of time in Turkey, even as the content of those policies has faced profound change. It could be said that the continuing power struggle between distinct political and social groups has been a more influential source of these contradictions than abstract pedagogical trends. Some of the significant controversial themes and issues underlined by scholars in this regard include: class differences in access to educational resources and reproduced social distinction (Gök, 2004; Gök, 2007; İnal & Akkaymak, 2012; Altinyelken et al., 2015); practices of nation building and modernisation/westernisation processes (Akın, 2004; Altınay, 2004; Gümüş, 2015; Tekeli, 1998; Akşit, 2013; Bahçekapılı, 2015); competing teachings on the subject of Islam/religion and the extent to which these are included in curricula (Eroler, 2019; Lüküslü, 2016); the definition of being Turkish and how different identities in Turkey (for instance, those who identify themselves as Kurdish, Alevis or non-Muslims) are represented (Çayır, 2014; Çayır, 2016; Eroler, 2019; Kaya, Aydın, & Vural, 2016); and how gender-based roles are reproduced in the education system (Akşit, 2013; Altınay, 2004; Gök, 2007).

In this context, the struggle between the 'conservative/religious' education model against the 'modern/secular' model shows itself as one of the dominant points of tension in the creation of education policies. Research and debate about the influence of secular education was at the forefront of the long process of modernisation and nation-state building (Akın, 2004; Altınay, 2004; Gümüş, 2015; Tekeli, 1998; Akşit, 2013). This focus shifted after 2002, in parallel with the governments established by the conservative and religious Justice and Development Party (AKP); at this time, discussion of conservatism and religion in education became more prominent (Eroler, 2019; Lüküslü, 2016; Altinyelken et al., 2015; Ural, 2015; İnal & Akkaymak, 2012). Of course, it would be oversimplistic to suggest that these two political standings in Turkey completely exclude the concerns of the other. In fact, the models overlap, as they contain similar nationalist aspirations (albeit with their own particular interpretations).

It is no coincidence that education is a significant area of struggle between different classes and political and cultural groups, as it seeks to determine what will be taught to whom and how. Any attempt to define which knowledge will have social recognition redefines the power relations between social groups. Thus, it is possible to speak of a struggle to confer validity and legitimacy on certain knowledge and skills that may be taught for social or political aims. This differs from a system where existing 'absolute' and 'true' knowledge, skills, and tastes are neutrally passed on to the youth (Bourdieu & Passeron, 1977; Reay, 2017). In this way, certain values can be imposed on individuals and 'new generations.' As a result, it is possible to track signs of power relations, struggles, and contradictions among social groups within ongoing education policies or practices (Apple, 1995; Reay, 2017).

In the last 15 years, there have been frequent changes to education policies in Turkey. Contradictory plans are placed on the agenda when new programmes are announced, and are usually introduced with reference to new and popular discourses among experts in education (Altinyelken et al., 2015). However, it is possible to say that, over time, the tendency towards religious and conservative influences has grown more pronounced in education institutions. Leading AKP politicians have stated the need to raise 'a pious generation' as a political goal; these types of statements have established more legitimate grounds for religious and conservative education practices (Eroler, 2019).

We were considerably concerned by controversial policies and practices while examining the national education policies and curriculum (Şentürk et al., 2018; Uçarol et al., 2019).[1] In recent contemporary debates regarding youth and education policy in Turkey, the deliberate attempts of authorities to implement more conservative, religious, and nationalist policies have begun to receive greater attention (Lüküslü, 2016, Eroler, 2019). However, as scholars of education, culture, and youth, we face serious challenges too: (1) reproducing prevailing binary oppositions, and (2) focusing mainly on top-down policies. While investigating the policies and implications of authorities and institutions acting according to particular binary oppositions, such as 'pious' vs. 'secular' and 'conservative' vs. 'modern', we might reproduce the same binary classifications in defence of one of the sides. Moreover, debates over related issues often deal with 'top-down policies' designed by those not subject to their effects (often authorities and institutions). Unfortunately, the young people who are directly affected by these policies do not often receive sufficient attention. Any concern for their practices, tendencies and attitudes is usually secondary. Instead, debates are held over an abstract conception of 'youth', which is perceived as being generally fixed across time and space. This means that young people are instrumentalised and objectified to support the good of a greater 'society' or the 'ideals' of a particular social group. We acknowledge that the prevailing power relations in a society have an impact on the content of culture: they attempt to reproduce their own concepts, classifications and perspectives in all social spheres related to culture, including education. However, when researchers try to identify and question such power relations or their outcomes in cultural spheres, we need to avoid reproducing binary oppositions. Further, as is true for other social issues, the

1 Here are some examples of how the implementation of education policy has changed over time: Values education (initially aimed to teach all students essential "universal values"; meanwhile, religion-based values became over-emphasised, including recent cooperation with religious foundations); 100 essential literary works (the content has changed depending on who designed the list, which authors and books have been selected, and how the foreign books are translated); Cooperation and collaboration with civil society organisations (organisations that strongly support the government receive more support and funds); Strengthening the local and national culture (generally, cultural practices with a conservative and religious interpretation of local or national culture); Increasing the number of elective courses (although there are opportunities to offer various elective courses, some school administrations tend to ensure that the courses about religion and Islam remain the most consistently open and 'available'). (Şentürk et al., 2018; Uçarol et al., 2019).

individuals, social groups, and organisations in the field influenced by such policies should not be considered as altogether 'passive' agents of educational policies implemented from above. The particular social field is also shaped by the practices and involvement of these agents, whether their engagement is collaborative or conflict-driven.

The basis for this concern is what happened when, after conducting our research on education policies for six months (Şentürk et al., 2018), we began to interview young people in their school environment in order to explore their high school experiences. When we were able to observe the practices of individuals and institutions on the ground, the process appeared both complex and promising. We found that actors in such education settings (primarily teachers, administrators, youth, and parents) are not merely passive implementers of education and cultural policies.

Our qualitative research findings in three different state schools (located in urban, semi-urban and rural regions of Turkey) show how the different practices or approaches of each setting may lead to different results, enabling us to understand the dynamics at play in this field in a more comprehensive manner.[2] Each school, with its own particular combination of actors, presents a different 'cultural package.' Our intention was not to create a fixed picture by considering each school as a 'package'. Instead, we used this concept to understand each school as a social space with a unique combination of human as well as non-human actors (the locations, facilities, connections of the schools, etc.) taking up different positions in the field. The ways in which these human and non-human actors interact change over time (Lefebvre, 1991; Latour, 2005). For instance, an especially crucial element of our research is the increasingly active use of digital communication and information technologies, as this shapes the young people's experiences of their formal education setting.

Throughout the article, we will compare our findings from each school to show how the realm of culture is dynamic and how each actor or institution

---

2 The urban school is a 'high quality public high school', accepting students using the central examination system. The semi-urban school also has traditionally held this status, but since the 2018–2019 academic year it has become a public high school that accepts students according to the address system. The meaning of the address system is that schools accept students regardless of their centralised exam success. The only condition here is residence in a neighbourhood close to the school. Similarly, the rural school's status as a high-quality school has been degraded since the 2018–2019 education year; it has also become a state high school accepting students according to the address system.

shapes its content. After a short description of the school locations, we explore the high school education experience of youth by presenting the various patterns and dynamics at play in the three schools. We then further elaborate on the cultural involvement of students in the formal education setting. Finally, on the basis of our interviews with young people, we try to understand their aspirations, interests, and excitements: these areas are often not considered as part of 'culture', even though they help us to grasp the cultural involvement of youth even when this is in a state of flux.

School locations

The urban and semi-urban regions were selected within Istanbul, the largest city in Turkey. Istanbul is commonly divided into two geographical regions: the European and the Anatolian sides. The urban school is located on the European side of Istanbul, whereas the semi-urban school is on the Anatolian.[3] Istanbul is the most developed city in Turkey in terms of cultural and educational opportunities (e.g. museums, theatres, libraries, galleries, and universities), which are predominantly located in the urban region. This is a district with socio-economic, cultural, and social diversity. The semi-urban district is easily accessible through Istanbul's main transportation networks. It was previously an important industrial centre (1950–1980), but during the post-1980 deindustrialisation period it was transformed into a mainly residential area. The cultural opportunities here are not as plentiful as in the urban region. The rural region selected is near Istanbul.[4] Although the rural region contains a smaller population, it has experienced intense internal and external migration movements from Syria, Iraq, Iran, and Afghanistan, as well as from the Eastern provinces of Turkey. The reason for high levels of migration to this place is its close proximity to Istanbul and its relatively easy life conditions. Thanks to migrant communities, increased cultural diversity has gradually started to shape the region's life as well. The region has limited cultural opportunities and facilities (for instance, the city has one university and two theatres).

The field study was conducted on March 29–May 9, 2019 at the urban and semi-urban schools and on May 13–May 22, 2019 at the rural school. All student and teacher interviews were conducted by two members of the CHIEF research team. The authors interviewed 79 students and 9 teachers in 3 schools. Later, we

---

3 The distance between the urban and semi-urban regions is 28 km.

4 The rural region is some 93 km away from Istanbul and can be reached by ferry in one hour.

also had the opportunity to conduct interviews with the parents of nine students at their homes.

High school as a new experience for youth in the shadow of the university entrance exam

In high school (upper secondary school, from ninth to twelfth grades), relationship modes between students and teachers differ from those of middle school (lower secondary school, from fifth to eighth grades). Many students stated that high school was a positive transition for them because teachers treated them like 'adults', through conversations about daily life. They described their student life using phrases such as 'becoming mature', 'bonds of friendship', 'close relations with the teachers' and 'better concentration in lectures'. In the urban school, the administration and the teachers seek to provide students with a participatory setting that enables them to better express themselves. Students choose the music used to indicate class intervals; although the school has a basic uniform, students are allowed to modify it to express their own styles; female students may wear light make-up; mobile phone usage is free in the school and the classrooms. In the semi-urban school, however, students have to more rigidly conform to the school uniform, the library is locked during lecture hours, and an atmosphere of discipline is felt by all students in the school setting. The rural school has the strictest rules of the three high school settings.

The courses offered in the curriculum significantly shape the youth's high school experiences. At high school, students take more courses – both compulsory and elective – than at the secondary level, and the content of the courses is more intensive. As was mentioned by many students during the interviews, a large number of topics are covered and these topics frequently change. Most of the students said that they had had difficulties with this, especially during the early periods of their high school life. Therefore, the ninth grade (the first year of high school) is mostly used as a period of adaptation to high school life, in which young people learn to balance intense school work and the wide variety of activities now accessible to them as high school students. For some, this adaptation stage continues into the tenth grade. By the 11th grade, especially among those who aspire to get a better score in the university entrance exam, students begin to limit their extracurricular activities or habits (mobile phone, computer games, social media usage, hanging out with friends) in order to improve their course scores. In the 11th grade, some students start to take private university exam preparation courses in addition to their regular school classes. In the twelfth grade, the university entrance exam is high on students' agendas. While private lessons, mock exams and additional studies were all mentioned, current students spoke more about topics such as exam stress, university preferences, and their anxieties over the future and their careers. Any kind of time-consuming activities, including cultural ones, are postponed until the end of the university entrance exam.

In this regard, the significance of university education, as mentioned by both the school and by individual students, is a determining factor in cultural participation. Pressure is felt especially intensely by students in the urban and semi-urban school settings. An additional 'stressful' process begins when many 12th-grade students attend additional courses to prepare for the university entrance exam. This exam is placed at the centre of their lives. In these success-centred schools, they concentrate more on Natural Science/Mathematics courses because these subjects are considered key to getting into a better university and department. Some of the students we interviewed complained about this situation:

> *I don't like that only Mathematics, Science and similar activities are abundant at school, because life is more than that. Life is not only the quality of the university that you enrol in. Of course, these are important, but general culture, life, social activities are also important.* (Mora, female, student, urban school)

At the rural school, the objective of attending university or getting into one of the best universities was expressed less often among the students. Students here tend to be more concerned with finding a 'reliable job'. Precisely for this reason, unlike the other two settings, in the rural school a significant number of students want to join the police or military forces as a career. This interest is supported by the somewhat stronger nationalist and conservative sentiments in the rural setting, but also by the employment security provided by these professions.

During their four years at high school, students take a number of different courses, from natural to social science. The interviews conducted in three schools show that students do not have a specific predetermined or preconceived attitude to any branch or course topic. An important criterion for youth to show interest in a particular course is the teacher offering it. Students need to be convinced of why they should learn a subject in the first place. In this regard, the teacher matters as a mediator. Students usually question one-sided and top-down imposed views and knowledge, and are willing to hear different perspectives and explanations. Today's young people are more capable of using digital sources to verify any information they feel is being imposed on them. If they mistrust information, young people will sometimes seek to confirm claims via digital platforms. Following on from this, they have higher expectations that teachers will have enough knowledge and enthusiasm for the subject they teach, as well as the skills to communicate with students. They prefer teachers who are able to establish connections between their course subjects and daily life, who are open to interacting with students, and have the experience and skills to make difficult topics enjoyable when necessary. However, it is also worth emphasising that teachers' creativity and level of subject interpretation have certain limits, as students will take a standardised multiple-choice university entrance exam at the end of high school. Indeed, some students complain if the course material covers topics other than the expected content of this exam.

In this respect, English language courses are among the most enjoyable ones in all three schools, as teachers are more open to integrating games and alternative teaching techniques into the language learning process. At the urban and semi-urban schools, Philosophy courses also provide students with inter-classroom debate opportunities. In interviews at both schools, students related how they participated in inter-school Philosophy debates with their teachers and prepared theatre activities (for example, Plato's *Socrates' Defence*). At the semi-urban school, one Philosophy teacher assigned homework readings from the works of Western thinkers such as More, Orwell, Sartre, and Camus, and gladly invited students to ask questions after class if they wished to talk further about them (Baykuş, female, teacher, semi-urban school). In our interviews, we saw how students started to realise with surprise that many contemporary topics had already been discussed by thinkers in the past. These philosophical readings seemed to help young people to gain a more inclusive approach to different cultures, societies, eras, and ideas. At the urban school, the students did not mention the names and works of specific thinkers as much. Instead, they stated that they could have discussions with their teachers on topics such as gender, equality, freedom, belief and identity, some of which were directly related to their own daily lives. As we saw in our field research, each teacher may interpret the curriculum of Philosophy differently. Some teachers placed more emphasis on Western philosophy, while others balanced Western and non-Western philosophers equally. In the rural school, the case was quite different, since this course was led by a Religious Culture and Moral Knowledge teacher rather than a Philosophy specialist. The interviewed students were not as interested in the subject and complained that their teacher placed more emphasis on religion, especially Islam, rather than non-theological philosophy. One student criticised his teacher for being 'judgmental' in this regard:

> *Actually, I am quite interested in researching other religions and their views, but the teacher judges more than explains the views of other religions.* (Yaşar, male, student, rural school)

One point that students care about is the connection between their courses and everyday life. In other words, they care about the relationship between the course material and the reason for learning it. Students questioned the subjects taught for exam preparation by asking 'what they will do in their life'. Many young people said that the courses they like most are the ones that increase their curiosity:

> *I like very much when sometimes examples from daily life are given during the lectures. For instance, giving the aeroplane as an example, explaining the mechanism of the aeroplane when examples are given about let's say about friction, I really agree with that in that case. And if there is anything I am curious about, I search for it by myself when I go home.* (Lusaac Smp, male, student, urban school)

Students not only pay attention to the content of the course and the teacher's narrative style, but also have thoughts about how to make the course practices 'more efficient'. In this context, in all three schools the need for illustrative visual materials is an outstanding issue, because the students like lectures to be supported by concrete examples and physical experiments. Students, especially in the History and Geography courses, said that narratives with catchy video content can be a way to make them learn better. Although there are laboratories in all three schools, they are not used. This commonality shows that even though the schools might have the facilities for a certain teaching technique, such as laboratories, these might become less available over time. They become a 'symbolic space' for students, physical proof that they are not receiving a proper education in a particular subject.

Course books are distributed for free to the schools by the Ministry of National Education, and it is not compulsory to use them. At the urban and semi-urban schools, teachers generally find the Natural Science books distributed by the state inadequate and recommend that students purchase additional resources. This puts economic pressure on some families. At the rural school, teachers do not offer additional resources due to the low income level of many families; instead, teachers dictate lecture notes to students. At all three schools, official course books are followed in Social Sciences, which the interviewed students often found 'boring', 'repetitive' and based on 'long expressions.'

At the urban and semi-urban schools, Philosophy teachers recommend utopia-dystopia novels to their students. Literature teachers use Turkish and 'the essential literary works', which are also named 'World Classics' in Turkey and mostly consist of Western literary works. The Literature teacher at the urban school pays extra attention to 'world literature books' by providing a list of 25 titles to be read by the students. Interviewed students stated that they initially had difficulty reading these books, but then they liked them, learned to read faster, and began thinking about the conditions of people living in different periods (Mora, female, student, urban school). Some students have started to understand different cultural settings through these works. Stating that she had learned to read more carefully by underlining, Darci suggested that her experience of literature has improved her own perspective and understanding: "*for example, I think I have better taste even when watching movies*" (Darci, female, student, urban school). At the rural school, Literature teachers mostly recommend classic Turkish novels. In other words, the teachers' interests, perspectives and skills also play a significant role in the choice of resources.

If we look at these examples of readings taken from classical works and philosophical texts, teachers can be important *mediators* in introducing students to certain fields, subjects, and cultural literacy. However, teachers can only be effective to the extent that they develop methods of attracting and holding students' attention. For example, a student who enjoys reading classical literary books also stated that he finds it absurd when such "*beautiful and enjoyable works*" are read only for thinking about their possible role in exam questions, and all "*the pleasure that could be taken from them is destroyed*" (Kalem, male, student, semi-urban school). We found a good example of how to encourage students without creating anxiety about grades at the semi-urban school, where a student without any previous musical training or experience started playing drums with the encouragement of his Music teacher. This teacher showed confidence in him by giving him the keys to the music hall, which enabled him to practice (Kalem, male, student, semi-urban school).

The school experience of youth in high school is not limited to their course content and their interaction with teachers. The next section will elaborate the cultural participation of youth in the school environment.

Schools as a package of cultural participation

Appearance of the schools

High school represents a new phase in terms of youth cultural participation. Each school offers a particular 'package of cultural participation' as the result of a flexible combination of the curriculum, its partial re-interpretation by the teachers, extra-curricular courses and activities, student clubs and their bodies, the profile of the enrolled students, school facilities, etc. When students enrol in the high school institutions, they begin to get their first impressions of these packages. Whether students are trying to register for a school based on their exam score or their home address, they make a choice by evaluating the potential of the schools they are eligible for and by consulting with their families. Although a school's success in university entrance exams is the primary criterion for many, the school's social and cultural activities also affect this decision. The school garden, interior design, general appearances, sports and other facilities are also effective in forming a perception of the school in students' minds. For instance, on the garden walls of the rural school, while there are pictures of historical characters (such as Atatürk, Fatih Sultan Mehmet and II. Abdülhamit Han)[5] and other nationalist historical figures, there is also an attempt to make the walls livelier with symbols (mathematical symbols, music notes, etc.). There are also human figures representing various sports activities. A few of the interviewed students shared that these kinds of images, which cannot be found in other public schools around their neighbourhood, make them feel closer to their school. The urban school's walls are decorated in a manner that can rarely be seen elsewhere, with pictures of youth-centred daily life in the city centre of Istanbul. There is also a mural of a pair of multi-coloured angel wings that is used during graduation for memory photographs by students, teachers, and families. The images on the walls in that school and its garden were chosen and implemented by students together with their teachers. As a result, the appearance of the urban school seems to better represent the taste and the style of young people. Many school activities are also represented by posters and images on its walls.[6] The semi-urban school gives the impression that it is a 'good and deep-rooted' public school, with numerous cups and medals exhibited in its building's entrance. Social media posts about the school have also gained influence recently: these are sometimes shared by students or alumni, and sometimes by the school administration. Video-style productions are also used on social media. For instance, a musical video published eight years ago about the semi-urban school has been watched over 7.5 million times, creating a positive image of the school among potential students. To what extent such fictional school presentations and images reflect school reality remains questionable. A student club promoted on the school wall may be inactive, for instance, or unknown to most students.

---

5 Mustafa Kemal Atatürk is the founder of the modern Turkish Republic; Fatih Sultan Mehmet is the sultan who conquered Istanbul and was represented in the periods when the Ottoman Empire was strong; II. Abdülhamit Han is one of the controversial sultans during the final phase of the Ottoman Empire, who is especially liked by the conservative nationalists.

6 For instance, maxims from various authors, promotional texts about screenings of Tim Burton films (such as *Edward Scissorhands* and *Corpse Bride*), short writings and notes on classroom doors about gender equality, etc.

The opportunities and physical facilities of the schools

The package of cultural participation and cultural literacy presented by each school depends on various factors. First of all, although all the schools are public, *the opportunities and physical facilities of these schools are not equal.* This inequality affects schools' conditions, especially in terms of social, cultural and sports activities. For instance, as the semi-urban school building was rebuilt in 2008 with the sponsorship of a private company, it has better facilities (sports hall and areas for various branches, laboratory, musical instruments, a music hall, camera, table tennis equipment on each floor, etc.). Although located in a central area of Istanbul, the urban school (built in 1967) is the one with the most limited facilities. School grounds within cities are usually small, so building facilities for sports and other activities remains challenging, demanding long hours of negotiation with relevant administrators and bureaucrats. Some students who were admitted after being successful in the entrance exam stated that they cried when they first arrived, because the neighbourhood is not a well-developed urban setting. However, they added that over time they began to like the school's atmosphere. Another important resource is the *endowments of the parents.* The parents of students who enrol in the school by examination have a greater tendency to make donations to the school in order for their children to get a better education. There is an obvious decrease in school donations from families whose children are enrolled based on address due to their lower income level. This directly limits the opportunities for social and cultural activities run by schools, including those that are part of formal education. Therefore, even though all public schools take their basic financial resources from the state budget, the material resources of the parents and their wish to support their children's education are important factors in increasing the capacity of the school.

Second, each school has developed *different methods and strategies* for arranging cultural and social activities as well as for increasing student participation. For instance, at the semi-urban school, some clubs are at the forefront of student life. Teachers may organise activities with interested students, as they do in the Astronomy Club, for instance. At the rural school, there is a Chess Club. In contrast, at the urban school, student clubs are less important; instead, some teachers (with the support of the headteacher and in collaboration with students) organise various activities, such as issuing a school magazine in English, field trips, and scientific projects. They also arrange "intercultural days". Thanks to these activities, students have the chance to take on responsibility, work together as a team, get to know their schoolmates and teachers, put their various talents and interests to practical use, and enjoy more of their time at school.

The school administration also has a significant influence on extracurricular opportunities. For example, the urban school teachers who currently take roles in organising these activities have worked at the school for a while. In the past, teachers did not organise such activities at this intensity. Although they stated that they were open to ideas, the new head teacher facilitated a suitable environment for extracurricular opportunities by supporting teachers and students (as well as parents). In the rural school, the headteacher decided to pursue a different approach due to the local conditions. He stated that, as his students are mostly from low-income families, he seeks to encourage them to participate in sports, despite the school's limited resources. He believes that sport helps to both "discipline" young people and to prevent them from "having bad habits" (smoking cigarettes, drinking alcohol). In this school, when students were asked about cultural activities they attended at school, most of them thought about parade, choir, music: activities organised alongside other schools and affiliated organisations or in the city centre as a part of national (official) ceremonies. The urban school facilitates a more open environment for graduation events, festivals, inter-school music competitions and theatre shows where students and teachers can come together and students take an active role.

Each school tries to 'manage the mobility and temporality' of their social and cultural activities based on their facilities' capacity and location. The school administration needs to take several factors into account, such as the transportation of students from school to sites; the schedule of shuttles; preventing the overlap of cultural activities with core academic programmes; the dilemma of whether to focus on extra-curricular activities or on university entrance exams, etc. Therefore, we should not consider the schools as isolated locations. The urban school in the city centre has better access to various museums, exhibitions and concerts. At the rural school, access to such areas is very limited. Managing the above factors and producing alternative opportunities can be difficult. Students at the rural school expressed their desire to organise trips to nearby cities more than young people at the other schools, as there are not enough cultural sites and alternative practices near them. The school has arranged trips to cities with attractive sights, such as *Eskişehir* and *Bursa,* in recent years, but only a limited number of students were able to attend these trips.

At this point, there is another issue that needs to be emphasised: at first glance, a school administration's list of activities carried out over recent years may seem impressive, but sometimes only certain students can participate in these activities due to the financial conditions of the school and the students' families. Some students are not even aware of these opportunities. The frequency of this lack of publicity must be questioned when considering how each school manages cultural and social activities. Another factor impacting participation in cultural and social activities is the *temporal management* of the events. Many of these activities are defined as extra-curricular activities, meaning that some students have to waive their normal classes in order to engage in them. (Mandatory classes are not disrupted.) This is a significant problem, especially for students and families who attach more importance to university exams. Alternatively, students may remain at school for a few more hours after class, but this is also difficult, especially for students who live in remote areas and come to school by shuttle. Parents are not always happy with after-school activities, either.

Extra-curricular activities

Reflecting changes in national education policies, more importance has been attached to extra-curricular activities at schools in recent years (Şentürk et al., 2018). There is strong emphasis placed on the idea that certificates acquired by participating in such activities have a positive effect on students' university enrolment as well as their career prospects. However, the best way to integrate these extra-curricular activities into the school curriculum remains uncertain. For now, teachers and students find intermediate solutions to timetabling issues and try to continue activities for as long as possible. Some students are disappointed when extracurricular programmes do not live up to their promises. For example, a student from the rural school was excited and prepared diligently for a debate event on 'globalisation and the use of technology', to be held at a university in the province. However, she experienced disappointment when an invited company manager instead used the time to promote his own company and young people were not given any room to speak (Afife, female, student, rural school). In other words, while extra-curricular programmes and events start with good intentions, they can sometimes turn into a mere formality, unable to attract or sustain the attention they expect from young people.

It is also important to consider how teachers manage to involve students in all kinds of social activities and cultural participation processes. Generally, administrators and teachers decide on the content and basic structure of the activity held based on their own experiences, and get students involved in the process by assigning duties to them. At the urban school, we observed that teachers try to include students more actively in determining the content and outline of the activities. Meanwhile, administrators and teachers work with students to find solutions together for any problems that may arise. For example, in the week of the May 2019 graduation celebrations, students wanted to have a water fight, which was allowed only when everyone agreed to wear black on the day of the game. Thus, they together took precautionary measures against students' clothes becoming transparent and possible criticism that could come from outside the school. Similarly, students wanted to use coloured water, but it was agreed that these dyes would not be permanent. Students also took responsibility for cleaning the entire school after the celebrations. In short, when administrators and teachers share concerns with their students based on their experiences, and try to create solutions with students rather than focusing on obstacles, they create a more effective communication channel between students and administrators. This helps to reduce the formal image of school and administrators, which is often seen as an 'obstacle' preventing students from having fun at school.

Finally, at all three schools we observed the presence of certain clubs and activities that students pursued with increasing interest, although they did not contribute directly to preparation for the university entrance exam. Both students and their parents predicted that these activities would positively improve the skills and careers of the participants in the long run. We observed a particular interest in foreign language programmes: students and parents considered that practicing languages such as French, German and especially English would allow the young people to study and perhaps work abroad as well. The Model United Nations (MUN) organisation is the most ambitious programme in which the schools are engaged.[7] MUN, which is an international organisation, has an active student group involved in arranging events, especially at schools that focus on English language learning. As part of the programme students hold a mock UN session, research how the countries they represent as delegates approach global issues, and hold a debate according to the UN format and style. MUN is an organisation that encourages learning by doing direct research on different countries and social issues. Of course, the programme is made more attractive for young people by including social events, interactions, and games. In Turkey, students at schools that offer more competitive English language education have more chances to attend this event. Similarly, coding courses or debate clubs offer education programmes as extra-curricular activities. Those promoting these activities suggest that they develop '21st Century skills' of leadership, innovation, critical thinking, creativity, communication and cooperation.[8] It is important to question the imposition and celebration of these skills as the "absolute" skills

---

7 For the Turkey branch of MUN see https://www.munturkey.com/.

8 The discourse continued under the 21st-Century skills in Turkey reproduce the themes in the following web page: Partnership for 21st Century Skills http://www.battelleforkids.org/networks/p21.

required for the 21st century. However, young people involved in these activities develop greater cultural literacy while honing their ability to communicate with people living in other countries. The opinion that such skills should be cultivated has become stronger at the urban and semi-urban schools in recent years. At the rural school, this approach is limited to learning English to improve students' job opportunities.

Youth aspirations and cultural participation: Interaction, fun and excitement

Students' cultural participation is not limited to what schools have to offer. Some young people develop hobbies before enrolling in high school, which they may continue in or outside the school environment. Interviewed students were most interested in sports (such as football, basketball, volleyball, martial art) or playing a musical instrument (such as classic or electric guitar, or *bağlama*). Those with a prior involvement in sports can easily be included in school teams and thus establish a stronger bond with their schools. Selim, who learned to play basketball in a secondary school with good sport facilities (and opportunities) in Istanbul, joined the basketball team of the rural school after his family moved to the region for financial reasons and has quickly become the school's Sports representative. Selim said that, in this way, he made friends from different grades at the school and established close relationships with teachers, especially the physical education teacher (Selim, male, student, rural school). Similarly, students interested in music and those who played a musical instrument were able to take part in the activities and performances organised by their schools. While the number of students playing guitar at the urban and semi-urban schools was higher, some rural school students played the *bağlama*, one of the important stringed instruments of the folk music tradition in Turkey. Other young people play the drums, piano, percussion, flute, and harmonica. Young people are also interested in listening to different types of music. Rock, Metal and Rap music are especially popular among young people. Those who consider music as an indicator of cultural literacy slightly disdain young people who primarily listen to native pop music. To many young people, it seems important to follow current music groups. Rarely do students listen to folk or European classical music; interest in these two genres is either transferred from their family and social backgrounds or necessitated by the musical instruments they learn (such as the piano and *bağlama*).

There are also students interested in different cultural activities, such as drawing, photography, dance, theatre, writing, and documentary. It is more difficult to observe a pattern in the formation of these hobbies, but interviewed students often referred to their social backgrounds in this context. For example, Miray mentioned that her grandfather, father and older brother enjoyed painting and that her grandfather's paintings hung on the walls of the house (Miray, female, student, semi-urban school). Even if young people spend relatively limited time and energy with their families during their adolescence, it is possible to say that cultural literacy and interests they acquired during childhood can remain relevant. On the other hand, the social background of young people makes it possible for them to critically examine the mainstream cultural practices they encounter at school and beyond, rather than to adopt them immediately. For example, students may have a sibling with high cultural literacy, a family with a liberal or oppositional approach, or an ethnic identity (such as Kurds, Rums, Armenians, Laz) or religious/sect background (such as Christians, Alevis) other than the dominant Turkish identity, which is widely considered to be *Sunni-Turk*. Ultimately, the social background of young people is a mediator in their cultural participation.

The fact that young people want to sustain and deepen their friendships in this period also has an effect in shaping their social and cultural activities. Making friends, spending time together, and having fun in club activities inside and outside school are important elements of young people's lives. As a matter of fact, 'spending time with friends', 'going to shopping malls', 'going to the cinema', 'sitting in the café', 'sitting in the park and talking' were common expressions that interviewed young people used to explain their free time activities. Depending on their school's neighbourhood, they try to spend time with friends in environments where they will not be disturbed and can act freely. Students form their close friendships according to their fields of interest – sports, books, music, computer games, cartoons, movies, TV series, etc. Therefore, the dynamics of friendship relations also shape the cultural tastes of young people. One student interviewed at the urban school defined the cultural setting of the school through the 'school alpha':

> *Friendship environments generally have an 'alpha'. This alpha is often a dominant character. He listens to such [music], and it spreads from him to the others, then to others, a certain section in the school becomes inclined towards that. I was, for example, before coming to this school, listening to Rock in English. Then I came to this school, the dominant section in this school led me more for instance to some groups in Turkish rock.* (Lusaac Smp, male, student, urban school)

These friendships are instrumental in both helping young people to get to know each other's cultures and for cultural exchange. Young people defined their identities, interests, and tastes through the relationships and conversations they have established during this period. One student explained the role he attributes to the school in this regard as follows:

> *I learn through the school but the school does not teach me. The school is only a mediator as it introduces me to friends. So, I am introduced to some other people in my friendship circle [...] Culture is thus those differences, different things, and also, I think I acquire culture with my accompanying research.* (Tim, male, student, semi-urban school)

In all observed schools, there was an interest in cultural discussion and talking with students different from them. Many issues, such as religion and atheism, sexuality, and politics in Turkey, were mentioned. Students stated that, inevitably, some debates could be profound and intense. Ultimately, high school education as a setting can be an occasion for different identities to come together, to be recognised and to transfer cultures through friendship. For example, while the rural school seems to be more limited in terms of cultural diversity at first glance, there are students from countries including Iraq and Iran, and some students from Iran are Christians. Therefore, as students meet these young people, they also start to interact with and get to know other cultures. As the urban school is in a district in Istanbul where there are relatively many non-Muslims, Muslim students may become familiar with non-Muslims in ways that they might not otherwise. Again, other encounters with identities such as Kurd, Alevi, Leftist, and Nationalist are also experienced in schools. On the other hand, a student who moved to the rural school from Istanbul and identifies as a left-wing person like his family, indicated that it is still more difficult to talk about such topics openly in the rural setting (Zethe, male, student, rural school). As mentioned earlier, there is a stronger nationalist and conservative tendency in the surroundings of the rural school. In sum, although education institutions prefer to avoid discussion of highly controversial issues, including local and national identities and politics in Turkey (Çayır, 2014), students seek to construct their own platforms to talk about these topics. Friendship and communication, which young people establish in and around their high schools, can also be considered part of cultural exchange and transfer. While enjoying time with friends, young people also have the opportunity to meet people with different types of cultural participation and levels of cultural literacy. In particular, these encounters give a direct impression of cultures and identities outside the country's mainstream discourse, although this is not always easy for the young people involved.

In terms of social and cultural activities, the potential of the neighbourhoods in which young people live is also important. Cultural offers are limited around the rural school, and the families' financial means are more limited. Students can attend courses run by public institutions, such as Youth Centres, that work mostly under the Ministry of Youth and Sports. However, Youth Centres have recently started to be given more responsibility to communicate the government's nationalist, conservative and religious policies with the local youth (Şentürk et al. 2018). Students can also access the activities of organisations that have direct organic links with the conservative-religious Justice and Development Party (AKP), such as the Turkey Youth Foundation[9] (TÜGVA) and the Turkey Youth and Education Service Foundation (TÜRGEV). In other words, young people at the rural school can only participate in activities provided by a narrow range of organisations and institutions. In the urban and semi-urban schools, students have more opportunities to pursue their interests in institutions that complement their own worldviews and lifestyles, and they can access different, private or non-profit courses in Istanbul more easily.

Apart from extracurricular youth organisations, digital home-based activities shape the social and cultural life of youth. These include communicating with friends or different people over the internet, following social media, watching TV series and movies, listening to music, and playing computer games with online teams (especially among the male students). When we consider these activities, we can say that cultural literacy of the youth is fed from a broader variety of channels than that of adults. Since young people follow news events on television less often, their sources of information about the world can differ greatly in both content and format. Instead of listening to a long story, their news is circulated through short videos or images. Thanks to new digital communication and information technologies, youth can gain impressions of different cultures and societies, receive information and become interested in some aspects of these cultures. For example, during the Cultural Days at the urban school, Sao Paulo, who also attracted our attention with her good English accent, started corresponding with Dutch followers in English when she opened a fan account on Instagram for Yolanthe Cabau, Spanish-Dutch actress and television host. She then started to watch TV series and videos in order to improve her English. Sao Paolo, who chose this nickname for our interview, also developed an interest in Latin America and started learning Spanish and making online friends. Other young people have started learning Russian and Korean, sometimes unintentionally. For example, when they are interested in Korean music and follow Korean TV series, they gradually pick up aspects of the language. Kim

9 http://en.tugva.org/

from the rural school explained how interest in K-Pop (Korean Pop) recently increased among young people in Turkey:

> *Now there is a 'Korean wave', they already name it [...]. The music groups of Korea are very interesting. Because they dance. As in Turkey we suffer from a famine of dance, look at half of the clips in Turkey, you just stand before the houses or stand before the white screen and dance, and it is over! But in Korea there is nothing like that, even the smallest dance has choreography, you make different movement for every second. The lights, those stage lights, are satisfying to the eye. That started to spread very widely nowadays.* (Kim, female, student, rural school).

Those people with more ability to use digital communication and information technologies are interested in materials with more visuality and mobility. The materials shared by the popular YouTubers in Turkey (such as *Barış Özcan* and *Ruhi Çenet*), who were frequently mentioned among the youth, tell stories that are supported by images. This establishes fast and interesting connections between different topics, providing information to capture the attention of young viewers.

Young people's curiosity drives them to research many areas of interest and to improve themselves. At each school, we encountered students whose aspirations developed from their initial experiences in different subjects. These students obtained further information about these areas, especially through digital platforms, and they established connections with different people and cultures during their research. For example, one student at the rural school was interested in cars: he watched different online videos to learn how to modify cars, connected with people who shared such materials, and finally began to modify cars himself. He said that it was a great pleasure to hear the new sound of the car engine. Later, he learned professional videography in order to share images of the cars he modified (Bahadır, male, student, rural school). Another student learned how to make a guitar by watching YouTube videos after he started to play that instrument (Zethe, male, student, rural school). Similarly, there are students who learned coding by watching videos and now earn income from this (Emir, male, student, rural school). An Iraqi student who, after coming to Turkey, started a bodybuilding course and became an instructor in the same hall two years later, now intends to open his own shop while preparing for national competitions. He follows bodybuilders from different parts of the world; he especially wants to go to Los Angeles because it is prominent in this area (Serhat, male, student, rural school). In sum, when young people have passions for certain topics, they become more determined to improve themselves, to learn very detailed information, and to establish links with different people and social groups over digital platforms. Thus, while developing their cultural participation and literacy, young people also gain a more culturally inclusive approach to learning. However, when the male students at the rural school choose their fields of interest, they tend to focus more on ways to earn money because their financial conditions are relatively limited. Although some of these students have interesting and promising hobbies, in their interviews they pointed out the jobs that come to the fore in their environment.

Discussion

This study first invites us to rethink the construction and implementation of education and culture policies. Since recent governments established by the conservative and religious *Justice and Development Party* have increasingly implemented conservative, pious, and nationalist policies in the realm of education and culture, researchers have started to pay increasing attention to the results of such policies. However, as mentioned above, these ongoing discussions also have the potential to unhelpfully limit our grasp of youth cultural practices, because they may lead us to approach these issues by reproducing binary oppositions such as 'secular' versus 'religious', 'modern' versus 'conservative', etc. Our intention is neither to underestimate the role of power relations in attempts to impose particular cultural practices, views, and beliefs on society, nor to ignore the conflicts among different social groups around these politicised positions. However, the realm of everyday cultural practices transcends the notion of culture as imposed by the power, and we need to find ways to approach this realm as well. The qualitative field research we conducted in three state schools helps us to acknowledge that the cultural practices of young people are more complex, diverse and dynamic than the notion of culture envisioned and promoted by the power. These practices are reproduced in certain performative ways, coming together through the interaction of various human and non-human actors around the setting of formal education.

As shown above, young people have many fields of interest, both inside and outside school, that reflect their cultural participation. Nevertheless, when we began to talk directly about 'culture' or 'cultural heritage' with this demographic, we noticed that they did not consider many of their own activities and interests as a part of culture. For interviewed young people, the concept of culture either only included certain 'high culture' activities (for instance, going to museums and classical music concerts),[10] or was perceived more generally as the 'essence' or 'heritage' of 'our' identity (Turkish in this case). Often, culture is seen as a type

10 Among the young people we interviewed, few of them went to a museum, exhibition, classical music concert or theatre; we saw that youth would prefer to go to a cafe, on a walk or to a cinema. For the study supporting our finding, see Erdoğan (2016).

of stable knowledge that is not directly related to people's daily practices but can be acquired by certain means.

In the formal education setting, cultural topics that youth encounter should gain meaning in their daily lives. Their relationships with friends take priority in sharing interests, knowledge, tastes and favourite subjects. Young people, especially though digital communication and information technologies to explore topics that attract their attention in the formal education setting, actually make cultural literacy more current, usable, and interpretable. While we were conducting our research, direct access to Wikipedia was blocked in Turkey. However, young people still use this platform for research.[11] This is a very concrete example of the discrepancy between the institutional and youth approaches towards access to knowledge. When young people use digital communication tools, they gain increased access to cultural knowledge platforms, and learn both different *content* and different *methods* through these technologies. Widespread knowledge as *content* is no longer limited to what teachers allow or what the course books say. Similarly, more rapid, interactive knowledge transmission *methods* are more frequently used with visually rich videos and diagrams, subjects and skills that are not learned in a classical lecture format. At the same time, young people follow (and may interact with) different individuals, social groups, and organisations through digital tools and platforms.

It is necessary to try to understand how youth is positioned within the formal education setting in relation to all of these developments. Recent top-down education and cultural policies in Turkey aim to 'encode' certain knowledge and approaches, which are concerned with promoting conservative, religious and nationalist content. Thus, those social groups with the political power assume that they know what is right and acceptable from the beginning, and are inclined to impose that 'knowledge' and 'approach'. Consequently, government-run youth organisations are insufficient to respond to the demographic's expectations, interests, and aspirations. However, teachers and administrators in direct interaction with youth in a formal education setting cannot stay totally indifferent to young people's expectations, as they have to include them in their programmes. Teachers and administers have to interact with youth cultural practices in one way or another. Ultimately, even though all state schools follow the same curriculum, each school presents a relatively unique 'package of cultural participation and cultural literacy' to its students.

11 From 29 April 2017 to 15 January 2020, Wikipedia was blocked in Turkey. https://en.wikipedia.org/wiki/Block_of_Wikipedia_in_Turkey

Conclusion

We will conclude our article with some proposals on how to improve cultural participation and cultural literacy in a formal education setting. First, schools should be encouraged to broaden the scope and to enrich the content of the 'package' they offer. Recent education policies have suggested that youth should be led to specific fields of interest and should improve themselves through elective courses and extracurricular activities (Şentürk et al., 2018). However, for the schools to take more meaningful steps in this direction, the complexities they face should be simplified. School administrators and teachers currently spend many hours 'managing the mobility and temporality of their social and cultural activities' in efforts to sustain such activities. All steps that simplify these processes are valuable. Second, the university entrance examination, which young people sit after four years of high school education, profoundly determines the shape of students' later formal education as well as their high school experience. Young people place more weight on spending time with their friends as they deal with novel cultural and social activities during the first 2 years (9th and 10th grades). In the 11th and 12th grades, however, they tend to withdraw from these activities, especially if they want to achieve a good result in the university entrance exam. University entrance exams determine the manner of teaching in schools to a great extent, as teachers must tailor the details of the subject content to the specific shorter format of the exam. This may restrict the teachers, even at the onset of high school, from selecting more open lecturing styles. Our research suggests that young people are more inclined to learn new educational content when it relates to their daily life and is delivered in a way that attracts their attention and curiosity. This is distinct from the university entrance examination format, which, as currently implemented, encourages rote learning and destroys students' enthusiasm for learning. However, our field research presents us with strong examples of how youth are often able to improve themselves by applying resources outside the formal education setting, especially when they are interested in a topic and wish to pursue it. Therefore, it is important to develop access to the kinds of alternative areas and resources through which youth can pursue their cultural practices outside school. However, significant inequality exists among schools and students in access to such courses of study. Due to the limited resources in the rural area, the state or pro-ruling party institutions are the main providers of cultural activities; at times, however, these organisations have issues of bias and sometimes seek to impose their political inclinations on the local youth. All institutions related to working with young people should be autonomous and free from the political agendas of the government or political parties.

The social background of young people is an important mediator in their cultural participation and their future aspirations. Young people are also introduced to certain cultural practices by their families and friends. The cultural literacy they develop through their social background enables them to question and evaluate cultural content offered by different institutions, including schools.

At the rural school, in particular, young people are turning to digital communication and information technologies for personal development in the face of limited opportunities. These platforms offer 'potential' and 'opportunity', but are not a guaranteed solution to all the shortcomings of the formal education setting, and should not be 'romanticised' or 'glorified' for their own sake. In fact, many young people navigate social media simply to 'kill/spend time'; some play computer games for the same reason. Even young people who professed more dedication to preparing for the university entrance exam confessed that they spent too much time on social media or their mobile phone. As a result, when talking about youth, both the opportunities and challenges of digital technologies should be taken into consideration.

Through these technologies, the cultural participation, literacy and interaction spheres of youth in Turkey transcend familiar Western/secular versus conservative/Islamic distinctions. The cultural practices of youth do not easily conform to traditional categories used to classify adults. For instance, young people from both secular and conservative families may be fans of the same rock group. Similarly, they may be interested in other cultures, societies and geographies, such as K-Pop and anime. As they do not totally conform to the current cultural positioning and codes in Turkey, young people have the potential of becoming interested in diverse fields. Finally, it is possible to say that young people with various interests and aspirations are open to establishing connections with distinct people, social groups and institutions while they try to develop their own knowledge and skills in these fields.

Of course, when making such a statement, one should be careful not to define youth as a 'homogenous' category and present a single 'prescription' to all young people. As with definitions made under the category of '21st Century skills', we may be imposing certain priorities on young people while excluding other qualities and challenges. Such an approach may ignore the variable material conditions of young people. For example, in the three schools where the research was conducted, while young people all felt intense anxiety over the future, there were clear differences among the ways they thought about shaping their future. At the rural school, enrolling in university is less common; instead, students look for relatively 'secure' employment within their own local context. At the urban schools, students have begun to feel that enrolling in a good university is no longer sufficient for a promising career, which has made the stress stemming from examination preparation and future plans more prevalent. This is why more effort is needed to understand the world of culture and the interests of today's youth, within all different social backgrounds.

Finally, when asked directly what culture is, youth usually answered that 'culture' and 'cultural heritage' is fixed, stable, 'high' or 'praised'. In other words, they may not consider many of their own activities or interests under the umbrella of 'culture'. Therefore, 'culture' and 'cultural heritage' needs to be redefined and presented as a field of practice that has a place in daily life. Culture is the part of our activities and practices that can be reproduced, interpreted and enjoyed; it is an area of practical endeavour that can enhance our lived experience.

Acknowledgments

We would like to thank Elina Marmer and Cornelia Sylla for their valuable comments on our article, and also Bahadır Ahıska and Graham Sheard for proof-reading and helping us to improve it.

References

Akın, Y. (2004). Gürbüz ve Yavuz Evlatlar: Erken Cumhuriyet'in Beden Terbiyesi ve Spor. İstanbul: İletişim Yayınları.

Akşit, E. E. (2013). Kızların Sessizliği: Kız Enstitülerinin Uzun Tarihi. İstanbul: İletişim Yayınları.

Altinyelken, H. K., Çayır, K., & Agirdag, O. (2015). 'Turkey at a crossroads: critical debates and issues in education', Comparative Education, 51(4), 473–483, https://doi.org/10.1080/03050068.2015.1089076 (Accessed on March 3, 2021).

Altınay, A. (2004). The Myth of the Military Nation: Militarism, Gender and Education in Turkey. New York: Palgrave Macmillan.

Apple, M. W. (1995). Education and Power, 2nd ed. Routledge.

Bahçekapılı, M. (2015). 'Türkiye'de Din Eğitiminin Politik Tarihi'. In A. Gümüş (ed.), Türkiye'de Eğitim Politikaları, pp. 371–403. İstanbul: Nobel ayıncılık.

Bourdiue, P. & Passeron, J. (1977). Reproduction in Education, Society and Culture. London: Sage.

Çayır, K. (2014). "Biz" kimiz? Ders Kitaplarında Kimlik, Yurttaşlık Hakları. İstanbul: Tarih Vakfı Yayınları.

Çayır, K. (2016). 'Türkiye'de Ulusal Kimliği Yeniden Tanımlama Yolunda Özcülük, Çokkültürlülük ve Kültürlerarası Eğitim', Eğitim Bilim Toplum Dergisi, 14 (155), 77–101.

Erdoğan, E. (2016). 'Türkiye'de Gençlerin İyi Olma Hali Saha Araştırması Bulguları', Habitat Derneği, https://habitatdernegi.org/wp-content/uploads/turkiye-de-genclerin-iyi-olma-hali-raporu.pdf (Accessed on February 17, 2020).

Eroler, E. G. (2019). Dindar Nesil Yetiştirmek: Türkiye'nin Eğitim Politikalarında Ulus ve Vatandaş İnşası. İstanbul: İletişim Yayınları.

Gök, F. (2004). 'Eğitimin Özelleştirilmesi'. In: N. Balkan & S. Savran (eds.), Neoliberalizmin Tahribatı: Türkiye'de Ekonomi, Toplum ve Cinsiyet, pp. 94–110. Istanbul: Metis Yayınları.

Gök, F. (2007). 'The Historical Development of Turkish Education'. In M. Carlson, A. Rabo & F. Gök (eds.), Education in 'Multicultural' Societies: Turkish and Swedish Perspectives, pp. 247–255. London and New York: I. B. Tauris & Co Ltd.

Gümüş, A. (ed.) (2015). Türkiye'de Eğitim Politikaları. Ankara: Nobel Yayıncılık.

İnal, K. & Akkaymak, G. (2012). Neoliberal Transition of Education. New York: Palgrave Macmillan.

Kaya, A., Aydın, A. & Vural, G. (eds.) (2016). Değerler Eğitimi: Eğitimde Farklılık ve Katılım Hakkı. İstanbul: İstanbul Bilgi Üniversitesi Yayınları.

Latour, B. (2005). Reassembling the Social - An Introduction to Actor-Network Theory. New York: Oxford University Press.

Lefebvre, H. (1991). The Production of Space. Oxford: Blackwell Publishing.

Lüküslü, D. (2016). 'Creating a Pious Generation: Youth and Education Policies of the AKP in Turkey', Southeast European and Black Sea Studies, 16 (4), 637–649.

Reay. D. (2017). Miseducation: Inequality, Education and the Working Classes. Policy Press.

Şentürk, Y., Uçarol, A.B., Oral, A., Mete, H., Esmer, E., & Kurban, S. B. (2018). In: Fooks, G., Stamou, E. & McNie, K. (eds.) National Cultural/Educational Policy Review, 237–284. Unpublished Report.

Tekeli, İ. (1998). Tarih Bilinci ve Gençlik. İstanbul: Tarih Vakfı Yurt Yayınları.

Uçarol, A. B., Oral, A., Mete, H., Esmer, E., & Kurban, S. B. (2019). In: Marmer, E. & Zurabishvili, T. (eds.), Qualitative Research in Formal Educational Settings: National/Federal Curricula Review. 210–237. Unpublished Report.

Ural, A. (2015). 'Temel Eğitime Örtülü Bir Saldırı: Değerler Eğitimi', Eleştirel Eğitim, 38, 21–24.

(by Chandrani Chatterjee, Swati Dyahadroy and Neha Ghatpande)

Chapter 2 Questioning cultural homogeneity: Negotiating cultural plurality by young people in formal educational settings in India

Abstract: The present chapter is the culmination of a study conducted in three schools in the state of Maharashtra in India, which aimed to understand the ways in which culture is perceived by young people and what roles institutional and family set ups play in shaping this. Data collected through interviews and observation reiterates the complex and nuanced nature of culture, and the particular issues of grappling with such a concept in a country like India. While there is a long tradition of 'Indian culture', this category is frequently contested, as there are competing claims about what 'Indian culture' represents; there have been several attempts by the nation state to explain what post-independence Indian culture should be. This makes it difficult to conceptualise one universally-applicable definition of 'Indian culture'.

In its legal institutional structure and its ideological positioning, the Indian nation state has adopted a substantially inclusive approach to culture. However, the practice of culture often tends to accommodate tendencies of exclusion. The co-existence of institutional and ideological inclusivity and spaces of exclusion in practice makes the Indian context both challenging and interesting. Interviews conducted in the schools helped us to examine the nuanced nature of cultural perceptions as well as the genesis of cultural identity in the young people, and the large trajectory that culture has. In this specific case, culture can perhaps be best described as being always 'in the making'.

It is important to underline that the school interviews proved to the difficulty of defining the concept of culture in any clear way. In the Indian context, the school has become a space where plurality can be highlighted and the ways in which culture has been mobilised/ homogenised can be mapped. The challenge is how to conceptualise plurality as difficult terrain that cannot simply be celebrated: there needs to be a critical review of the ways in which plurality often translates into inequality within Indian culture.

Through interviews with both teachers and students across three schools, it became clear that the students (who came from various class, caste and religious backgrounds) primarily participated in mainstream Hindu festivals celebrated publicly and at home.

Keywords: culture, youth, hegemony, diversity, caste, identity and gender

Introduction

Ever since its independence from British rule in 1947, India has had a complex way of dealing with culture. On the one hand, there is a rather unproblematic vision of culture as a homogenous 'national culture'. Most policies related to culture have propagated the idea of a legitimate culture as that which contributes to a wider programme of nation-building (WorldCP, 2013). On the other hand, governments have tried to develop a narrative of celebration of diversity. However, the idea of the nation projected in such discourses inevitably presents a homogenised version of culture, which is needed to produce a seamless narrative of harmonious, democratic nationhood. The debate over whether India should have a national cultural policy has been prevalent for a while now, but it has been widely rejected on account of the sheer heterogeneity and diversity of Indian culture and the complexity involved in classifying the country's many art forms.

As a nation-state still emerging from its colonial past and making its mark on the trajectory of global politics, India stands as a unique case compared to other countries with or without a history of colonialism. The country's status as the largest democracy in the world, and as a plural society with inequalities of many kinds, is at loggerheads with the primarily right-wing politics of the recent past. While the spread of right-wing politics is a global phenomenon, India's case is distinct in the way this large democracy still manages a high level of inclusion, be it in terms of caste, religion, or language – thus, varied cultural aspects. This is perhaps difficult to compare to Europe. Much has already been written on the post-colonial condition and the ways in which this narrative is often given an easy linearity, with the hegemonic discourse being necessarily highlighted. Such an approach tends to overlook plural articulations and even out the possibilities of heterogeneous existences and negotiations between individuals and communities in an attempt to produce a homogeneous understanding of the nation-state and its culture. Contrary to this, our attempt here is rather to emphasise the plurality of Indian cultures and to suggest the dialogic nature of culture in India.

This 'dialogism', to borrow a Bakhtinian[1] concept (Bakhtin, 1981), plays a vital role in how cultures keep reshaping and renewing themselves. This rather

1 The Russian philosopher, literary critic and socio-linguist Mikhail Bakhtin (1895–1975) developed a philosophy of language and social theory that questioned notions of authoritarianism. He developed the concept of the 'dialogic' in juxtaposition with 'monologic' discourse. Bakhtin saw the novel as a genre with the potential of the dialogic, which he believed could subvert the monologic form of the epic. Bakhtin's philosophy, metaphorically, can be read as a challenge to the autocratic structure of Stalinist

fluid understanding of culture enables us to move beyond generic definitions and to situate culture as an entity forever in the making. Once we move beyond the closure of definitions, it becomes possible to locate the various entities that become interlocutors in this process. Education, undeniably, can be identified as an important player in facilitating the dialogism: it is essential to the making of cultures and can play a key role in strengthening the principle of equality in a hierarchised, graded society. Education often initiates a process of socialisation that plays a vital role in how cultures are understood and play out in practical terms. It also facilitates a dialogue between the past and the present, which is often reflected in how readings of the past shape and reshape our understanding of history as well as the present.

The interviews conducted for this research article help to reiterate the rather complex and intricate nature of connections that one can trace between formal education and the formation of ideas about culture, which in turn feeds into the creation of a nation-state. We have also tried to indicate the many ways in which issues of diversity and plurality often simultaneously play out in the narrative of homogeneity that has become a national hallmark. These rather curious juxtapositions are perhaps also indicative of the agency of the consumers of culture and education (young people, teachers, family members) and how they participate in the (re)making of ideas about cultures. We felt the need to emphasise this two-way exchange within the construction of cultures, as well as their circulation and consumption in the Indian context. The present article studies the state of Maharashtra in western India, further narrowing the focus by focusing on chosen schools in the city of Pune and nearby semi-urban settings. Given the sheer geographical expanse and diversity of India, it would be incorrect to assume that this study can be regarded as a representation of India in general. However, some patterns and tendencies that emerged from the interviews conducted in Pune may be also seen in other parts of India. So, though not indicative of the entire country, this article will provide a glimpse of the diverse ways in which culture is articulated in India.

Three schools were selected, two in the urban and one in the semi-urban area.[2] The two urban schools are located in the old quarter of Pune, as this area

---

Russia, where he lived. Though the idea of the dialogic and dialogism was developed across his entire writing career, the most cited work in this regard is his book *The Dialogic Imagination: Four Essays* (1975).

2 In Maharashtra, it is not common to find high schools in rural areas. Most students from rural areas migrate or travel long distances daily to continue their secondary or high school education in semi-urban as well as urban schools. This is why no rural school was selected for the CHIEF fieldwork.

contains caste diversity and is also considered a hub of cultural activity. There is substantial socio-economic diversity among students and teachers. The language of instruction in the two urban schools is regional (Marathi).[3]

The semi-urban school is based in Lonavala.[4] This location allowed us to work with students from diverse backgrounds Young people from neighbouring villages and industrial estates (migrants from different parts of Maharashtra, as well as some from other states) come to study at this school. Here, the language of instruction is English.

A total of 69 interviews were conducted in the 3 schools by 4 interviewers. Out of these, 60 interviews were conducted in Marathi, 3 in English, and 6 in dual or multiple languages including Hindi and English. All informants were Indian citizens.

School experiences: Location, composition and culture

The characteristics of the selected schools have inevitably impacted the ways in which culture and cultural activities are taught and practiced in each of them. 'Culture' has been invoked in the name of nation, religion, caste and gender. The challenge is to make sense of this concept in an enabling and empowering way. Modes of negotiating with culture(s) and its various ramifications deserve deeper critical analysis. Interpreting culture may 'mark' the differences between individuals, label cultural practices as 'high' or 'low', and distinguish the 'elite' from 'the masses.' Culture is not a product that is produced, circulated and consumed. Rather, it is a process of understanding lives, worldviews and systems at large. There is a need to address culture in more nuanced ways; we especially need to understand culture as a means through which individuals find meaning in their everyday lives and the ethos produced around it. In this case, we concentrate on the interplay of culture in the daily lives of adolescents between the ages of 14 and 18.

A common experience in all the three schools lay in the detailed explanations that had to be given by the researchers in order to encourage students to share their thoughts. A lot of warm-up exercises were needed to make the students comfortable, and then researchers had to frame the questions not in a direct

---

3 In Maharashtra, the language of instruction in schools can be both English and Marathi, along with a few examples of other languages. However, as the main language of the region, Marathi is generally the language of instruction in most of the schools in Maharashtra.

4 Lonavala is a semi-urban area located between Pune and Mumbai.

fashion but rather in a way that was both explanatory and facilitated the interview aims. Often these interventions would take the form of informal, casual and friendly conversations with the interviewees to make them feel at home. In the semi-urban school, this almost amounted to coaxing: the interviewer had to resort to innovative practices to make students share their feelings and opinions.

This general unwillingness can perhaps be attributed to the fact that students in Indian schools are not accustomed to such interviews. One of the concerns that surfaced time and again, both in the interviews and in our analysis of them, was the question of whether we can really interrogate a concept like culture in a country like India. How does one even go about introducing such a complex concept to young people?

In Urban school 1, it was observed that the students had particular difficulty in articulating their understanding of culture. There was a certain desire to maintain 'political correctness' in the answers, which seemed too neat and organised. This has much to do with the sense of pride that most students of this school exhibited; their school played a pioneering role in promoting women's education in Maharashtra as well as in constructing ideas about who they are (cultural identity). This sense of pride was also clearly visible in interviews with the teachers, who must have inculcated it in the students. Discipline, punctuality and cleanliness were cited as virtues on which the school insists. Students of Urban school 1 seemed to announce themselves as arbiters of the culture of Pune city and of democratic values. While the students and teachers at this school seemed to be confident and prepared to uphold a grand narrative of what they considered the school's glorious tradition, we recognised a homogenous discourse emerging from this sense of pride. A student in the 11th grade, who had transferred from a different school, indicated that the idea of culture should not be restricted to the state but should embrace all humanity. In its zeal to bolster Marathi culture and an associated pride, this school came across as the most elite and fixed in its agenda.

In Urban school 2, the interviews had to be conducted in a short span of time, primarily because it is a public school that is very short on staff and students. Many students commute from diverse social locations and come from economically underprivileged classes, especially those in the 11th and 12th grades. Most of the students studying in this school were also working to make their ends meet, and so were not attending lessons regularly. During the interviews, it seemed that this was perhaps the first time the students were asked to voice their opinions with a sense that their opinions mattered. The articulation of caste identity was much clearer and more forthright here. This being a public school (fully funded by the state), students from underprivileged castes and classes form the majority of the school. However, marginalisation of students from different religious identities continues.

Teachers from all three schools celebrated a sense of rootedness in culture. There seemed to be a high level of exposure to mainstream Brahmanical culture,[5] with less attention paid to anything diverse or at odds with the mainstream. This rather feudalistic behaviour in an otherwise democratic school (housing a majority of students from so-called lower and marginalised castes) is perhaps indicative of a larger shift towards a monolithic projection of culture and an outright rejection of the nuances and multiplicity has contributed to India's cultural diversity.

In the semi-urban school, the students and teachers articulated their views on culture in a much more detail than the other two schools. Two of the basic reasons for their greater cultural awareness are the Central Board of Secondary Education curriculum[6] and the very composition of the student body. In this school there are many students who have migrated from other Indian states and rural populations. Students originally from Karnataka, Jharkhand, Uttar Pradesh and Bihar bring distinct cultural diversity to the school environment and politics, which was visible despite the school's attempts at homogenisation. However, what initially appeared to be a happy, harmonious group gradually revealed a different narrative of discrimination and marginalisation. Interviewees had a tendency to adopt a more regional and linguistic identity, which resulted in othering the students from states outside Maharashtra.

With access to cultural and economic capital, the students in this school were very well versed with technology, showed familiarity with hip hop and rap music, and had aspirations of looking West. While the students' exposure to digital media was discouraged by most teachers, there was a clear indication that the idea of culture articulated by the young people was primarily mediated through new media and technology. This cannot be seen as a passive reception of technology, but as active participation in a technology-enabled world, which also contains within it possibilities for intervention and subversion. Technology

5 The term *Brahmanical* refers to those who are born into a caste group labelled Brahmin or linked with Brahmanism, the dominant ideology codified from earlier religious texts and practiced in everyday life. Brahmanical refers to those norms and practices that privilege the Brahmin and their way of life in cultural and religious terms. It is also a set of practices bound by the principle of purity vs pollution, which allow for the continued hegemony of the Brahmin.

6 The other two schools follow the Maharashtra State Board of Secondary and Higher Secondary Education (SSC) curriculum.

allows young people to access a larger world, something that they do not necessarily experience in their day-to-day lives. While technology was regarded by the teachers and parents as a threat to what they saw as rootedness in their own culture and traditions, the students explored an alternative way to experience what they perceived as their culture. For young people, WhatsApp, YouTube, Facebook and other social media platforms have become a means of straddling the local and the global, the universal and the parochial. The use of the internet to complete school assignments was reported as a regular practice among students and yet they were apprehensive about discussing their social media accounts. This apprehension could perhaps be attributed to how the school authorities project social media as a constant threat to students' growth and development. It appears that the students use new digital platforms as a shared space within their peer groups to engage in activities discouraged by the institutional space of the school. Often, youth culture and cultural practices are mediated through technology, and there can be no denying that the appeal of these technology-mediated cultural practices (and sharing these with a peer group) have become a major form of cultural participation among young people.

Notions of 'culture' and 'cultural heritage'

The interviews suggested that there is a lot of confusion about the concept of culture among the young people, especially in how they comprehend culture as a part of everyday life. For the interviewees, special events, celebrations and holidays were seen as part of culture. This is an obvious break from treating culture as ideational/sacred, instead underlining the everyday impact of culture and its mundane nature. These cultural events and festivals are celebrated both in private spaces – at home with family – and in public spaces. Thus, the line between sacred/ ideational and everyday/mundane can become blurred.

Of the many interpretations of culture that emerged through the interviews, one stood out as the most recurrent in the Indian context: culture was most often understood as a synonym to tradition. Traditions include customs, beliefs, festivals one celebrates, the food one eats, and festivities. The interconnectedness of these ideas cannot be overlooked, as was repeatedly exemplified by the informants' attempts at grappling with the concept of culture. By locating their examples of culture in festivities (mostly religious and celebrated publicly), interviewees invoked the intricate and complex connections that are at the core of any understanding of homogenised Indian culture; these connections reinforce the idea that society in general is upholding authentic culture. This projection of an authentic culture brings corollaries like cultural pride, cultural superiority and cultural divisions, which in turn form the basis of cultural identity.

The interviewed teachers and students understood culture differently. For example, a student from Urban school 2 talked about festivals as cultural pride and a way to connect to the past:

> *Culture means our language and the various festivals that we celebrate. We preserve our culture through them. By celebrating Gudi Padwa we start our new year. After that we celebrate* Diwali *and other festivals. To remember things [that] happened in ancient days we celebrate festivals.* (Sheetal, female, student, urban school 2, India)

On the other hand, a teacher from Urban school 1 indicated that cultural preservation is often mistaken as cultural education:

> *One of the main objectives is to look after it (culture), protecting your culture, this is the main purpose. In preserving culture, one does not think about the thoughts or feelings behind it, it tends to be more prone to blindly preserving it than it is to preserve it for that…* (Varsha, female, teacher, urban school 1, India)

Cultural identity

Cultural identity is often constructed through a set of binaries that are created and furthered by a process of socialisation. The school environment, curriculum, student-teacher interactions, and interactions between students and their peers all create conditions of socialisation that play vital roles in the formation of cultural identity. In our interviews, we noticed that the concept of cultural identity, like the concept of culture itself, was not clearly defined or understood by the young people. When asked about cultural identity, they tended to juxtapose their individual and their families' experiences with those of their peers. The family plays a crucial role in forging cultural identity, and in an Indian context the caste norms and cultural practices are intertwined in such a way that it is difficult to find a universal definition of culture. Many of the interviewed students identified themselves in relation to their everyday practices at home and within the family. They spoke about values and norms they had learned at home, such as respecting elders, pride in their religions and traditions, and clothing and culinary habits: in other words, values and norms that are generally learned more in the family than at school.

Even the values and norms related to a particular caste or a social or economic class are associated with the family setup and young people's practices there. At school, these values and norms are shaped further through a formalised system of socialisation. In none of the interviews did we witness reports of any radical transformation through processes of socialisation. Rather, existing values seem to be strengthened at school. For example, the role religion plays in a country like India in instituting a sense of identity cannot be overemphasised. An English teacher from the Semi-urban school, Kalpana, regarded religion as a value to be inculcated and internalised in the students:

> *First of all, I would like my students to know about the religion because I believe that religion can control the actions of anyone. If they know their religion well, if they know the teachings of their religion, definitely the fear would come for doing the wrong things, and that would restrict them into the wrong path. So, first of all I would like to tell them that they should follow the religion, they should know about the religion.* (Kalpana, female, teacher, semi-urban school, India)

What also emerged from the interviews was a strong opposition to the reservation policy in higher education.[7] This sentiment was common among teachers and students from the so-called upper and middle castes. For example, a student from Urban school 1, while answering a country-specific question about uprisings and marches for caste-based reservation rights in 2018–2019, said that she and other members of her family had participated in a march in support of the reservation for the Marathas[8] in education institutions and government jobs. However, she also held the opinion that discrimination based on caste needs should be annihilated in order to change reservation policy. This is a broader debate in contemporary India, which corresponds with the agony over the outcome of the reservation policy. The decision to implement the recommendations of the Mandal commission[9] was divisive; this led to violent protest by the so-called upper caste groups, who responded negatively to the greater presence of Dalits felt in public spaces that were previously occupied by the so-called upper

---

7 The reservation policy is an affirmative action policy that has been present in India since the 1950s and aims to empower those who come from a disadvantaged background when it comes to their educational and employment opportunities.

8 From 2007–08, the Maratha community, which is a dominant upper caste in Maharashtra, held silent marches across the state of Maharashtra to demand reservation in government jobs and educational institutions.

9 The Mandal Commission was established in 1979 by the government of India to identify the socially and economically disadvantaged classes that could be given reservations in government jobs. This commission recommended that 27 % of jobs in the public sector should be reserved for Other Backward Classes (OBCs), who constituted 52 % of India's population. This recommendation was implemented in 1990 and led to mass protests by upper caste students at colleges and universities across India, who opposed the reservation policy.

caste group. Thus, the reservation policy has in a limited way changed a few spaces, which has made the upper caste anxious about maintaining their hegemonic position. This anxiety was further aggravated thanks to an acceptance of neo-liberal state model, which has promoted privatisation and reduced the power of the state:

> *Yes, if we refuse to believe in caste discrimination then there won't be any need for reservation. If we stay together then everyone will get this equally. […] these differences of upper caste and lower caste should not be there.* (Payal, female, student, urban school 1, India)

By taking this position, Payal, who belongs to the upper caste Maratha community, is adhering to the argument made above: that reservation provided to the lower castes should either be cancelled or be provided to the dominant upper caste communities as well. Her understanding of reservation policy, which was very similar to that of other participants, comes from looking at the reservation policy as a type of reverse discrimination against the upper caste population. This entirely dismisses the idea of stigma and centuries-long discrimination.

Cultural participation

Cultural participation often begins in the family and continues in schools. Many of the interviewees said that the most common form of cultural engagement is participation in religious festivities. Of the festivals that were repeatedly mentioned in the interviews, the most important is the Ganesh festival, which has special significance in Maharashtra because it was initiated in the late 19th century by Bal Gangadhar Tilak (1856–1920), ideologue and nationalist leader of the Indian Independence Movement, in order to mobilise the population. These are religious and cultural celebrations in honour of the elephant god known as God Ganesha. Another celebration the students often mentioned is Diwali, festival of lights. The students expressed their familiarity with these celebrations and reported enthusiasm for participating in them. It is noteworthy that these celebrations seem to bridge social, religious, economic and caste divides, as students from different communities and different social and economic strata reported participating in these festivities. While these festivals provide occasions for celebration, one cannot forget the fact that the origins of these festivals (and others) are imbued with caste and religious hierarchies. They may thus be regarded as a curious combination of social hierarchy and divide. These festivities aim to propagate a sense of fellow-feeling and brotherhood, which a closer look exposes as being missing.

Another form of cultural participation mentioned in the interviews was the so-called special days, which are celebrated in schools and colleges. These special days can generally be divided into three types: (1) days of national importance, e.g. Independence Day, Republic Day or commemorations of national leaders (October 2 is celebrated across the country as Gandhi Jayanti, the birthday of Mahatma Gandhi); (2) different celebrations, like Traditional Day;[10] (3) days that are marked by state or national authorities, such as National Yoga Day (to propagate the practice of yoga as an ancient Indian cultural practice). In addition, the school authorities often organise visits to heritage sites or activities pertaining to environmental causes, like planting trees.

Negotiating other cultures

Indian students' knowledge about Europe is, usually, very limited. While the world history taught in the schools does include European topics, there is a general lack of awareness about Europe, and European culture in particular. Surprisingly, students showed a greater familiarity with Japanese and Korean cultures, perhaps owing to exposure through popular culture. For example, Pallavi (student) from the Urban school 1 said:

> *Me and my sister watch Japanese cartoons together. ... I really like the discipline that is there, they say 'sorry' and 'thank you' to each other all the time, and they continue the conversation. And they help each other, too... They have a nice culture. They preserve their culture and live like that, that is why I like it, and I feel that India should also do it.* (Pallavi, female, student, urban school 1, India)

Her comments on the hierarchisation of the linguistic communities in India and the growing importance of English as the most dominant language, indispensable for social, cultural and economic mobility, were also very interesting:

> *There is this curiosity that develops, their language is Japanese. And Maharashtra's language is Marathi. Whenever I watch [Japanese] dramas and cartoons, they always speak in Japanese, not so much in English, here it's a bit opposite. Marathi is less spoken and English is more spoken. We should preserve our Marathi as a Maharashtrian, or else even if not Marathi then at least Hindi should be spoken.* (Pallavi, female, student, urban school 1, India)

---

10 The schools and colleges in Pune city have annual day functions every year when schools and colleges celebrate occasions such as Chocolate Day, Rose Day and Traditional Day. On the latter occasion students wear costumes that are considered traditional (sari for women, salwar kurta for men).

Here, Pallavi is not only commenting on linguistic hierarchy but also on a cultural narrative that has always privileged Europe and America as the much sought-after destinations in which to fulfil one's aspirations. Pallavi aspired to do 'something different', and the popular culture of Japan and Korea represents an alternative space for her to nurture her dreams and aspirations:

> *Till now, I have seen that everyone likes to go to America, or in Europe; England, Paris, France, Germany, other countries they would like to go to, so I thought if it's the same, then I should do something different. … I like Japan, Korea, China more. [Laughs].* (Pallavi, female, student, urban school 1, India)

Europe was often not understood as a continent by the interviewees, but as a country. Moreover, in the binary of the West vs the East, it is America, not Europe, that was generally highlighted as the bigger influence on Indian culture. America and Europe were also used as synonyms for the West in general, especially where topics of fashion and clothing were concerned. Western fashion is often contrasted with the traditional clothing of Maharashtra.

Another strong opinion about the bad influence of 'western culture' was exemplified by a student from the Semi-urban school:

> *I feel it's not good. It has entered our country through European people. They will party late at night, sleep the whole day. But they have less population so they can earn well. Their total income doesn't get affected whatever they do. There is a big difference between their and our culture.* (Jinku, male, student, semi-urban school, India)

He further stated that:

> *Foreigners party whole night, drink beer, and their parents don't live with them. Children stay separately that's why they are so spoilt. But now that culture is gradually spreading in India. [I] Don't know how but it has spread more since the arrival of the British.* (Jinku, male, student, semi-urban school, India)

The above remark is symptomatic of the arbitrary synonymisation of the culture of the 'other' within colonial history. This creates the binary of 'our' versus 'their' culture, with the primary aim of aggrandising the former. Thus, one can see that an understanding of 'western culture' is always related to the British rule over India and its impact on what is understood as Indian culture and values.

Understanding the indian context: Impossibility of imagining a homogeneous culture

In India, questions of cultural awareness pertain to both the regional and the national level. Given the sheer geographical expanse of the country, it is very difficult to legitimately ascribe the label 'Indian culture' without accounting for the specificities of different regional and local cultures that contribute to the formation of what we may then loosely call 'Indian' culture. Nevertheless, the plurality of cultures has to be emphasised. It is perhaps more conducive to talk about Indian 'cultures', in the plural, from the very outset.

This plurality can be witnessed in the recurrence of caste and gender-related issues in the interviews. The question of the reservation of seats in formal education for marginalised communities was looked upon with a certain degree of concern by both teachers and students. While this is in line with the provisions made in the constitution of India, a certain kind of elitism rules rampant when it comes to executing reservation rules. This can be observed in the teaching community, including those members we interviewed. In spite of the fact that some interviewed teachers themselves got their jobs thanks to reservation rules, they were pessimistic about this, claiming that the rules are responsible for the declining quality of education. Young people from more privileged backgrounds in terms of caste hierarchy often look upon their less privileged peers as a threat to their existence. A discourse of caste and class privilege erases nuances that would perhaps have enabled an alternative history of the school. This was notable in Urban school 1, where the headteacher, despite herself being from a marginalised community, refused to be critical of her experience of caste and class at the school. There was a visible attempt at this school to project one form of regional Brahmanical orthodox culture as the dominant culture, though the number of teachers and students coming from privileged backgrounds was very low. This priority was evident in the ways in which caste barriers seemed to be overcome during the Ganesh festival, while there was no mention of Ambedkar Jayanti[11] or Buddha Purnima[12] as other occasions or days to be commemorated. Strikingly, in Urban school 2, which takes on a majority of students from middle- and lower middle-class backgrounds who belong to the Dalit community, they still mark Brahmanical celebrations. A certain kind of Brahmanical

11 Ambedkar Jayanti is a celebration of the birth anniversary of Dr Babasaheb Ambedkar (1891–1956), the architect of the Indian Constitution and the leader of the Dalit movement. It is celebrated by the Dalit community across the nation.

12 Buddha Purnima is a celebration of the birth anniversary of Gautam Buddha, the founder of Buddhism. It is celebrated in India on the national level, especially by the Dalit community, which converted to Buddhism following Dr Ambedkar in order to break the shackles of the oppressive Hindu caste system.

culture – that of the Ganesh festival, Shivaji Jayanti[13] and Diwali – seemed to be predominant in the minds of these young people, which was apparent in their understanding of culture. Thus, though the demographic compositions of these two schools are very different, their students and teachers did not exhibit the diversity that would have been expected.

An interesting example in this regard is the case of Kabir, the only Muslim student interviewed at Urban school 2. When asked about the events on the calendar that he would consider cultural occasions, Kabir's answer was Diwali; when asked about holidays, he mentioned Dussehra.[14] Although he comes from a Muslim community with Hindi as his first language, events like Ramazan or Eid did not occur to him until prompted by the interviewer. He further said, "*My opinion is that everyone should have one religion*" (Kabir, male, student, urban school 1, India). He could not state what religion this should be.

Similar dichotomies emerged with regard to gender during the interviews. Though gender equality is on the school agendas and both teachers and students talked about its importance, few practical steps have been taken to change the situation. For example, discussions of menstruation or the reproductive system are often conducted separately for male and female students. This primarily owes to the fact that it is considered taboo to speak about one's sexuality in public in general, and more so in the presence of the other gender. Even in the all-girls school, the students expressed their discomfort in discussing matters pertaining to the menstrual cycle. Certain taboos associated with gender kept surfacing in how gender roles played out in the schools, with a hint of gender discrimination. We noticed particular discrimination in the case of parenting, where families treated their male and female children differently.

Discussion: Post-coloniality and beyond

The study of cultural literacy practices in the schools of Maharashtra cannot be contained within any singular framework. This pushed us to look beyond post-coloniality to a more contemporary understanding of 'India' as a nation-state and 'Indian' culture as a corollary of that. It was therefore necessary to revisit the idea of the nation-state in its multiple forms and formulations, both when it comes to its structured institutional function and in the minutiae of its non-formal and

---

13 Shivaji Jayanti is a celebration of the birth anniversary of the Maratha Emperor, Shivaji. It is celebrated in Maharashtra and is a public holiday.

14 Dussehra, also known as Vijaya Dashmi, is a major Hindu festival that culturally marks either the goddess Durga's or the god Ram's triumph over evil.

loose execution. Ideas of inclusion and exclusion, and their ramifications in the circulation and consumption of the concept of culture, formed the cornerstone of our investigation.

The schools' practices of exclusion, for example, operate on several levels: linguistic, caste, gender and economic hierarchies, among others. What is challenging is the fact that not only are these forms of exclusion interrelated in important and rather complex ways, but that they are also instrumental to the maintenance of a democratic political structure that continues to carve its position in world politics. Moreover, the inclusivity-exclusivity contestations in the case of India also stem from, and to a large extent overlap with, the history of colonialism and colonial modernity. To say this is not to reiterate an unmitigated complaint against colonialism that renders the task of the cultural/social historian unbearably complex through its project of rewriting codes of dominance. Rather, colonial modernity, for most non-western societies, affords an important moment of departure that helps in situating pre-colonial hierarchies against post-colonial ones. This is suggestive of the influences that determined the emerging structure of mobility.

One of the many ways in which colonial rule restructured prevalent social hierarchies was by introducing 'high' and 'low' as a binary that would manifest itself in different spheres of socio-cultural and political existence. This began with a reconfiguration of the relation between 'high' and 'low' languages, the ripples of which could be seen in the various facets of everyday existence. These consequent changes were not merely of a discursive nature. By virtue of determining access to rungs of political power, these shifts had important implications that fundamentally restructured social and cultural life. The introduction of English, and the reshaping of the modern Indian/regional languages under English influences, determined the ideological orientation and social position of new generations. This included the regional sections of the intelligentsia, their access to state power, and their attitudes towards less privileged social groups. Though such a proposition will not help us unravel all the subsequent connections of social structuring, it provides a vantage point from which to embark on an analysis of how the restructuring of the linguistic field under colonialism has defined political identities and possibilities in contemporary India. This debate has had a continued relevance far beyond colonialism, in post-colonial and contemporary reconfigurations of the nation state in terms of linguistic communities' access to languages of power and mobility (English and other European foreign languages).

The refashioning of regional languages was an important axis along which the transformation of social relationships (from a vastly hierarchical order to one premised on egalitarian ideas) proceeded. However, linguistic changes also put further strain on the already difficult and dichotomous relationships between caste hierarchies. Several telling instances of this discursive effect can be seen in the bristling antagonism between English-speaking and regional intellectuals, as well as the interdependence of these groups. There was a simultaneous cultural marginalisation of the regional sphere, leading to its valorisation as a site of particular political legitimacy; this most significantly culminated, perhaps, in the consolidation of regional identity along linguistic lines at the time of the reorganisation of states after Independence. While this was a clear trend across India, in Western India the politics of the Samyukta Maharashtra movement, which eventually resulted in the bifurcation of the old state of Bombay into Gujarat and Maharashtra in 1960, merit special mention. Most interestingly, the campaign for Samyukta Maharashtra mobilised support by combining a demand for a monolingual state with the language of class resistance, demonstrating yet again the shifts in the links between language, structures of domination and the political arena (Naregal, 2000).

The history and hierarchies that have determined the types of exchanges stated above have also been instrumental to the many 'modernities' with which India continues to grapple. The empirical data collected in interviews held in state-run educational institutions in western India point towards asymmetries of many kinds, which urge us to be mindful lest we too hastily define modernity or contemporaneity. This empirical data is indicative of narratives that can be traced back to colonial times, yet cannot be contained therein. A link between linguistic and caste hierarchies recurred as a dominant understanding of culture in these interviews, for example. While English has typically been seen as the language of privilege, elitism, opportunities and the like, there is a counter-discourse that envisages a future for the preservation of niche cultural markers – linguistic identity being one of them. Thus, while it might sound presumptuous to consider linguistic hierarchy as centre stage in the nation state, there is no denying that the linguistic hierarchy (as well as its corollaries in religion and caste) carries more weight in the contemporary political arena.

The rise of a majoritarian government and of political appropriation is mired in a larger politics of linguistic, religious and caste hierarchies. The steady rise of a dominant, mainstream ideology since 2014 – in the Indian context, Hindu ideology and a claim to a Hindu nation – is evident in the empirical data collected. There were also indicators that a counter-hegemony seeking to uphold a linguistic monopoly is simultaneously on the rise. This was witnessed in cases where students who constituted a linguistic minority felt discriminated against. The tentacles of this majoritarian dominant politics perpetuate other existing forms of marginalisation (such as caste and gender). There were noticeable cases of this marginalisation across the schools, involving young people and teachers alike.

What deserves reiteration are the instances where these otherwise discriminatory and exclusionary sites become locations of inclusion and project solidarity. This happens most notably during religious festivals, where students across caste, class and religious divides are seen to participate in the celebrations. However, one cannot overlook the genesis of these religious and ritualistic performances in Brahmanical politics; in that context, what appears as inclusion becomes a double-edged strategy for appropriation and rejection used as needed by the dominant power.

While the mainstream discourse on culture seems to wield considerable power and its dissemination is rapid, resistance and counter-narratives are part of the contemporary India that we witnessed. The interviews allowed us to engage with varied viewpoints on India's diverse social and cultural practices, and to glimpse some contemporary political debates and their ramifications. It is in this process of the making of a contemporary India that citizens, who are at once the consumers and producers of culture, have a vital role to play.

While investigating questions related to what constitutes Indian culture, it became clear that no homogeneous definition of this was possible. Rather, the question seemed rhetorical in the face of the plurality of concepts jostling for space in the very idea of culture. The rather hierarchised relation between linguistic, religious, and caste denominations proved vital in understanding the shifting contestations that have determined the intricate cultural space that is often loosely labelled as 'Indian'. We realised that this 'Indian' culture is a mediating and mediated one – one that is constantly struggling to make its presence felt in a larger global context, with its contemporary politics and post-colonial past contesting for space. This gave rise to several interesting patterns of symmetries and asymmetries when comparing ideas about "European culture" and "Indian culture". In the schools where the interviews were conducted, these patterns further manifested themselves in elitism around linguistic competence in English, as opposed to regional languages. This can be regarded as a continuation of a colonial legacy, which defined English as the sole language of higher learning and thus relegated the regional languages to primary education. This, as we know, not only fixed the modern Indian regional languages within an intellectual hierarchy but had a major impact on the country's social structure – this constituted a kind of subalternisation of the regional sphere in the emerging cultural and political hierarchy. A linguistic hierarchy was visible in the interviews conducted in the schools. Another hierarchy, symptomatic of a nationalist discourse, was also seen in how the students and teachers understood culture. This nationalist discourse began as a need to consider English as alien and extraneous to an essentialist understanding of India. This understanding, as the interviews illustrated, was based on a homogeneous and monolithic view of the nation-state. Increasingly, there is now a noticeable propagation of this view, which works to erase a heterogeneity that was until the 1990s considered to be at the core of modern India (Menon and Nigam, 2007). While there is a fear that this will be detrimental to India's status as a secular democracy, a contesting view suggests that a new India is being created in the process. The India that is striving to make a mark on global politics is also aware of the ways in which regional languages can play a determining role in the transformation of relationships, both in the nation state and on the global stage. In most cases, the state supervises regional culture through educational curricula and determining tenets of nationalist solidarity at different strata of society. We saw this in how certain religious festivals were repeatedly emphasised as crucial markers of culture and were hailed as being synonymous to the notion of India and its heritage.

The proliferation of similar views and their legitimisation through state mechanisms (of which educational institutions are but one), helps to perpetuate a grounded, exclusionist view of culture that is not accommodating to its minority communities. This system meticulously undermines anything that threatens its propagandist agenda of circulating a uniform cultural programme. The individual becomes the bearer of this sense of legitimate culture: through this process, a culture emerges that is upheld as "pure", guarded against "pollutants", and is exclusionist in nature.

Institutional practices of inclusion and exclusion often work in tandem, which may be regarded as a unique feature of Indian culture. Social, cultural and political historians in India have generally assumed a direct connection between the formulation of state policies and their execution. This understanding presupposes a seamlessly linear, uninterrupted progression, conflating intention with effect. However, our study reveals that this process is not as direct or linear as may have been expected. We suggest that one should not overlook the possibilities for subversion and intervention that individuals can (and do) have within the larger systemic and institutional apparatus, even when that apparatus is as dominant and powerful as state machinery. In fact, in the conducted interviews, moments of interruption and intervention revealed a pattern, be it in the ways in which a predominant cultural trait was highlighted, caste and gender markers questioned or accepted, or in how texts on the curriculum were understood. In each case, one can identify the possible agency of the cultural consumers – in this case the students and teachers. For example, a teacher from Urban school 1 suggested that

> *I think that the things that have happened in the history which are related to culture, from which we introduce ourselves as Indians, all things related to this are important to be told to them [the students]. Be it our natural diversity, diverse geography, different languages … I feel that it should be introduced in these terms. And along with that the sentiment of being Indian, … how our diversity is strength for us, is something that I feel is important to tell them.* (Varsha, female, teacher, urban school 1, India)

This is an important moment of intervention, because the actor disseminates a view that has within it the possibility of subverting the mainstream dominant discourse of homogenisation.

Conclusion

Through recent advances in post-colonial discourse and its assessment of the colonial moment, there have been noticeable shifts in understanding and defining the 'colonised.' One important shift is the way in which the consumer, who was previously regarded as being a passive recipient, is now looked upon as an active agent in the formation of colonial modernity. The narrative of India's colonial encounter is being, and needs to be further, revisited from the perspective of dissent and consent, cooperation and subversion. Though this exchange was largely unequal, and also perhaps unequally motivated, it can still, despite its unevenness, be characterised by ideas of exchange.

We felt that it was important to situate the present set of interviews on such a continuum and to identify the myriad ways in which post-colonial discourse has been furthered by India's contemporary understanding and projection of her culture in relation to a larger global politics. For instance, in the post-colonial period, the 'modernists' wanted India to identify with the future and the path of 'progress' previously set by Europeans. They wanted India to build a secular democratic nation with a new industrial economy free from agrarian dependencies. Some were also looking for an opportunity to build post-colonial India through majoritarian cultural practices.

The school interviews proved the difficulty of defining the concept of culture in any clear way. It may be more useful to understand these institutional spaces of formal education as participants in the making of Indian cultures. The plurality of 'cultures' cannot be ignored, because doing so disregards the history of exchange and transaction that is constitutive of any idea of culture. The notion of culture cannot be understood only in terms of patterns of social behaviour and practices; its more invisible forms of meaning – systems and discursive power – must also be recognised. Thus, culture needs to be understood as a critical category of social reproduction and as a political articulation of power.

Having said that, we must also remind ourselves that plurality in the Indian context is always a contested term: what is our aim by claiming plurality and is it practically possible? There are two ways of understanding plurality in the Indian context: one is to celebrate plural histories, cultures and ways of life, and the other is to take a critical look at this claim in order to challenge the way plurality has historically been present in India. This latter concern became predominant with the upsurge of 'majoritarian politics' and its aim of making everyday life more like the practices of the upper caste Hindu community. Although this was an attempt to homogenise Hindu practices and, eventually, to make India a Hindu state, this has also led to more inclusion of marginalised groups. The incorporation of diverse and heterogeneous cultural histories into a single world signified a cultural and intellectual intersubjective configuration equivalent to the articulation of all forms of control, which has had such a significant impact on all experiences, histories, resources, and cultural products that it has ultimately become hegemony. This is evidenced by the finding that interviewed students from various class, caste and religious backgrounds reported having participated in mainstream Hindu festivities. It is perhaps in witnessing and participating in such a discourse that one could locate the contemporaneity of the Indian case.

The interviews conducted with students and teachers point towards a reality that is imbued with a state of confusion. There is a lack of clarity about the definition of culture and its place in the curriculum. The complexity of this concept notwithstanding, the interviewees' sweeping, generic conclusions – which are made without the desire to probe further into any nuances – may be considered indicative of institutional homogenisation, despite the schools' facades of plurality and diversity. While this is, we feel, a larger global trend, India's participation in this, and its rapid erasure of attributes of plurality and diversity, is alarming. This global and domestic proclivity towards homogenisation cannot be understood without considering the crucial role of capitalism in encouraging and even necessitating it. Modern right-wing politics (in the Indian and in a more general western sense) draws its power from this process of homogenisation, a result of the expansion of capitalism.

The phenomenon of schools being sites for cultivating such feelings is steadily increasing and there is a need to understand the larger socio-cultural politics at work here. It would be rather reductive to ascribe these socio-cultural transitions to a straightforward link between the rise of a right-wing government and the unleashing of a particular ideology. Although this element cannot be overlooked, we have also observed other emerging patterns that are indicative of a more nuanced process at work in the formation and dissemination of the notion of culture. These patterns include the circulation of different perspectives on culture, and their consumption and appropriation by certain sections of society. One also cannot dismiss the fact that, within our overall heritage, history and political evolution, there has always been an element of homogenisation. This has been seen historically in the Brahmanical project,[15] and continues to manifest itself in modern capitalist social formations: modern elites and the penetration of capitalist mores often lead to the homogenisation of norms, cultures and behaviours.

We found it rather difficult to situate the role of culture in Indian social and political life within any one model or structure. Our reference points in approaching culture were neither singular nor homogeneous. We identified three modes of talking about culture: (a) the accepted notion of a long and ancient tradition of Indian culture; (b) the idea that there are contestations as to what 'Indian' culture is because there are competing claims to that title; and (c) the theory that the post-independence nation state may have initiated the process of shaping contemporary Indian culture. It is not easy to either cull or reconceptualise any one definition of 'Indian culture' amidst the confusion and contestations that already form a part of the discourse around (and the varying points of departure from) 'culture'.

We initially located our argument on culture within an established post-colonial discourse. The works of Arjun Appadurai (2013), Dipesh Chakrabarty (2008) and others informed our study. However, we also felt the need to look beyond post-coloniality to a more contemporary understanding of 'India' as a nation state and to 'Indian' culture as a corollary. Postcolonialism explores how the western colonial and imperial domination that began in 1492 ultimately encompassed the globe and how this shaped – and continues to shape – our world's social, political, and economic structures, as well as the knowledge and identities of colonisers and colonised alike (Patel, 2017). Both nationalism (as practiced during the anti-colonial movement and after 1947 in independent/post-colonial India) and the Indian state as a legatee of the colonial state wanting to carve out new paths of statecraft, have helped to forge India's contemporary approach to culture.

15 The Brahmanical project refers to a set of practices bound by the principle of purity and pollution, which allow for the continued hegemony of the Brahmin.

References

Appadurai, A. (2013). *The Future as Cultural Fact: Essays on the Global Condition.* London: Verso.

Bakhtin, M. M. (1981). *The Dialogic Imagination: Four Essays.* Austin: University of Texas Press.

Chakrabarty, D. (2008). *Provincializing Europe: Postcolonial Thought and Historical Difference.* Princeton: Princeton University Press.

Chatterjee, C. & Dyahadroy, S. (2018). *Review of Making of Cultural Policy.* India (Unpublished submitted as part of the work Package 2 of the project Cultural Heritage and Identities of Europe's Future).

Government of India. Ministry of Human Resource Development. (2005). *Integration of Culture Education in the School Curriculum. Report.* https://mhrd.gov.in/sites/upload_files/mhrd/files/document-reports/Culture.pdf (Accessed on January 9, 2020).

Government of India. Ministry of Culture. (2014). *High Powered Committee Report.* http://www.indiaculture.nic.in/sites/default/files/hpc_report/HPC%20REPORT%202014.pdf (Accessed on January 9, 2020).

Lukose, R. (2009). *Liberalization's Children: Gender, Youth, and Consumer Citizenship in Globalizing India.* NC: Duke University Press.

Menon, N. & Nigam, A. (2007). *Power and Contestation: India since 1989,* New York: Zed Books.

Naregal, V. (2000). Language and Power in Pre-colonial Western India: Textual Hierarchies, Literate Audiences and Colonial Philology. *Indian Economic and Social History Review,* 37 (3), 259–294.

Patel, S. (2017). Colonial Modernity and Methodological Nationalism: The Structuring of Sociological Traditions of India. *Sociological Bulletin,* 66 (2), 125–144.

WorldCP. *International Database of Cultural Policies.* (2013) *India.* http://www.worldcp.org/india.php (Accessed on January 9, 2020).

(by Monika Bagalová and Ľubomír Lehocký)

Chapter 3 Threatened? The understanding of culture, identity and diversity in the Slovak educational system

Abstract: This paper aims to examine how the national guidance on cultural literacy is reflected in classroom practices in Slovakia. Slovak policy and curricula contain specific goals relating to teaching young people cultural literacy, but they present almost no guidelines on how to achieve these goals. The study analyses cultural literacy practices in formal education in reference to fieldwork from three different schools. The main focus is on intercultural interaction and multicultural education, which present many interesting insights and issues. Topics such as diversity, inclusion and multiculturalism do not have clear definitions and their integration into practice still seems challenging. The subject of segregation is associated with persistent prejudice against the Roma. Researchers also encountered stereotypes, othering and the use of racist language. Tensions were particularly strong in one school. It was observed that national / ethnic identity was considered the most important aspect of identity among teachers and students.

Keywords: culture, education, youth, identity, diversity, inclusion, integration, extremism

Introduction

This chapter is a case study that deals with the issue of how culture, identity and diversity are understood in the Slovak educational system. The main content presented here is obtained from the analysis of educational policy texts, academic texts and curricula, as well as ethnological research with teachers and students at three different schools.

The main focus here is on how the national guidance on cultural literacy is reflected in classroom practices in Slovakia. Although Slovak policy documents and curricula aim to present some specific goals relating to teaching young people cultural literacy, the definitions of essential terms such as culture, identity and diversity are very vague (Bagalová, Lehocký, Deák and Karásek, 2018). Therefore, it is important to explore the use and understanding of these words in practice.

In terms of the current Slovak situation, national identity, inclusion and extremism are the most current topics in cultural contexts. Themes of national identity are mainly connected with unequal relationships between majority and minority groups. We can observe that (inter)cultural interaction has become a major trigger for the defence of national integrity and sovereignty. The inclusion and acceptance of others is, in most cases, accompanied by a hidden power structure and perceived as a potential threat. Growing patterns of essentialist social judgment call for more reflection and new approaches to move the situation in a new direction.

A brief overview of the schools, locations and context are first introduced, followed by an examination of cultural literacy practices in formal education. The analysis looks at learning about culture in general terms such as how cultural topics are taught in schools and what is presented under the umbrella of the word 'culture.' Concepts of cultural heritage and identities will then be discussed, analysing the different layers of using these themes within educational texts or classes. The topics of cultural participation and sources of information deal more with the practical sides of how culture operates in students' lives, with new information verified by the students themselves. Special attention will be paid to intercultural interactions and multicultural education, which are presented with several interesting examples, discussions, issues and tensions. In the discussion section, the findings are contextualised through various theoretical approaches, followed by recommendations on future policies or actions. A summary of findings and final thoughts are presented in the conclusion.

Context and information about the fieldwork

Three public schools in different regions of Slovakia were selected for the fieldwork: one urban school in Bratislava, the capital; one sub-urban school in Martin, a medium-sized town; the third is in the small town of Rimavská Sobota, a predominantly rural location. Bratislava is among the six most developed districts in Slovakia, Martin ranks 23rd, and Rimavská Sobota 79th (the least developed district in Slovakia).[1] The selected district of Bratislava is 'ethnically' rather homogeneous, with the majority of residents identifying as ethnic Slovaks and a small number of people identifying as Roma. The same is true for Martin. Rimavská Sobota is a more heterogeneous district, with a higher proportion of people identifying as ethnic Hungarians and a large share identifying as Roma (Mušinka et al., 2014). We also looked at support for nationalist parties according to the 2016 election data. In Bratislava, none of these parties got any

1 The Slovak Government Office identified the most and least developed districts of Slovakia: http://www.nro.vlada.gov.sk/podpora-najmenej-rozvinutych-okresov/.

significant electoral support; in Martin, the Slovak National Party and People's Party Our Slovakia got average electoral support; and in Rimavská Sobota Party of the Hungarian Community got high electoral support, while there was average backing for the Slovak National Party and People's Party Our Slovakia. In order to consider different types of schools, we chose a grammar school in Martin and secondary vocational schools in Bratislava and Rimavská Sobota.

The Martin school is attended by students from the Martin region (which mainly consists of nearby villages). The school has many activities for students. For example, G8-gate is a voluntary student club, created as a continuation of activities organised under the 'Connecting classrooms' international project begun by the British Council. This club organises cultural, sports and beneficial events for students and the public. The school also encourages students to develop their creativity and a strong sense of self by, for instance, publishing a collection of writing by students. There is an annual event attended by students' family members where students present their contributions to the collection. The school also has a student parliament, and students regularly participate in extracurricular learning events. Throughout the academic year, students are able to attend dances, sporting events, competitions, language courses, handicraft classes, local and international excursions, among other activities. The gymnasium is involved in the Erasmus programme, so students are eligible to apply for study exchanges to visit other European countries. The school also collaborates with several NGOs.

The Bratislava school is attended by students from Bratislava and the surrounding area. The school participates in two major international projects. It offers international exchanges and practical training in several countries (for instance, Japan), and excursions in Slovakia as well as abroad. Students have the opportunity to visit theatres, galleries and other cultural events. Other cultural activities the school participates in include traditional crafts. This school also has a student parliament.

The school in Rimavská Sobota is attended by students from the city and nearby villages. Students can participate in several cultural activities, which are usually focused on vocational education. They have the opportunity to go on excursions to Slovak and foreign cities to visit local galleries, museums and theatres and take part in a student parliament. The students are eligible for practical training exchanges through Erasmus+. The school participates in the *We love Slovakia* (Máme radi Slovensko) project, the aim of which is to create a multimedia guide to interesting locations in Slovakia.

Analysis of cultural literacy practices in formal education

The interviews with students confirmed our assumption that social networks and friendships are more important today in shaping young people's cultural identity than the formal education process in schools. We were surprised by the marked differences in students' ability to understand and meaningfully answer questions. In general, students who often participated in their school's cultural activities (e.g. school parliament, school magazine) gave more complex answers. However, these active students were a minority among all interviewed pupils. We also observed the efforts of the school representatives to choose stronger students to participate in the project. This effort was most visible in Rimavská Sobota, where the project was presented only in selected classes, which were considered better ones by teachers. This phenomenon was probably due to an attempt to look good in front of us, although it was thoroughly explained to school representatives that we were not testing or inspecting their school.

Learning about culture

The students said in interviews that they mainly "learn about culture" in their Slovak, English, geography and history lessons. Usually, the teacher explains a concept and then asks the students to discuss it. Differences of opinion are rare in these discussions, and generally the more active students engage while many others are left out. The teachers at the school in Bratislava said that there is not enough time to discuss issues fully during lessons.

The students gave a wide range of views on culture in general, reflecting their personal understanding. They often expressed the view that their generation's culture was more open and tolerant than that of their parents and grandparents, but that older generations were politer and more responsible. In almost all cases, they had positive views of "traditional Slovak culture", which they perceived mainly as a heritage of folk culture, such as traditional crafts, costumes, songs and gastronomy. Slovak policy documents contain no clear definitions of essential terms such as culture and cultural identity. The texts emphasise the majoritarian classification upholding ethnic Slovak culture, but also mention that traditional culture is a result of multi-ethnic endeavours. For example, 'The Conception of Maintenance of Traditional Folk Culture till the year 2020'[2] focuses on how to support, document, and maintain traditional folk culture. Traditional folk culture is said to have an inclusive character based on its creation by both ethnic

2 http://www.rokovania.sk/Rokovanie.aspx/BodRokovaniaDetail?idMaterial=24176

Slovaks and minorities, and people of different religious creeds. This diversity can be seen as bringing feelings of fellowship and as culturally beneficial for the society's quality of life. It is described as "a living heritage, a source of people's cultural identity, historical consciousness, learning, knowledge about cultural diversity, as well as a tool of tolerance and civic unity" (Bagalová, Lehocký, Deák, and Karásek, 2018: p. 184). However, in practice, most respondents perceived traditional Slovak culture as primarily made up of ethnic Slovaks, without a deeper knowledge of the historical context and influences that contributed to its creation.

Some students showed a keen interest in various folk groups or in traditional craft courses. However, most of them did not engage in what they considered traditional culture, nor were they curious about exploring it. Some informants in Bratislava and Martin showed great interest in "other countries' cultures", such as Austria, France, and Japan. They liked these cultures because they thought that people in these countries were decent and responsible and that everything worked better there than in Slovakia. In general, the students were more interested in the cultures of 'economically developed' countries. Some responses indicated a degree of contempt for 'economically underdeveloped' countries, and the informants were on the whole less attracted to these countries' cultures. This could be interpreted as a result of Eurocentric views of policy and curricula designers, in which the binary of "developed us" and "undeveloped others" is still present.[3] The students also reported that in school they had learned primarily about "European cultures". That reflects the dominance of Eurocentric themes apparent in the Slovak curricula, which either does not mention the cultures and history of Asia, Africa and Latin America, or only does so in a limited way (Deák, 2019: p. 14).

Several teachers expressed the view that the maturity of a culture is directly related to a nation's economic development. On the question of this connection, teacher Petra answered:

> *The culture of a nation reflects whether ... the culture is still developing in some way, and I think it certainly reflects the nation's maturity, that if the nation is stagnating somewhere, or if it can respect those traditions but let go of them a little bit to advance the nation (economic development).* (Petra, female, teacher, urban school, Slovakia)

Some students, especially those from Rimavská Sobota, did not answer the questions about their views on culture.

3 These relations have been discussed further in Said (1985).

Cultural heritage

The students often thought that 'cultural heritage' referred to different customs and traditions. Slovak cultural heritage was thought to refer to costumes, traditional cuisine, crafts and folk songs; some interviewees also mentioned traditional Slovak alcohol (*Borovička*) as an example of 'cultural heritage'. Students were familiar with the UNESCO World Heritage List, and were able to recall the included Slovak sites, but had greater difficulty naming European or world UNESCO cultural heritage locations. A few students gave examples of other cultural artefacts, such as literary works, statues, and so on.

Students in their first year of study at secondary schools often could not answer, or even understand, questions about cultural heritage. This may be because of the sequencing of subjects taught at Slovak secondary schools; geography and civics lessons often begin in the second year of secondary school. Students from upper grades at the school in Bratislava, on the other hand, stated that they had mainly covered this topic while studying geography and tourism, where they learned about Slovakian heritage sites such as Banská Štiavnica, Vlkolinec, the Altar of Master Paul in Levoča.[4] As part of their lessons, these students prepared various presentations, for which they also had to cook meals and dine according to different culinary traditions. Thus, they have an opportunity to practice various elements of 'foreign' cultural heritage, especially culinary customs.

The students at the school in Martin mentioned various school excursions to places of cultural heritage. They most often reported having been on trips to local cultural sites, many of them sites of national importance, such as the National Cemetery in Martin. These students also had the most extensive knowledge and strongest views on cultural heritage of all the students interviewed. In contrast, students from the school in Rimavská Sobota often had no idea what was meant by the term 'cultural heritage'. They did not mention having visited cultural places with their school. The students from Bratislava did not give many examples of school excursions either, and often could not remember if they had visited places, or, if so, what places they had visited.

In general, the students thought about cultural heritage in terms of what they had learned about great cultural works from the past, rather than as something that they could create or that could directly influence their lives. Some students

---

4 Banská Štiavnica is a historical town in central Slovakia; Vlkolinec is a village with traditional houses. These places and the Altar of Master Paul, a Gothic altar in the church of Saint Jacob in Levoča, are the most famous Slovak monuments listed as UNESCO World heritage sites.

were able to grasp this distinction, such as Joseph from Martin, who said that Slovak cultural heritage was his roots, but that it certainly was not part of his everyday life. While answering a follow-up question about why he had mentioned it as his "roots", he expressed through body language that he did not really know and answered: *"Um, that's so learned"* (Joseph, male, student, semi-urban school, Slovakia). Joseph used 'learned' in the sense that he had just learned about/memorised an idea of Slovak cultural heritage; he was taught at school that it was his roots, but he did not have any personal connection to it. Several students admitted that their ideas about Slovak cultural heritage were just stereotypes they had learned at school. While Bruman and Berliner talk about UNESCO cultural heritage sites as "linchpins of global imaginaries" (Bruman and Berliner, 2016: p. 3), for Slovak students they are simply names to learn. Because they are Slovaks, they think they should know the primary Slovak cultural heritage sites.

The interviewed teachers showed similar thinking processes. When asked about cultural heritage, they responded by listing the different elements covered during the term. For example, a geography teacher from Bratislava said the following about her method of teaching cultural heritage:

> *I talk about cultural and historical monuments, natural heritage and so on … about the historical figures who also formed our heritage.* (Jana, female, teacher, urban school, Slovakia)

To ensure that students do not just have an abstract conception of cultural heritage, schools try to make the topic more relevant through various practical activities. The most active in this respect was the school in Martin, which, in addition to several excursions, also arranged for students to learn about various topics from their grandparents and then present their findings at school. Similarly, the school in Bratislava organises various workshops and projects. The students' responses showed that many of them had become interested in 'traditional' crafts (woodcarving, basketry, tinkering, lacemaking, etc.). The school in Rimavská Sobota lagged behind in the number of activities it offered students, which probably contributed to the truncated responses of the students from this school.

Identity(ies)

Researchers approached identities as categories rather than groups, which allowed them to understand "how categories get institutionalized and with what consequences" (Brubaker, 2004: p. 184). Informants, however, thought about identity, especially national/ethnic[5] identity, as a group of people (Slovaks, Roma, etc.) with whom they identified themselves and others. When answering questions about identity, most of the teachers and students first reported their sense of belonging to an ethnic group. According to the informants, national/ethnic identity is strongly represented in the teaching process. Students are taught "national identity and pride" in the context of cultural heritage developed by ethnic Slovaks. This is consistent with policy documents and curricula, which are also mainly nationally-oriented in terms of identity issues (Deák, 2019: pp. 142–182). Most informants stated that they felt they were Slovaks. Far fewer students said that they also felt like Europeans. Several students from the Rimavská Sobota school did not find the European identity attractive: "*Europe … It's not appealing*" (Bruno, male, student, rural school, Slovakia).[6] Surprisingly, only a few students named their religious affiliation as part of their identity. When answering questions for the participant notes, several respondents stated that they were practicing Christians, but this did not come up during the interviews.

In general, the teachers said that there was not much opportunity to cover other types of identity in teaching, such as religious, political, or gender identities. Only the subjects Ethics and Religious Education have space to discuss these aspects, but most students did not remember whether they had ever talked about them at school. Several teachers mentioned off the record that they did not feel confident talking about multiple forms of identities with students because they were not trained in how to approach these themes. Teachers also mentioned that students are influenced by online role models in thinking about their identities.

> *Young people are following their role models (mostly YouTubers) strongly.* (Jana, female, teacher, urban school, Slovakia)

When asked about their identity, Slovak students were clearly able to answer questions about whether they felt they were Slovak, European, and Christian. However, many did not understand questions about subcultural, political, and opinion-based identities; it was not something they were used to thinking about. There were, of course, exceptions, with some students identifying with (for example) hip hop, liberal, patriotic, or Satanist groups. Only one student, Eve from Bratislava, said that she was also dealing with the question of her own

5 In Slovakia, the terms 'nation/nationality' are used more as a synonym for 'ethnicity' than to refer to citizenship.

6 Several students answered that European identity is not important to them, but they could not explain why.

gender and sexual identity. She mentioned that a Slovak language teacher had made an inappropriate joke in the classroom that she found very offensive:

> *'Why can't the sun have children? Because it is warm!' Then the teacher said that it doesn't matter, none of you here are warm.*[7] (Eve, female, student, urban school, Slovakia)

(Inter)cultural interaction and multicultural education

Slovak curricula state that pupils should learn to "tolerate diversity" (Deák, 2019: p. 159). This goal is addressed in various ways in different subjects.

It is necessary to reflect on the concept of tolerance to gain a deeper understanding of this particular context. According to the Declaration of Principles on Tolerance in the UNESCO constitution, tolerance refers to respect, acceptance and appreciation of the rich diversity of our world's cultures, forms of expression and ways of being human. Tolerance is also understood here as an active attitude prompted by recognising the universal human rights and fundamental freedoms of others.[8]

In policy documents and curricula, the use of the term "tolerance" is mainly essentialist or employed in a way that implies a power struggle within society, putting emphasis on divisions between a majority and minorities. In Slovak academic discussions, academics deal with these issues by trying to re-evaluate unequal power relationships and suggesting ideal models of cultural diversity for Slovakia. According to more experts, it would be more appropriate to create an inclusive model of society where "it is not necessary to define and specify particular minorities and their rights." This would theoretically give everyone a sense of belonging and acceptance, rather than relying on tolerance. Building society on a civic basic may be more appropriate; at the same time, certain cultural, social, economic, historical and political frameworks should be taken into account (Filadelfiová and Hlinčíková, 2010: p. 140).

The theme of the cultural security of ethnic/linguistic minorities was mentioned by Tatiana Podolinska in her 2017 article 'Roma in Slovakia - Silent and Invisible Minority'. Podolinska argues that the concept of the constitutional protection of minorities in Slovakia is based on two principles: the principle of equality and non-discrimination, and the principle of guaranteeing special

---

7 'Warm' means being gay.

8 The complete Declaration of Principles on Tolerance is available online at: http://portal.unesco.org/en/ev.phpURL_ID=13175&URL_DO=DO_TOPIC&URL_SECTION=201.html.

rights to members of national minorities and ethnic groups. These rights include practicing their culture with other members of the minority or group, disseminating and receiving information in their mother tongues, joining national minority associations, and establishing and maintaining educational and cultural institutions. However, according to the Constitution of the Slovak Republic, exercising the rights of citizens belonging to national minorities and ethnic groups must not threaten the sovereignty and territorial integrity of the Slovak Republic or to discrimination against other populations (Podolinská, 2017: p. 139).

As is shown above, the hidden power structure is key to understanding the term "tolerance" in a research context. Here, tolerance is intertwined with the themes of cultural safety and is often coloured by vigilance and a sense of potential threat.

The most important concept regarding cultural tolerance seems to be multicultural education, which is a cross-cutting (interdisciplinary) theme within certain subjects, namely History, Civics, Geography, Ethics, Religion, and Art and culture. However, the interviewed students had rarely encountered the term "multiculturalism" in their lessons. Those who could remember covering the topic at school said it had come up mainly in English lessons and to a lesser extent in Civics, Geography, and Ethics:

> *I know it was in English class, … when we did cities like London and they said that it was a very multicultural city, that there are a huge number of nationalities, that it is one city, but basically that every part of the city is almost like a different country, that they have Chinatown, the Indian Quarter, and that there are many places in one place.* (Marko, male, student, urban school, Slovakia)

"Multicultural society" was also part of the English-language graduation exam for the students at the gymnasia.[9] A geography teacher from Bratislava said that multiculturalism came up only marginally in her lessons, because there is not enough time to talk about it fully. A history teacher from the same school said that she included multicultural education in her subject as follows:

> *Kollar (Slovak historical national figure), he asks which should we prioritise, our country or nation? So, let's start talking about migration, for example, the current connection (with Kollar's question) is that foreigners come here, but we go abroad, too.* (Božena, female, teacher, urban school, Slovakia)

9 The students at vocational schools do not have this exam.

Matej from Bratislava recalled that they had talked about Islam in civics lessons: *"terrorism is also related to it, so that is what we remember"* (Matej, male, student, urban school, Slovakia). Bruno, also from Bratislava, did not even know the name of Islam, so he called it *"Muslim Christianity."* He said he did not like Muslims because the people he had met from the Middle East during his internship at a hotel were always very rude.

In general, the students considered multiculturalism to be the coexistence of several cultures in one place; some said they did not understand the concept at all. Multicultural education does not seem to have made its way into Slovak formal education yet.

> *It is always the problem with all the Ministry of Educations cross-cutting themes … Very often, when something is given as an obligation and there are no resources, there is no teacher training behind it.* (Jana, female, teacher, urban school, Slovakia)

Some teachers openly expressed their prejudices about multiculturalism. Speaking about a student whose mother is white and whose father is black, one teacher said:

> *I think that even though [they are] a Negroid race, their nationality*[10] *can be Slovak. It must be accepted. As the influence of a time period that came from that multiculturalism, open borders and everything. And still who knows what awaits us. Nobody knows that. [laughs] … But now we see her [the student] as normal.* (Blanka, female, teacher, semi-urban school, Slovakia)

All three selected schools work with various non-governmental organisations that offer multicultural education lectures and projects. As mentioned above, the schools in Bratislava and Martin are also involved in several international projects, such as Erasmus, where students encounter other cultures. Slovak students can go to France or Japan, for example, and foreign students visit Slovakia. The students found these exchanges enriching, and consistently claimed that the exchange students in their schools were accepted positively. Eva from Bratislava admitted that she had chosen to study at this school because there was the possibility of an internship abroad. The students from Bratislava and Martin did not mention conflict between classmates based on (sub)cultural or ethnic differences, nor did they encounter any opinions or statements at school that they would consider extremist. Our experience was that students from these two schools showed a high degree of 'tolerance' towards other cultures and opinions.

---

10 As explained above, in the Slovak language the terms "nationality" and "ethnicity" are used as synonyms.

By contrast, students in Rimavská Sobota openly talked about various tensions and conflicts at school. These were particularly common between students from the majority population (in this context, ethnic Slovaks and Hungarians) and Roma students, who represent approximately half of the school's intake:[11] *"There are only two groups, white and black"* (Bruno, male, student, rural school, Slovakia). Students from Rimavská Sobota often spoke about the segregation inside and outside school. They also mentioned various fights, which did not take place at the school building. Some of the boys identified themselves as "patriots", but other interviewees said that those students proudly talk about themselves as skinheads or Nazis. During interviews, some of them wore T-shirts with slogans typical of the neo-Nazi subculture. They also mentioned that they went to Bratislava to support the football club Slovan, whose Ultras are known to sympathise with neo-Nazi ideology and racist actions.[12] Researchers had the feeling that this group avoided talking about topics related to neo-Nazi ideology.[13] Several mentioned that they sometimes conflicted with the teacher over lesson content, for example about the WW2-era Slovak Republic, Andrej Hlinka (a Slovak national figure of the late 19th and early 20th centuries), and the so-called Hlinka Guard, a militia during WWII:

> *[The teacher] said that everyone in the Hlinka Guard was fascist, and then we … began to talk because my grandfather had told me that his family was also in the Hlinka Guard and that the Hlinka Guard weren't all fascist.* (Boris, male, student, rural school, Slovakia)

Some of these boys said they would welcome more content about Slovakia, Slavs and Slavic culture in the school curricula, and less content about other European nations, because everyone should know most about his own culture.

The school organises special lessons for students from this group. In cooperation with NGOs, they cover various topics as part of multicultural education.

> *This year, we've had these kinds of interviews all year, just because of us. There was a "blackie" (černoško) here from a gang and he started telling us about his life … we can*

---

11 Most of the Roma students identified themselves as ethnic Hungarian on the school's records. This is why, in official statistics, the Roma ethnicity represents less than 10 % of students.

12 For example, in August 2019, UEFA ruled that Slovan Bratislava fans had abused Albanians and called for violence against them, for which the club was punished. For more information, see: https://www.skslovan.com/clanok7234-Rozhodnutie_UEFA_za_spravanie_fanusikov.htm.

13 They also felt that they were being watched at school by teachers and could be reported to police for their activities.

accept that, multiculturalism, but not in our own country. (Bruno, male, student, rural school, Slovakia)

Students from other classes did not attend these lessons and these boys felt that they and their opinions were being directly targeted. Another student, Peter, said he had previously belonged to this group, but later became dissatisfied with it, because he found their opinions and actions to be extreme. He changed his group of friends completely.

Teachers and other students who did not belong to this group did not express discriminatory and ultra-nationalist attitudes. However, they also confirmed a certain division within the school. The fact that most Roma students speak Hungarian better than Slovak, although they study in the Slovak language, contributes to the separation between 'whites' and 'blacks'.

I have [in the classroom] Roma children … [and] I have children of Slovak nationality, too. And there is no … racial or national problem in this class. Rather, the problem is that it is a class with Slovak as the language of instruction and many children from elementary schools came to this class, where the language of instruction was Hungarian, and … there are children who do not know Slovak at all. This is because … [in] some schools, especially the village's smaller schools, they pay no attention to the Slovak language. (Iveta, female, teacher, rural school, Slovakia)

One result of the mixed political agendas between Hungarians and Slovaks shows that accommodation of Hungarian-speaking people is still ambivalent at school. This situation affects Roma students as well. However, ethnic tensions do not manifest themselves violently on school grounds. Students from Rimavská Sobota who had negative attitudes towards their Roma peers explained that this was the result of their own negative experiences. They said that they had experienced violence and criminal activity (stealing) from Roma in their towns and villages, but not at the school. As explained above, according to school representatives, no Roma pupil from the chosen classes volunteered to participate in the project. The situation in Rimavská Sobota shows that the tensions between several minority groups are still not properly discussed or addressed. Unresolved conflicts and prevailing stereotypes have become the main source for perceptions of Roma students.

Cultural participation

In terms of cultural participation, the interviewed students were generally very active. Some were members of folk, art and other interest groups, such as scouts. Many were interested in culture, formed communities, and went to museums, concerts and the like without belonging to any formal group. In the latter case, joint visits or events were primarily organised through social networks. Some informants also created cultural content individually, such as writing blogs or producing music, which would then be disseminated. Students arranged their leisure activities spontaneously, usually through social media. They used these platforms to connect with each other to instigate visits to museums, concerts, sport events, etc. Students were also involved in various environmental activities, as many considered the destruction of nature to be the greatest problem in the world today.

Participation in other political activities was rarely mentioned. In civics lessons, the students studied the political systems of Slovakia and the European Union in a fair amount of detail, but most were uninterested in politics. Interviewees said that discussions about politics usually only took place in the classroom in the run-up to elections. This was also true of students who were eligible to vote. Although they were not very interested in this topic, most said that they would vote; they made their electoral choices based on conversations with their parents and friends, as well as information from the media.

Schools encourage their students' civic engagement. Through student parliaments, they can directly influence the management of their school, while clubs can improve their skills in various areas. Schools also run civic engagement projects. At the school in Martin, for instance, there is a thematic group in which students simulate G8 meetings and discuss important social issues. Some of the students involved in this project were excited about it and thought it was very beneficial to them. Although teachers claimed that participation in this group is voluntary, there were also students who felt they had been slightly manipulated into taking part by the school's deputy (i.e. felt pressure to participate). The school's representative perhaps chose them to join this group because they are students with impressive academic records.

At the school in Bratislava, students had to prepare a community project for a hospital. The project was devised and organised by the students themselves: "*We made a variety of snacks and we sold them at school and then actually donated the money to [the hospital]*" (Matej, male, student, urban school, Slovakia). Most students rated the project very positively and felt good about participating, because they helped children with serious diseases. Others joined in simply because it was mandatory; these students found the project boring.

The schools in Bratislava and Martin publish a school magazine, and students contribute articles on various themes. The school in Rimavská Sobota was, again, substantially behind in terms of student participation in extracurricular activities. The main reason for this is that students have to travel to school from the surrounding villages. The buses run only a few times a day and so if they were involved in after-school clubs or activities they would get home late. Another reason is that there are generally fewer cultural economic and civic activities in the region. Many students from Rimavská Sobota did various sports in their free time. Most of the students in this school are boys, and football was the most popular leisure activity among them. Boys from the group of "patriots" also took part in various marches and activities organised by the political party People's Party Our Slovakia, which is, according to Slovakia's General prosecutor Jaroslav Čižnár, "an extremist party with fascist tendencies."[14] However, they did not want to give more details about these activities.

Sources of information

Accessing credible information is key to cultivating cultural literacy in young people. Young people obtain a lot of information online. In their interviews, teachers stressed that they were trying to keep students away from unreliable sources on the Internet. The school in Martin had even set up digital literacy classes covering these topics. Some of the students from this school were more knowledgeable about fact-checking than interviewees from other schools. Most of the interviewed students, though said that they had received only limited guidance from teachers on how to find and use resources. The teachers would only tell them which sources should be removed. Some students said they were taught to compare multiple resources, and that generally books offer more reliable information than websites. However, some students had received no guidance at school.

As part of the teaching process, students at all three schools are given tasks to prepare individually, such as presentations on various topics. Wikipedia seems to be an especially popular source of information. If students are interested in a topic, they will try to verify the information from several (Internet) sources. If they find the same information on more than one site, they consider it trustworthy. However, if they are not interested in the topic, they will usually use the information from the very first webpage they come across without verifying it. Students obtain information that is not related to the school curriculum from their family and friends; various Facebook, Instagram and YouTube influencers represent another big source of knowledge, as students follow quite a few of them.

14 See https://dennikn.sk/775198/ciznar-podal-na-najvyssi-sud-podnet-na-zrusenie-kotlebovej-lsns/.

Discussion

The findings of earlier CHIEF project reports (Bagalová, Lehocký, Deák and Karásek, 2018; Deák, 2019) have shown that Slovak policy documents and curricula contain no clear definitions of essential terms such as culture, identity and diversity. The concept of cultural heritage is described as 'something worth preserving'. However, this approach reproduces the cultural heritage philosophy of conservation (Brumann and Berliner, 2016), without enquiring as to "why the legacy of the past should be evaluated" (Deák, 2019: p. 172). According to this study's findings, teachers usually explain cultural heritage as a collection of material and intangible artefacts from the past. The interviewed students perceived it in a similar way, and felt that the artefacts of cultural heritage do not feature in their daily lives. Researchers reported only a few exceptions, where some students saw cultural heritage as something "alive."

The policy documents and curricula indicate that several perspectives apply to the acquisition of knowledge about cultural heritage, cultural identity and diversity: "On the one hand, they attempt to deconstruct the nation-state narrative," while, "on the other hand, the nation-state identity is clearly preferred" (Deák, 2019: p. 167). National/ethnic identity was mentioned most frequently by teachers and students, who mainly felt that belonging to the Slovak nation was the most important aspect of their identity. In this way, the category of culture becomes essentialised because it is constantly evoked, whether in terms of the nation, an individual's personality, or some imagined other. Essentialisation occurs despite all these elements potentially referring to "a very different set of practices-cum-knowledge and their historical antecedents" (ibid.: p. 173).

According to Brubaker, nationality can be seen as a strong understanding of "identity" because it emphasises continuity over time and across persons (Brubaker, 2004: p. 37). Interviewed teachers and students had a strong sense of their nationality. National identity was also strongly represented in formal education. According to most teachers, there is not enough class time to discuss other types of identity.

Teachers in the Slovak Republic are poorly paid and have lower general skills than people in other professions (OECD, 2017a); their poor training and skills in sensitive topics could be another reason that other types of identities are not discussed in schools. In terms of perceptions of diversity, Slovak policy documents and curricula are tied too closely to a Eurocentric approach (Deák, 2019: p. 179). Teachers perpetuate stereotypical images of others and even employ the language of stereotypes (ibid.: p. 173). Researchers observed a few cases of staff directly using racist language (i.e., "~~Negroid~~ race"). According to some teachers, they receive insufficient training on how to incorporate new topics, such as the diversity of identities, into the formal teaching process. Slovak students often supposed the cultures of 'economically less developed' countries to be underdeveloped, and showed more interest in the cultures of 'economically developed' countries.

Slovak state regulations aim for an inclusive system with regulations calling for effective management of those pupils with specific educational needs. However, several studies have shown[15] that this system enables the creation of special classes, which indirectly allows for the segregation of some, mostly Roma, pupils. This is exemplified by the case of Šarišské Michaľany, where the court decided that the school practice of racial separation (Roma/ Non-Roma) was unwarranted. After mixed classes were enforced by the court's ruling, non-Roma parents enrolled their children in different schools. Another example is the case of Rokycany, where pupils being transferred to a private school for children with specific needs (mental health problems) led to the closure of the public school. Contemporary re-diagnosis of pupils is ongoing, and the public school has been re-opened under a Teach for Slovakia[16] custodianship (ibid.: p. 148).

Researchers did not encounter strong manifestations of extremism or prejudice at the schools in Bratislava and Martin. Only a few students manifested prejudices directed against "terrorists", who these students identified generally with "Muslims" or "refugees". The situation was different at the school in Rimavská Sobota. It was clear from what the students said that they were internally divided into "white" (Slovak and Hungarian) and "black" (Roma) students.

This "white" and "black" segregation in the school can be associated with ongoing high levels of prejudice against the Roma in Slovak society in general. In recent years progress has been made in putting together a legal and policy framework to tackle discrimination against the Roma. However, 80 % of surveyed Slovak Roma were unaware of the existence of any organisations that can offer

---

15 Huttová, Jana; Gyárfášová, Oľga and Sekulová, Martina (2012) Segregácia alebo inklúzia Rómov vo vzdelávaní: Voľba pre školy? (Segregation or inclusion of Roma in educational system. Is there an option for schools?) Bratislava: Open Society Foundation; Rafael Vlado, ed. (2017), Školy proti segregácii. Metodická príručka na prevenciu a odstraňovanie segregácie rómskych žiakov (Schools against segregation. Methodological guideline for prevention and removing of segregation of Roma pupils). Bratislava: eduRoma.

16 Teach for Slovakia is an NGO (a partner of the 'Teach for All' educational network https://teachforall.org/) that implements new methods of education and works for the improvement of education available in Slovakia.

support or advice to people who have suffered from discrimination, and 50 % of all Roma were unaware of anti-discrimination laws.[17] Students' interactions, seen through different concepts representing collective identities, also relate to the question of power. In the education context, this is most visible in the cases of unequal access to education, which results in the segregation of Roma, who are seen as culturally and racially 'other' and as bearing signs of an 'underdeveloped culture'. Even recently, there the declaration of integration policy has been introduced,[18] but implementation results in separate school divisions or an "allocated school branch". This is an educational facility established within the reach of a marginalised community to boost access to education, which brings to mind an image of the majoritarian 'helping hand' that sets all the conditions for its acceptance (Deák, 2019: p. 177).[19]

In Rimavská Sobota, no Roma students were interviewed, despite about half of the school population being Roma. This could have been because most Roma students do not understand the Slovak language very well. The Roma constitute the second-largest minority ethnicity in Slovakia after the Hungarian, which, at the number of 520,528, makes up 9.7 % of the total population. However, the number of people reporting the Roma nationality does not correspond with the number on the census, because the number of those who consider the Romani language their mother tongue is greater than the number of those who have officially declared themselves to be Romani.[20]

---

17 FRA, (2016), "Second European Union minorities and discrimination survey" European Agency for fundamental rights, Luxembourg: https://fra.europa.eu/en/publication/2016/eumidis-ii-roma-selectedfindings.

18 Východiská pre integráciu marginalizovaných rómskych komunít KSK na roky 2016-2020. (The departure points for integration of marginalised Roma communities of Košice higher territorial unit for the years of 2016–2020). Košice: Košický samosprávny kraj. [online]: https://web.vucke.sk/files/socialne_veci/2016/vychodiska-integraciu-mrk-ksk.pdf.

19 For more on the majoritarian attitudes in the Slovak educational system, see Gállová-Kriglerová, E. and Kadlečíková, J. eds. (2009) Kultúrna rozmanitosť a jej vnímanie žiakmi základných škôl na Slovensku (Cultural diversity and its perception by the pupils of primary schools in Slovakia). Bratislava: Centrum pre výskum ethnicity a kultúry. See also Huttová, Jana; Gyárfášová, Oľga and Sekulová, Martina (2012) Segregácia alebo inklúzia Rómov vo vzdelávaní: Voľba pre školy? (Segregation or inclusion of Romas in educational system. Is there an option for schools?) Bratislava: Open Society Foundation.

20 https://www.romaeducationfund.org/wp-content/uploads/2019/05/web_slovakia_report_slovak.pdf?fbclid=IwAR1JvFfSyIUccjDTLTNbqPFbUtn4UJBGYCHTC5C4JvYdiT3aFVZc8MJgoFY.

Only one-third of Roma consider Slovak their first language. This represents an important barrier, as proficiency in the language of instruction is a fundamental determinant of successful educational outcomes. Students who have not mastered the language of instruction are at a significant disadvantage in schools. Very few schools provide Romani as a support language or Romani-language textbooks (Gallová-Kriglerová et al., 2012). Most teachers and support staff do not speak Romani, and Roma teachers are significantly under-represented: only 10 primary and lower secondary teachers have declared a Roma origin.

As well as this barrier to being part of this study, there is also the possibility that Roma students could be afraid of any kind of interview in case it could be something like a test (Roma are often stigmatised as less gifted students). Teachers could also have simply not informed them about the CHIEF project, although we do not have any data to prove this. The teachers from Rimavská Sobota expressed their opinions as to why the Roma students have generally worse results at their school. According to them, Roma students had problems expressing themselves because they had to overcome the language barrier in the educational process; some did not speak Slovak or Hungarian. In an interview with the school principal, language problems and poor educational results due to a less stimulating family environment were identified as the most common reasons for educational problems. Roma pupils often do not show interest in education, do not have the support of legal representatives, and their further progress is often limited by unfavourable social conditions. Some students take care of securing financial resources. Generally, only one-third of Roma attend pre-school compared with almost 80 % in the overall population and 90 % in most OECD countries. Due to the high demand, pre-schools prefer the children of working parents and families with permanent residences, conditions which often effectively disqualify Roma parents (To da Rozum, 2018). According to the Education Act, in addition to the right to learn the state language, the right of minority groups to an upbringing and education in their language is ensured. In this school year, education in the language of the national minority took place in a total of 352 pre-schools, 271 of which were Hungarian and 74 bilingual Slovak-Hungarian. There are three Ruthenian pre-schools, two Ukrainian, one German and one Bulgarian. None are Romani.[21] The language of instruction in most schools is Slovak, but the possibility of education in a minority language, including Romani, is formally enshrined in the constitution. The Romani

21 https://www.narodnostnemensiny.gov.sk//pravo-ucit-sa-v-materinskej-reci-vyuzilo-viac-ako-50-tisic-deti-vsetky-mensiny-vsak-tuto-moznost-nemaju/

language is used at the Department of Roma Culture and Language at the Faculty of Social Sciences, University of Constantine Philosopher, at the Secondary Art School in Košice, at the Gandhi School in Lučenec, and at a private grammar school in Košice.[22]

As has been shown above, Slovak policy documents and curricula focus mainly on general descriptions of terms such as culture, identity, diversity, inclusion and extremism without expanded reflection on their applications in practice. Slovak academic studies have thus sought to research these topics. Academic studies indicate that Slovak young people who attend vocational schools are more prone to adopt extremist views, which is reflected in their support for extremist political parties (Velšic, 2017). Other research has confirmed that students from grammar schools have a better knowledge of history and civic education than those at other types of schools, and that grammar school students also have a 'more tolerant attitude' towards minorities (Milo, 2017). Recent research findings show that having a better knowledge of history does not automatically lead to students having a higher 'level of tolerance' (ibid.). However, this formulation again only replicates an image of the majoritarian 'helping hand' that sets all the conditions for acceptance of marginalised groups (see above).

Based on the study presented in this chapter, several areas for future research on how to improve the existing curricula and teaching materials can be proposed. A clear definition of culture and direction of policy is a necessary step, as is trying to develop policy coherence through consistency. There is also a need to find an efficient way to train teachers on the topics of broader cultural learning, expanding this subject beyond the essentialisation of concepts such as multiculturalism, diversity and inclusion. Further research should be conducted to find new techniques and communication channels through which teachers can effectively engage more students in formal education projects and activities designed to develop cultural literacy.[23]

Conclusion

This study aimed to examine how the national guidance on cultural literacy is reflected in classroom practices in Slovakia. Slovak policy documents and

22 https://www.romaeducationfund.org/wp-content/uploads/2019/05/web_slovakia_report_slovak.pdf?fbclid=IwAR1JvFfSyIUccjDTLTNbqPFbUtn4UJBGYCHTC5C4JvYdiT3aFVZc8MJgoFY

23 Further reading and a complete list of recommendations is available on the CHIEF website: http://chiefprojecteu.com.

curricula contain specific goals for teaching young people cultural literacy, but they contain only very vague definitions and almost no practical instructions or guidance. This may be part of the reason for the observed lack of professional awareness among many teachers of how to incorporate topics such as multiculturalism or cultural identities into their teaching. Some teachers educate themselves on these topics independently, while others are less active and follow the curriculum.

In addition to the responsibilities set out in the curricula regarding the subjects within which the topics of culture, heritage and cultural identities are covered, the teaching process also includes educational visits to museums, galleries, theatres, concerts, and other sites of local, national, and European cultural heritage. The observed schools participate in various local and international projects and related events, depending on the financial and human resources available to them. They often cooperate with NGOs and invite external experts to visit. At the school in Martin, teachers work with NGOs to develop their own methodologies for talking to students about topics like global education or multicultural education.

The students were generally willing participants in the interviews. One of the reasons for this was that the interviews were conducted during the school day, which meant the students were allowed to be absent for part of their lessons. During the interviews, most of the pupils were very open and had no problem sharing their opinions with the interviewers. They were not afraid to criticise the school, some of the teachers and their methods, because they were guaranteed confidentiality and trusted us as researchers. One group of boys from the school in Rimavská Sobota (about one third of the interviewed students) were an exception. This school is attended by students from Rimavská Sobota and nearby villages and has a technical focus, with 90 % male students. Rimavská Sobota is a more heterogeneous district than the other researched locations, with a higher proportion of ethnic Hungarians and a large share of the Roma population (Mušinka et al., 2014). It is also the least developed district in Slovakia. In Slovakia generally, experienced teachers are in short supply in schools in socio-economically disadvantaged regions (Santiago et al., 2016). As has been shown in the field, further research is needed to devote more time and focus to such an environment. Spending more time in this location is essential to building closer connections with locals, which could potentially lead to better trust between researchers and respondents. Greater involvement of Hungarian and Roma speaking researchers is required in future studies of this area.

As we learned from other students, some boys were known within the school to be neo-Nazis. However, they did not mention this during the interviews, and they were very careful in how they answered questions. Their participation was also apparently not entirely voluntarily, but was coerced by teachers. They did not trust researchers and did not want to give open answers. These boys felt that they were being monitored by teachers and even the police, but they did not want to share any details about this. They felt that some of the school activities they had to attend deliberately targeted them and their opinions. Interestingly, most other students in the school did not want to talk about this group of boys, as if they were afraid of possible retaliation. This could be an indication of how much power the neo-Nazi boys have among other students.

Teachers responded positively to our interviews. Some were initially nervous, as if they were afraid that they were being inspected. These concerns generally dissipated during the interview and the teachers opened up. However, they did not want to make comments that could be interpreted as criticism of school management, and avoided controversial issues relating to their school. If the teachers criticised anything, it was the Ministry of Education regulations (excluding funding). They were most critical of the scale of the curriculum, and the small number of lessons allocated to the subjects they were teaching. This means they lack time to discuss the topics; nevertheless, the teachers try to encourage discussion. In general, the teachers rated our interviews positively, with most giving scores of 9 or 10.

The teachers approached the term 'cultural heritage' as a set of individual elements, such as cultural and historical monuments and the key figures associated with them. Some also mentioned that cultural heritage is an ongoing process in which we are all co-creators. As for cultural identity, Slovak national identity was covered most in the three schools. Teachers thought that this concept was mainly represented by costumes, traditional dishes, crafts, folk songs and key figures/national heroes. All the interviewed teachers said they felt proud to be Slovak and encouraged their students to be patriotic. Their Slovak identity was more important to them than the European identity, while local/regional identity was important to only a few teachers.

In all the schools, there was significant ethnic diversity among students. There was less religious diversity; respondents were Christians or atheists, and teachers were not aware of any students subscribing to other religions. Students experienced ethnic diversity through international or local exchanges, especially at the Rimavská Sobota school, where there is a large number of students of Hungarian and Roma ethnicity. During the lessons, some teachers revealed their prejudices, for example against Muslims in connection with terrorism, or against sexual minorities.

The students usually described learning about cultural heritage in stereotypical ways, as a set of lessons. Few were interested in the topic, and some believed that what they knew about cultural heritage from school had little effect on their everyday lives. Like the teachers, most students felt they were far more Slovak than European. Their reference points were primarily their friends and role models, both virtual and real. Online platforms seem to dominate the spontaneous organisation of leisure activities among young people today. Students perceived diversity positively, both in their own school and in society. The only exception was, again, the group of patriot boys from Rimavská Sobota, where, in addition to negative attitudes towards Roma students, anti-immigrant attitudes were often expressed.

In Slovakia, there are very few academics and teachers with Roma origins. This is a result of the unfavourable reality of the Slovak education system, where Roma students have to face a lot of barriers to graduate from university. Slovak academics, the EU and NGOs have all made several recommendations for how to make the situation better. To boost the participation of Roma children in pre-school education it will be necessary to increase the number of pre-school facilities through more investments. Empirical research has confirmed that early interventions are more cost-efficient than remedial education later in life (OECD, 2011; Schweinhart, 2006; Heckman et al., 2009). At the same time, additional Slovak language support for Roma students should be introduced. Teachers should be able to identify those in need of extra language training. This additional language support can start even before primary school.

More support should also be offered to teachers; it is crucial to attract the best teachers to disadvantaged schools. Teacher quality can have a large effect on the performance of students, significant enough to close the achievement gap between advantaged and disadvantaged students (Chetty et al., 2014; Schacter and Thum, 2004).

The schools where the interviews were conducted offered several activities aimed at developing students' cultural literacy. All the schools created sufficient opportunities for the students to participate in projects, giving them practical experiences of European and national cultural heritage through formal education. NGOs and the students' families were also involved in some projects. Participating students often evaluated these activities positively. The problem, however, is that the schools fail to stimulate interest in these topics and events among the majority of students. Themes such as cultural heritage, multiculturalism and civic engagement are of interest to a very narrow group: these are usually elite students, who are often members of the school's parliament or contribute to the school's magazine. Meanwhile, the majority of students are not interested in participating in these activities, even when they are coerced into doing so.

References

Bagalová, M., Lehocký Ľ., Deák, D., & Karásek, M. (2018). '*CHIEF project Deliverable: 1.2 National Cultural/Educational Policy Review*', http://chiefprojecteu.com/wp-content/uploads/CHIEF-WP1_D1.2_National-Cultural-Educational-Policy-Reviews_v1.1_KM.pdf (Accessed on May 3, 2021).

Brubaker, R. (2004). *Ethnicity without Groups*. Cambridge, MA: Harvard University Press.

Brumann, Ch. & Berliner, D. (eds.). (2016). *World Heritage on the Ground. Ethnographic Perspectives*. New York: Berghahn Books.

Deák, D. (2019). '*CHIEF project Deliverable: 2.1 National/federal Curricula Review*', http://chiefproject.eu/wp-content/uploads/Chief-WP2_D2.1_National-Curriculum-Review-Reports_v1.0_14.01.19.pdf (Accessed on May 3, 2021).

Filadelfiová, J, Hlinčíková, M. Diskusia o kultúrnej diverzite a migrácii: trendy a výzvy pre verejnú politiku in Filadelfiová, J., Gyárfášová, O., Hlinčíková, M., & Sekulová, M. (2010). *Sondy do kultúrnej diverzity na Slovensku* (Bratislava: Inštitút pre verejné otázky, 2010), 103–146.

Milo, D. (2017). Vychovávajú dezinformačné a konšpiračné médiá Kotlebových voličov? (Are misinformation and conspiracy media raising the Kotleba´s voters?). In: Nociar, T. (ed.), *Mládež a Extrémizmus. Výskumy, úvahy, odporúčania (Youth and Extremism. Research, Considerations, Recommendations)*. Bratislava: Inštitút pre medzikultúrny dialog, pp. 12–14.

Mušinka, A., Škobla, D., Hurrle, J., Matlovičová, K., & Kling, J. (2014). *Atlas rómskych komunít na Slovensku 2013*. Bratislava, UNDP.

Podolinská, T. (2017). 'Roma in Slovakia - Silent and Invisible Minority (Social Networking and Pastoral Pentecostal Discourse as a case of giving voice and positive visibility).' *Slovak Ethnology*, 2 (65): 135–157.

Said, E. (1985). 'Orientalism Reconsidered.' *Cultural Critique*, 1 (Autumn 1985): 89–107.

Velšic, M. (2017). *Mladí ľudia a riziká extrémizmu (Young people and the risks of extremism)*. Bratislava, Inštitút pre verejné otázky.

Weblinks

Declaration of principles on tolerance by UNESCO constitution (1995). Available from: http://portal.unesco.org/en/ev.php-URL_ID=13175&URL_DO=DO_TOPIC&URL_SECTION=201.html (Accessed on July 12, 2021).

Mikušovič, D. (2017) *Čižnár filed an appeal with the Supreme Court for the dissolution of Kotlebas ĽSNS.* Available from https://dennikn.sk/775198/ciznar-podal-na-najvyssi-sud-podnet-na-zrusenie-kotlebovej-lsns/ (Accessed on December 12, 2019).

Official webpage of ŠK Slovan Bratislava. *UEFA decision for fan behavior.* Available from: https://www.skslovan.com/clanok7234-Rozhodnutie_UEFA_za_spravanie_fanusikov.htm (Accessed on December 12, 2019).

(by Eleni Stamou, Anton Popov and Ebru Soytemel)

Chapter 4 Normative multiculturalism and the limits of inclusion in school lives: Qualitative insights from three secondary schools in England

Abstract: This chapter provides empirical insight into teaching practices and learning experiences around issues of culture, heritage and belonging in secondary education in England. The study is located within a broader context of social developments, including a retreat to nationalism, growing migration, the increasing internationalisation of the economy and culture, and conditions of 'superdiversity' (Vertovec, 2007). Against this bedrock, we draw on semi-structured interviews with students and teachers in an urban, a semi-urban and a rural school to shed light on pedagogic practices and schooling experiences.

Our findings indicate that teachers critically engaged with education policy, describing their teaching practices as bounded by the opportunities and constraints facing their schools or localities. We observed teachers looking beyond their direct roles and connecting their lessons to wider issues and learning objectives. Yet, throughout their narratives, they often evoked conceptualisations of culture as external to pupils' embodied experiences, thus reproducing dominant hierarchies of cultural value and foregrounding forms of cultural capital related to strategies of distinction. In relation to the above, we identified that teachers' narratives were underlined by a 'deficiency' model, preoccupied with establishing a given value system, one largely underpinned by normative accounts of culture and multiculturalism.

Students' narratives of school experiences echoed their multifaceted social positioning. We observed habitual class elements in their accounts of their learning strengths and weaknesses, their possible future pathways and their perceptions about the horizons of possibilities ahead. In terms of ethnic positioning, we observed that young people who identified as having ethnic minority backgrounds were significantly more engaged with issues of culture and identity than those who identified as belonging to the ethnic majority. In all cases, we found that the "politics of belonging" (Yuval-Davies, 2011) emerged as embodied, intersectional and context-specific. Across young people's narratives, schools were constructed as inclusive places, though inclusion was either couched on single-dimensional notions of culture or superficially focused on certain manifestations.

Overall, pupils and teachers' narratives revealed the limits of inclusivity in school contexts through: (a) a lack of consideration of the interplay of differences involved in cultural belonging and (b) the deployment of essentialist ethno-cultural understandings of culture, which focus on accepting difference rather than on seeking more dynamic inquiry, in-depth understanding, recognition and the incorporation of diversity at an institutional level.

Keywords: culural diversity, multiculturalism, cultural deficit, inclusion, cultural belonging

Introduction

Intensifying divisions over issues of nationhood and sovereignty, and immigration and diversity, have defined contemporary political environments. Manifestations of these trends are particularly pronounced in the UK, where the departure from the European Union, along with the effects of economic austerity, feature prominently in the current policy context. The emergence of new nationalisms (Halikiopoulou and Vlandas, 2019) and the spread of Euroscepticism (Leruth, Startin and Usherwood, 2017; Harmsen and Spiering, 2004), and of debates on immigration and free movement, have signalled a retreat from post-nationalism. On the other hand, the increasing internationalisation of economic production, culture and higher education, as well as conditions of 'superdiversity' (Vertovec, 2007) in the country's demographic make-up, work towards eroding existing dominant forms of national belonging. Within this landscape of contradictory trends and developments, issues of cultural identity and diversity are at the forefront of policy and public debate. Recent education policy has reflected this through exchanging multicultural models for a greater focus on Britishness (Fooks et al., 2018; Stamou et al., 2019). Since 2014, as part of their safeguarding duty, schools have been required by the Department for Education to teach the Five Fundamental British Values (FBV).[1] These consist of democracy, the rule of law, individual liberty, mutual respect, and tolerance of those of different faiths and beliefs. The FBVs are part of the wider Prevent Strategy, which was introduced by the Home Office in 2011[2] to tackle 'radicalisation'. Additionally, the teaching of the FBVs has been added to the criteria against which school performance is assessed by the Office for Standards in Education (Ofsted), as well as being incorporated into teacher training programmes. These shifts in education policy encapsulate the government's "muscular intervention"[3] to revive a shared sense of Britishness, while declaring multiculturalism failed

1 https://www.gov.uk/government/publications/promoting-fundamental-british-values-through-smsc

2 https://www.gov.uk/government/publications/prevent-duty-guidance/revised-prevent-duty-guidance-for-england-and-wales

3 https://www.gov.uk/government/news/british-values-article-by-david-cameron

and redundant. Critical remarks have been made regarding the securitisation of education through an extension of the policing agenda and a shift to focusing on security above cultural diversity (Raggazi, 2017).

Taking into account the above trends, educational researchers (Osler and Starkey, 2018) have identified a number of challenges for teachers and schools, particularly when it comes to teaching democratic cosmopolitan citizenship. These include the securitisation of education, Islamophobia and new forms of racism (ibid.). Youth studies exploring attitudes towards diversity over time have identified young people as displaying different opinions about different aspects of diversity. Jannmaat and Keating (2017) found their informants to be more open to racial difference and homosexuality, but less accepting of "immigrants" and "foreign workers" (Janmaat and Keating, 2017). Other research has demonstrated how schools can play a significant role in the development of cosmopolitan dispositions (Keating, 2016). At the same time, a significant amount of educational research has indicated how class and racial positioning have an ongoing effect on young people's educational experiences, pathways and life chances (MacDonald, Shildrick and Furlong, 2019; Reay, 2017, Ball; Maguire and Macrae, 2000; Shildrick et al., 2012; Allen, 2016; Ingram, 2009).

Within this wider context, our aim is to shed light on formal learning experiences and to explore how young people develop a sense of culture, heritage and belonging in secondary schools in England. Our broader objective is to offer a bottom-up conceptualisation, bringing to the fore empirical insights through teachers' and young people's accounts of schooling. Drawing on critical and post-colonial frameworks, we approach culture as fluid, contextual, relational and dynamic (Hall, 2000); that is, as related to groups of people with shared meaning rather than something drawn along national boundaries (Halbert and Chigeza, 2015). Following Hall's (2000) critique of cultural identity as a "continuous, self-sufficient, developmental, unfolding, inner dialectic of selfhood" (p. 42), we seek to embrace his "new logics", which point towards an "open-ended and continuous process of construction" (Hall, 2000: p. 16). Similarly, we understand cultural heritage in terms of process and the 'discursive practices' of collective memory (Rowlands, 2002), rather than in terms of heritage-as-object. In this respect, heritage feeds into the formation of cultural identities through "ideologically loaded and politicised" (Franquesa, 2013) forms of practice.

Our understanding of the formation of culture and identity, which draws on Bourdieu's work (1979, 1980), recognises systems of inequality and social positioning. While focusing on social practice, Bourdieu examines the making of inequalities, moving beyond economic accounts to show how certain forms of culture are exchangeable and intertwined with privilege and distinction. In this respect, he provides a valuable set of tools (Ball, 2006) for understanding young people's cultural accumulations and practices within a nexus of wider social divisions and hierarchies. The main concepts that Bourdieu developed across his analyses, and which we will deploy to interrogate our data, include the concepts of cultural capital, habitus and field. Cultural capital is used to make sense of the accumulations that social subjects gain through practice, and may take objectified, embodied and institutional forms. Bourdieu puts forward a wider conceptualisation of culture that embraces material and non-material forms, and multi-sited and multi-scalar manifestations. Irrespective of the forms it takes, cultural capital can never be understood as neutral or static, as it is examined along with its exchange value and its potential to work as an asset. Habitus, on the other hand, is always embodied and enacted; it refers to the workings of cultural dispositions in the structuring of subjects' practices. Habitus and cultural capital are relational concepts, and need to be approached and understood in their interactions within a given field at a certain time.

Our empirical research focused on three schools in England in an urban, a semi-urban and a rural area. The urban school is located in an area with a high level of disadvantaged students, among the 10 % most deprived places in England. Many of the pupils here are entitled to free school meals. The local population is highly diverse in terms of ethnic and religious background. Accordingly, many students have English as an additional language. In the recent European Union (EU) referendum, there was moderate support here for the Leave vote. The location of the semi-urban school has moderate ethnic diversity and low deprivation. Overall, this is an area with an above average level of affluence, yet it includes small pockets of high deprivation. In the EU referendum there was strong support for remaining in the Union. Finally, the rural school is located in a predominantly white, working-class area with high rates of unemployment and very low ethnic and religious diversity. The vast majority of the population in the area voted to leave the EU in the recent referendum.

During our fieldwork in secondary schools in England, we witnessed first-hand a number of challenges facing teachers and schools. We came across the problems and struggles in the teaching profession, such as heavy workloads, working overtime, and the limited opportunities for reflection, recollection and development in teachers' daily professional lives. The above issues have increasingly become an object of research, and public debate has begun to highlight the risks of teachers' burnout and lack of retention in the teaching profession (Bamford and Worth, 2017; Foster, 2018). Existing neo-liberal regimes of performative accountability – target-setting, universal assessment criteria and school rankings – have also been identified as eroding teachers' autonomy, undermining democratic professionalism (Biesta, 2017), and fuelling managerialism (Skinner, Leavey and Rothi, 2019). These issues, along with their effects on teachers' practices and subjectivities, have been vividly illustrated as the 'terrors of performativity' (Ball, 2003). The above research provides some context within which teachers' narratives and accounts of pedagogic practices need to be read and considered.

Teaching culture and engaging with diversity in the classroom

Teachers' reflections on school lives

The teachers we interviewed talked passionately about their subjects and spoke of going beyond their prescribed roles, working creatively and taking initiatives to meet their pupils' needs, with a focus on linking their subjects to wider social issues. Teachers' answers regarding how they taught their particular subject pointed towards a combination of knowledge, skills and general values that they wanted their students to develop through their classes. They demonstrated how their subjects connect to and help raise awareness of wider social issues:

> *It teaches you about society, it teaches you about culture, it teaches you about different places and different time periods. I think you learn a lot about yourself through reading and you learn a lot about society. ... ... The reason I enjoy teaching that is because you can, to all students, you can teach really high level stuff.* (Nina, English Literature Teacher and Deputy Head, Urban School, UK)

Teachers also stressed the importance of developing critical thinking and an in-depth understanding of wider social issues, particularly in the current context of an overflow of information, some of which may be considered fake news, from the media and social media. In addition, teachers described their subjects and teaching practices as aiming to contribute to the development of pupils' skills-base, with a focus on transferrable skills, creativity and adaptability.

> *I'm passionate about making sure that all of our students have the opportunity to be able to be successful in whatever it is they do in life. I strongly believe that my job goes beyond being a drama teacher. ... My job is making sure that they can work in a group, they're able to speak and listen, they can work to a deadline, they can work on a project, I can give them a theme and they can create...to access those soft, those transferrable skills* (Ben, Drama Teacher and Head of Drama, Urban School, UK)

As the final lines of the above quotation showcase, when talking about their subjects and teaching approach, teachers emphasised instilling certain values in young people; these values often included kindness, empathy, open-mindedness, and respecting and accepting diversity. Overall, teachers' grasps of their subjects, as well as their teaching objectives, encompassed expansive notions of learning.

At the same time, teachers highlighted their heavy workloads, tight schedules and tough working conditions, which they related to wider pressures facing the sector. They particularly referred to the pressures of league tables and the focus on performance and results. Apart from adding pressure to their working lives, these also impacted how schools were forced to think about the curriculum. This included limiting time spent on general learning experiences and activities that do not directly translate into boosting attainment, such as 'pulling them off timetable to watch a play'.

In the rural school, teachers outlined a number of significant infrastructural issues including problems with their school buildings, facilities and funding, with which they struggled. The highlighted problems with old buildings 'falling apart', with heating, lack of insulation and broken windows, as well as having limited or outdated equipment for practical lessons. All of the above posed obstacles to their teaching practices and to pupils' learning.

Beyond school-specific issues, which were discussed as contextual elements of learning experiences, our interviewees also referred to local characteristics as influences on the possibilities and barriers of student experiences and learning. In the case of the rural school, a lack of ethnic diversity and significant levels of socio-economic and educational deprivation were highlighted as factors that narrow pupils' learning horizons. In the case of the urban school, teachers stressed challenges related to socio-economic deprivation and problems that occur in the immediate inner-city locality, such as gangs, knife crime, and drug abuse.

> *They live in an area of intense social deprivation, they live right in the middle of a massive drugs culture, gang culture, prostitution, it's all there literally on the doorstep. They walk through this, or they live in it.* (Vicky, Drama Teacher and Senior Vice-Principal responsible for inclusion, Urban School, UK)

Teaching with and beyond the curriculum

In relation to the wider context of teaching and learning, teachers critically engaged with different aspects of education policy and the curriculum, as definitive of the conditions where cultural learning takes place. Recent changes in the curriculum include a shift to knowledge-rich courses that slim down the teaching content, focusing on the acquisition of hard facts and core knowledge. The national curriculum has been replaced with a set of guidelines, which allow schools to decide on the particulars of the taught content. This reportedly put strain on schools and teachers' workloads, and was followed by the government's announcement of designated funding to support schools in building up their curriculum content and related resources.

Some teachers talked about the challenges, the additional work and time investment that the first phase of implementing the new curriculum has required. They highlighted this as indicative of the tendency for each successive government to introduce its own education policies and changes, creating disruption and discontinuity. Teachers stated the need for stability in education policy and longer-term planning. Overall, our participants appeared to feel positive about the change in the curriculum format, noting the heavily prescriptive and bureaucratic nature of its previous form.

> *Piles of folders, thick folders…with the national curriculum, down to almost what issue you'd be teaching in each lesson, you know?… It was so prescriptive, it was crazy! Obviously, rightly, gradually, that was refined.* (Luna, Teacher of English Literature and Deputy Head, Rural School, UK)

While welcoming the new curriculum format, our interviewees did raise some critical points, mainly in relation to the predisposition towards subjects like English, Maths and Sciences. They explained how this focus results in other subjects becoming marginalised or squeezed out of the curriculum:

> *Now it's gone much more towards STEM[4]…This morning I heard it on the radio coming to school, 20% increase in the film industry during the last couple of years. I mean the market is there, the jobs are going to be there, in the media, in the arts, there are going to be opportunities and the arts actually earn phenomenal amount of money for this country.* (Vicky, Drama Teacher and Senior Vice-principal Responsible for inclusion, Urban School, UK)

Processes of undermining the value of certain subjects was also discussed, by some teachers, as an outcome of the new assessment procedures, which predominantly focus on exams. This marks a change from the previous combination of assessment techniques (essays, exams etc.). Additionally, in some cases, the new assessment methods were criticised as creating a lot of stress for pupils; we captured examples of teachers describing the exam focus as fit for private rather than state schooling, as well as disincentivising students from taking up particular subjects.

> *So it has actually prohibited a lot of my students from doing A Level languages. They've made the subject so much more difficult, compared to other subjects… Well, the government has*

4 STEM is a widely used acronym to refer to subjects related to Science, Technology, Engineering and Mathematics.

kind of shut the door on language learning in this country…It's a very monolingual society that our education system is developing. (Lila, Languages Teacher, Rural School, UK)

Finally, we encountered cases where teachers criticised changes in the actual content of curricula. Some interviewees pointed out how contemporary literature and international texts have been pushed out of the English curriculum, replaced by older English literature, which they denounced as elitist and less appealing to their students.

At GCSE[5] you have to teach English authors, we don't have a choice. There's no writers from other cultures on the spec, so we can't, there's nothing we can do. But we teach it at Key Stage 3[6] and then at Key Stage 5[7] it's a bit more diverse. We teach metanarratives at Key Stage 5. We teach post-colonialism, we teach feminism, we teach Marxism and we cover a range of writers from different social classes, genders and races through that module. Also, we teach Margaret Atwood, she's Canadian (laughs), so yeah, there's more flexibility. (Nina, English Literature Teacher and Deputy Head, Urban School, UK)

Teachers' accounts of culture and heritage in the school classroom

Notions of culture, cultural heritage and diversity were described as central to school life and were often discussed as the main reasons that attracted teachers to work in their particular schools.

Our interviewees talked about issues related to culture and heritage as involving certain values, emphasising respect and openness to diversity. They generally understood culture in juxtaposition with ethnicity and religion, and in some cases with class background. The teachers generally understood cultural heritage as having local and national dimensions, as well as a set of wider humanistic values, which were often articulated through human rights discourses.

The values that we really need to embed would be accepting differences, accepting different cultures…And it's actually about being a good human, not really about being British. (Jannis, Teacher of English, Rural School, UK)

---

5 GCSE (General Certificate of Secondary Education) is an academic qualification taken by students in England at the end of compulsory secondary education, and is based on exams sat over the course of two or three years.

6 Key Stage 3 is the term used to refer to the three years of school (years 7, 8 and 9) for pupils aged 11 to 14 years old.

7 Key Stage 5 refers to the two years of school (year 12 and year 13) for pupils aged 16 to 18 years old.

Obviously bringing together the different cultures and the different ethnicities and the gender differences is very important to us. … … We work with those values and everything that we do we try to relate to those values. (Mary, Art Teacher, Urban School, UK)

The approaches to culture, heritage and diversity we identified were predominantly underscored by liberal political theories and legal concepts. While welcoming and celebrating diversity, teachers referred to the need to have shared values, which may not be necessarily linked to Britishness but frame co-existence and guide young people's behaviour in this context. From this viewpoint, teachers understood the introduction of Fundamental British Values (FBV) as a positive addition to the learning experience. While in some cases they questioned whether these constitute British-only values, they still positively embraced them as a set of fair and useful principles that all students should share. The interviewees often discussed the FBVs as humanistic values in their essence, and therefore accepted them as positive and useful signposts for pupils' cultural identities. In other words, the teachers focused more on the content of those FBVs rather than on questioning the underpinning logic and potential effects of claiming this set of values as a presupposition of British national identity.

Particularly because of the nature of our students, to try and ensure that they understand some of these principles that we believe are fundamental for everyone to understand, particularly if you are part of the United Kingdom…We do remind them of it, particularly about the importance of law and what is expected in this country, the bottom line is the law of the land. So that cultural practice, if it flies in the face of the law of the land, is not acceptable. … For example, you don't go around using the word 'gay' disparagingly…You respect. Now, culturally that's difficult for some of our kids. (Vicky, Drama Teacher and Senior Vice-Principal responsible for inclusion, Urban School, UK)

Going beyond the celebratory discourses of diversity, and moving beyond legal and humanistic approaches, we can also capture how perceptions of culture interweave with ideas of ethnicity and religious belonging. Teachers' accounts of inclusive practice, as well as their discussion of the challenges entailed in dealing with cultural diversity, predominantly focused on religion. In their narratives, certain cultural attitudes were construed as interwoven with religious belonging, while in some cases class was added as another layer reinforcing these connections.

In their accounts of inclusive practice in their schools, the teachers talked about recognising and respecting diversity, one example being celebrating major festivities from different religions.

We have a room devoted, which is their worship room, where they can go and do their Friday prayers. They have different time periods for the girls and the boys. They have their wash room where they can do their ablutions. We've tried to accommodate it in the school. During special periods of time, for example during Ramadan, we're allowing 16+ to wear their religious wear underneath their jackets. It still meets the school expectations, but we're compromising so they can express who they are and what's important to them. (Josh, Social Sciences Teacher and Assistant Principal, Urban School, UK)

We celebrate virtually every holiday. The majority of our students are Muslim, so we do a lot of celebrations at Eid and obviously we have to work with the community, with Ramadan because it falls around exam period at the moment ... Then we celebrate all the festivals really. We do Diwali in November; a lot of the staff here celebrate Diwali. So we have Diwali parties and obviously we celebrate Christmas, we study A Christmas Carol in Year 11 in the run-up to Christmas. Yeah, loads of celebrations and stuff like that. (Nina, English Literature Teacher and Deputy Head, Urban School, UK)

To a great extent, we observed that inclusion was perceived in terms of allowing young people to practice their religions in the school space. Recognising and respecting their differences, and making space to accommodate their needs, were the main features of the teachers' descriptions, with religion being the main focus of their inclusive ethos. Furthermore, while elaborating on the challenges of everyday school life, our interviewees often talked about cultural diversity in terms of the barriers they perceived as being embedded in their pupils' religions and ethnic backgrounds.

I think in a school like this, I've been here a long time and culturally, within families, particularly within Islamic culture, there is a big barrier to any kind of performing arts. That is a wall here, it really is. It's a difficult wall for people to break through, for staff to break through, it really is. (Ben, Drama Teacher and Head of Drama, Urban School, UK)

In the above quotation, we can observe the racialisation of educational orientations and wider social practices, as belonging to an ethnic minority group is assigned certain cultural dispositions. Ethnicity is essentialised as a normative unifying feature that is predominantly believed to be overshadowed by religious identity. Furthermore, these aspects of students' identities are understood as posing barriers to empowerment, which reinforces fixity in educational and social terms.

Teachers' understanding of cultural identity and cultural participation

At the different research sites, teachers highlighted different aspects of cultural identities and experiences of cultural participation. In our rural school, the key challenges teachers mentioned were the lack of ethnic diversity in the local population, the high deprivation of the area, and the socio-economic disadvantages facing families. These factors were discussed as limits to pupils' cultural horizons that lead to low aspirations. Furthermore, teachers referred to students' strong connections with the locality – despite poor its future prospects – as 'narrow-mindedness'. These assumptions regarding lack of skills or ambitions in mind, their teaching priorities consisted of exposing pupils to new cultural experiences, raising their career prospects and aspirations, and developing their critical thinking in relation to news and the media.

> *Their cultural identity around here is very, very narrow. If they live in [name of rural location], they possibly haven't been into the town centre, and they certainly wouldn't have been across town… And that hasn't really changed in the time that I've been working in this county. And even when I lived in this county, you didn't really leave your town or your village.* (Lila, Languages Teacher, Rural School, UK)

In the urban school, teachers stressed the challenges of teaching a highly diverse student population in terms of ethnic, religious, cultural and socio-economic backgrounds. Their priorities were to expose pupils to diverse cultural experiences, as well as to enrich and increase pupils' cultural knowledge. In several instances, teachers talked about families' assumptions about education as restrictive and narrow, due to their expectations that their children would follow certain professions and their mistrust of aspects of students' arts and culture education.

> *For example, we were just talking about homosexuality, which is traditionally an area of concern for quite a lot of our students. It's something that's been brought up with which is wrong, so we've got to bring down those barriers. So in that sense when we're broadening their horizons, trying to educate them about that and not sticking to their principles or their foundations, which they might have had at home.* (Josh, Social Sciences Teacher and Assistant Principal, Urban School, UK)

Although this was often framed differently, the teachers generally pointed out the narrow cultural horizons available to young people and identified limitations in young people's cultural literacy skills. Irrespective of the particulars, they all understood the role of the school as exposing young people to wider cultural experiences and forms of participation, which they more or less lack otherwise. Thus, teachers' starting points were regularly based on an identified deficiency in cultural learning.

Learning experiences of culture, heritage and belonging

Insights into school experiences

Young people talked about their school experiences and their views about school more generally, with reference to their preferences and frustrations regarding school life and to their ideas about the future. We encountered different opinions about school, ranging from young people being perfectly happy with their education to young people who highlighted negative experiences and grievances. The latter were either related to personal preferences or to particular incidents and disappointment with how the school dealt with them. Across all the interviews, pupils appeared to be overwhelmed by the pressures and demands of school life, especially in relation to their forthcoming exams. They all reported tiredness, or even exhaustion, due to their preparation for these exams, and underlined their limited free time.

> *I do a lot of revising. I think that's probably my main thing that I go to when I have any free time, because I have loads of exams coming up and I want to make sure that I'm getting as much information known to me.* (Ronnie, 15 years old, Semi-urban school, UK)
> *I have no idea what I want to do when I'm older. Working really hard for the exams that are coming up. Obviously I want to do well but I can't see myself in the future. I'm not even sure what I want to do yet, whatever.* (Courtney, 15 years old, Semi-urban school, UK)

Interestingly, we observed that, in most cases, our interviewees did not necessarily link these exams to their future plans for studying in further/higher education or to their employment prospects. Instead, they talked about them as stressful events and purposes in themselves, that is, not as part of a longer-term trajectory to which they aspired. In this respect, exams were conceived of as aims in themselves, rather than as a means to an end. This may exemplify the increasing presence of an exam culture and focus on attainment in secondary education in the UK.

Within this broader context, pupils talked about their most and least favourite subjects. Their discussion of preferences was often linked to their learning strengths and weaknesses, and in some cases to ideas about future education and employment. Their narratives evoked their family's experiences of education and parental ambitions. In these cases, we observed a reluctance to think about the prospect of higher education; when students did so, they referred to the university or further education college in closest proximity.

> *I've picked three sciences for my GCSE.... My mum always bought me science books when I was smaller. Then she bought me my first science kit. When I was smaller, I was really girly. I guess it was the idea of making cosmetics and things like that. But now it's more working with chemicals and acids and seeing what happens then.* (Zara, 14 years old, Urban school, UK)

Generally, young people appeared to be less confident and comfortable with the idea of university in cases where parents had no university education.

> *I know that I want to eventually go to college; I don't really think I could handle university. … My aunty went and she just said, like the money that you get, then you have to pay it back, that I just don't think I could, that would stress me out a lot. My grandparents think I should get an apprenticeship…. I want to be an assistant care person, I can't remember what it's called but I need to go to college for that, do health and social and then I can hopefully go onto that. … I think I will search later. There's a few around me.* (Anne, 14 years old, Semi-urban school, UK)

We observed that pupils' outlooks on the future emerged in the context of the financial and educational resources available to them in their immediate family and local environment.

> *I'm not sure what I want to do because my mum would still like me [to] becom[e] a hairdresser and I know it would improve my concentration because you have to keep steady and stuff …my dad does it… It's easy money, kind of like, and it just helps you with your skills.* (Raj, 15 years old, Urban school, UK)

This discernible differentiation in young people's accounts could be by and large related to the material and symbolic conditions young people find themselves in. In this context, our interviewees' framing of their learning strengths and weaknesses, as well as their ideas about future education and employment, can be read as a reflection of wider social hierarchies and a manifestation of their unequal positioning in terms of resources.

Embodying and practicing culture

The influence of family background was evident in young people's experiences of cultural participation. In some cases, the location of their residence also played a role in the choice of activities available. We identified some examples of class reproduction, with middle-class pupils participating in a wider range of hobbies and after-school activities. These activities were costly and often required parents' active involvement with transport, etc. Pupils from less disadvantaged backgrounds also appeared to engage with activities in a more consistent way and for longer periods of time. Young people who did not engage in structured activities spent time with friends at parks or at home.

In terms of their school lives and opportunities to practise their culture in a school context, our interviewees portrayed their experiences in positive terms. Once again, their narratives focused predominantly on religious practices and beliefs. Students at the urban school described how their school respects and accommodates their needs, making special arrangements and providing space and time for religious practice. They conveyed that a non-judgmental and accepting ethos dominates the institutional setting.

You could walk around school and you'd hear about people and their experiences and stuff like that, especially to do with festivals and stuff like Eid, because I'm Muslim and Ramadan and stuff like that. We do talk about it and the serious events that happen around, outside of school, we talk about those and we have the minute silences. I don't think anyone is very judgmental, I think from being here with each other we learn that we're all, we might be different skin colour, different religion, but in the inside we're all the same people. (Safia, 15 years old, Urban school, UK)

We can practice our culture in school. Like, for example, we are allowed to wear scarves, which is very important for us because in some schools you may not be allowed to wear a scarf, or you might get picked on for wearing it. In certain schools there are some incidents like that. In our school, I think they're very open-minded about it. Also, we have a prayer room. For my culture, we pray five times a day and some of those prayers happen during school time. For example, one would happen during our lunch time, so we have this prayer room which we can go and pray in, but the boys would go first and then girls would go after. So, we would have our own separate times. (Aisha, 16 years old, Urban school, UK)

Young people's perceptions of culture and cultural heritage

Young people talked about culture in both direct and indirect terms: directly by giving their own definitions of culture, and indirectly by identifying and reflecting on certain aspects or manifestations. Throughout the interviews they were asked to discuss culture generally as well as in the specific context of their self-identifications.

The most common approach to culture that we encountered was in terms of family origins, which was often related to ethnic background as well as to religion. Ethno-cultural definitions of culture were dominant in young people's accounts. Religion was also identified as a dominant marker of culture and, in many instances, was considered by young people as synonymous to culture.

AISHA: *For me, I believe in Islam and that's my culture, but if someone else was Christian or Sikh I would not be like, "Oh, you should convert to Islam", because for me that's their thoughts and their opinions and that's their religion and that's what they believe in.*

INT: *So, is culture only restrained to religion or is it something else?*

AISHA: *I think it could be something else, but I mainly believe it's more religion.*

(Aisha, 16 years old, Urban school, UK)

We thus captured culture as being widely understood by young people through rather essentialist schemas, which focus on a single visible parameter of belonging at the expense of other reference points. In some cases, we also witnessed interpretations of culture that touched on aspects of everyday lives and experiences.

Your background, your beliefs, your morals, what you think is right, and what you think is wrong. (Liz, 14, Semi-urban school, UK)
It depends on probably where you're from, your family background, the people you associate yourself with, stuff along those lines. Or if you… even to do with religion probably, as well. (Rita, 16 years old, Semi-urban school, UK)
Just like how we live and how they live their lives is different to other people, and like how things are different in different places. So, if you go to France, things are run differently and things happen differently and if you go to America, things are run differently. (Becky, 15 years old, Semi-urban school, UK)

In other cases, culture was discussed in conjunction with language, while for a few young people it was related to the arts and participation in cultural activities:

Culture to me is like artsy stuff, like going to the cinema, like theatre, that's what I think of really when I hear culture, but I don't know exactly, like I wouldn't be able to define it, write it down. (Rahma, 17, Urban school, UK)

We generally observed that young people who identified themselves as belonging to ethnic majority groups were less aware of issues related to culture, diversity and identification.

I have a friend, actually, who is Spanish, I think, or French. I always get mixed up. She's either from Spain or France. The amount of stuff she knows is amazing and I think she's so clever. She's half the language, because her mum's English and then her dad's side is that. I know people that are Muslims. I have some classmates who are Muslims. When we're in our RE lesson, I find it crazy how they know all that stuff and I don't know anything about it. (Rita, 16 years old, Semi-urban school, UK)

Pupils who identified themselves as being of ethnic minority heritage displayed greater engagement with struggles of identification and cultural belonging. This may indicate how identities are inextricably connected to experiences of diversity (Hall, 2000). Overall, however, pupils predominantly showed awareness of cultural diversity in terms of ethnic and religious background. This awareness was mainly constituted on the basis of tangible – embodied or objectified – manifestations of cultural difference. Through these youth narratives, we captured lived experiences of ethnic and cultural diversity, formed, by and large, in the private sphere, in the context of the young people's family lives and traditions. Learning experiences in formal and semi-formal settings were said to predominantly involve events celebrating a certain country (Chinese New Year, Brazilian Day, Somalian Day) or theme (Refugee Awareness Day). In the former case, events had more or less the same structure, including national flags and food. In effect, the majority of these learning experiences appeared to focus on visible, objectified markers of culture and diversity: a rather limited and superficial engagement with 'otherness'. This also exemplifies the focus and framing of inclusive practice within schools, as perceived by pupils.

> *Yeah, I think when you're putting your sum on, to check your money for buying food and stuff, there's little posters, like world, I don't know, this is an example, World Brazilian Day or something and there'll be like we're selling, and they'll sell like Brazilian food in the restaurant and stuff. The posters are cool but I don't think they actually do anything, it's just for show. I've seen it once, like the posters are nice but the actual thing is a bit of a let-down. I remember to celebrate Chinese New Year they were like selling Chinese food or something, but it was just like the same as normal food, just in different pots. [Laughter.]* (Rahma, 17 years old, Urban school, UK)

Religion emerged as the main locus of inclusion in the public sphere, as well as being a main definitive feature of cultural belonging identified across young people's interviews. Thus, inclusion in the public sphere appears to involve recognition of religious belonging, and occasional opportunities to experience diverse cultural artefacts. In the school context, this supports the critical argument that there is little incorporation of diversity within formal, institutional settings. This argument has also been made as part of calls to diversify the content and modalities of pedagogic practice (examples include calls for de-colonising the curriculum, incorporating black history into formal learning, and rethinking learning interactions in the classroom).

Discussion

The narratives by teachers and pupils offer insights into the experiential elements of school life, as well as the particularities and complexities of teaching or learning about culture, cultural heritage and belonging in contemporary UK secondary education. These findings may not fully capture young people's experiences in schools, but they provide rich illustrations of formal learning practices and exemplify widespread ideas. Our findings captured teachers developing their practices as they navigated changes to curriculum guidelines and assessment methods. They also faced the dominant culture of measurement (Biesta, 2017) and the financial constraints posed by fiscal consolidation policies in the UK public sector.

Within these conditions, teachers' enactments (Braun, Maguire and Ball, 2010) were also bounded by the opportunities and constraints specific to their institutions and were mediated by their lives and professional identities. In the rural school, teachers highlighted infrastructural and financial constraints and the challenges of working in a locality with so-called ethnic homogeneity, significant socio-economic deprivation and high rates of unemployment (the area is populated by predominantly white working-class families). At the urban school, teachers stressed the challenges of working within an inner-city location with high levels of crime, economic deprivation and a highly diverse population in terms of ethnic and religious background. Although facing different types of challenges, all teachers talked passionately about their work. Each teacher described their efforts to set learning objectives and to develop teaching practices with a wider, public-minded focus.

Despite the particularities and differences of the contexts in which teaching and learning take place, we captured some shared elements in teachers' understanding of culture and their teaching approaches. Firstly, in several instances, the teachers' narratives evoked conceptualisations of culture as external to pupils' own embodied experiences. While teachers worked passionately to widen pupils' cultural horizons, they often did so based on the assumption that pupils' cultural backgrounds were limited or not directly relevant. In this respect, young people's embodied culture and cultural practices were not always or fully acknowledged, nor were they recognised as resources for building up further learning experiences. Despite this general outlook, we did glimpse some exceptions. One example was a reading programme designed to trigger pupils' interest and attention by starting with books written by "Youtubers" popular among young people, before then moving on to other genres. In this case, cultural learning was couched in young people's previous experiences, which were recognised and used as a starting point from which to build up further learning. Yet these examples were marginal; the overall approach to the development of cultural literacy drew, by and large, on rather normative perceptions of culture.

In pedagogic terms, these findings encapsulate a shift away from dialogic pedagogy and the scaffolding approach to knowledge development (Bruner, 1996; Vygotsky, 1978; Edwards, Fleer and Bøttcher, 2019), as well as differing from experiential learning models of knowledge co-construction (Freire, 1993). From a sociological viewpoint, following Bourdieu (1979, 1980), teachers' practices were pervaded by a dominant account of cultural value and foregrounded forms of cultural capital that related to strategies of cultural distinction. In some cases, this was a conscious teaching strategy: one of our interviewees explained how this focus would equip young people to achieve greater upward mobility, highlighting the potential exchange value of amassing valid forms of cultural capital. However, Bourdieu's analyses and contemporary research has showed the classed (Savage, 2000; Skeggs, 2004), gendered (Adkins and Skeggs, 2004) and racialised (Gillborn, 2014) foundations of such valuation systems and the ways in which they reproduce existing hierarchies by degrading and silencing 'less' valuable cultural practices.

Secondly, and in relation to the above, we identified that teachers' narratives were underpinned by a model of 'deficiency'. Although teachers championed the need to expand pupils' cultural horizons and develop their appreciation of cultural diversity, they worked on the assumption that pupils lack certain forms of knowledge and skills and that school should provide them with these. We encountered several examples of teachers describing their efforts to introduce young people to cultural activities, knowledge and experiences. To a great extent, teachers' accounts echoed aspects of Bernstein's (1982) theorisation of codes: pupils' cultural knowledge was predominantly perceived in terms of a 'restricted code', while the teaching focus was on 'elaborated codes'. In Bernstein's theory, codes incorporate and manifest wider principles of power and social control in the field of education, constituting pedagogic modalities that are engraved with the principles of social hierarchies and regulatory regimes. Thus, teachers who understand pupils' communicative codes and cultural knowledge as 'restricted' – as opposed to the 'elaborated' codes of school – may be seen as reflecting, incorporating and reproducing dominant power/control configurations. In one school, the 'restricted codes' were related to the cultural politics and lived experiences of the working class, while in the urban school they were attached to certain racialised perceptions of cultural background.

We observed teachers' practices as predominantly focusing on the development of cultural literacy through establishing shared value systems for all young people, irrespective of their positionality and background. Their approach embraced rather normative notions of culture and diversity in a mixture of what Kiwan (2008) has described as legal-based and values-based models. We found that approaches to culture, heritage and diversity mainly drew on liberal political theories and legal concepts. According to a theory by Torres and Tarozzi (2020), these may exemplify the workings of 'normative multiculturalism', which they define as "an institutional perspective that is rooted in a political project based on a culturalized interpretation of the public sphere, requiring a rigid conception of culture" (p. 11). Following this analysis, such an approach has been deployed in both conservative and progressive political agendas. In a conservative context, it has fed into arguments regarding class and the need to protect national culture from hybridity. In the latter case, normative multiculturalism has been used to campaign and advocate for the rights of minority groups. However, a shared problematic feature is the understanding of culture as being rigid, unifying and essentialist.

We encountered little evidence of teachers exploring pupils' cultural references and background in detail. Instead, their teaching of diversity predominantly deployed a top-down approach to cultural literacy development. While lessons focused on raising awareness of and celebrating diversity, little attention was paid to incorporating individual pupils' cultural reference points. Thus, while teachers advocated for a commitment to inclusion, there was little concern with expanding or remaking the boundaries of culture by accommodating its varied forms.

At the other end of the pedagogical practice, we captured young people's narratives of their school experiences (their perceived learning strengths and weaknesses as well as their ideas about future pathways). These were framed in ways that echoed their social positions in terms of material and symbolic/cultural resources.

We identified that pupils' accounts differed in ways that echoed their class positions. Notably, we observed that their engagement with education and their relationships with the future developed in part habitually and in part reflexively, depending on familial resources. Habitual processes were identifiable in young people's perceived horizons of possibilities, as well as in the affective elements of their narratives. For some pupils, continuing their education appeared to be a common-sense route that was taken for granted (Ball, 2003; Vincent and Ball, 2007), while for others the idea of going to university created insecurity, uncertainty and reluctance (Ball, Maguire and Macrae, 2000). Additionally, we observed that some young people thought of their future strictly within the locality, while others considered themselves open to a number of opportunities and were not necessarily constrained by their immediate local context. We found that this was closely linked to families' educational experiences and views on education and future employment. In the narratives of young people, habitus structured their cultural experiences and present/future cultural horizons, as well as manifesting the emotional politics of class (Skeggs, 1997).

Throughout youth narratives of educational experiences and perceptions of the future, young people linked their ideas to those of family members. In these cases, we observed how families and their cultural resources worked to facilitate or limit young people's perceived horizons of possibility in their engagement with education and imagined future pathways. The differences we captured showcase how certain cultural resources operate as capital while others do not.

Conclusion

Taken together, teachers' and pupils' accounts illustrate the lived experiences surrounding formal teaching and learning about culture, heritage and belonging. They offer insights into learning in formal educational settings by bringing to the fore the multifaceted process of how young people develop a sense of cultural identity and belonging. Overall, these empirical insights are in line with current social and educational research findings. The findings stress the enduring and profound effect of socio-economic positioning on the lived experiences and life chances of young people in the UK. In Bourdieu's terms, we observed the continuation of cultural reproduction through habitual inclinations and the workings of economic, cultural and symbolic capital. In all cases, irrespective of the different orientations or forms of engagement with present and future learning, young people reported being overwhelmed by exam preparation. This was discussed as having implications for their free time and, for some, was stress-inducing. We thus glimpsed aspects of the so-called culture of measurement (Biesta, 2017) and its implications for young people's lives.

In addition to manifestations of class positioning, we identified the workings of ethnicity in pupils' educational experiences. Although we found that all young people were aware of certain aspects of diversity, young people who identified as part of the majority ethnic group appeared to be less engaged with issues of culture and belonging. For young people from ethnic minority backgrounds, ideas about culture and identity appeared to be a lot more relevant and guided their overall accounts of schooling as well as wider life experiences. In these cases, their family culture was considered to be more or less distinct from the school culture, while young people suggested that they themselves drew on both contexts. In Yosso's (2005) terms, this raises questions of whose culture constitutes capital and whose does not.

Young people from minority ethnic backgrounds talked about their cultural identities as being predominantly performed in the private sphere. Schools were described as culturally distinctive fields; nevertheless, they were felt to be non-judgmental and accepting of difference, and therefore were experienced as relatively 'safe' spaces with respect to cultural diversity. By unpacking young people's accounts, we can not only examine their lived experiences of inclusivity at school but identify its limits. The schools' inclusive ethos was portrayed in terms of recognising and accommodating young people's religious belonging, such as allowing time and space for religious practices. Yet inclusivity in schools was experienced through lessons about other cultures that predominantly focused on certain objectified markers like food and flags. In this respect, we observed that learning experiences were underpinned by limited, superficial or partial notions of culture, which could be subsumed by religious belonging. The schools' commitment to inclusivity emphasised accommodating pupils' rights to diverse religious practices rather than driving a dynamic understanding of the many aspects of cultural diversity. As a result, we found that there were limited opportunities for pupils to utilise their culture as 'cultural capital' in the learning process.

This wasted opportunities for students to develop a more rounded and in-depth understanding of culture and diversity, one that could look beyond superficial manifestations (Dixson, Rousseau-Anderson and Donnor, 2017).

References

Adkins, L. and Skeggs, B. (Eds.) (2004) *Feminism After Bourdieu*, Oxford: Blackwell.

Allen, K. (2016) Top Girls Navigating Austere Times: Interrogating Youth Transitions since the Crisis, *Journal of Youth Studies*, Vol. 19 (6), pp. 805–820.

Ball, S. J. (2003) The Teacher's Soul and the Terrors of Performativity, *Journal of Education Policy*, Vol. 18 (2), pp. 215–228.

Ball, S. J. (2006) The Necessity and Violence of Theory, *Discourse: Studies in the Cultural Politics of Education*, Vol. 27 (1), pp. 3–10.

Ball, S., Maguire, M., and MacRae, S. (2000) *Choice, Pathways and Transitions Post-16: New Youth, New Economies in the Global City*, London: Routledge Falmer.

Bamford, S. and Worth, J. (2017) *Teacher Retention and Turnover Research. Research Update 3: Is the Grass Greener Beyond Teaching?*, Slough: NFER.

Bernstein, B. (1982) *Pedagogy, Symbolic Control and Identity – Theory, Research, Critique*, (Revised Edition), Maryland: Rowman and Littlefield.

Biesta, G. (2017) Education, Measurement and the Professions: Reclaiming a space for Democratic Professionality in Education, *Educational Philosophy and Theory*, Vol. 49 (4), pp. 315–330.

Bourdieu, P. (1979) *Distinction: A Social Critique of the Judgement of Taste*, Cambridge, MA: Harvard University Press.

Bourdieu, P. (1980) *The Logic of Practice*, Stanford, CA: Stanford University Press.

Braun, A., Maguire, M., and Ball, S. J. (2010) Policy Enactments in the UK Secondary School: Examining Policy, Practice and School Positioning, *Journal of Education Policy*, Vol. 25 (4), pp. 547–560.

Bruner, J. (1996) *The Culture of Education*, Cambridge, MA: Harvard University Press.

Dixson, A. D., Rousseau Anderson C. K., and Donnor, J. K. (2017) *Critical Race Theory in Education* (Second Edition), New York: Routledge.

Edwards, A., Fleer, M., and Bøttcher, L. (Eds.) (2019) *Cultural-historical Approaches to Studying Learning and Development: Social, Institutional and Personal Perspectives*, Singapore: Springer.

Fooks, G., Stamou, E., and McNie, C. (Eds.) (2018) *National Cultural/Educational Policy Review: Deliverable report*, Cultural Heritage and Identities of Europe's

Future. European Commission, Available at: http://chiefprojecteu.com/wp-content/uploads/CHIEF-WP1_D1.2_National-Cultural-Educational-Policy-Reviews_v1.1_KM.pdf (Accessed on March 1, 2021).

Foster, D. (2018) *Teacher Recruitment and Retention in England*, Briefing Paper Number 7222, 4 June 2018, London: House of Commons Library. Available at: https://dera.ioe.ac.uk/31729/1/CBP-7222..pdf (Accessed on March 1, 2021).

Franquesa, J. (2013) On Keeping and Selling: The Political Economy of Heritage Making in Contemporary Spain, *Current Anthropology*, Vol. 54 (3), pp. 346–369.

Freire, P. (1993) *Pedagogy of the Oppressed* (New Revised Edition), New York, Continuum.

Gillborn, D. (2014) Racism as Policy: A Critical Race Analysis of Education Reforms in the United States and England, *The Educational Forum*, Vol. 78 (1), pp. 26–41.

Halbert, K. and Chigeza, P. (2015) Navigating Discourses of Cultural Literacy in Teacher Education, *Australian Journal of Teacher Education*, Vol. 40 (11), pp. 155–168.

Halikiopoulou, D. and Vlandas, T. (2019) What is New and What is Nationalist about Europe's New Nationalism? Explaining the Rise of the Far Right in Europe, *Nations and Nationalism*, Vol. 25 (2), pp. 409–434.

Hall, S. (2000) Who Needs Identity? In: P. du Gay, J. Jessica Evans and P. Redman (Eds.), *Ideology, Genealogy, History, Identity: A Reader*, London: Sage.

Harmsen, R. and Spiering, M. (2004) *Euroscepticism: Party Politics, National Identity and European Integration, New York*, New York: Rodopi.

Ingram, N. (2009) Working-class Boys, Educational Success and the Misrecognition of Working-class Culture, *British Journal of Sociology of Education*, Vol. 30 (4), pp. 421–434.

Janmaat, J. G., & Keating, A. (2017) Are Today's Youth more Tolerant? Trends in Tolerance among Young People in Britain. *Ethnicities,* Vol. 19 (1), pp. 44–65.

Keating, A. (2016) Are Cosmopolitan Dispositions Learned at Home, at School or through Contact with Others? Evidence from Young People in Europe, *Journal of Youth Studies*, Vol. 19 (3), pp. 338–357.

Kiwan, D. (2008) Citizenship Education at the Cross-Roads: Four Models of Citizenship and their Implications for Ethnic and Religious Diversity, *Oxford Review of Education*, Vol. 34 (1), pp. 39–58.

Leruth, B., Startin, N., and Usherwood, S. (Eds.) (2017) *The Routledge Handbook of Eurescepticism*, Abington: Taylor and Francis.

MacDonald, R., Shildrick, T., and Furlong, A. (2019) 'Cycles of Disadvantage' Revisited: Young People, Families and Poverty across Generations, *Journal of Youth Studies*, Vol. 23 (1), pp. 12–27.

Osler, A. and Starkey, H. (2018) Extending the Theory and Practice of Education for Cosmopolitan Citizenship, *Educational Review*, Vol. 70 (1), pp. 31–40.

Ragazzi, F. (2017) Countering Terrorism and Radicalisation: Securitising Social Policy? *Critical Social Policy*, Vol. 37 (2), pp. 163–179.

Reay, D. (2017) *Miseducation: Inequality, Education, and the Working Classes*, Bristol: Policy Press.

Rowlands, M. (2002) Cultural Heritage and Cultural property. In: Buchli. V. (Ed.), *The Material Culture Reader*, Oxford: Berg.

Savage, M. (2000) *Class Analysis and Social Transformation*, Milton Keynes: Open University.

Shildrick, T., MacDonald, R., Webster, C., and Garthwaite, K. (2012) *Poverty and Insecurity: Life in 'low-pay, No-pay' Britain*. Bristol: Policy Press.

Skeggs, B. (1997) *Formations of Class and Gender*, London: Sage.

Skeggs, B. (2004) *Class, Self, Culture*, London: Routledge.

Skinner, B., Leavey, G., and Rothi, D. (2019) Managerialism and Teacher Professional Identity: Impact on Well-being among Teachers in the UK, *Educational Review*, (published online), DOI: 10.1080/00131911.2018.1556205.

Stamou, E., Popov, A., and Zurabishvili, T. (2019) National Curricula Review in England, in Marmer, E. and Tina Zurabishvili, T. (Eds). *National/Federal Curricula Review: Deliverable report*, Cultural Heritage and Identities of Europe's Future. European Commission, pp. 238–276. Available at: http://chiefprojecteu.com/wp-content/uploads/Chief-WP2_D2.1_National-Curriculum-Review-Reports_v1.0_14.01.19.pdf (Accessed on 15 May 2022).

Torres, C. A. and Tarozzi, M. (2020) Multiculturalism in the World System: Towards a Social Justice Model of Inter/Multicultural Education, *Globalisation, Societies and Education*, Vol. 18 (1), pp. 7–18.

Vertovec, S. (2007) Super-Diversity and its Implications, *Ethnic and Racial Studies*, Vol. 30 (6), pp. 1024–1054.

Vincent, C. and Ball, S. J. (2007) Making-up the Middle Class Child: Families, Activities and Class Dispositions, *Sociology*, Vol. 41 (6), pp. 1061–1077.

Vygotsky, L. (1978) *Mind in Society: The Development of Higher Psychological Processes*, Cambridge, MA: Harvard University Press.

Yuval-Davies, N. (2011) *The Politics of Belonging: Intersectional Contestations*, London: Sage.

Yosso, T. (2005) Whose Culture has Capital? A Critical Race Theory Discussion of Community Cultural Wealth, *Race Ethnicity and Education*, Vol. 8 (1), pp. 69–91.

(by Elina Marmer)

Chapter 5 "Who is a German?" Young people's cultural identification and the issues of belonging, memory and participation in Hamburg schools

Abstract: This chapter analyses processes of young people's cultural identification and how these are shaped by the dominant German discourses on culture, memory and belonging, as well as by structural inequalities and participation opportunities. It looks at how culture has been conceptualised and how these concepts became apparent in the young people's reflections on their cultural practices. It further examines the contribution of schools in this regard. Data was collected from students and teachers at three very different secondary schools in the city of Hamburg. The CHIEF-produced questionnaire was complemented by a country-specific question on German history, because of the important role *Erinnerungskultur* (commemoration culture) plays in German discourse. Questions on German Nazi history revealed a problematic aspect of German identity, prompting defensive responses and claims of hurt national feelings, especially from those who identified as 'normal' or 'standard' Germans. Confirming results of previous research, Germany's colonial past and its impact on the present were largely absent from the curriculum and there was no or very limited knowledge of this issue. Traces of the colonial and nazi ideologies in terms of cultural hierarchy persist in the way teachers and students speak about culture. In schools, culture was often prone to a reductionist approach based on 'ethno-national origin'. This functioned as a marker of 'othering' and was often used (by teachers and students alike) to define boundaries and emphasise differences. The 'ethno-national origin' construct defined and guarded the access to the dominant 'German culture', to Germany as a country, and even to Europe. However, over the course of the interviews, boundaries sometimes shifted and differences became relative. Culture was also understood as a combination of more universal human achievements, expressed through arts and sports or through political, social, digital and other spheres of life. Unequal access to cultural participation was observed across schools, and could be linked to what we have termed a *school culture*. This was determined by various aspects, such as the students' environmental and familial backgrounds (particularly their socio-economic, educational and cultural capital). Other relevant factors included educational policy, as well as institutional and individual decisions. The German selective school system can produce, increase or reduce these barriers. By highlighting and analysing relevant discourses and practices, and the barriers to participation they create, this study hopes to contribute to the development of more inclusive cultural education policies and approaches in schools.

Keywords: cultural identity, cultural dominance, memory, belonging, diversity, migrantization, formal education

Introduction

CHIEF's unique approach is to study discourses, conceptions and practices of culture, cultural heritage and identity from both top-down and bottom-up perspectives. Having previously analysed Hamburg's school curricula (top-down) (Sylla, Marmer & Seukwa, 2019), the current study was particularly interested in understanding how cultural literacy is acquired and enacted in selected schools in the city (bottom-up).

Curricula analysis showed that 'culture' was primarily used to make binary distinctions between 'our' and 'other' cultures. 'Culture' was assumed to change with time, but cultural diversity, hybridity and fluidity in a given time and space were hardly taken into account. While diversity was often discussed within curricula in the context of conflict, 'cultural identity' was understood as something acquired mainly through comparison. Rarely was 'cultural identity' framed beyond national and ethnic categories. Sporadic attempts to shift the dominant discourses on culture and identity towards more inclusive notions have been observed, as exemplified by the following quote:

> *Culture should not be understood only in the sense of ethnicity – rather, every society consists of a plurality of constantly changing cultures. These are determined by the social milieu, the geographic region, gender, generation, belief, sexual orientation etc. Every individual therefore bears various cultures and can contribute different facets of his or her cultural imprint to different situations (model of multiple belonging).* (Hamburg District School Curriculum 2011 Grades 5–11, General Tasks, Intercultural Education, p. 27. Translated by author)

However, this approach to culture and identity is an isolated example that was not followed through in the curricula. In fact, it often contradicted the dominant narratives of cultural identity as developed through comparison with other cultures – conceived of in ethno-national terms – and through understanding and manifesting differences (Sylla, Marmer & Seukwa, 2019). Explicit claims in the curricula to inclusion, equality and participation were found to be in conflict with the selectiveness of the German formal education system, as curricula are set up to educate young people in accordance with their position in the neo-liberal world.

Selectivity as a principal of formal education is common all over Germany, but each state has some particularities. In Hamburg, students are split after four years of primary education into two major secondary school streams – the district school (*Stadtteilschule*) and the academic secondary school (*Gymnasium*). Each offers three hierarchical graduation levels: basic secondary graduation *(ESA)*, middle school graduation (*MSA*) and the general qualification for university entrance (*Abitur*). However, there are significant disparities between the school types. In the academic year 2019/20, while nearly equal shares of students graduated with either *ESA* (29%), *MSA* (30%) or *Abitur* (34%) qualifications from Hamburg *district* schools, 87 % of *academic* secondary school students graduated with the *Abitur* qualification (ifbq, 2021). White German middle- and upper-classes are over-represented in *academic* secondary schools (Chzhen et al., 2018), while students "with [a] migration background"[1] are more often than not referred to district schools (ifbq, 2021). In district schools, more emphasis is put on vocational prospects. All these facts taken together certainly indicate the reproduction of cultural capital by the school system, which inhibits social mobility.

While the curricula for the two school types differ in some aspects, they are both in line with the dominant German discourse when it comes to the dichotomous hierarchy between so-called 'German' and 'migrant' cultures. This discourse is also reflected in cultural policy praxis. For example, the Hamburg Ministry of Culture and Media[2] offers various funding pots directed at categories such as 'visual arts', 'film', 'literature', 'music', 'theatre and dance', etc. These are dedicated to predominantly white-majority German projects. In addition, there is a single funding pot for "intercultural cultural exchange", which encapsulates projects of any type of cultural expression that are initiated and/or participated in by people considered 'intercultural'. (This became clear during personal communication with Hamburg's artists and cultural managers during CHIEF fieldwork.) But who is considered 'intercultural'? Mecheril (2003) coins the term 'natio-ethno-culturally other' to describe the interlinked othering processes certain people face in Germany. An example of this is migrantisation, when "children and grandchildren of migrants of colour [are considered] as second and third generation migrants and not first or second generation citizens" (El-Tayeb, 2015: p. 15). Black Germans and Germans of Colour (BPoC), German

1 Here the term refers to students with at least one parent born outside Germany (ifbq, 2021) or to those without German citizenship.

2 https://www.hamburg.de/bkm/downloads/

descendants of South European and Turkish 'guest workers', immigrants from Eastern Europe[3] and the Global South, and their German descendants, as well as German Jews, Muslims, Cinti and Roma, are treated as "eternal newcomers, forever suspended in time, forever 'just arriving'" (El-Tayeb, 2011: p. xxv).

However, when referring to Hamburg youth, it is no longer possible to speak about a white German 'majority' and a migrant or migrantised 'minority'. According to school statistics, over 50 % of all Hamburg school students have a "migration background"; many more migrantised young people of Colour do not fall under this category because their families have been living in Germany for generations. Therefore, defining who is German and who is the Other is not a question of statistics, but one of power.

Regardless of their theoretical, political or ideological orientations, most German researchers of youth and cultural identity are concerned with the identity of the 'natio-ethno-culturally others', i.e. those who are perceived to be different and whose cultural identity is often questioned by the white German population (Mecheril, 2003). For instance, Riegel and Geisen (2010) analysed what they called the ethnically-gendered attributions and natio-cultural associations that confront young people with a 'migrant background', making their belonging a precarious issue. Meanwhile, the cultural identities of those who self-identify or are identified as "German" remains under-researched.

The purpose of the present study is to understand how young people in Hamburg schools view issues of cultural identity, to gain some insight into their cultural practices in school and beyond, and to analyse how issues of culture and identity are approached by teachers as part of their pedagogical practice in different school environments. To achieve this aim, qualitative, semi-structured in-depth interviews with 11 teachers and 60 students between the ages of 14 and 19 were carried out at three selected schools – one *academic* secondary school and two *district* secondary schools. As a result, an extensive data set was produced that reflects a rich and multifaceted experience of young people.

After referring to some issues surrounding the fieldwork and describing the three schools, this chapter will analyse findings that address students' and teachers' concepts of culture, identity and diversity, and some differences between the schools in terms of access and participation. The chapter closes with some concluding remarks.

---

3 Except for those who migrated in the aftermath of WW2 from former German territories in Eastern Europe and whose descendants are fully recognized as Germans.

Notes on the fieldwork

During the fieldwork undertaken from April to June 2019, political discourses in Germany were strongly influenced by the EU Parliament Elections in May and the rise of right-wing extremism in the country and elsewhere. The Hamburg city-state has traditionally been governed by the centre-left, but since the 2015 Hamburg state election the far-right party *Alternative für Deutschland* [Alternative for Germany, AfD] has been represented in the city hall. Since March 2021 the party has been under investigation by the Federal Office for the Protection of the Constitution for extremist activities. In the autumn of 2018, Hamburg AfD launched a portal for Neutral Schools[4] (sarcastically referred to as the 'denunciation portal'[5]), which asked students and parents to report supposed "violations of neutrality" by teachers. The AfD forwarded over 100 complaints, mainly about anti-fascist stickers and Fridays for Future[6] banners, to the Hamburg school authorities. Cases of schools being forced to remove Antifa and anti-AfD stickers made some headlines.[7] Anti-racist and feminist discourses also gained some momentum in Germany during the period of fieldwork, especially on social media platforms like YouTube, Twitter, Facebook and Instagram. Since autumn 2018, people have reported cases of everyday racism using the #metwo hashtag, which received coverage in a few mainstream print and online news outlets. These stories have revealed that racism is often exerted by white German teachers towards BPoC students and other racialized groups.[8]

Access to the three schools proved quite difficult. After several schools had been approached without success, we found three schools that gave their consent to participate in the study. School U (urban) is an *academic* secondary school located in the city centre, in a historical quarter with a rich cultural infrastructure as well as an economically and otherwise diverse population. Due to its specific profile, which emphasises art and culture, this school attracts students from all over the city. Since culture was the topic of our study, the school headmaster was relatively easy to convince. School S (semi-urban or sub-urban) is a

4 https://afd-fraktion-hamburg.de/aktion-neutrale-schulen-hamburg/

5 https://www.ndr.de/nachrichten/hamburg/Ein-Jahr-AfD-Meldeportal-Mehr-als-100-Faelle,afdmeldeportal100.html

6 In December 2018, students in Hamburg joined the global youth climate movement Fridays for Future, organising strikes, demonstrations and other public events.

7 https://www.ndr.de/nachrichten/hamburg/Antifa-Aufkleber-in-Schule-sorgen-fuer-Wirbel,schule1798.html

8 https://www.zeit.de/2019/03/deutschsein-ali-can-metwo-alltagsrassismus-migranten

district secondary school in a major social housing project erected during the 1960–1970s, which is economically disadvantaged and cut off from the city's underground network. Most students live in the project but others come from a very wealthy sub-urban neighbourhood in the vicinity. The intercultural coordinator[9] of school S was initially sceptical about whether her students, whom she described as disadvantaged, would benefit from participating. It was possible to convince her by promising that (1) the interviews would focus on the students' experiences and opinions, and (2) a researcher of Colour would conduct the interviews. The aim of this was to create a more comfortable space for the many students of Colour, in light of their experiences of racism in white German spaces, to address issues of culture and identity. Another idea behind this was for the interviewer of Colour to serve as 'role model' for the disadvantaged and predominantly migrantised students. Finally, School R (R stands for rural, though the school was located in a sub-urban area), a *district* secondary school located on the city's borders that also serves surrounding rural areas in the neighbouring state of Schleswig-Holstein, was approached via personal contacts. The coordinator reluctantly agreed participation for students from grades 11–13, those aspiring to the highest graduation level. During fieldwork, the two schools that negotiated conditions for their participation (schools U and S) proved to be much more committed than school R, which agreed reluctantly as a personal favour. The level of commitment was also reflected in the respondents' attitudes towards the interviews. At schools U and S, most students and especially teachers were engaged with the interview topics, and a rapport was often easily established between interviewers and respondents. At school R, however, students sometimes seemed to be annoyed by certain questions or gave brief replies, while teachers were often in a hurry. However, most respondents were open to and interested in at least some of the questions.

Culture as a 'place of origin' (*Herkunft*)

Students and teachers alike often struggled to define their understanding of culture, which they first and foremost associated with the idea of *Herkunft* ('place of origin'). Students often referred to customs, traditions, norms and values,

9 Intercultural coordinators are teachers who have participated in special voluntary training organised by the State Institute for Teacher Education and School Development, which "prepares Hamburg teachers in a period of two years for their commitment as 'change actors' who initiate and support intercultural school development processes" (https://li.hamburg.de/iko/).

but also the "mentality" and temper of a certain group, with a strong focus on ethno-national interpretations. Here, the alleged geographic 'place of origin' of the group – usually a nation-state – seems formative. According to the students, it is where someone comes from that determines their culture: "*Actually, when I think about culture, I always think about the origin*" (Ali, male, student, school S). 'Place of origin' and 'nationality' were also often used synonymously. For example, when asked about his friends' culture, Lars (male, student, school R) replied, "*It always depends on nationality, where they come from.*"

Culture was usually attributed to religious practices, festivities, languages, traditions, food and dance. These practices are mostly carried out within the family, which often occupies a central space in learning about and enacting culture. Participants often ethnicised ideas of upbringing, norms and values set by the family, suggesting that cultural differences are explicitly produced along ethno-national lines. Students named two main sources of cultural knowledge: at home (sometimes in their community), where they learn 'their own culture', and friends and schoolmates, where they learn the 'culture of the others' through social interactions in class or during leisure time.

Teachers' interpretation and their answers were usually more careful and elaborate, with different layers and facets. However, most of the interviewed teachers explicitly or implicitly associated culture with a 'place of origin' as well, even, as in the following example, in an ambivalent way:

> *I mean, from my own biography I can give examples that… it is not exclusively the origin that necessarily constitutes culture. But [culture] is also related to the origin.* (David, male, teacher, school S)

'Culture' was often locked into a closed geographical space, usually a nation-state (Irish, French, and Canadian culture were used as examples). Only one teacher explicitly deconstructed this view:

> *The extended definition of culture is for me obviously… that as humans we are universally connected. […] And then we socialise in different groups, in family, in peer-groups. At school as well. […] And there are many parts of this puzzle in which I navigate and collect cultural experiences, in these different groups.* (Hülya, female, teacher, school S)

The dominant framing of culture and cultural differences was not consistent and was often fractured by participants, even within the same interview. For example, when asked about culture, Amina postulated cultural differences with certainty:

> *Every country has its own culture. The customs and how people act is always very different from other countries.* (Amina, female, student, school R)

However, such rigid differentiation by 'place of origin' was no longer valid when it comes to her friends:

> *I have a friend from the Balkan and two from Asia. And when we compare ourselves we realise how similar we are.* (Amina, female, student, school R)

Amina then emphasised values that seemed equally important to her and her friends' different 'places of origin', hereby dismantling her initial conception of cultural difference. Over the course of the interviews, such disruptions and fragmentations of constructed cultural difference lines were often observed, especially when the migrantised (El-Tayeb, 2015) respondents spoke about their actual experiences. It seemed that they had internalised the dominant discourse of cultural differences – a paradigm that they were taught in school – despite the fact that it often contradicted their own experiences.

Cultural identities

When speaking of cultural identities, the most commonly raised issue – explicitly or implicitly – by students and teachers alike was the definition of 'being German'. What do 'German' and 'not-German' mean in statements like "*I am the only German in my class*" or "*In my class, we are all foreigners*", when nearly all interviewed students were German nationals?

Only one teacher, himself migrantised, claimed to challenge this notion of 'being German' in his class:

> *I am also perceived as a foreigner. What is German? Well, I sometimes feel more German than someone who (…) Unfortunately I experienced it once again recently in East Germany; someone who harassed and racially offended me. I feel more German than him. But what is German?* (David, male, teacher, school S)
>
> *I try to create fractions in their [students'] [German] identity to make them think. To break it up in order to open them up to this question: What is German?* (ibid.).

Exclusivist discourse on 'being German' was often taken up by those who unquestionably identified themselves as 'German'. These respondents usually described their own culture as "normal", "typical", "standard", "classic", and in opposition to those with 'different' culture. The use of the term 'cultural' often denotes something that differs from the dominant 'German' norm (similar to the English use of the word 'ethnic'). Some interviewees also linked being German with being "*blonde and blue-eyed*", being silent or being uptight. When speaking of being German, one main topic was the German past and the associated loss of national pride. Quite a few of the young people regretted that Germans cannot show their national pride or even say where they come from when travelling abroad without being judged for the country's Nazi past.

> *I believe we Germans lost the national pride quite a bit. I have noticed that. For example, if I called myself a proud German, others would call me a Nazi.* (Grimm, male, student, school R)

Meanwhile, most teachers, when asked about their students' cultural identity, seemed to be preoccupied with the identities of the migrantised youth, problematising them in many different ways. Sophie (*f, teacher, school R*), reproduced the 'German-not German' dichotomy by saying that in the schoolyard "*Germans and non-Germans are at loggerheads with each other*". Sophie actively migrantised students she perceived as 'non-Germans', and blamed them for insisting on

> *an artificially knitted identity based on their parents' history, which they assign to themselves in order to distance themselves from the place where they live. Like, 'I live here, but I am not a German. Have nothing to do with Germany. Stupid country. Potatoes*[10] *everyone.' That's what you often hear in the school yard with an aggression in their voices.* (Sophie, female, teacher, school R)

Many of the migrantised young people we interviewed, however, saw their identity as problematic only when dealing with migrantisation:

> *I was born here. Only, I have black hair and brown eyes. I don't look like a German, but I actually am one.* (Amira, female, student, school S)

Saying that she doesn't look like a German reflects what Amira has been told, and the need to insist that she "*actually is one*" is something white students do not face.

Over the course of the interviews, the migrantised respondents often constructed their cultural identities in a fluid and dynamic way: 'in between', 'multiple', 'mixed' or 'unique', or a combination of these. The following are some examples:

> *Someone can belong to many cultures.* (Minnie, female, student, school U)
> *My culture is somewhere in between.* (Elsa, female, student, school U)
> *I am a Hamburger Kurd and that's it. I am from Hamburg.* (Emre, male, student, school S)
> *I am half Asian, half European. But I don't want to be European, I want to be Asian.* (Sel, female, student, school S)
> *My own culture is a bit mixed.* (Max, male, student, school R)

---

10 Potato (Kartoffel) is a common pejorative nickname for white majority Germans from the perspective of migrantised Germans.

Some of my ways of thinking have a touch of Iranian, but otherwise I am quite German. (Azita, female, student, school S)
You should do what your ancestors did, what your parents taught you. That should impact you. But you should try to be unique. (Ali, male, student, school S)
I see myself as European. However actually I would rather say Asian, but not really. I would say both. But I would say rather European, because not really German. However, Germany is my home. (Asli, female, student, school S)

Cultural diversity

Often, the question about diversity in the classroom prompted answers that focused on the perceived 'ratio' of 'Germans' to people with 'migration background' or 'foreigners', terms that were used interchangeably (as noted above, this distinction cannot be citizenship-related). Thus, diversity was understood as a '*mixture*' of the two different groups:

My class is really quite diverse, also in terms of, for example (…) how do I say that? (…) Well, we have quite many foreigners, we have a good ratio, I mean a mixing ratio, foreigners, Germans. And we are in great harmony with each other, therefore my class is great. (Inis, male, student, school R)

The breaks (…) taken by Inis in order to think about his phrasing indicate unease with these terms. Yet he continued to call his migrantised peers "foreigners", excluding them from belonging to the country.

'Place of origin', commonly paired with religion, is the common departure point when speaking about diversity, but students often broadened this narrow definition of culture to encapsulate more categories:

Uh, of course we have many people from different nations. We are also very diverse in our interests and simply different personalities. Everyone is different, some [are] a bit loud, some – a bit shy. (Asli, female, student, school S)

The otherwise monolithic and exclusionist concept of culture of origin became fractured and distorted:

We have children from many different countries and many different religions and such. That's why I would say that we are diverse. And we have different opinions on different topics. […] People from different cultures can also have the same opinion. (Yasemin, female, student, school S)

Some students even understood 'diversity' completely outside the ethno-national sphere:

We have people who can draw, others are great at sports, or have a talent for languages or math. And then if you need help you can always ask someone, and they can explain it all to you very well. (Mia, female, student, school S)

In this case, only after the interviewer insisted on different meanings did countries of origin come into play:

[INT.] Can you think of other things which make them diverse? I mean something other than talents?
[MIA] Uh, the countries of origin, I guess. Yes, we have different countries. I am not sure which ones but it is also quite interesting. (Mia, female, student, school S)

Though an '*interesting*' aspect, 'place of origin' seemed not to be central to Mia's understanding of diversity.

Without being asked, students overwhelmingly evaluated diversity as positive, mostly emphasising the benefits of mutual exchange:

And we learn a lot [...] sometimes we sit in a circle in class and we talk about things we do. [...] And I believe we need this kind of learning. Because we (...) are a bit limited in our culture. We think our culture is the best culture. [...] But I believe, talking to others makes one think. Why is it like this in my culture? There can be something I would like to change. It can become like a vision. (Zara, female, student, school S)

Students also pointed out the benefits of being able to get along well despite being different:

Everyone is unique in their own way. We are all very different. That's what I have noticed. And for being so different, we get along quite well. That is something very positive. (Amina, female, student, School R)

However, some white German students positioned themselves outside this 'diversity'. Both classism and racism were evident in an interview with one student from an affluent neighbourhood in the vicinity of the deprived area in which school S is located:

My class is diverse in terms of how they live their lives [...] for instance [in regard to] hobbies. I do horse riding, and it keeps me busy every day. But them, they go home, do some homework and go to sleep and then come back to school the next day. Personally, my impression is that they actually don't have a proper life. (Marie, female, student, school S).

By enforcing a solid line between '*me*' and '*them*', '*their*' life is imagined as not being '*proper*' because of a lack of typical (and expensive) white upper middle-class hobbies like horse riding, which also runs in Marie's family, as she later explained. Despite perceiving '*them*' as a homogenous group in terms of lack of cultural activities, she nevertheless acknowledged lessons learned from that very group as '*exciting*', personally beneficial and a positive contrast to her former, homogenously white German school:

> *I am this kind of person, I can imagine going on a world trip in order to get to know other cultures and other people. [...] This is very exciting. That's why it is so cool here, because in my old school, there were ONLY Germans. And there were no such conversations [about culture]. [...] That's truly exciting. That's something that I actually personally benefited from.* (Marie, female, student, school S)

Such devaluation of the 'diverse others', paired with the benefits for the privileged 'global citizen' of learning from those 'diverse others', is characteristic of German neo-liberal diversity discourse. In this way, a push for 'diversity' can coexist with segregation at the intersection of classism and racism.

How cultural concepts varied across the different schools

While ethno-national origin was the main cultural framework for most of the interviewed students across all schools, significant differences between schools can be noted: at school U, an academic school with emphasis on art and culture, this idea was much more often complemented by various other concepts. Some interviewees, for example, referred to micro-cultures within different neighbourhoods of the city. Others mentioned more general concepts of culture like "*everything that enriches you*" (Alex, male, school U) or "*whatever makes a person unique*" (Ilhan, male, student, school U). School U students associated culture much more frequently with art, theatre, film, music and sports, and with the digital sphere:

> *I post photos on Instagram. But in those discussions where there is always hate... I never comment at all. I am staying out of it. And I read it but ... for me personally I have decided not to be a part of this culture.* (Ella, female, student, school U)

Consequently, students from school U often classed their free time activities as cultural practices:

> *I live my culture through my hobbies... because I enjoy them and can share with other people.* (Luna, female, student, school U)

In the two other schools, however, students rarely regarded their hobbies or free time as 'culture'; exceptions were religious or family activities, which they classified as 'origin related' and ethniticised (food, celebrations, upbringing, etc.).

Asked about their hobbies and talents, many students at schools R and S also mentioned playing musical instruments, sports, writing, digital activities, handicrafts, languages and other activities they participated in either individually or in an informal group of friends. Fewer students at schools R and S mentioned non-formal educational settings than at school U. They spoke about artistic and aesthetic consumption in the forms of music, films, TV series or digital culture (Youtube, Instagram, etc.). However, unlike school U students, they did not often understand activities outside ethno-national categories as 'cultural' or a part of 'their own culture'. For example, Sel talked in detail about her hobbies:

> *I love singing. And acting. Sometimes I write songs. I love reading. I also write stories. I listen to music. I watch series. Sometimes I go outside with my cousin. Talents? I can draw, sing and act. I am good with people. I am very empathic, for example.* (Sel, female, student, school S)

However, later in the interview, when explicitly asked how she practices *her culture*, she replied:

> *Honestly speaking, I do not practice my culture. Because in my culture, let's say (…) I don't know much about culture. […] I just know that we (…) for example, only Ramadan. And how do you say in German? The Festival of Sacrifices. I know that we have these things. But other things that we have, I don't even know them. I don't know much about our culture, nor about dress or food.* (Sel, female, student, school S)

Despite having a broad range of interests and talents, Sel presented herself as 'not practicing her culture' just because she is not familiar with religious and ethno-national cultural practices that constitute what she called *"our culture"*. Students often adapted the mainstream discourse that reduces 'cultural' to anything different from the activities popular among white majority Germans. Discursive barriers to participation such as this inhibit some of the young people from recognising their own contributions to culture beyond ethno-national terms.

Cultural participation in and outside schools

Although most of the interviewed teachers mentioned several cultural activities they undertake with students, these did not always resonate with the young interviewees. The only cultural activities at school that nearly all of them mentioned were annual cultural events, which take place at each school. These have significant differences. For instance, the cultural night at school U is a compulsory event, and the whole school prepares for and participates in it collectively. Even months after the event, when the interviews were conducted, traces of decorations and symbols were visible in the school's halls and recreational area. Meanwhile, the event at school R mainly involves students who chose to study arts, music or theatre as one of their subjects, which pertained to only a few interviewees in our sample.

In terms of cultural participation, there was an obvious difference between students of different schools. Due to its artistic profile, school U actively introduces students to 'high culture' as part of the curriculum; in addition, many participants said that they visit the theatre or concerts with family and friends. It is likely that families with a particular interest in the arts prefer to send their children to school U, since its students hail from all over the city. Various curricular activities take place at school in the afternoon, offering different interest groups, clubs, choirs, orchestras, theatre, etc. Many school U students seem to have a family background that enables them to engage in a broad variety of cultural practices in and outside the school – most of their parents have university degrees. Many young people are members of sports clubs, play a musical instrument or participate in a special interest group. Only at this school did some of the students say they volunteered, and many took part in international student exchange programmes.

The situation is quite different at the two other schools. As a senior high school branch of the district school, school R does not offer many optional courses or clubs for students, probably because its main aim is to get the students through the *Abitur* rather than to provide opportunities to participate in creative activities. Although information about afternoon clubs and activities can be found on the school S website, students interviewed here did not mention them at all. Most of the students interviewed at schools R and S did not have the financial means to benefit from cultural offers outside the school, as can be assumed by their parents' occupations (mainly working class). Many students also work after school to support their needs; only two students from these schools, both from economically privileged backgrounds, mentioned participating in international exchange programmes. Some, like Brooke, used the necessity to earn money as a chance to pursue their own cultural practices:

> *I work at a bookshop and I need to have a broad knowledge for that and therefore I need to learn a lot. And to be open-minded in this regard. And yes, I also write books myself.* (Brooke, female, student, school R)

For school S students, the isolated location of the neighbourhood presents an additional obstacle to participation in Hamburg's rich cultural life.

Barriers and inequalities

Discursive and tangible barriers to participation in society limit access to cultural participation; at the same time, not all cultural practices receive equal recognition. In German cultural policy documents, as well as in the Hamburg curricula

(Seukwa, Marmer & Sylla, 2018; Sylla, Marmer & Seukwa, 2019), 'participation for all' is a declared priority. In this context, it is important to understand how various barriers are addressed and/or experienced by teachers and students.

Gender and sexual orientation

Only female respondents raised the issue of gender inequality, saying that gender discrimination in the family and/or society is discussed at school and among friends. Few students were engaged in feminist cultural activities. The role assigned to mothers, sometimes praised as feminist role models, is especially notable:

> *I think my culture is closely related to that of my mother […] I have this European-Pakistani mentality […] My culture is equality. This (…) equality between men and women.* (Zara, female, student, school S)

Sometimes mothers were criticised for perpetuating gender discrimination:

> *They do not understand that if you lock up a girl so much, I would say, it is like locking up a bird for a long time. And when the door suddenly opens, the bird will fly away. You know?* (Amira, female, student, school S)

Sexual orientation was explicitly cited by one student, who self-identified as homosexual, while another said she is at the age of confusion in terms of her sexual orientation and finds support in reading novels on the topic. Hülya (female, teacher, school S) was the only teacher who touched on how both gender and sexual orientation are reflected in her teaching practice.

Ableism

Hamburg's schools consider themselves inclusive, as they admit students regardless of whether or not they have special needs. Although mainstreaming inclusion has been prioritised for years on the educational political agenda, this was not reflected in the interviews conducted with students. None of the students claimed to be affected by ableism; apparently those who are were not selected for interviews by their teachers. The researchers did not make any additional effort to include such students. When teachers spoke about discrimination, there were no references to ableism at all. However, David (male, teacher, school S) complained of a lack of staff to cater for students with special needs, naming them according to their official status (which determines whether the school receives additional resources to accommodate these students' needs). Dinovefa (female, teacher, school S) mentioned the difficulties faced by a student with autism, while Layla (female, teacher, school U) was *"fascinated"* by the inclusive ways in which her students treat their peer labelled as 'disabled'.

Socio-economic status

Socio-economic background is much more of an issue, especially at school S, which is located in a deprived community. The people living here were often characterised by teachers (who do not live here) and by some of the students from affluent nearby suburbs as *"badly articulated", "being verbally abusive and disrespectful", "having to deal with precarious living conditions", "affected by domestic violence", "being neglected", "not having books at home"*, and as *"coming from families lacking educational aspirations."* When speaking about economic barriers their students face, school S teachers noted the intersections with racist discrimination. According to David (male, teacher, school S), students face discrimination when applying for jobs due to a combination of "*a photo with a hijab*", "*a foreign sounding name*" and "*the address*". He claimed that this intersectional discrimination produces frustration and contributes to "*fractioned identities*", which according to him has led to radicalisation by the IS in the past.

Racism and antisemitism[11]

Racism was an important topic in the interviews conducted at school S, and was predominantly raised by migrantised teachers and students. Though taking an active stance against racism, here (like at the other schools) teachers sometimes reproduced racist language during the interviews. Many participants spoke about their own experiences with racist discrimination and exclusion, either direct or subtle, or about racism in Germany. They sometimes made connections to the German past and/or expressed their concern about the future. One young woman even broke down in tears recalling discrimination she experienced at primary school. The fact that an interviewer of colour conducted the student interviews at school S may have created a safer space to speak openly about racist experiences.

---

11 Antisemitism is not spelled out "anti-Semitism" following the recommendation of The International Holocaust Remembrance Alliance (IHRA): "IHRA's concern is that the hyphenated spelling allows for the possibility of something called 'Semitism', which not only legitimizes a form of pseudo-scientific racial classification that was thoroughly discredited by association with Nazi ideology, but also divides the term, stripping it from its meaning of opposition and hatred toward Jews." https://www.holocaustremembrance.com/spelling-antisemitism

Racism, however, was less of a topic at school U interviews. Only Bert (male, teacher, school U) expressed his criticism of racist reproductions in textbooks and curricula, and the colonial heritage of geography as a discipline. Bert further recalled an incident, also mentioned by Jorja, in which an anti-racist banner was created by students as a form of protest against the invitation of a politician from the extreme right AfD party to the school. However, while Bert expressed his support of the action, Jorja stated her disappointment in the lack of support by the school authority:

> *After all, it is written in the constitution, that being racist is not ok. But the headmaster said to take [the banner] down. I would actually wish there was more support here.* (Jorja, female, student, school U)

It seems that despite his commitment, Bert was not aware of the ban on students' anti-racist activism. The headmaster did not mention the incident in her interview at all. It can be speculated that the fear of being denounced on the AfD webpage and having to deal with education authorities (see *Notes on the fieldwork*) contributed to her decision to take down the banner.

At school R, two teachers, both white, perceived themselves as victims of 'reverse' racism. While Sophia (female, teacher, school R) lamented the aggressive behaviour of "*non-German*" students, calling '*German*' students '*potatoes*' (see *Cultural identities*), Lehrer (male, teacher, school R) claimed that

> *The Muslims among my students take it for granted that they build mosques and then pray when they want. But they would never consider a Jew or a Hindu or a Christian who might also want to exercise his right. And that's a fact, and when you say something like that, you are quickly accused of being anti-Islam or reactionary or even racist by both students and left-wing intellectuals.* (Lehrer, male, teacher, school R).

It is a paradox for white people in power to feel racially discriminated against, especially when they use racist language and express racist views. Grimm (male, student, school R), who is also white, complained defensively that "*Germans are often accused of racism*", and said that he never witnessed how teachers or the school system "*erected barriers*" for those he perceived as non-Germans. Contrary to their views, Leonie (female, student, school R), also white, practiced a form of allyship by pointing out that "*racism is sometimes, like, subconscious*"; she saw a need to tackle subtle racism and to study this topic in more depth.

Unlike racism, none of the participants claimed to be affected by antisemitism. They mostly mentioned this in relation to German history. Two school U students spoke affectionately of their former Jewish history teacher and his commitment to combatting antisemitism. Emilie, who travelled to Israel last year with her history class to visit the Yad Vashem Holocaust Remembrance Centre, said that this visit left a long-lasting impression on her:

> *It was very emotional and we have never been that quiet ever before. Really, people who always chat in class were completely silent.* (Emilie, female, student, school U)

David is also engaged in anti-antisemitism pedagogy, but his focus is the antisemitism of his students:

> *I ask them a few questions: Who believes Jews rule the global capital? Who believes we are remotely controlled? And there we get several partly open, partly subtle antisemitic opinions. […] That made the students think about to what extent antisemitism might be a problem in their own circles.* (David, male, teacher, school S).

In terms of antisemitic expressions, an association between Jews and money was apparent in one student interview. In another, the Palestinian-Israeli conflict was used to justify the idea of Jews as a personal enemy when speaking about the Shoah:

> *Yes, it was a terrible time. And if I had lived then, I would surely have ended up in a concentration camp, or I would have had to leave the country. And, yes, it is sad. I want to be sincere. If I see a Jew somewhere, I wouldn't do anything, but I would be always thinking: We can never be friends, because I saw this conflict between Palestine and Israel. […] So I guess I could never speak to a Jew.* (Amira, female, student, school S)

Even though Amira identified with the victims of violence by saying she would have ended up in a concentration camp had she lived during that period, she reproduced antisemitism by blaming every Jew for the Palestinian-Israeli conflict, refusing to recognise the humanity of any given Jewish person.

Clearly, that does not mean that antisemitism is confined to some migrantised young people in solidarity with Palestinians; on the contrary, it is deeply rooted in German history. David remarked that he has found Nazi symbols at every school in which he has ever taught, a number of which are in various Hamburg neighbourhoods. He ironically suggested that the AfD should be more concerned with those than with antifascist stickers.

The German culture of remembrance

In terms of the post-National Socialism remembrance culture, two of the schools, S and U, have fixed annual commemoration rituals. Students from all three schools said they have visited a concentration camp with their teachers. Hitler, Nazis, Holocaust and WW2 were always mentioned when talking about German history. Much was said about how this history has affected Germany's image in the world. Many participants believed that the past should not be 'transferred' to the present, because they themselves did not have anything to do with it. While some pointed out that Germany has a certain responsibility "*not to repeat the history*", they mostly spoke defensively about feelings of guilt and shame:

> *I would not say that I should feel guilty or, um, in any way, or that I should show penitence for anything.* (Johann, male, student, school U)

While some migrantised students adopted the 'guilt' discourse as a part of their German identity, others distanced themselves:

> *I think it is good that they [Germans] are ashamed, because it will prevent them from doing other horrible things to other cultures or religions or minorities. Because now they know how other countries hated Germans as a result.* (Zara, female, student, school S)

Lina was the only person who claimed that her grandparents were affected by the Nazis, although she did not know the details of what happened. She spoke at length about the lack of awareness among her peers of the horrors of the past. According to her,

> *The topic is being suppressed here at school. … [B]ecause many do not (…) I mean, they know it happened and sometimes they make little jokes about it, but (…). But many don't realise (…) that it ACTUALLY happened and it was REAL and it was not good and it should have NEVER happened.* (Lina, female, student, school U)

In contrast, the topic of colonialism was largely unheard of; at most, it was something distantly remembered from a lesson. If anything, students recalled that Germany was "*quite a minor colonial power, not as extreme as England, France or Spain*", (Sakura, female, student, school R). It is significant that only one student – who identifies as Gambian, following her father's country of origin (Yasemin, female, student, school S) – spoke about colonialism and its impact even before the question arose, naming her family as her main source of knowledge about the issue. David (male, student, school U) also seemed to be exceptionally well informed about Germany's colonial past. He said, however, that in his history class "*colonialism was not even touched upon*". Two students from the same school, who had a different history teacher, reported having just attended a post-colonial city walk with their history class. They talked quite passionately about colonial traces in the city and how the colonial past impacts the present. Such lessons seem to be an exception and depended on the individual teacher's engagement with the topic.

This situation was also reflected in teachers' interviews, as most admitted that German colonial legacy is not a part of their teaching practice. School U's headteacher seemed to be aware of German colonialism, but said that the curricula of her subjects (art and literature) are already too overloaded for the topic to be included. She assumed that there was some postcolonial content in history lessons. David (male, teacher, school S) claimed that colonialism and post-colonialism were part of his teaching practice, but speaking about it he uncritically used the term "*discovery*". This gives violent colonial expansion progressive and positive connotations, a practice recognisable from German textbooks (Marmer & Sow, 2015). The headteacher at school R (who teaches literature) admitted that he would not be able to teach this topic as he himself has no knowledge of it.

However, even without having much knowledge about colonialism in general or the German colonial past in particular, several students spontaneously replied that colonialism may well have paved the ideological ground for the Nazi regime.

Europe

When asked about Europe, students mostly mentioned western European countries, often associating Europe with the West and with Christianity as well as with ancient Greece and Rome. To many, Europe means unity and cooperation, and some remarked that this is a result of numerous historical wars. 'Europe' was often used synonymously with the EU, and Brexit and elections to the EU Parliament were also discussed several times.

Opinions were divided between those who thought that diversity, openness and '*tolerance toward different cultures*' are what constitute European culture, and those who believed that there is no such thing as European culture because of the diversity of individual countries' cultures:

> *[B]ecause it makes a big difference, if you are born in Germany or in Spain, for instance. A huge difference.* (Dominik, female, student, school R)

Along with 'unity' and 'cooperation', 'open borders' and 'solidarity with the neighbouring countries' were often seen as part of European culture. Europe was also described as a culture of order, functionality and regulation, democracy, hard work, modernity, freedom, peace, security and prosperity. Some considered it a privilege to be born in Europe.

Very few were critical of the glorification of anything European. David (male, student, school U) said that what Europeans have in common is the history of intolerance towards everything non-European and non-Christian, adding that this "*wouldn't be a good basis for a common culture*". Yasmin (female, student, school S) believed that European culture is related to "*slavery, because Europeans went to Africa to colonise*". Amina (female, student, school S) said that European culture is a culture of "*narrow-mindedness and isolation*", while Amira (female, student, school S) criticised European migration politics, closed borders and the deportation of refugees.

Being European was mostly understood as being born in Europe and/or feeling at home in Europe. However, some associated being European with being blond and white. Asked if he sees himself as European, Marat (male, student, school S) replied

> *I do somehow identify with Europe. But sometimes I think, yes, it is fine that I am European, but in Germany [...] I am still considered a foreigner and not European.*

In a similar vein, some migrantised students did not consider themselves European, while others resisted any label, saying that they want to see themselves simply as human beings.

Discussion

The most prominent feature in the data collected at the three Hamburg schools is the prevailing reductionist discourse that narrows the meaning of culture to 'ethno-national origin'. Constructing culture and cultural difference in this way has several implications. First of all, due to the fact that 'nation' is confined by physical borders, while 'ethnicity' is often constructed in relation to kin and thus biologically confined, 'ethno-national' framing promotes a rigid understanding of culture with fixed rules of exclusion and inclusion. Secondly, each particular 'ethno-national culture' is imagined to be rather homogenous, leaving little space for the plurality of individuals who share the same 'ethno-national origin'. Thirdly, the emphasis on 'origin' constructs culture (and belonging) in association with a geographical place that was once home to one's ancestors, rather than with the place in which one actually lives.

The central role that 'origin' plays in defining and perceiving culture marks processes of inclusion and exclusion according to the dominant German narratives of migration, which tend to migrantise (El-Tayeb, 2015) certain groups of people in this country irrespectively of their actual experience with migration. Nearly all interviewees were born and raised in Germany and hold German citizenship. Nevertheless, migrantised students and teachers are not perceived (and often do not perceive themselves) as German; they are constantly addressed as the 'ethno-nationally-culturally other' (Mecheril, 2015). Taking into consideration historical and current ethno-national-cultural power relations (ibid.), and the apparent lack of recognition that migratory processes have historically shaped (and still shape) 'German cultural space', it becomes clear that the reductionist understanding of culture serves to reinforce the status quo rather than to induce greater equality or inclusion.

The dominant discourse was replicated but also complicated multiple times by the respondents. Students and teachers alike felt the limits of a reductionist approach, especially when it came to defining 'their own culture'. Nevertheless, ethno-national framing was dominant. In constructing their cultural identities, nationalist and exclusionist tendencies could often be observed in the cases of students who self-identified as German on the one hand, and the struggle of those who were excluded to define their place in society on the other. Most of the interviewed teachers, however, seemed to be preoccupied with the cultural identities of the 'ethno-nationally-culturally others', rather than all students. The so-called 'self-ethnicisation', "the insistence on ethnic difference on the part of migrant children who grew up here [in Germany]", which is "a response to the everyday racist experience and the impossibility of belonging to the mainstream society" (Soufiane Akka, 2007: p. 197), was not recognised by the teachers as a reaction to exclusion, but as an unwillingness to belong.

The next interesting finding is that most of the students whose understanding of culture goes beyond the ethno-national were from school U. One could theorise that this broad concept corresponds with Appiah's idea of a "more cosmopolitan picture in which every element of culture – from philosophy or cuisine to the style of bodily movements – is separable in principle from all the others" (Appiah, 2018: p. 207), which makes "all cultural practices and objects mobile [...] and themselves creations of intermixture" (ibid.: p. 208). Culture is thus conceived of as 'diverse' and 'intercultural' in every aspect.

While students at school U are encouraged to participate in a broad range of cultural activities by their school and their families, at schools S and R students often lack the cultural and financial capital and infrastructure to enable them to participate. Additionally, existing discursive barriers confine many of the migrantised S and R school students to ethniticised concepts of culture and prevent these students from recognising their own diverse practices as cultural.

Some students are involved in cultural practices in and outside school that actively tackle inequalities, like the (failed) anti-racist activism at school U, the participation of young women in feminist cultural groups (school S), or Brooke's (school R) use of her job as a reason to read and write literature.

Based on familial and environmental socio-economic, educational and cultural resources and infrastructure, to which the unequal distribution of the selective school system has obviously contributed, each school seems to have developed its own school culture. Institutional, personnel and individual decisions have impacted each school culture, and vice versa, as was reflected for example in the interviewed teachers' attitudes towards their students. As was observed from first contact and teachers' interviews, school S places emphasis on empowering young people. While acknowledging the vulnerable situations of most young people living in the neighbourhood where the school is located, teachers stressed their students' resilience and solidarity, as opposed to the engagement and self-esteem praised by school U teachers. Empowering students was not found to be the priority of interviewed teachers at school R. They highlighted academic achievement, but were often judgemental about their students, made negative comments about them, and, in several cases, took derogatory and racist attitudes toward migrantised youth. Despite the fact that school R is a part of the network Schools without Racism (*Schule ohne Rassismus*),[12] openly racist comments from teachers seem to be tolerated by the school culture.

However, these assumptions about school culture should be viewed with caution, considering the recruitment process: school culture deduced from the interviews at schools U and S could correspond with how these schools wished to represent themselves, as interviewed teachers, who selected students at both schools, were themselves chosen by the headteacher (U) or intercultural mediator (S), while at school R all interviewees were selected completely at random.

In each of the schools, a culture of remembrance, which "developed into a fundamental element of the country's self-image and international representation after 1990" (Messerschmidt, 2015: n.p.), is practiced as part of school culture. As a result, when speaking about German history, the Nazi past, the need to learn from history or Germany's responsibility for 'never again'[13] were often participants' first associations. However, the damage caused to Germany's image and an aversion to feelings of guilt seemed more relevant to many interviewees, especially those who identified themselves as German. Speaking about Nazi history often prompted praise of contemporary Germany. This is reminiscent of Bodemann's remembrance theatre (Bodemann, 1996), whereby the official culture of remembrance represents the self-construction of the white German majority as free of guilt and responsibility rather than for a structural, consistent reappraisal of National Socialism and its current perpetuation (Czollek, 2018: p. 24). Similarly, antisemitism was commonly confined to historical context of the Holocaust; only at school S, which is predominantly attended by

12 https://m.schule-ohne-rassismus.org/startseite/

13 Historical responsibility for the 'never again Auschwitz' – through raising awareness and the prevention of nationalistic tendencies – is the cornerstone of the concept 'Education after Auschwitz', introduced by Adorno (1966/2005).

migrantised young people, is it taught as part of students' 'worldview'. Such "singling out immigrants and specifically Muslims" as "the main contemporary antisemites", as observed by Özyürek (2019: p. 42), is mirrored in some political educational programmes (Seukwa, Marmer & Sylla, 2018). Placing antisemitism outside the mainstream contemporary society creates an image of "a new Germany that has fully liberated itself from any anti-democratic tendencies surviving from its Nazi past", but also "obscures connections between anti-Semitism and anti-Muslim racism, both of which are active forces in mainstream German society" (Özyürek, 2019: p. 42).

The culture of remembrance as practiced in the formal education setting does not extend to the horrors of colonialism and its continuities. Interviewees were largely ignorant about issues of the German colonial legacy that still defines and affects today's discourses and practices, especially in regard to racism and migration (Kilomba, 2016; Eggers et al., 2005). This is not at all surprising, as the colonial past has long been erased from the white German collective memory (Zimmerer, 2015). Despite some recent political attempts to establish post-colonial approaches to commemoration culture within Hamburg museums, academia and, most recently, at the ministry level,[14] this is not yet reflected in formal education. On the contrary, colonial and racist narratives of '*discovery*' and derogatory representations of Black people, for example, are still present in textbooks and curricula. Messerschmidt (2008: p. 45) argues that this collective amnesia in regard to colonialism has a double effect: it declares German colonial history irrelevant, and it fails to recognise the continuation of colonial practices under National Socialism. In rare cases, students seemed to be sincerely invested in these topics, usually with the encouragement of individual teachers committed to anti-racism and anti-antisemitism rather than any institutional commitment by the school. True emotional engagement with Germany's historical legacy was also obvious in cases of students from affected families. As Messerschmidt remarks, "[f]or the descendants of the colonized this option [to ignore historical crimes] does not exist, because for them colonialism is a much deeper cut in their history, culture, their self-image and their position in the world" (Messerschmidt, 2006: p. 1). It is striking that, although most of the interviewed pupils had only a faint inkling of the colonial past, they were usually able to make an intuitive connection between the colonial and Nazi ideologies when asked about this. Closer scrutiny of these ideologies and their continuation in contemporary Germany would be a more inclusive – in the sense of who

14 https://www.hamburg.de/bkm/koloniales-erbe/

is addressed as well as who is commemorated – approach to commemoration culture.

While discussing these findings, it is important to reflect on the impact of the recruitment process, the interviewers' and the researchers' choices. As mentioned above, there may have been a difference in responses to an interviewer of colour and a white interviewer. How the three interviewers formulated their questions might have led to answers that seemed more socially desirable, while different recruitment procedures in the three schools could have also influenced the results. Last but not least, observations of lessons, leisure time and in the staff room would have provided deeper insight into the general *school culture*.

Conclusion

In this chapter, empirical findings obtained from data collected in three Hamburg schools are discussed in terms of young people's and their teachers' concepts of 'culture' and 'cultural identity'. Culture has an interesting double meaning: on the one hand, it can be interpreted as related to the place of origin (of the 'other') and as a deviation from the 'German' norm. In this context, 'cultural' is used similarly to the English 'ethnic'. This sense of the word refers to ethnicised norms, values, family relations, upbringing, character and behaviour, as well as food, clothes and celebrations, often combined with religion. This representation of culture constructs solid lines of difference and defines what constitutes 'German' identity or belonging to German society. On the other hand, culture also connotes creativity, artistic production and consumption, hobbies, social and political engagement, digital culture, and communication. This concept of culture is potentially more inclusive but may have restrictions based on socio-economic, cultural and educational capital.

The concept of commemoration culture has the potential to scrutinise ideologies that support nationalisation, essentialisation, culturalisation and exclusion, as well as their impact on contemporary German society or the European self-conception. Currently, however, it is often used to affirm the progressive and democratic state of contemporary German society. Mechanisms of exclusion (racism, antisemitism, classism, as well as sexism, ableism, heteronormativity, etc.) are not systematically assessed and challenged in formal education.

Each school can be characterised by its own *school culture*, which is based on structural, institutional and political decisions, but also on various input from staff and students, and the socio-economic school environment. This school culture, in turn, seems to have an impact on students' cultural participation, where the lines of exclusion are sometimes drawn.

Most participants seemed to be interested in the interview topics and enjoyed the fact that the questions made them re-think some otherwise unchallenged concepts. They were actively involved in the production of meaning over the course of the interview and often expressed their eagerness to learn. Interviewed young people assessed diversity positively and understood it as normal, unlike the Hamburg curricula, which often problematise diversity in the context of conflict. Young people pointed out how they can learn from each other; thus, informal social interactions often may be more important elements of cultural education than the lessons and curricula themselves.

'Cultural knowledge' was mostly interpreted by the interviewed students in ethno-national terms, referring to the 'place of origin'. This kind of cultural literacy seems to help young people navigate a pluralistic society. For many interviewed students, knowing how others celebrate, worship, eat and interact within the family, as well as the amount of freedom or restrictions others possess as compared to themselves, constitutes basic everyday cultural literacy, as at all three schools students speak from within an 'ethnically' diverse environment.

The expressed wish to learn more about other cultures, however, was often paired with the creation and reinforcement of differences through locating these cultures in distant places and exoticising the unknown. Believing that something is located far away and is 'exotic' makes it look vastly different. A curricular approach to cultural literacy that questions and deconstructs differences produced by historic power relations, as well as the continuities of colonial and Nazi ideologies, could offer a helpful framework for more inclusive cultural education.

Acknowledgments

I would like to thank my assistants Öykü Coskun and Rosa Lüdemann for collecting the students' data and the latter for discussing the results. Her bachelor thesis in education, based on the same data, was also a source of reflection (Lüdemann, 2019). Many thanks to Cornelia Sylla for valuable discussions and constructive comments, as well as for support in establishing contacts with schools, Awista Gardi for useful comments and Louis Henri Seukwa for inspiration.

References

Adorno, T. W. (1966/2005) Education After Auschwitz. In *Critical Models: Interventions and Catchwords* (S. 191–204). New York: Columbia University Press.

Appiah, A. (2018) The Lies That Bind: Rethinking Identity, Creed, Country, Color, Class, Culture (First edition). New York, NY: Liveright Publishing Corporation.

Bodemann, Y. M. (1996) *"Gedächtnistheater". Die jüdische Gemeinschaft und ihre deutsche Erfindung*. Berlin: Rotbuch.

Chzhen, Y., Gromada, A., Rees, G., Cuesta, J. and Bruckauf, Z. (2018). An unfair start: Inequality in children's education in rich countries, Innocenti Report Card no. 15. Florenc: UNICEF Office of Research.

Czollek, M. (2018) *Desintegriert Euch!* München: Carl Hanser Verlag.

Eggers, M. M., Kilomba, G., Piesche, P., & Arndt, S. (Eds.). (2005) *Mythen, Masken und Subjekte: Kritische Weissseinsforschung in Deutschland* (1. Aufl). Münster: Unrast.

El-Tayeb, F. (2011) European others: Queering ethnicity in postnational Europe. Minneapolis: University of Minnesota Press.

El-Tayeb, F. (2015) Anders Europäisch: Rassismus, Identität und Widerstand im vereinten Europa (First edition). Münster: Unrast.

Hamburg District School Curriculum (2011) Hamburger Bildungsplan Stadtteilschule, Jahrgangstufe 5–11, Aufgabengebiete. https://www.hamburg.de/contentblob/2372700/39806d625c1b4e86f03af54244443454/data/aufgabengebiete-sts.pdf (Accessed on January 14, 2022).

ifbq (2021) Schulstatistik Hamburg 2020/2021, https://www.hamburg.de/schuljahr-in-zahlen/4662018/sus-migrationshintergrund/ (Accessed on January 14, 2022).

Kilomba, G. (2016) *Plantation Memories: Episodes of Everyday Racism* (Fourth edition). Münster: Unrast.

Lüdemann, R. (2019) *Perspektivwechsel – Eine Gegenüberstellung der bildungspolitischen Darstellung von Diversität und der Wahrnehmung von Vielfalt von Schülerinnen und Schülern*. University of Hamburg, unpublished bachelor thesis.

Marmer, E., & Sow, P. (Eds.). (2015) *Wie Rassismus aus Schulbüchern spricht: Kritische Auseinandersetzung mit „Afrika"-Bildern und Schwarz-Weiss-Konstruktionen in der Schule-Ursachen, Auswirkungen und Handlungsansätze für die pädagogische Praxis*. Weinheim: Beltz Juventa.

Mecheril, P. (2003) *Prekäre Verhältnisse: Über natio-ethno-kulturelle (Mehrfach-) Zugehörigkeit*. Münster: Waxmann.

Mecheril, P. (2015) Kulturell-ästhetische Bildung. Migrationspädagogische Anmerkungen. *Mission Kulturagenten – Onlinepublikation des Modellprogramms „Kulturagenten für kreative Schulen 2011–2015"*. www.kulturagenten-programm.de (Accessed on January 14, 2022).

Messerschmidt, A. (2006) *Solidarität unter postkolonialen Bedingungen. Vom Umgang mit uneindeutigen Realitäten in einer globalisierten Welt* [Lecture]. ESG, Jena. https://www.mangoes-and-bullets.org/solidaritaet-unter-postkolonialen-bedingungen/ (Accessed on January 14, 2022).

Messerschmidt, A. (2008) Postkoloniale Erinnerungsprozesse in der postnationalsozialistischen Gesellschaft. *Peripherie, 28*(109/110), 42–60.

Messerschmidt, A. (2015, Januar 25) Bildungsarbeit in den Nachwirkungen von Auschwitz. *Praxisforum – Workshop 5: Erziehung nach Auschwitz – 2015.* Internationale Konferenz zur Holocaustforschung: Der Holocaust als Erfahrungsgeschichte 1945–1949, Berlin.

Özyürek, E. (2019) Export-Import Theory and the Racialization of Anti-Semitism: Turkish- and Arab-Only Prevention Programs in Germany—CORRIGENDUM. *Comparative Studies in Society and History, 61*(04), 986–987. https://doi.org/10.1017/S0010417519000355 (Accessed on January 14, 2022).

Riegel, C., & Geisen, T. (Eds.). (2010) *Jugend, Zugehörigkeit und Migration: Subjektpositionierung im Kontext von Jugendkultur, Ethnizitäts- und Geschlechterkonstruktionen* (2., durchges. Aufl). Wiesbaden: Springer VS..

Seukwa, L. H., Marmer, E. and Sylla, C. (2018). In: Fooks, G., Stamou, E. & McNie, K. (Eds.) National Cultural/Educational Policy Review, 74–104. http://chiefprojecteu.com/wp-content/uploads/CHIEF-WP1_D1.2_National-Cultural-Educational-Policy-Reviews_v1.1_KM.pdf (Accessed on January 15, 2022)

Soufiane Akka, A. (2007) „Wir sind alle Schwarzköpfe“, Selbstethnisierung als Strategie der Selbstbehauptung. *Überblick, Zeitschrift des Informations- und Dokumentationszentrums für Antirassismusarbeit in Nordrhein-Westfalen* (1).

Sylla, C., Marmer, E. and Seukwa, L. H. (2019). In: Marmer, E., & Zurabishvili, T. (Eds.) National Curriculum Review, 70–110. Unpublished Report.

Zimmerer, J. (2015) Humboldt Forum: Das koloniale Vergessen. *Blätter für deutsche und internationale Politik* (7), 13–16. https://www.blaetter.de/ausgabe/2015/juli/humboldt-forum-das-koloniale-vergessen (Accessed on January 14, 2022).

Part II Cultural literacy in non-formal education

In this part of the book, the results of profound qualitative research in non-formal educational settings are presented. These settings are considered an integral part of young people's cultural education and development. A bottom-up (re-)production of various forms of cultural knowledge and practices is attempted here to show how 'cultural heritage' and 'cultural literacy' are articulated and adopted in the civil society sector.

Research questions

The central questions addressed in the following chapters are:

- Which bottom-up cultural practices are relevant to local communities and young people?
- How are diversity and pluralism negotiated in different contexts of intercultural communication in non-formal educational settings?
- What different views on 'European culture' do members of civil society institutions hold? What are the origins and conditions for the emergence of these differences?
- How do non-formal education settings affect young people's cultural participation and their acquisition of cultural literacy?
- How can cultural literacy in local communities be enhanced?

Method

Research in non-formal educational settings is challenging, because these exist in many different organisational forms and tend to change a lot more quickly than schools. Thus, individual research procedures may need to be adapted for the settings and dynamics found in the field. However, all chapters in this section present results of a common research design. Practices were mainly revealed through participant observation, while articulations of knowledge and concepts were gathered in the form of semi-structured topic-focused interviews with cultural/educational practitioners and with young people who took part in the activities at the research sites.

For each site, one or two participant observations of group activities were conducted and documented, separating descriptive and analytical or critical observations. Participation in the research field was designed to gather first-hand information about the practices and experiences of young people and practitioners within the field. The researchers were meant to experience what it could feel like to take part in the activities.

Semi-structured in-depth interviews were conducted with one to three practitioners and about 5–10 young people aged 14–25 per site. A gender and age balance between selected groups was attempted but proved difficult in some cases. For both groups, separate interview schedules were prepared and translated to the national/regional languages. The questions for practitioners focused on organisational structures, cultural identities of participants, and notions of culture and practices prevalent within the organisation. The interview schedule for young people consisted of four question blocks that focused on

1. Young people's motivation to participate in the organisation,
2. Their notions of culture and cultural practices,
3. Relationships/friendships and identities,
4. One block focusing on national issues, selected by national research teams.

Analysis of all data was first done inductively, leaving lots of room for individual researchers to select the theoretical literature most fitting to the emerging themes from the qualitative data. This led to a broad variety of theoretical approaches in the different chapters of this section. Overall, the intent of Part II is to present a spectrum of cultural and educational practices in the non-formal sector to highlight as many key points in the development of cultural identity as possible.

While non-formal youth groups are not strictly tied to the curricula of formal education, they are influenced by national education policies and are situated in specific institutional structures that may encourage or limit certain practices. Therefore, the differences in the national circumstances concerning funding, and the relationship between formal and non-formal education in each country, are another dimension of the broad spectrum of opportunities through which young people acquire cultural literacy. Further dimensions were introduced through the sampling process, when each national research team was asked to select two diametrically different cases. This request was answered in diverse ways, since what researchers considered important differences was influenced by their respective perspectives on culture, youth, and the question of what role the organisations played in the acquisition of cultural literacy. The Slovakian research (Chapter 6) focuses on the differences among organisations concerning youth's relationship to national history. The Georgian research team takes on a perspective within the Georgian mainstream discourse on culture (Chapter 7), exploring what is perceived as "ethnically Georgian culture", including aspects of language, religion and certain art forms, and what is considered "traditional" within this discourse. The selected sites are similar in that regard but differ as regards the organisational structures. In Chapter 8, the German research team looks at differences in inner organisational communication and the relationships between young people and their peers, themselves and social structures in general. The sites also differ in which concept of culture their programmes represent, and in the socio-demographic profiles of their clientele. This can also be applied to the Indian research (Chapter 9). Here, both the structures and the clientele of the organisations are representations of different points along the spectrum.

(by Matej Karásek)

Chapter 6 The past as a dream and a nightmare: Cultural heritage and identity in a Slovak non-formal educational environment

Abstract: This case study is based on ethnographic research in a Slovak non-formal educational environment. The study deals with the reproduction and distribution of emic discourses related to culture, cultural heritage, cultural diversity and identity. Research was conducted in two groups whose activities mainly target a youth demographic. The first group is a neo-pagan new religious movement (re)constructing the spirituality and lifestyle of pre-Christian Slavs; the second group is a liberal, pro-diversity non-governmental organisation providing non-formal education on human rights, democracy, cultural diversity and cultural memory. This study discusses the criteria used to select the elements of the past that represent cultural heritage within these groups, and examines how these representations of the past and of cultural heritage are actualised for the groups' present and/or future purposes. Finally, the study considers how such constructions of cultural heritage affect the identities and daily activities of the young participants.

Keywords: cultural heritage, identity, cultural diversity, youth, non-formal education, neo-pagan movement, pro-diversity non-government organisation

Introduction

The tradition of non-formal youth education in Slovakia can be traced back to at least to the First Czechoslovak Republic (1918–1938). The birth of the fascist Slovak state in 1938 put an end to diverse youth organisations, with many either becoming part of *Hlinková mládež*[1] (Hlinka Youth) – an imitation of the *Hitler Youth* – or being dissolved (Milla, 2008: 23). After a short post-war boom in youth organisations, the beginning of the communist era saw the prohibition of many of them (e.g. Scouts); others were integrated into the *Národný zväz mládeže* (National Youth Association). Besides the National Youth Association, the Communists established the *Pioneers*, an organisation for children. In terms of foundation and structure, these organisations took inspiration from the Soviet

1 Named after Andrej Hlinka (1864–1938), the Catholic priest and the leader of the Slovak autonomy movement in the First Czechoslovak Republic. Hlinka was posthumously proclaimed a national hero by the Slovak fascist government.

Pioneers and the *Komsomol*. These groups were state controlled and aimed to cultivate the 'new man' in the 'new society'. Besides providing leisure activities, the main purpose of both organisations was to teach children and young people communist ideology. All children had to become members of these groups. After the intervention of the Warsaw Pact troops in Czechoslovakia, the *Socialistický zväz mládeže* (Socialist Association of Youths) was founded to replace the former National Youth Association.

With the fall of communism, the Socialist Association of Youths was disbanded and some of the youth organisations forbidden under communism were re-established. Formerly prohibited Christian clubs and the Scouts became very popular, for instance. Nowadays, there is a wide range of organisations open to young people with various interests. Generally, young Slovaks belong to sports and hobby clubs, political organisations, artistic and cultural groups or religious groups. Volunteering organisations for the preservation of environmental, social and cultural heritage are also popular. In rural areas the volunteer fire brigade has a strong following. The Youth Council of Slovakia is the biggest 'umbrella' association, encompassing 25 children's and youth organisations. In total these organisations have 25,000 members.

The objective of this chapter is to examine the discourses on culture, cultural heritage, identity and cultural diversity constructed within two non-formal groups, and subsequently to investigate the dissemination of these discourses amongst their leaders and young participants. This case study explores how the emic theory of culture, identity and cultural heritage is constructed within the context of the group on the one hand and through the practice of sharing and disseminating knowledge on the other.

The first group, Slavic Natives (SN), is a new religious neo-pagan movement with a pre-Christian 'Slovak/Slavic cultural and spiritual heritage' orientation; it aims to (re)construct the 'original, natural Slavic spirituality'.

The second group, anonymised as Civil Liberties Organisation (CLO), focuses on teaching young people about democracy, civil rights, discrimination, cultural memory and cultural diversity. The CLO's agenda is based on ideas of multiculturalism,[2] cultural diversity, intercultural tolerance and democracy.

2 There is not enough space here to discuss the meaning of this highly problematic concept. For the purposes of this study, I understand the term in the sense of Eriksen, who describes multiculturalism as the doctrine that ethnic groups have the right to be culturally different from the cultural majority, just as the majority group has the right to its own culture (Eriksen 2008: 337). The research data indicates that this definition

The main criterion for selecting the non-formal groups was their contrasting approaches to discourses related to culture, cultural heritage and cultural diversity. Both groups hold significantly different attitudes towards these concepts. While SN has an essentialist view of culture or ethnicity, CLO adopts a constructivist approach that problematises or relativises these concepts. While SN leaders and members emphasise their Slovak or Slavic ethnic identity, CLO instructors tend to identify as Central Europeans, Europeans or humans. In general, the interview data shows that CLO and SN differ in their attitudes to the main public discourses on immigration, Islam and LGBTQ+ rights, and in their opinions of Slovakia's geopolitical orientation. CLO agitates for Slovakia to continue its membership of European and transatlantic organisations, while the SN is very critical of the EU and thinks military neutrality is the best option for the country.

This research was focused around the following research questions:

- What is the emic meaning of the term *culture* in the group?
- What are the criteria for selecting elements of the past that are used to represent cultural heritage within the groups?
- How are these representations of the past and cultural heritage 'actualised' for the group's present and/or future purposes?
- How does the way in which the group construes cultural heritage affect the identities of its members and their sense of belonging within a particular collective category?

Slavic natives

Site description

Slavic Natives can be described as one of the many neo-pagan revivalist organisations that have appeared in the former 'eastern bloc' since the fall of the communist regimes. SN first formed in a medium sized city in western Slovakia in the 1990s. Veleslav is the SN's founder and charismatic leader. All the group's activities are related to 'pre-Christian culture and values'. SN places a strong emphasis on its 'Slavic and Slovak essence', especially the glorification of the so-called 'Ancient Slavs and Slovaks'. SN members conduct rituals pertaining to the Slavic pagan religion[3] and its embrace of nature. Veleslav defines the philosophy

of multiculturalism is very close to the emic understanding of the CLO informants (and the meaning used by formal education policymakers).

3 Pre-Christian Slavs worshipped a pantheon that is similar (in terms of the Gods) to other Indo-European pantheons (there is a God of Thunder, the God of the Underworld

of SN as 'original, natural spirituality'. SN also exhibits strong Euroscepticism, radical linguistic purism, and seeks to declare itself an oppressed dissident group. Since the group has no formal membership, it is hard to say what its exact size is. For a rough estimate we could use the number of Facebook followers: the *Veleslav* profile has 697 followers, the *Veleslav–Slavic Natives* page has 2,126 followers, and the related *Farmer and Craftsman Revival* group has 620 members (data from 10.10.2019). According to the participant observation, approximately 200 people took part in the summer solstice festivals, indicating that the number of active followers is smaller than the number of Facebook followers.

The SN gives talks promoting 'native culture', holds native spirituality workshops, and puts on concerts by the band *Spirits* (consisting solely of SN members). There are also celebrations of festivals such as the summer and winter solstices. These activities are usually connected: the talk is part of the concert, and each celebration includes discussion and music. Recent activities include a podcast broadcast by an online radio station that is well-known in Slovakia as part of the alternative and conspiracy theory media. Other research (Puchovský, 2017) has shown that many young followers became aware of the group thanks to the radio station. The SN target audience seems to be anybody interested in pre-Christian spirituality, folk music and folklore, history or ecology.

According to SN, the summer and winter solstices are among the most important festivals of the year. While the winter solstice is more of a closed celebration, usually organised just for close followers, the summer solstice is a three-day event open to anybody wishing to attend. The main event is four ritual bonfires. The solstice is also an initiation ceremony for new followers, at which they gain new Slavic and spiritual names. Other rituals are *postrižiny*, or spiritual purification, and a 'protect the new-borns' rite that takes the place of a Christian baptism.

SN does not have a permanent base in which to meet or hold talks. SN gatherings are usually held in the mountains in central Slovakia, where the festival takes place. However, they also organise events all over the country (especially near Veleslav's house in the middle of the forest), including in towns or cities, where they meet in tearooms or health food shops.

Veleslav holds the central, decisive role in the group. He delegates the management of some tasks to his closest and most loyal followers. The group is funded by membership fees and voluntary contributions.

---

or the Goddess of Spring, etc.). Besides personified natural powers, Slavic pagans worshipped sacred forests, springs and other elements of nature.

The religious cult of cultural heritage

Slavic Natives is a new religious movement propagating a return to an 'original, natural spirituality' based on the 'ancient traditions of the ancient Slavs'. It is worth stressing that SN, led by its founder Veleslav, is about (re)constructing the religious beliefs and rituals of the 'ancient Slavs'. Veleslav himself denies that his movement is reconstructivist. He argues that his group does not follow the spiritual practices of the pre-Christian Slavic religion in a strict sense, but adds innovative elements. These innovations come from his spiritual inspiration, gained by 'joining with the pure source'. This 'pure source' could be described as the higher consciousness of the Universe, the reservoir of all knowledge. Otherwise, the SN rituals are centred around materials selected from ethnological, historical, archaeological and linguistic literature. This is why Veleslav alternatively calls his spiritual system a "new-ancient spirituality" (*novodrevné duchovno*). The key concept of Veleslav's teaching is *vedomectvo* (spiritual wisdom).

Although Veleslav shares his messages with all sorts of audiences and his followers belong to different social and age groups, young people make up a significant proportion of those attending his events. The events organised by SN can be characterised as non-formal education. Veleslav and his followers take every opportunity to spread the teaching and philosophy of the 'original, natural ancestral spirituality'. Veleslav conveys his teachings through songs[4] and concerts, workshops, lectures, magazines, books, websites, radio broadcasts and rituals.[5] His workshops cover various topics and activities, such as traditional Slovak musical instruments; using a scythe or gardening; traditional cooking; crafts; and performing rituals. Whatever the topic of the workshop, Veleslav stresses the spiritual dimension of these activities, encouraging participants to understand the deeper meanings of the various actions involved and to follow his teachings by working in tandem with nature and *vedomectvo*.

4 Veleslav's songs are composed for musical instruments typically associated with Slovak folk music. He also uses folk music rhythms or even whole melodies, accompanied by his own lyrics. In his lyrics, he presents his worldview and spiritual teachings. He often performs with his band at concerts.

5 Although our research focuses on non-formal youth education, it is interesting to note that SN provides activities for children as well. Veleslav holds summer camps at which he teaches children traditional crafts, farming and woodcraft skills alongside his philosophy. Woodcraft and the Scouts inspired him to organise these camps, which he wants to expand across the country.

To shed light on the general approaches of SN and the emerging themes of our research requires us to have some knowledge of what Veleslav and his followers understand by the term culture. According to Veleslav, "*culture and spirituality are parallel concepts*" (Veleslav, practitioner, male, 52). Veleslav's teaching does not follow a nature/culture dichotomy. In fact, he does not distinguish between them but views culture as being on a continuum with nature. He does not consider cultures to be just "*ways of thinking, speaking or dressing*", suggesting instead that culture is everything that is inheritable. DNA, blood groups and stomach enzymes are examples of this: "*Stomach bacteria are also cultures*" (Veleslav). This view corresponds to his worldview of nations, humankind, earth and even the universe as living beings.

The cultural extension of nature should be moderated by spirituality. For Veleslav and most of our informants, culture only makes sense in relation to nature. SN followers are convinced that Christianisation has severed the tight bond between culture and nature because Christians ignore and suppress the worship of nature. Veleslav draws on the idea that Slavic culture was more sensitive to the hidden powers of the natural world and was a "*culture prohibited in the 9th century*" (Veleslav). It was clear from many of our young informants that this idea is common among SN followers. Veleslav and SN followers believe that there are still remnants of "*the original culture*" (traced back by SN members to before the 9th century, when Christianity spread across the area that is now Slovakia), and they said that they are trying to conserve this for the future. In other words, Veleslav and his fellows are (re)constructing the cultural heritage of the pre-Christian Slavs. The terms 'ancestors' and 'heritage' were frequently used by SN interviewees, suggesting that the organisation is engaging in 'heritage in the making'.[6] The following statement by a young informant is illustrative of this:

6 In basic terms I agree with Graham et al., who understand the term 'heritage in making' to mean the process whereby stakeholders "assign diverse cultural meanings and socio-political functions to heritage, and heritage may become a component of broader economic and/or political strategies" (Graham et al., 2005: p. 30). However, I would add that heritage can be used not just in economic or political ways, but as a component of ideological (including religious) strategies. This case study on SN is an attempt to show that particular meanings can be assigned to cultural heritage in an effort to legitimise a modern religious worldview.

> *Actually, we ourselves are cultural heritage. I wear a tunic*[7] *[…] and that is culture too and we are encouraging it. I arrive in a tunic, someone likes it and they start wearing a tunic as well.* (Borislav, young person, male, 19)

Although this heritage stems from their idealised view of pre-Christian Slavic culture, it is one that has been largely constructed in a stereotypical manner by Veleslav. For Veleslav, cultural heritage is "*spiritual heritage and thus all the good and bad […] we have inherited*" (Veleslav).

SN followers attribute spiritual meaning to various tangible and intangible artifacts of traditional culture. They see spiritual references in the embroidery on folk costumes, in folk lyrics, traditional dances, and so forth. A typical example of this is the traditional whistle, which is called a *koncovka*. In the eyes of the SN, it is the perfect medium for meditation and connection with the four natural elements (water, earth, fire and air). SN followers frequently use the *koncovka*, a simple whistle without holes, in individual and group meditation. A series of steps are followed when playing the *koncovka*. Before starting to play, players should greet the instrument by lifting it over their heads using both hands, and then touch their chakras (known as *čarokolá* in the SN, a Slavicised term thought up by Veleslav) with it. The *koncovka* plays a very important role in many SN rituals. However, there is no scientific evidence indicating that the *koncovka* was traditionally used for meditative or ritual purposes; Veleslav has made no attempt to deny that this is his own invention. Nonetheless, his followers fully accept the *koncovka* as a traditional instrument used for spiritual purposes. Hence, in SN, cultural heritage has acquired a new and unusual meaning and has become part of their spiritual practices. One could say that this Slovak/Slavic cultural heritage has shifted to spirituality, and that members of the group worship the cult of cultural heritage.

While the informants shared relatively clear ideas about Slovak and Slavic culture, most of them found questions about Europe and/or European cultural heritage confusing. They claimed that they couldn't think of was any examples of European culture or heritage. One young informant stated that "*It is an empty concept which is based on nothing*" (Bojana, young person, female, 15). Apart from one respondent, who tried to define European culture as "*rich, but rich with money*" (Chranibor, young person, male, 19), there was only one other person who thought there were cultural commonalities across Europe. He mentioned

7 SN members frequently wear tunics or other clothes made from natural materials in reference to the 'Ancient Slavs' or traditional Slovak costume as a visible means of identifying themselves with their purported lifestyle and worldview.

Roman law and Greek democracy as being common to Europe (Dalibor, young person, male, 19). It is worth mentioning that this informant was the only one who had no problem identifying as European. This was rare: Veleslav's followers are critical of the European Union and of Slovakia being an EU member.

Nevertheless, in Veleslav's teachings we observed an element of European culture, which was referred to as Indo-European culture. This Indo-European reference is a means of legitimising the historical authenticity of Slavic culture on the one hand, and the spiritual authenticity of his teaching on the other. According to Veleslav, Indo-European culture and spirituality were linked to nature and therefore have something in common with SN's 'original, natural spirituality'. However, other cultures are based around the same 'universal natural values', which Veleslav often mentions (especially the cultures of the Indigenous peoples of North America) in his speeches. Neither he nor his followers consider Slavic culture and spirituality superior to other cultures that have preserved their 'original spirituality'. Veleslav claims to view all cultures as equal, although he speaks about some with disdain. The value that Veleslav ascribes to other cultures depends on how close the culture is to Veleslav's view of universal, natural spirituality. Notably, he considers Islam too anthropocentric and removed from nature rather than "*open to coexistence alongside other cultures*". Veleslav welcomes the diversity of cultures, but at the same time believes that cultures should not be excessively mixed, because mixing cultures leads to the cultures losing their uniqueness and the world becoming less diverse. Most of our young informants had negative attitudes towards 'mixing cultures' (which they understood as people coming together from different ethnic backgrounds). Some used arguments similar to Veleslav's to support their views, but others went further, claiming that having a child with a person from another 'race' was the equivalent of "*betraying their own blood*" (Bojana, young person, female, 15). Most SN members shared an essentialist view of the nation and ethnic group membership. They thought a person belonged to an ethnic group by birth and that ethnicity is 'in the blood'. The informant mentioned previously expressed this essentialism, saying that if she had children with someone from another ethnic group the "*children would fall somewhere between the two, they would be neither one thing, nor another*" (Bojana, young person, female, 15). For SN members, culture and ethnicity are rooted in nature in both biological and genetic senses. This may be why many SN members claimed that 'Slavic DNA' is very old. Proof that Slavic DNA had ancient historical origins would help root SN members more deeply in their newfound Slavic identities.

Civil liberties organisation

Site description

The Civil Liberties Organisation is a mid-size NGO founded in 1991. CLO is one of the oldest Slovak NGOs. It was founded to 'develop democracy, culture, tolerance and civic society'. CLO activists have implemented many human rights projects in schools: oral history (e.g. remembering the genocide of Jews and Roma during the Holocaust); activities with socially-excluded Roma communities (e.g. helping youth to attend high school, research, community work, seminars); teaching children to be active citizens; and promoting transatlantic cultural exchange.

CLO is developing a new strategic plan based on three pillars: diversity, inclusion and memory. As part of diversity, CLO runs projects and activities aimed at training teachers to provide innovative intercultural instruction.[8] CLO provides various training sessions, workshops and seminars on diversity for people who work with youth or immigrants, NGOs, and state institution staff. It also organises an annual multi-genre festival. The main purpose of the festival, according to CLO, is to promote cultural diversity and respect for all kinds of minorities.

The pillar of inclusion is primarily related to poverty and Roma communities. CLO draws up public policies and works with Roma grassroots activists.

The last pillar is historical memory. CLO organises courses, workshops and seminars for teachers and students to learn about the Holocaust, totalitarianism and other historical traumas affecting Slovakia. For the purposes of our research, the most important project is a travelling exhibition, *The Diary of Anne Frank – historical message for the present day.* The exhibition, which has toured high schools, is a non-formal educational project about the Holocaust, totalitarianism, antisemitism, racism, discrimination and human rights violations. This project is based on 'peer education': the CLO team trains students to give a guided tour of the exhibition for their classmates. The idea of the project is to present the story of Anne Frank, and to find links between historical and current forms of discrimination in contemporary society.

Students attend a two-day workshop and training on how to give a guided tour of the exhibition. They are also expected to discuss similarities between

---

8 Intercultural instruction refers to teaching that aims to improve understanding and tolerance of different cultures. CLO's approach to intercultural education is explained in more detail below.

historical and present-day forms of discrimination. Students are instructed to read the *Diary of Anne Frank* before attending the event. The observed workshop was held in Bratislava (at the end of April 2019) and was attended by 16 students from three high schools in the city. Two of the workshop instructors prepared a substantial programme of non-formal educational activities on anti-discrimination. There were two goals. First, the participants were encouraged to think about or even problematise their identities (ethnic, local, gender, political, religious, etc.); the instructors wanted to show the participants that identity is not stable, but flexible and fluid. The second goal was for the participants to realise that anyone can become the victim of discrimination, since people are targeted for different reasons (e.g. physical appearance, sexual preference, faith, supporting a particular team). The message the instructors wished to convey was that we are all different and any difference can potentially be considered dangerous by a collective. Since everyone is unique, one can never know which difference will be selected as the reason for discrimination.

In one game, students had to cross a line drawn on the floor depending on whether they agreed or disagreed with the instructor's statement (e.g. I'm Slovak; I'm a feminist; I like football). According to the instructors, this task helps students to realise that, depending on the criteria, everyone can be in the minority. In another activity, participants were asked to write a word on a label that other people had used to unfairly describe them. The students had to stick the label on their clothes so everyone could see it. They then had to introduce themselves using the negative word (e.g. wonk, bighead, dressy girl, crazy). The students were told that the goal of this 'exercise' was to help them to understand Anne Frank's situation: she was similarly identified (with a Star of David) and nobody was interested in the fact that she was a complex person with her own inner world. There is not enough space here to describe the workshop in detail, but the instructors mainly used experiential learning, dramatic methods, discussions and peer learning. The last few hours of the workshop were spent on practical preparations for the guided tours of the exhibition. Students had to learn the relevant historical facts, and were trained to present the topic in a fluent and interesting manner to the audience. Several weeks after the workshop, the exhibition's opening ceremony took place at the Comenius University arts faculty in Bratislava. The exhibition was opened by the Ambassador for the Netherlands. The guests of honour included representatives of local religious communities (Jewish, Christian and Muslim). Over the next month, the students gave guided tours of the exhibition to groups of visitors from elementary and high schools.

CLO is currently running four other educational projects (for youth and teachers). Two of these are about the Holocaust and two focus on totalitarian regimes and the relationship between memory and attitudes.

CLO is based in the Slovak capital of Bratislava, but collaborates with schools across the country to provide educational programmes for students and teachers. The organisational structure of CLO consists of an administrative board, the founders, internal and external workers, volunteers and, of course, the CLO programme participants. Most of CLO's funding comes from European Union projects.

Relativist universalism

As is apparent from the above, CLO's most important work is intercultural and anti-discrimination instruction. However, CLO instructors reject the belief (typically found in Slovak education policy and academic writing) that children and youth should be taught about *other* cultures, as that presupposes the dominant characteristic of *culture* is ethnicity or religion. As one of the CLO instructors stated,

> *We are trying to disrupt that kind of approach by using a transcultural approach. It takes the links between into account and the idea that every single individual is unique, that they can draw on for example an ethnically defined culture, but absorb different influences. [...] We don't avoid speaking about other cultures, but we don't see them as constant things but as conditioned by the long-established closed community which created the norms. [...] However, in instruction we follow a norm-critical approach. That means we question our norms and look at how norms are conditioned by the environment.* (Adam, practitioner, male, 39).

According to the CLO instructors, instead of using the term 'culture', they focus on identity, stereotypes, prejudices and views of diversity. Another CLO instructor stated that their courses were aimed at problematising concepts students do not question. The CLO instructors focus on deconstructing seemingly obvious concepts related to ethnicity, identity and culture (Eva, practitioner, female, 31). They call this *personality-based intercultural instruction*. Here, the emphasis is placed on personal experience and the characteristic nuances of each individual life story, which supersede collective criteria. This is conducted in "*a safe and controlled environment*" (Eva). The link between the tragic story of Anne Frank and stories of discrimination against real people today – the main idea of the exhibition – is an example of this method.

Our youth informants were very positive about the CLO approach. One female informant said: "*It was a great experience that opened my eyes*" (Barbora, young person, female, 15). Others stated that, thanks to the workshop, they had started to view "*things*" differently and had become more sensitive to discrimination. However, it is crucial to note that the workshop attendees were privileged children from elite high schools in the capital city, and that they had to write an essay about Anne Frank in order to be accepted into the workshop. In that sense, the organisers created conditions under which students interested in topics surrounding discrimination, the Holocaust and human rights were selected. Those who were not interested – or, even worse, who were interested in extremist ideologies – stayed at home.

When we asked the organisers if they thought it productive to try and persuade those who were likely already persuaded, they defended themselves by saying that the exhibition was predominantly based on the principles of 'peer learning'. This means that the beneficiaries or secondary target group of the project are primarily classmates, peers, friends or relatives, who will then have informal discussions with the young attendees of the CLO workshops (Adam, practitioner, male, 39).

However, our young informants, who were supposed to spread the CLO's message amongst their peers, did not entirely share the views of their instructors. To some degree, they articulated a constructivist approach to culture (and displayed an understanding of cultural dynamics), stating for instance that "*A culture is the people who create it*" (Katarina, young person, female, 17). The young interviewees suggested that we should respect all cultures, but many of them had negative attitudes towards migration and the 'mixing' of people from various cultural backgrounds.

Paradoxically, their arguments against 'mixing' relied on concepts and terms that are key to the CLO agenda: "*Discrimination against people, or even the aggressive oppression of people, is not mature. Developed people from developed cultures have no reason to do it*" (Katarina, young person, female, 17). Another informant said:

> *The Middle East has no place in Europe, because we have a totally different culture. Moreover, their culture tends to dominate. They have spread their culture to other people and cultures. And that is totally the opposite of what we are taught: 'Be kind to everyone and don't force people into things.' They are taught the opposite.* (Emil, young person, male, 16).

When we asked the instructor if the CLO covered cultural heritage, she immediately mentioned human rights (Eva, practitioner, female, 31). She referred to human rights as 'universal laws'. Suggesting that these are a product of Western culture and history, she considered that the concept is universal and should be upheld across the world. The paternalistic bias of this belief is aptly explained in Gayatri Chakravorty Spivak's *Righting Wrongs*:

> *Thus 'Human Rights' is not only about having or claiming a right or a set of rights; it is also about righting wrongs, about being the dispenser of these rights. The idea of human rights, in other words, may carry within itself the agenda of a kind of social Darwinism—the fittest must shoulder the burden of righting the wrongs of the unfit—and the possibility of an alibi.* (Spivak, 2004: pp. 523–4)

Eva is sceptical of spreading of human rights by force, since that approach has often failed. She thinks that the most effective solution is to educate people and support those trying to change their countries. When Eva was asked whether she implicitly said that shared European or Western knowledge was superior to the knowledge of those countries that did not develop the western concept of human rights, she responded:

> *In essence yes, I said that. I now think that human rights are the best thing we have, but that does not run counter to the fact that we can change our views, adjust or reform [them] and through dialogue with other countries we can figure out that maybe some things don't work as well as we thought. [...] So yes, I think there is a degree of superiority hidden behind my words, but I'm not against entering into dialogue with other countries in relation to what they consider right.* (Eva, practitioner, female, 31)

Despite her openness to dialogue with other types of societies, she did not deny that she regards the Western cultural appropriation (or in her terms cultural heritage) of the concept of human rights as superior to other socio-formative models. For Eva, discussion with other types of societies seemed to be possible only within the Western human rights framework. Although CLO states that respecting cultural differences and sharing cultural relativist attitudes to different customs is crucial, in a more detailed interview we detected bias in the organisation's thinking about particular cultural products and practices. The same bias was apparent in relation to the point of reference for interpreting different cultures and societies. The superiority of what is conceptualised as Western ideas of human rights, the stress on the need to distribute (culturally-determined and perhaps also power-based) knowledge to other countries, and the search for ways to implement the human rights agenda by using local agents in foreign countries are all principles underpinning colonial practices. As Spivak states:

> *Colonialism was committed to the education of a certain class. It was interested in the seemingly permanent operation of an altered normality. Paradoxically, human rights and 'development' work today cannot claim this self-empowerment that high colonialism could. Yet, some of the best products of high colonialism, descendants of the colonial middle class, become human rights advocates in the countries of the South.* (Spivak, 2004: pp. 524)

Therefore, there is a contradiction in the CLO's discourse: while on the one hand they insist on respect for different cultures, they are willing to participate in the establishment of a cultural hegemony based on human rights on the other. Similarly, some of the young participants viewed 'developed cultures' as those that respect different cultures, a view that mirrored that of the instructor, for whom 'developed cultures' were viewed through the concept of human rights. Human rights serve as an ideological source for the superior attitude towards cultures that, in the CLO´s view, are not established or do not practice liberal democracy.

However, while the CLO instructor provides non-formal education without paying much attention to the potential contradictions between the relativistic 'pro-diversity' approach and the universalism of the concept of human rights, in formal education the situation seems to be more deep-rooted. Critical academics claim that Slovakia's multicultural education policy is half-baked and *pro-forma;* the concepts are vaguely formulated; the ideas coming out of the ministry are cut off from the everyday reality in schools; and there is a lack of resources or technical support or guidance on the goals of education policy reform (See Petrasová, 2010). A teacher and informant who participated in Alena Chudžíková's ethnographic investigation into multicultural education practices in Slovak schools had the following to say:

> *In Slovakia, multicultural education has been reduced to the teaching of facts about other cultures. I think that if we teach children to respect other people, they don't need to know everything about their culture. Our multicultural education is merely about presenting other cultures. Let's teach them about the Roma flag and then they will better understand the Roma […] That teaching is not based on values but on knowledge of characteristic things. It does not help them to understand other cultures or understand why we should live with them. It is just stereotyping.* (Chudžíková, 2015: p. 18)

This case study points to the continuation of a common phenomenon in Slovakia that can be observed in all the 'pro-diversity' materials relating to the various research areas of the project (including academic writing about multicultural education, policy documents, curricula and formal instruction). While many of our interviewees – either on the personal or textbook level – adopted the vocabulary of multiculturalism and 'pro-diversity', detailed research at both the formal and non-formal education level showed that they had not internalised 'pro-diversity' attitudes.

Discussion

Using the data obtained from our field research among the leaders and participants of the two groups, we will now try to answer our initial research questions. The first research question (What is the emic meaning of the term *culture* in the group?) was about the notions of and general discourse about culture in each group. We can conclude that the two organisations take very different approaches to culture. The first group, the neo-pagan Slavic Natives, holds an essentialist view in which culture is inseparable from nature. Religion, or 'original, natural spirituality', should ideally serve as the bond between the two. In other words, culture was born out of a spiritual understanding and connection to nature, and should continue to evolve in that way. The charismatic leader of the group understood culture more broadly as 'everything we have inherited'. He did not exclude phenomena usually classified as belonging to the natural world (e.g. DNA, stomach enzymes, blood groups). Culture and ethnicity are, our analysis shows, 'coded' or latent natural features. To be a Slovak or Slav is not just about being socialised in a Slovak community, but is determined by biological conception and birth. People are born as members of a particular ethnic group and are bearers of that culture (or, rather, their blood is), as membership is biologically driven. The data obtained from the SN members contributes to the problematisation of the view (found in structuralist thought and elsewhere) of the nature–culture dichotomy. The scientific paradigm, according to which the culture/nature dichotomy is a crucial anthropological category, often points to the common cross-cultural phenomenon of members of a society describing it as a group of cultural beings and classifying 'others' as belonging to chaotic nature (see Levi-Strauss, 1999). This tendency is often linguistically expressed by comparing other groups to animals. Claude Levi-Strauss claims that humankind ends at the limits of the tribe, village or linguistic group, and many social groups are convinced that others do not share human virtues or human nature. These groups are called "human apes" or nits (Levi-Strauss, 1999: p. 16). The SN position contrasts with the structuralist one: nature is not chaotic and unpredictable, but has a valued order. The most authentic human virtues are those directly relating to the natural order, and valued cultures recognise that order. The superiority of a culture does not, therefore, depend on its distance from nature in civilization terms, but on its close contact with nature and commitment to its principles.

In contrast with the SN philosophy of biologically-defined cultural and ethnic essentialism, CLO occupies the opposite cultural relativist position. The CLO instructors rejected the notion that cultures are 'closed entities' inseparable from an ethnic or other collective category. They understood culture to be the result of various interactions, which are not limited to any collective category. Moreover, they emphasised the role of the individual in absorbing a range of cultural influences. According to the CLO instructors, cultures are mutually pervasive and influence each other. This is why the CLO's non-formal educational programme deconstructs, or at least problematises, collective categories and identities. While SN is about belonging to an ethnic group on the basis of nature and spirituality, CLO talks about belonging at the level of individual personal feelings. The intellectual thinking of CLO focuses on the social constructions of collective categories and encourages young people to adopt a 'norm-critical approach', which leads them to question the norms and 'truths' of their own culture. CLO representatives claimed that their approach crosses ethnic and religious cultural boundaries, calling this a 'transcultural approach'. This has two practical consequences. First, unlike in SN, where the available cultural sources for constructing young people's worldviews and identity are ethnically-defined, in CLO individuals can look for the potential sources of their own identities out of their ethnically or religiously defined 'box'. This is not necessarily limited to a mono-ethnic family and history, and represents a geographical area in which country and ethnic borders overlap, as is the case in Central Europe thanks to intercultural dialogue and coexistence. Second, CLO leaders draw on this transcultural approach when they criticise education about *other cultures*. According to CLO instructors, that approach, which is common in formal and non-formal education in Slovakia, reinforces the narrow understanding that cultures are the product of particular ethnic groups and fosters existing stereotypes.

Here we can see the clear distinction between the two dominant approaches to culture and cultural diversity in Slovak pedagogic theory. The first, represented by prominent Slovak theorist of multicultural education Erich Mistrík, is based on the notion that culture is stable and monolithic. In short, to achieve intercultural tolerance, the education system has to provide students with knowledge and experience related to *other cultures* (Mistrík, 2009: p. 92). Hence, people 'in' these cultures are passively captured within them. CLO instructors, along with advocates of the second approach, are critical of this view of culture and diversity. A younger generation of academics argues that a discourse that defines cultures as stable and discrete entities with clearly-marked boundaries has more risks than benefits because it creates borders between groups rather than spaces for mutual interaction and coexistence (Gállová-Kriglerová, 2009: p. 12).

However, there is a surprising similarity between SN and CLO. Despite the cultural relativism and respect for cultural differences (and relativisation) articulated by CLO and the young participants, our interviews revealed biases in the way cultures are compared and judged. While the spiritual tie with nature was the reference point used by SN members when comparing and judging other cultures, data from CLO informants shows that they also rely on *criteria* for classifying and judging cultures or societies. These criteria or referential points related to human rights and respect for other cultures, and for some CLO informants was crucial. For some young informants, only those societies that observed human rights and respected others were developed cultures. Those that did not were categorised as 'underdeveloped'. One of the CLO's non-formal education programme leaders exhibited a similar bias when she admitted that she considered Western knowledge on human rights superior to that of societies where human rights were not important. The cultural relativist position appears not to be as rigid as proclaimed and as it initially seemed. Respect for other cultures is limited by the perceived ability of others to respect difference. The belief that all cultures are equal is undermined by the belief that the Western cultural appropriation of human rights is superior. As we can see, cultural relativism can also become relative. This relativity can perhaps be grasped through Bruno Latour's 'particular universalism':

> *One society – and it is always the Western one – defines the general framework of Nature*[9] *with respect to which the others are situated. This is Levi-Strauss's solution: he distinguishes Western society, which has a specific interpretation of Nature, from that Nature itself, miraculously known to our society. The first half of the argument allows for modest relativism (we are just one interpretation among others), but the second permits the surreptitious return of arrogant universalism – we remain absolutely different.* (Latour, 1993: p. 105)

The privileged position of the Western cultural product of human rights, as articulated by the CLO representative, can be explained using Latour's 'grand Western narrative'. This is based on the belief that the West is set apart from other cultures due to its privileged access to (the 'knowledge' of) Nature (ibid.). CLO is relativist when comparing cultures with their, as one might say, Latourian Natures, in the sense of 'non-human' natural and cultural products. The CLO's relativism is enabled by bracketing the cultural product of human rights. When we have to consider other cultures in terms of human rights, this criterion is no longer bracketed and the CLO worldview suddenly becomes universalistic or, as Latour would probably say, "particular universalistic". In other words, while

9 For Latour, Nature does not necessarily mean nature alone, but the whole range of 'non-human entities.' Consequently, Nature is not the same as the natural science conception of nature, but is about understanding the ontological essence of the world of *things-in-itself*.

SN does not make a nature–culture distinction, the CLO holds that 'developed' cultures must consistently be set a distance apart from natures (and Natures) that could negatively affect the pursuit of human rights, which has become possible thanks only to 'developed' cultures' privileged Knowledge of the world of things.

Our second research question was designed to identify the criteria used to select the elements from the past that represent cultural heritage within each group.

SN informants highlighted elements from the past that gave evidence of their belief that their Slavic ancestors had a connection with nature. These SN members searched for spiritual meanings in tangible and intangible artifacts of Slovak and Slavic folk culture. They, especially their leader Veleslav, not only interpreted such artifacts in terms of 'natural spirituality', but also introduced new practices that took spiritual inspiration from the original and 'pure source', according to the leader. That is, the leader's reflections help to connect the spiritual source for the most authentic interpretations of historic cultural elements and at the same time guarantee that the newly-invented practices, words or rituals reflect the 'original culture of the ancestors.' This phenomenon can be explained using the concept of *invented tradition*, which Hobsbawm defines as

> *a set of practices, normally governed by overtly or tacitly accepted rules and of a ritual or symbolic nature, which seek to inculcate certain values and norms of behaviour by repetition, which automatically implies continuity with the past. In fact, where possible, they normally attempt to establish continuity with a suitable historic past.* (Hobsbawm, 1983: p. 1)

The instrumental function of inventing tradition is apparent in SN's case. It affirms the leader's authority (as a channel for the paradoxical historical *authenticity* of his innovations and inventions) and legitimises the group's existence and – again – its historical authenticity. The absence of face-to-face intergenerational transmission of the ancient Slavic tradition is substituted with knowledge of literature about the Slavs, which has to be confirmed by the tradition. In this context, continuity is not easily identified but exists within a hidden spiritual source. This provides Veleslav with inspiration for his invented traditions and consequently lends them sufficient credibility to be adopted by his followers.

However, there is a relatively strict set of criteria for selecting and actualising elements from the past for present purposes. Veleslav selects and decides which elements fit into the group's practices and which should be excluded. Selected elements must have originated in Slovak or Slavic folk cultural heritage. This ethnic principle excludes many elements of Slovak folk culture that were first introduced or sustained by non-Slovak/non-Slavic groups. However, SN members can accept exceptions that are not of Slovak/Slavic origin but are considered useful to their practice. Generally, elements that fulfil the second condition for selection – natural origin – can be integrated. The ethnic origin requirement excludes non-Slovak and non-Slavic elements from SN's conception of folk cultural heritage, while the natural requirement excludes elements of folk heritage belonging to the urban classes on the grounds that this culture was not sufficiently connected to nature. It is worth noting that this view is a variation of the dominant Slovak discourse that the Slovaks are a nation of peasants and shepherds, an idea that is reproduced culturally and politically, especially through the formal education system (see Bagalová and Lehocký, 2020).

As we can see, there are two major criteria for selecting the elements to be actualised and re-interpreted by SN. These criteria often serves as a means of excluding a particular historical element, but occasionally the natural origin criteria can be used to include elements that do not fit the ethnic origin criteria. Moreover, since Veleslav claims that "*cultural heritage is everything we have inherited, all the good and bad customs*", elements that are considered bad have to be excluded from the concept of folk culture (or what is left of this once other ethnic groups and the urban classes have been disregarded). Veleslav gives the example of the Slovak 'tradition' of drinking alcohol to excess.

As already noted, SN members mainly (re)construct their visions of cultural heritage practices from literature (ethnographic, historical, archaeological, linguistic). Therefore, the SN begin their 'heritage in the making' when spiritually contemplating certain books.

While SN members emphasised the constitutive role of folk culture and folklore in cultural heritage, the CLO instructor believed that developing folklore is pointless. She stated that the glorification of folklore has no useful application in the current era, and explained that nowadays nobody performs folk traditions in their authentic form. The same instructor thought that there was much more inspiration to be found in folk uprisings against landowners and the Habsburg monarchs, because these historical events can be used to discuss the conditions under which citizens have the right to resist the government. As noted above, this CLO instructor believes that the most precious cultural heritage artifact is the achievement of human rights. For the CLO leaders, human rights and civil liberties are the criteria to be used for selecting elements from the past that are worth actualising. Our CLO instructor even wondered whether the aesthetic appeal of old dances or crafts was enough to be considered part of cultural heritage or sufficient reason for conserving folklore (Eva, practitioner, female, 31). However, another CLO instructor thought there was a good reason to conserve folklore. Although critical of reducing culture to folklore (which is very common in Slovak educational practice and public discourse), he thought folk events were occasions for people to experience their local identity. He stated that 'cultural heritage' was not a common expression in his vocabulary, but that he recognised the values of humanism and democracy and thought them an accurate representation of cultural heritage – a similar principle to his colleague's. The young participants of the CLO workshop did not entirely adopt this viewpoint; they thought folklore and folk culture (along with historical architecture) were the most accurate representations of cultural heritage. Their characterisation of folk culture was vague and limited to artifacts like costumes, songs or dances. This reflects findings from our research on formal education settings (see Bagalová and Lehocký, 2020).

Our third research question was about how constructions of the past and cultural heritage are actualised for each group's present purposes and agenda. In SN, rituals are the main means of actualising past cultural heritage (as developed through SN ideology). Ritual practices are also used to disseminate SN discourse and knowledge. Participants play an active role in the rituals, performing them as designed by Veleslav. These rituals, which take place several times a year, on occasions including the summer or winter solstices or the welcoming of spring, are means of explaining the broad thematic scope of SN ideology. Participants are presented with topics such as SN cosmology, ecology, spirituality, the nation, policy and social issues. Veleslav's songs are an effective tool for communicating SN messages about such issues and form an integral part of the rituals. For example, one song invokes the god Rod and implicitly asking him to revitalise the nation.

The American anthropologist Clifford Geertz identified two aspects of religion. Religion, and especially religious rituals, provide a *model of reality* and a *model for reality.* While the model of reality is based on "*the manipulation of symbol structures so as to bring them, more or less closely, into parallel with the pre-established nonsymbolic system*", the model for reality is based on "*the manipulation of the nonsymbolic systems in terms of the relationships expressed in the symbolic*". Therefore, the model of reality provides the theory or model "*under whose guidance physical relationships are organized*" (Geertz, 1973: p. 93). We can describe the instrumental and, most importantly, the non-formal education function of SN rituals using Geertz's terms. Essentially, the SN's religious rituals provide participants with symbolic sources that help them to organise their (re)interpretation of the non-symbolical world around them (e.g. cosmology or principles of nature) and consequently offer symbolic meanings for their actions in the world; meanings are thus subjected to the SN interpretation. The SN rituals provide participants with a theory of the world and symbolic manual for future behaviour in the world. They are highly effective in fulfilling a non-formal educational function by offering both a theoretical explanation of the world and practical advice on how to live. Moreover, the rituals enhance the effect of non-formal education through the intense collective emotional and spiritual experience of the participants. For our informants, participation in the rituals is their contribution to the continuation of the remnants of Slavic spirituality. These rituals are a means of engaging with an exclusive community of those continuing the old tradition, those who carry the old wisdom into the current era. They also represent models for interpreting cultural heritage and for living in the present and future in accordance with the symbolic messages of this (constructed) heritage.

Interpretations of the past have practical consequences for the lifestyle of SN members. They often wear clothes made of natural materials that are similar to 'Slavic' clothing; they perform personal and collective rituals and exercises recommended by Veleslav; they play traditional musical instruments and learn traditional crafts; they grow organic products; they prefer natural medicines to modern western ones; they leave the cities, buying land to farm or joining existing farm communities. Our informants try to live in harmony with nature and their 'original' culture, and – as a quote from an informant earlier showed – they consider this to be cultural heritage.

The SN members' adherence to their interpretations of the past affects their civic life. They are actively engaged in ecological issues, participating in campaigns against hunting or deforestation in Slovakia. They are also involved in an initiative to propagate and teach people about traditional crafts, agriculture and breeding farm animals.

According to the CLO instructors, those past moments that are worth actualising are related to the development of civil liberties, human rights, democracy and intercultural tolerance. Their actualisations of the past mainly relate to commemorating historical events or eras that CLO interprets as conveying useful messages from the past. A good example is the exhibition and workshop *The Diary of Anne Frank – historical message for the present day*. The way the exhibition was conceived illustrates how notions of the past are connected to the CLO's current purposes. The exhibition, depicting the life story and inner world of a young Jewish girl under the Nazi regime, ends with panels about the life stories of members of minorities in Europe today (e.g. a Muslim girl, a man with disabilities, a transgender woman). Present-day discrimination against minorities and the failure to acknowledge their unique personalities and inner worlds is, according to our informants, the central idea that connects the past with the present. CLO leaders select historical events and eras appropriate for guided commemoration, especially those involving dramatic confrontations between the individual and the socio-political system. They usually choose stories of the Second World War, fascism or communism. Individuals defending human rights and civil liberties in the totalitarian era offer a sufficient number of role models for young people participating in the CLO's programmes. The focus on eras when there was little respect for human rights and civil liberties aims to cultivate a deeper appreciation of the socio-political circumstances of young people's lives, as well as an awareness that democracy is vulnerable and has to be constantly protected. Actualising the past for present purposes is a systematic part of CLO's work with youth. CLO leaders call this *memory education*.

The last research question is about how the group's construction of cultural heritage affects the identity of its members and their feelings of belonging to a collective.

Amongst SN informants, we observed intense demonstrations of ethnic identity. A clear line can be drawn connecting the organisation's interiorised discourse about history and cultural heritage and the growing ethnic identity of the young people. This process of reinforcing Slovak/Slavic identity begins with the young people discovering hidden and spiritual meanings (constructed or even invented by Veleslav) in traditional folk culture. After their first meetings with Veleslav, the young spiritual seekers suddenly discover that the 'boring' folk culture widely propagated by state cultural and educational institutions, appreciated only by 'backward pensioners from the countryside', has deep spiritual meaning. They come to realise that there is no need to search for wisdom in foreign cultures or 'exotic' religious traditions, as their country has enough cultural heritage of its own. Young SN members no longer feel the need to admire the imposing history of the pagan Vikings or the ancient spiritual traditions of India. Under the influence of Veleslav and his followers, they learn that pre-Christian Slavic culture was just as rich as that of the Vikings, and that Indo-European Slavs and Slovaks are the direct heirs of the Vedic Indian tradition. The usually unexpected depth of their own folk culture elicits greater appreciation for Slovak folk culture; the young people start to feel proud of Slovak traditions and gain a greater sense of belonging to the Slovaks and Slavs.

SN youths demonstrate their sense of belonging to the Slovak ethnic group by wearing traditional clothes, using 'purist' language with no calques and living a lifestyle reminiscent of the imagined lives of their ancestors. However, they still use modern technology such as computers, cars and mobile phones. They claim that these modern achievements are good if used within reason and for good purposes. Despite strongly identifying with their ethnic group, these young people are unable to identify with modern Slovaks and their lifestyle, which they see as "detached from nature and their cultural and spiritual roots".

Instead, young SN members seek their place in the world by identifying with an idealised group that is more about the past than the present and more imagined than real. SN members are a classic example of Benedict Anderson's 'imagined community', which is bound together not through daily face-to-face contact but by reading the same materials (namely Veleslav's books and webpages) and listening to the same music (see Anderson, 2006). The only direct personal contact SN members have with one another is at the rituals and workshops. Like the large groups described by Anderson, small religious groups require techniques or ideology to connect the members of the virtual community. What connects this particular imagined community is the construction of a historical community of ancestors, predecessors or forebears, which strengthens the identity of the community members. This type of community thus has what is known as an 'invented tradition', which binds the SN members together as an imagined community of the living and the dead.

In contrast to the SN members, whose identity is captured in the group's specific construction of cultural heritage and *idealised past*, the CLO discourse relies on a *demonised past*, which generally cannot offer a positive collective that is worth identifying with. The axiological reference points for the demonised past are where it deviates from its ethos. These deviations are not represented through ethnically or religiously framed collectives, but through the resistance of individuals to the socio-political ethos of their era. CLO proffers life stories as an example for young people to follow. While SN idealises the historical collective of Slavs or 'Ancient Slovaks', CLO tends to offer a demonised picture of historical collectives and an idealised portrait of historical individuals. Their instruction methods build this picture exclusively from the historical person's relationship to the regime or ethos of the time, which may be a reductive perspective of history. While SN discourse encourages its members to identify with historical collectives and with the past, CLO discourse encourages its participants to maintain a safe distance from their 'own' history. In SN the word 'own' is accentuated, and in CLO it is questioned and relativised.

However, we observed a difference in the extent to which the young people adopted each organisation's discourse. In CLO there was a greater divide between the answers given by the young respondents and those of their leaders than in SN. This can be explained by the fact that SN has a charismatic leader and by the nature of the community, whose members are in close, frequent, intense contact with one another. Meanwhile, CLO generally organises temporary groups that last only until the end of each educational programme and workshop. There was a notable discrepancy between the discourse of CLO instructors and the attitudes of the young participants in articulating ethnic identity. Belonging to the Slovak ethnic group seemed to be more important for the CLO youth than the instructors. It is worth noting that, in most cases, CLO members overtly rejected nationalism. However, nationalist tendencies were observed in responses to questions on controversial topics such as the Muslim community's position in Slovakia. It is hard to tell whether the 'soft' demonstrations of ethnic identity and efforts to be 'politically correct' are a result of the CLO's work with youth, or, more likely, because the informants who attended the CLO workshop came from the best high schools in the capital and were selected on the basis of an essay.

Conclusion

Our research focused on how discourses about culture, cultural heritage, identity and cultural diversity are disseminated in non-formal instruction. We selected two groups with contrasting approaches to these concepts. The first was the neo-pagan Slavic group *Slavic Natives,* which has formed around its charismatic leader and founder Veleslav. *Slavic Natives* focuses on the Slavic and Slovak ethnic identities of its members and claims to follow the "original spirituality of Ancient Slavs." The link between religion or spirituality and the strong sense of ethnic identity generates a specific nationalist discourse "*hyperbolized to cosmic proportions*" (see Bakić-Hayden, 2004: p. 34). SN members reject multiculturalism on principle and are critical of the European Union.

The second group, *Civil Liberties Organisation,* adopts a contrasting 'pro-diversity' approach. Its main activities are teaching human rights and democracy, social inclusion, discrimination, cultural diversity and memory. CLO members reject nationalism and encourage educational programme participants to be critical of their own cultural norms and to problematise identity.

These groups sometimes represent very contradictory attitudes, but also share commonalities, mostly in the way the non-formal educational practices are organised. In both groups, talks are just one part of the instructional process, and apparently not the most important part. Frequently, ideological content is transmitted through collective games or exercises designed to promote introspective and experience-based understanding of the issue being contemplated, alongside creative activities and even rituals. Through these activities, the leaders of both groups convey to the young participants specific interpretations of the surrounding world and thereby specific cultural literacies and worldviews.

The data gained from the participant observations and interviews in both groups has revealed significant patterns. Looking at emic meanings of culture, we realised that there is no strict nature/culture dichotomy in the SN community. For SN members, culture is on a continuum with nature, which is moderated by spirituality. SN discourse holds that cultures in close contact with nature are more developed and valuable than cultures disconnected from it. Culture includes elements that are part of natural phenomena, from the etic viewpoint at least. Consequently, SN's cultural essentialism is biological in nature – culture and ethnicity are to be found in DNA and blood cells.

In contrast, CLO adopts a cultural relativist and constructivist position. CLO leaders reject outright the idea that culture should be approached through collective categories such as ethnicity or religion. CLO members stressed that culture has the potential to overlap and that the individual plays a role in drawing together different cultural influences. However, the data indicates that the rhetorical cultural relativism of CLO is limited, since we observed that 'human rights' and 'intercultural tolerance' are, according to CLO's practice, emphasised as privileged cultural products that assert superiority over cultures assumed not to have these concepts.

SN and CLO also differ in how they work with the past and cultural heritage. SN members construct an idealised Ancient Slav/Slovak past and add spiritual references to various tangible and intangible artifacts of Slavic and Slovak folk culture. In fact, SN members worship the cult of cultural heritage. They actualise an imagined continuity with their Slavic ancestors, predominantly through rituals and practices invented by the group's leader. Such *invented traditions*, which Veleslav presents as the products of spiritual inspiration, are generally accepted in the group and are considered to exhibit the authentic spiritual meaning of the Ancient Slavic faith.

While SN produces and uses idealised versions of the past and historical collectives, CLO demonises the past and idealises individuals. CLO's educational focus is on working with historical materials and stories from aspects of the totalitarian regimes and their morally corrupted collectives; this organisation's programmes glorify strong individuals who resisted the collective ethos of the time to fight for human rights and civil liberties.

The cases of CLO and SN confirm that multiple pasts can coexist within a single contemporaneity. For SN followers, the past is an idealised dream of harmony with nature and its spirits, and they do their best to re-actualise this image. Meanwhile, for CLO members the past is a nightmare, with demons whose return should be prevented. However, both groups – intuitively or rationally – understand that whoever masters history will conquer the future.

References

Anderson, B. (2006) *Imagined Communities: Reflections on the Origins and Spread of Nationalism*. London: Verso.

Bagalová, M. and Lehocký Ľ. (2020) 'Cultural literacy in formal education (Slovakia)' In T. Zurabishvili and Elina Marmer (eds.), *Country based Reports: Cultural Literacy in Formal Education,* Cultural Heritage and Identities of Europe's Future (Grant Agreement No: 770464). European Commission, pp. 214–248.

Bakić-Hayden, M. (2004) 'National memory as narrative memory, The case of Kosovo'. In M. Todorova (ed.), *Balkan Identities: Nation and Memory*, pp. 25–40. London: Hurst.

Chudžíková, A. (2015) *Budúci učitelia budúcej multikultúrnej školy.* Bratislava: Centrum pre výskum etnicity a kultúry.

Eriksen, T. H. (2008) Sociální a kulturní antropologie, Praha: Portál.

Gállová-Kriglerová, E. (2009) 'Kultúrna rozmanitosť'. In E. Gállová-Kriglerová and J. Kadlečíková (eds.), *Kultúrna rozmanitosť a jej vnímanie žiakmi základných škôl na Slovensku,* pp. 12–26. Bratislava: Centrum pre výskum etnicity a kultúry.

Geertz, C. (1973) *Interpretation of Cultures.* New York: Basic Books, Inc., Publishers.

Graham, B., Ashworth, G. J., and Tunbridge, J. E. (2005) 'The uses and abuses of heritage'. In G. Corsane (ed.), Heritage, Museums, and Galleries, pp. 26–37. London, Routledge.

Hobsbawm, E. (1983) 'Introduction: Inventing Traditions'. In E. Hobsbawm and T. Ranger (eds.), *The Invention of Traditions*, pp. 1–14. Cambridge: Cambridge University Press.

Latour, B. (1993) *We Have Never Been Modern.* Cambridge, MA: Harvard University Press.

Lévi-Strauss, L. (1999) *Rasa a dejiny.* Praha: Atlantis.

Milla, M. (2008) *Hlinkova mládež 1938–1945.* Bratislava: Ústav pamäti národa.

Mistrík, E. (2009) 'Odporúčania pre prípravu učiteľov'. In. E. Gállová-Kriglerová and J. Kadlečíková (eds.), *Kultúrna rozmanitosť a jej vnímanie žiakmi základných škôl na Slovensku*, pp. 91–95. Bratislava: Centrum pre výskum etnicity a kultúry.

Petrasová, A. (2010) 'Realizácia multikultúrnej výchovy v základných a stredných školách'. In *Cesta ku vzdelaniu*, pp. 76–88. Zvolen: Quo Vadis.

Puchovský, M. (2017) 'Vedomec na rozhlasových vlnách: Prípadová štúdia významu novopohanského rozhlasového cyklu Rodná cesta v kontexte dejín slovenského rozhlasového vysielania'. *Sacra*, 15 (1), 17–34.

Spivak, C. G. (2004) 'Righting Wrongs'. *The South Atlantic Quarterly*, 103 (2/3), 523–581.

(by Rati Shubladze and Anano Kipiani)

Chapter 7 Attempts of simultaneous preservation and modernization of traditional Georgian culture: Observation of martial arts and folk-dance groups in Tbilisi

Abstract: The paper discusses how non-formal education settings understand traditional Georgian culture and facilitate its preservation. More specifically, the focus of the study lies in young people aged 14–25 years in two different settings: a Georgian national dance studio and a Georgian martial arts group. The key finding of the study is that the observed young Georgians unanimously interpreted culture as something related to history, tradition and etiquette. The interpretation of Georgian culture in this context is predominantly ethno-religious in nature, meaning that only 'ethnic Georgian' and orthodox Christian cultural artifacts are usually associated with Georgian culture. Beyond this, young people try to reinterpret and modify existing cultural norms and practices in their own ways. Sometimes they do not mind 'borrowing' knowledge and traditions from cultures they define as foreign if this would 'enrich' what they consider to be Georgian culture. This process is carried out using bricolage – taking pieces of international and local culture and making new, hybrid versions of cultural practices. Nevertheless, for the interviewed young people, it was important to stay within the context of what they believed to be the core values of Georgian culture and the preservation of 'Georgianness'. These non-formal education settings provide opportunities to engage in cultural acquisition and engagement, as long as the participants declare alignment with the 'core Georgian values'. Non-formal education settings are also important for providing space for practicing culture in 'its natural environment', as formal education settings often lack orientation on the practice while engaging with cultural topics.

Keywords: bricolage, cultural modernization, cultural preservation, non-formal education

Introduction

The goal of this research was to identify how non-formal education settings influence young people's cultural acquisition, as well as how they facilitate the preservation and modification of traditional cultural practices. According to the DVV[1] International Georgia Country Office report (2017), participation levels

1 DVV International is the Institute for International Cooperation of the Deutscher Volkshochschul-Verband e.V. (DVV), a German organisation that works in adult education.

of Georgia's general adult population in non-formal education is low. The first appearance of non-formal education in the legislation domain goes back to 2011, when it was mentioned in the context of accrediting non-formal education within regulated vocational education (Order of Minister of Georgia, document number 8/ნ). Elaboration of this legislation and further public policy documents concentrated on vocational education, lifelong education and the validation of non-formal and informal learning (NECE, 2015). The only legislative issue related to the non-formal education in the context of youth is 2014's Youth National Policy, which defines this as *"any scheduled, voluntary programme of individual and social education, which is not part of the formal educational programmes and is designed to develop competencies (knowledge, skills, and attitudes)"* (The Georgian National Youth Policy Document, 2014). Non-formal education in the Georgian context lacks a grassroot approach whereby non-formal education groups are self-organised, interest-driven and operate independently from education institutions, both government and non-government funded. The majority of the non-formal education activities facilitated by the state and non-governmental actors focus on the development of employability skills and, to a lesser extent, on civic education. The challenges described in the situation analysis of the non-formal education settings in Georgia by the NECE (2015) were their concentration on the urban areas (including rural settings close to urban areas), and the fact that activities are mostly driven by donors or NGOs rather than requested by the communities and young people.

Before explaining the reasons behind selecting the observed non-formal education settings and presenting the essential findings, it is important to describe how *culture* was perceived in the context of this study. The researchers never provided participants with any explicit definition of the term. This was done deliberately, so that interviewees were not bound to specific definitions of culture, but had to develop their own interpretation and understanding. Thus, the perceptions of culture and the spectrum of cultural activities listed in the text are entirely derived from respondents' points of view.

The role of non-formal education in cultural practices is underrepresented in the Georgian policy and academia. This research tried to fill those gaps. The purpose of initiating the study was to understand how non-formal educational sites create and transmit culture through working with young people. A typical case sampling approach was chosen to identify non-formal education groups. As Patton (2002) suggests, this method ensures the selection of the most 'average' case from all possible options (Ritchie et al., 2013). Two non-formal educational settings, both self-organised and focused on cultural heritage, were selected based on the researchers' perceptions of the most widespread non-formal educational settings in Georgia. The interviewed traditional dance and martial arts performers strongly associated their activities with the country's cultural heritage. In Georgian society, too, those fields are also predominantly perceived as essential parts of Georgian national cultural heritage. The sites include one of the most well-known dance companies in Georgia and a group of young people practicing traditional Georgian martial arts. Both groups are based in the capital city, Tbilisi. Though they both aim to preserve aspects of culture they consider to be traditionally Georgian, each organisation performs its mission differently, thus making it possible to observe different approaches to non-formal cultural education.

The concept of 'Georgianness' or 'ethnic Georgian identity' is an essential factor to consider while examining and interpreting the study outcomes. Being Georgian is often given ethnolinguist and religious dimensions: Georgian literature and history, and subsequently the school curricula, strongly connect Georgian identity with Orthodox Christianity, having Georgian parents and speaking Georgian as a native tongue (Mindiashvili et al., 2016; Khoshtaria et al., 2018; Tabatadze et al., 2020). The elements of Georgian national heritage, or any understanding of what is 'Georgian' or not, are therefore understood through this lens. This is important to consider when reading the quotes and remarks by young people.

The chosen dance company is one of the country's leading cultural organisations, with a long history of collaboration and support from the state. Such collectives have been described as embodying 'invented tradition', a term coined by Hobsbawm and Ranger (1983, cited in Shay, 1999). Since its formation, the dance company has been part of mainstream traditional and popular culture; despite many innovative experiments with traditional Georgian dance, it is widely accepted as part of the country's culture (Chincharauli, 2014; Kadagidze, 2015). The Georgian martial arts group is less conventional and more of a grassroots organisation. While the dance company has a long history, dating back to the Soviet era, organised groups like the selected martial arts association only started to emerge in the 1990s. Usually self-organised and without much publicity, such groups conducted ethnographic expeditions to rural and mountainous areas of Georgia to recover old martial arts traditions and techniques (Navrozashvili, 2015). In this regard, the selected martial arts site is a scion of the larger Georgian martial arts movement, which is more subculture than an established means of preserving and transmitting Georgian culture.

The non-formal educational settings studied in this chapter have similarities and differences in terms of their understanding of culture, thematic scope, missions, and target groups. The dance company is well-established, with a strong institutional legacy as a non-formal educational setting associated with mainstream Georgian culture. In comparison, the martial arts group is a relatively new, small non-formal educational organisation with less visibility and public presence. The following subchapters will present the key descriptive findings per site.

Case 1: Dance group

Site description

The selected dance company was one of the first professional state dance ensembles in Georgia. Like many of the State Dance Companies established under the Soviet Union, the company sought to create a national ballet founded upon the traditions of folk dance. Its work became widely popular, promoting the traditions of Georgian dance throughout the country and overseas. Dances were both influenced by and themselves influenced Georgia's cultural heritage. The dance company is well-known not only in Georgia but outside the country, predominantly in the post-communist space. The academy has subdivisions to teach ballet, 'traditional' and 'modern' Georgian dance, and traditional dances from other countries. After the dissolution of the Soviet Union, the family members of the founders managed the dance company independently.

The dance company has a reputation for innovation, having created a number of different dances in the second half of the 20th century. Its current artistic director seeks to uphold the ensemble's history of innovation, regularly working on the creation of new dances, which sometimes become subject to intense discussion in Georgia. They also sometimes use arranged versions of older Georgian dance music combined with more international instruments. The dance company organised two well-acclaimed projects that are, as was reported by both young people and practitioners, modern visualisations of Georgian folk dances.

The studio affiliated with the company offers a range of classes to students, including Georgian and international folk dance, ballet, ballroom dance, modern dance, gymnastics and Zumba. New ensemble recruits are drawn from the studio, with new members entering the company at around 20 years of age as interns.[2] Interns join the company's principal performers on stage at corporate events, festivals and regular stage shows, in addition to joining tours abroad. The

2 Interns, in the context of the dance company, are people who work for free, with the hope of gaining experience and potentially a job in the academy.

studio also provides amateur classes, which do not have age limitations. Many former dancers stay and work in the organisation as tutors or in an administrative capacity.

The group of interns consists of young people of all genders, mostly under the age of 25. For this group, the non-formal education setting is rather formal, led by experienced instructors identifying as female and male. The instructors are typically former members of the ensemble, although at times classes may be led by current performers. Observations showed that trainers were strict and actively involved throughout the entire practice session. Training is intense and each session lasts about 3 hours, 3–4 times a week. Young people in the intern group mostly wear tight-fitting black outfits, and some dancers need to continuously control their weight. While exercising, members who identify as female typically wear a black scarf as a skirt around skinny leggings, in order to feel more covered. However, this practice is not mandatory.

The amateur dance group is comprised entirely of young women. The dance academy administrators and tutors reported that "men dance only for special occasions if they are not professionals," and thus the studio offers their services to women only. Training lasts for 1.5 hours three times a week. The amateur trainer is a graduate of the dance academy and currently an intern. She leads two groups of amateurs – beginners and experienced dancers – both of which contain participants aged up to 55. Despite limited opportunities in this regard, most of the young amateurs hope they will be noticed by academy heads and asked to join the ensemble. Older members of the group are typically former professionals from other ensembles or amateur enthusiasts.

Being part of 'Georgian cultural heritage' as a motivation for practicing

The so-called 'national dance' is considered a major part of Georgian identity, often framed as "Georgian cultural heritage". Most respondents reported studying folk dance in their childhood, although not necessarily at this dance company. Respondents also frequently noted that, whilst they loved to dance, taking lessons was often their parents' decision. Amateur group members had less frequently danced in their childhood, but reported wanting to keep themselves close to the activity that makes them happy. All of them wanted to improve their dance skills, with the innovative versions of folk dances a popular reason for engagement. Many cited the skill of professional performers and the prestige of the company as a motivating factor: *"[Dance company name] has the best practitioners"* (Lika, female, young people).

For interns, dance has become a lifestyle; most of them joined this dance company because *"[it] is one of the lead folk ensembles which promotes Georgian dance"* (Toma, male, young people). Young people from both groups, as well as practitioners, mentioned that being part of this ensemble was their childhood dream. Many practitioners also expressed great pleasure in teaching others, sharing their knowledge and receiving positive feedback from students and peers.

Respondents were overwhelmingly positive about their experiences, and many of them felt that this community is perfect without any need for change. Young people in the study appreciated both the company's contemporary approach to performance of Georgian dances and its stewardship of traditional dance. They were also overwhelmingly enthusiastic about dance itself, describing it as pleasurable and interesting, despite the inflexible rehearsal schedule. They highlighted the role played by the practitioners in the training process, praising their ability to create a friendly and engaging atmosphere during classes.

> *The choreographers give us the freedom to dance in our own style. This freedom makes me love the [dance company] more than any other company, and makes me not want to miss lessons.* (Sopo, female, young people)

The amateur respondents valued their learning experience, with many reporting that better understanding Georgian traditions and the stories behind the dances has allowed them to better express themselves onstage. Young people in the intern group shared similar sentiments, and also highlighted the opportunities for international travel and learning.

Practitioners understood the amateurs' efforts and their positive attitudes towards the dance ensemble community, and sought to sustain this enthusiasm by offering additional activities:

> *It is bad that amateur groups are not able to attend gymnastics, world dances, ballet, and acting classes. [...] Therefore, I choreographed Spanish dance for their performance.* (Nino, female, practitioner)

All young people interviewed reported that they planned to continue their lessons with the dance company, and expressed hope that, with sufficient study and practice, they might be able to join the full ensemble. Whilst interns may well join the troupe as full members, and indeed do participate in concerts, some practitioners were dismissive of amateurs' hopes:

They do not have a chance [...], because they are older, and do not have applicable background. One must be the highest-level professional with nice looks. (Tsisana, female, practitioner)[3]

Intra-organisational culture in the dance group

Practitioners expressed pride in the dance company's originality of approach, with respondents reporting that they never imitate others, and always work to create something new yet influenced and guided by traditional elements. This blending of innovative approaches and traditional themes provides a complex dilemma for the organisation. On the one hand, respondents reported that there is the expectation for the ensemble to be innovative, but on the other they receive lot of criticism about such innovations when new approaches are tried. However, practitioners felt confident that, with time, experimental interpretations are usually accepted by the public: *"After several months or years, those dances always become hits"* (Nino, female, practitioner).

The practitioners believed that the ensemble's activities are more popular among young people now than previously, which is evidenced by the opening of five new branches in the capital over the last couple of years. Respondents felt that the mixture of 'traditional' and 'modern' approaches may play a key role in the ensemble's continued success. Young people from both the amateur and intern groups suggested that the aim of the dance company is to promote Georgian culture among young Georgians and to export it to the whole world. They noted that conducting cultural events is one of the main ways to commercialise Georgia's cultural heritage. Practitioners likewise mentioned that one of the main goals of the dance company is to spread Georgian culture across the world.

Dance group community as a family

The interviewed practitioners were proud of their role in sharing Georgian culture with future generations. Furthermore, they adore working with amateurs, as they *"dance just for kicks and text me that they're fulfilling their childhood dreams"* (Nino, female, practitioner).

Practitioners believed that young people apply for the ensemble because of the reputation the organisation has, as well as its programme, which makes it possible to reinterpret, alter and change what were once considered traditional

3 All of the ensemble members look like models. There is an implication of lookism here, but we did not follow up on this question.

dances using contemporary techniques, novel 'moves', and music. They viewed their students as unique individuals with different skills, personalities and motivations, and were aware that some students are motivated to become professionals, while others do it just for fun or *"just want to be able to dance in wedding parties"* (Nino, female, practitioner). One tutor noted the therapeutic value of participation in classes, saying that they had taught students with mental health problems, for whom amateur class was a rehabilitation opportunity.

Many instructors noted that young people are sometimes highly ambitious and want to dance in the front rows and perform solos. There are, however, only so many opportunities for these leading roles, which may lead to disappointment and distress. Whilst the limited number of leading roles generates competition, practitioners said that this rarely leads to conflict: *"We are low-conflict staff. [...] There are stressful situations, however it is notable only for [some] people"* (Tsisana, female, practitioner).

Practitioners reported that sometimes friends take the dance company lessons together, and that classes are an opportunity to make close friends. Students are encouraged to help each other understand and/or improve their dance moves: *"that works as a team-building activity and makes [...] friends"* (Tsisana, female, practitioner). It is not unusual for children to give paintings to their tutors, while older students and tutors often socialise together. Students variously described practitioners as friendly, demanding, hard-working, and strict but fair. They frequently noted that their tutor has made them love Georgian dance even more.

Cultural practices and personal culture

Young people and practitioners alike linked culture to traditions and 'national identity'. They underlined that Georgian folklore and wine-making heritage are important parts of Georgian culture. Young people also highlighted the importance of cultural events as a tool for sharing traditions with future generations and for encouraging foreigners to enjoy Georgian culture.

Practitioners saw themselves as cultural educators and as part of a centuries-old identity. Some defined 'cultural heritage' as a heritage linked to ancestry. Others believed that Georgian dance is a form of cultural heritage because of its individuality and 'uniqueness' compared with other folk dances. At the same time, practitioners believed that, when teaching youth, they should also talk about Georgian history, traditions, and any relevant related topic; these discussions are important in helping young participants to fully understand what Georgian national dance means.

The young people interviewed for the study saw culture as traditional and individual, and based on Georgia's culture. One respondent reported that *"the aim of my life and my job [as a dancer] is to promote Georgian culture"* (Toma, male, young people). Outside of dance company activities, many attend classical, jazz, blues, or rock concerts. Respondents also attend cultural festivals such as the Art Gene festival, visit the cinema and theatre, and enjoy folk dance concerts and exhibitions. The majority of the young people interviewed had jobs or were studying, with most enjoying professions of their choice. For most interviewees, their primary source of information about culture is the internet: *"if I missed [an] interesting cultural event, I can find information about it on the internet"* (Archili, male, young people). Practitioners frequently noted that the internet has contributed significantly to popularising the dance company among young people, as it provides easy access to videos of their work. Young respondents from both groups mentioned that family, friends and university are also important information sources.

In both observed groups, young people claimed to have diverse friendship networks beyond the ensemble community with whom they share common values. Some of their friends are interested in cinema, books, poetry, and/or computer science and coding. For some of their friends, the dance company and/or a love of dance are also a part of culture. Young people said that they had good friends, and that a good friend should be faithful, friendly, and supportive in good times and bad.

National and international topical issues, work, and politics were frequently reported as key conversation topics amongst friends. Respondents reported that they and their friends hang out together, and attend the cinema, theatre and annual celebrations together. Talking about friends from within the ensemble community, young people said that they are like another family. They hang out together and have the same goal:

> *We have the same goal, to become a member of the main ensemble of [name of the dance company]. […] After that some of them want to become a practitioner.* (Shota, male, young people)

Contrasting Georgian and European culture

Young people love Georgian culture, but also disapprove of some traditions. For respondents, Georgian culture means the traditional *supra*,[4] dance, music,

4 'Supra' in the Georgian context means a traditional Georgian way of feasting, led by a 'Tamada', a person who makes toasts. Festive 'supras' are usually accompanied by music, songs and dances.

hospitality and traditional clothes. They like *"the beautiful synthesis of many traditions [...] you can see the combination of cuisine, wine-making, dance, music at a Georgian supra"* (Sopo, female, young people, Dance group, Georgia). However, young people do not like traditions that are seen as insincere. For example, they think that the traditional funeral wake *"is sometimes focused on wining and dining more than respect to the dead"* (Kristina, female, young people). Respondents regularly attend Georgian dance and music concerts and join in with Georgian *supras* with their family and/or friends – they express Georgian culture through their activities.

The majority of respondents considered themselves both Georgian and European. As one of the respondents noted, *'I would consider myself fully European if I were free enough'* (Leila, female, young people). Young people saw Europe as being on a constant trajectory of progress. They associated Europe with personal freedom, innovation, freedom of expression, and good manners.

> *The most important topic in the European culture is personal freedom and importance of every person in the world. [...] [name of the dance company] are exactly representative of European cultural identity, because they do not limit their community members and are always oriented on development.* (Toma, male, young people)

Young people did not have much to say in relation to knowledge about Europe. They could not provide specific answers to questions about the EU or Europe in general, and did not have established ideas of what European culture is like. Therefore, it can be assumed that they are not well informed on this topic. Their information about Europe came from history classes at school, the internet and TV.

Case 2: Martial arts group

Site description

The martial arts group observed in this study was founded in 2000, and in 2011 was rebranded with a different name. In 2019, they rebranded again, because the previous name was associated with several Georgian far-right groups. This group is a historical society that seeks to regenerate traditional fighting techniques by operating in several different fields, like ethnography, physical education, and art related activities. The martial arts community is less well-known among young people than the first case in this study (the dance company). However, they have their own audience and followers, especially among those who are engaged in the exploration of national cultural heritage and history.

The organisational structure of the martial arts group is not strictly vertical. There are two groups of members: practitioners (teachers) and students. As a rule, practitioners are former apprentices, who have developed enough skill and 'privilege' to guide others. Being a practitioner also entails a readiness to dedicate free time to the organisation's activities; some experienced and skilled students do not want to be promoted to be practitioners due to the time commitment involved. Respected practitioners, former and current, form the organisation's council. This council is not involved in the day-to-day activities of the collective, but rather manages the group's strategic development.

The martial arts group brings together young people regardless of gender from a wide variety of backgrounds. Whilst practitioners are typically men aged 30 and above, the majority of students are 14–29 years old. The martial arts group's target audience is predominantly a younger demographic, with an expressed goal of including as many young people as possible in their activities in order to popularise traditional Georgian martial arts. The organisation's board communicates with schools and youth centres in an effort to promote their events and expand their membership.

The group is a predominately self-funded volunteer organisation. Whilst it has received external funding in the past, financing has been irregular, and it currently has no material or organisational support from any governmental or non-governmental body. The sole source of income comes from performances, which are irregular and limited in profit, leading to continued financial struggles. Respondents reported that the organisation's financial constraints have resulted in problems with accessing training facilities and equipment, and shortages of funds for other administrative expenses.

Motivations of practicing culture in the martial arts group

Younger people reported three major motivations for their engagement with the group: family influence, an interest in Georgian history, and a desire for physical activity and exercise. These factors were also reported by the practitioners. Family influence was predominantly cited by those with family members who are currently or had been previously involved with the martial arts group:

> *I am involved through my family. My brother was, my father was, and so am I […] My father was the [name of the martial arts group] practitioner and he is supervising one of the groups in my hometown. My brother is currently not a member, but he was training for four years.* (Lazare, male, young people)

A general interest in Georgian history and tradition was a frequently-cited motivation for joining the group among both young people and practitioners.

Respondents agreed that the group provides an opportunity to understand a very specific dimension of Georgian history and culture that they would not have access to elsewhere. Interviewees were enthusiastic about history, particularly military history, and reported that membership enables them to learn more about this passion:

> *… because of our past. I think everyone should know the history of [Georgian] combat and if one has the possibility to learn these techniques you should definitely learn that.* (Keti, female, young people)

The interviewed young people mostly joined the group during their late teens or in their early twenties. Many reported having found this martial arts group whilst searching for identity and their place in society. Most interviewees felt that this group was a place where they were able to make friends and learn about what friendship means, and that the group has helped them to express themselves more effectively:

> *Before I started training at [name of the martial arts group] I was more of a closed person, with limited contact with the outer world […] I did not enjoy contact with others too much, but I learned [to enjoy other people's company] here. I could say that I have become more open.* (Dato, male, young people)

The martial arts group helps young people to master traditional Georgian weapons and combat techniques. Whilst learning these skills provides the historical understanding and the engagement with a sub-culture that its members enjoy, some respondents also saw the group as a means for learning self-defence. Some female members of the group reported feeling safer and more confident since joining:

> *Martial arts, including wrestling, boxing or other physical exercises, have helped me a lot. […] women are generally more vulnerable […] I was afraid to walk the streets alone at night. However, after I learned [self-defence] I am not afraid anymore. I know I can defend myself in any situation.* (Eto, female, young people)

For members of the group, martial arts are as important a part of Georgian culture as folk dances, songs, literature and visual arts. Respondents reported their participation is driven by a desire to expand their understanding of what constitutes Georgian culture:

> *I want to show people how rich [a] culture we have […] Martial arts are not widespread and I want it to be popular like Georgian dance.* (Eto, female, young people)

Relationships inside the group: Horizontal relations between young people and their teachers

Both field observations and semi-structured interviews indicate that there are few formal boundaries between the younger and more senior practitioners. Some respondents did, however, report a sense of discipline within the organisation:

> *There is some sense of order, strictness. We need to have a serious approach while training to do anything.* (Gia, male, young people)

The decision-making process regarding the organisation's development was described by respondents as highly inclusive:

> *We make decisions jointly, we think about pros and cons. There is no absolutism, democratic principles are here.* (Nika, male, young people)

As a creative organisation, interviewees reported that this horizontal governance structure also applies to performance:

> *We argue, which specific element should be done better [while practicing for public event]. We argue on such things, but eventually we all come to the same point of view.* (Lasha, male, young people)

All interviewees stressed that there are no divisions in the organisation on the basis of gender, class or age:

> *Girls, boys all train together, seniors and juniors and everyone has the opportunity to spend time together* (Dato, man, young people)

Female respondents also reported that they feel an absence of traditional cultural norms that portray women as 'weak and vulnerable':

> *When I first came to [name of the martial arts group] I thought that the teacher would be softer on me as I am a girl, and he would not make me do [particular] exercises, but [during the training] he collapsed me on the training ground. After that I realised there is no distinction between boys and girls here. This is also true [outside] the training.* (Keti, female, young people)

Similarly, having different ideological points of view does not lead to strained attitudes among group members. Both young people and practitioners reported that they respect each other's values, whilst not always agreeing with them. This diversity of values and ideas was considered important in sustaining a strong team:

> *If we want to have the team, the team should be diverse and diversity means that we should accept people that are different from us.* (Lazare, male, young people)

Despite some differences of opinion, respondents described having very close relationships with other members of the group. Interviewees named their common interest in Georgian history as key to building relationships; for older respondents, who have known each other for a particularly long time, the duration of their friendships was also cited as important. Younger respondents were less likely to describe their relationships with other members in strong terms, drawing distinctions between themselves and their older peers:

> *Personally, I am still in a state of self-reflection, searching and finding myself […] they [the older generation] are more settled down and they know what they are doing.* (Gia, male, young people)

Understanding of culture

The idea of culture as an intersection of nation, historical factors, traditions and norms was a recurring theme during conversations with members of the group. Respondents reported the belief that culture serves as a bridge between contemporary reality and the realm of ancestors. This imaginary 'bridge' makes it possible to retrieve the knowledge and experiences of the past. This experience is essential in terms of continuing their cultural legacy and values, as well as helping the formation of modern nations.

Culture as a means of understanding other people was mostly related to the ability to interpret and correctly understand norms and traditions that may be unfamiliar to a given person. Young people reflected on diversity when answering questions about culture: "*When thinking about culture different countries and their clothes come to my mind*" (Dato, male, young people). These respondents also felt that an understanding of a culture is crucial in avoiding misinterpretations: "*[without having knowledge of cultures] you may make big mistakes*" (Nika, male, young people). Young people saw the concept of culture as a building block of society, and something that unites people:

> *I think that [culture] unites people and connects them with each other. People need this very much to feel that they are part of something big […] If there was no culture and history it would be hard [to stand together] […] people would disintegrate.* (Eto, female, young people)

Young people also pointed out that aesthetics is also part of culture. A variety of masterpieces in poetry, music, paintings and dance gives people a sense of appreciation and pleasure, and facilitates the creativity of human beings. Many interviewees felt that creativity is important in making life more interesting: "*One can say there is no need for culture, but […] people like diversity, uniformity is dull*" (Dato, male, young people).

The word 'culture' has many meanings in the Georgian language, including alignment with perceived established rules of behaviour in society. Respondents linked public behaviour and conformity with cultural norms: "*[culture involves] being friendly, courteous, helping others, being polite and respecting other's opinions*" (Elene, female, young people).

Being part of an organisation with a strong and specific cultural mandate, respondents also linked culture with martial arts. Practitioners were more explicit than young people in this respect:

> *What I [think about] culture is all in relation to my organization. At the end of the day I still base [my definition] on that. Something that is based on traditions and creativity.* (Gogi, male, practitioner)

Though generally agreeing that culture is important for personal development, both young people and practitioners reported little involvement in other cultural activities outside of the martial arts group. For some, this lack of broader engagement was due to constraints on free time, and for others it represented a perceived scarcity of cultural activities. Regardless of their rates of participation, for the majority of young people interviewed, cultural activities were important elements of practicing culture. They were enthusiastic about the potential for events as a mechanism for transferring cultural knowledge:

> *All sorts of cultural events should be organised. If they are not organised, it [culture] will not be transferred to people.* (Lasha, male, young people)

Identity of young people: Influence of family and friends

Respondents saw family as an important and formative influence with regard to youth culture:

> *My culture comes from my family, from my father, mother, my brother. In general, the family influences the formation of a child.* (Eto, female, young people)

A recurring theme was the attempts of family and young people to combine what they each see as traditional and modern values. Interviewees said that they respect Georgian norms and traditions that they had learned through socialisation within their families and social environments. However, at the same time, they adapt these norms to suit modern life:

> *[Family culture] is respecting our past and considers the reality of modernity. We are not observing all traditions and customs. We try to modify them and interpret them in our own way.* (Elene, female, young people)

Though family was frequently cited as an important factor in the formation of personal culture and identity, for the most part young people interviewed felt detached from their families with regard to cultural expression. This manifested in how rarely they went to any cultural event with their parents or discussed culture with them. Typically, respondents felt that friends had a greater influence on their identity. Some respondents felt that shared culture and interests are an important precondition for friendship: *"personally I can't be friends with a person that is not interested in Georgian culture or heritage"* (Keti, female, young people). Other young people stressed the importance of sincerity and depth in relationships:

> *My friends, in general, are characterised by having deep interests [...] We are not some 'faint', indifferent society.* (Lazare, male, young people)

Besides friends and family, the identities of young people are shaped by the influence of the organisation itself. When young people compared their friendships inside and outside the martial arts group, there were clear, distinguishing patterns associated with how young people self-identified. The majority of respondents described their friends and acquaintances from the martial arts group as being more 'traditional' than other people they knew, and that friends from the martial arts group valued 'Georgianness' above all. Friends from other circles were considered more open towards 'other cultures', with values that do not bind their identity to 'being Georgian':

> *My friends are very different from each other, because I have contact with many people. I study at the art academy and people there are more open-minded and think more or less in a European way, although not entirely. People at [name of the martial arts group] are more oriented towards Georgian traditions.* (Nika, male, young people)

Activities outside the martial arts group also influenced the young people's identities. Those involved in civic activities outside of the group often described themselves using terms such as 'feminist' and 'European', or noted that they value universal virtues and do not identify solely with Georgian culture. One quoted a prominent Georgian politician to describe Georgia as a natural part of Europe: *"I am Georgian, therefore I am European"* (Sandro, male, young people). Respondents with less diverse hobbies outside of the martial arts group more strongly identified themselves solely with 'Georgianness'.

Contrasting Georgian and European culture

When questioned on what they understand by Georgian culture, respondents frequently discussed history, tradition and Georgian orthodox Christianity. For young people, the concepts that make Georgia unique were the most important features of Georgian culture, with the Georgian language,[5] alphabet, wine and folklore cited as examples of Georgia's unique cultural heritage. Interviewees saw Georgian culture as very diverse, and agreed that, whilst it should take new ideas from other cultures, it should maintain its core values:

> *It is 50/50. We can take other things from all cultures in order to improve [Georgian culture] but making the strong emphasis on [changes] and neglecting Georgian culture is not a good idea.* (Nika, man, young people)

Though Georgian culture is important to respondents, they do not enjoy every aspect of it. On the one hand, young people had unconditional respect for many cultural norms, like hospitality and Georgia's ability to sustain itself in the face of adversity:

> *I like that throughout so many centuries, despite so many enemies we sustained ourselves and did not lose our national identity.* (Keti, female, young people)

However, despite a strong desire to promote and preserve Georgian culture, young people also expressed frustration with the strong dogma that constrains cultural development. Several young people noted that the stress on conservative values by the majority of Georgian society limits the country's ability to adapt with contemporary times:

> *In fact, what we have now [culture], it was not in the same form as we have it at the moment. That was also changing over times. Consequently, we must try to adapt to the modern reality and we should shape our traditions and habits accordingly […] it should not be all about past.* (Elene, female, young people)

Young people found it difficult to speak about European culture, which was predominantly interpreted as a phrase for a geographic and political space:

> *When I hear European culture for the most part modern European countries come to my mind.* (Dato, male, young people)

Compared to their knowledge of Georgian culture, respondents' understanding of European culture was limited and mostly associated with 'European values'. Young people frequently linked European values to respect for the opinions of others, freedom of thought, the rule of law, and order. Europe also received praise for its ability to achieve reconciliation:

---

5 By the 'Georgian language', respondents mean the literature standard of Georgian language.

> *I recall the old time, when they [Europeans] were in constant disagreement, but I like that they make it possible to reconcile and to establish relationships with each other. That was possible because of their culture.* (Gia, man, young people)

European culture was believed to be more rational and purposeful than that of Georgia: "*The European culture is some sort of consequentiality that is present in every individual's everyday routine*" (Lazare, male, young people). Others associated Europe with progress, development and welfare: "*I have positive associations, I associate it [Europe] with developed and well-organised countries*" (Dato, male, young people).

Europe and Georgia were understood on different levels. Respondents saw Georgian culture in terms of traditions, history, art and material heritage, while Europe was associated with values such as freedom of thought and self-expression. In this regard, being European was seen in the abstract:

> *[Being European] does not depend on the location or specific country. Probably being European is based on the ideology or etiquette, how to behave.* (Nika, male, young people)

Expressing culture through group activities

For young people, the martial arts group's activities extended beyond conservation to creativity. In general, young people and their peers considered all activities associated with their community traditional and in complete alignment with the demands of Georgian society (it is interesting to note that young people also believed that society perceives their activities similarly). However, they also stressed that the group does not merely replicate existing practices but reproduces traditional Georgian cultural norms in their own way. The organisation undertakes ethnographic trips to mountainous parts of Georgia to rediscover martial art techniques, and works to document the history of Georgian martial arts:

> *The information [about traditional martial arts] was researched during research expeditions. [We also discovered a lot from] archive data and museum exhibits.* (Tengo, male, practitioner)

This information is then passed onto newcomers in the group and to the public through history lectures:

> *Our lectures can be on many topics. It can be on history, folklore, it could be about the songs, martial arts, or battle tactics, that is also more or less part of [the] culture of every country.* (Dato, male, young people)

By engaging in the typical activities of the martial arts group, like dressing in traditional attire, preparing copies of the traditional fighting armaments and, at the end, by staging centuries-old martial art performances, young people believe that they are reviving Georgian culture. However, their goals extend beyond re-enactment. Respondents noted that the organisation also wants to "update" and "upgrade" traditional martial arts, and to offer "broader society" their own vision of Georgian culture: *"[Our activities] are dedicated to the renewal of culture. Without it, culture will not survive"* (Lazare, male, young people). Young people want to renovate and upgrade Georgian traditional martial arts by modifying and modernising their techniques. Their interests also lie in the fields of traditional attire, decorations, and accessories, like bows, axes, swords, shields, etc.

When it comes to the modification of martial art moves, the group members not only recreate old techniques, but also incorporate new approaches from other cultures:

> *Sometimes there are moves from films, like stunts they are doing in movies. The manoeuvres and tricks can be also adapted to Georgian culture as well, though [nothing] too unrealistic.* (Sandro, male, young people)

Some members have worked in the film industry, performing stunt and traditional combat techniques. The practitioners are currently working on expanding the opportunity presented by Georgia's growing film and television industry:

> *We have talks [with movie directors] and we hope that we will [do more] martial art scenes in the movies, not only in Georgia, but on a higher level too.* (Gogi, male, practitioner)

Discussion

The non-formal education settings represented two different cases of cultural acquisition, characterised by one common feature: an attempt to modernise traditional Georgian culture. However, that understanding itself contains a number of contradictions and ambiguities. The culture discussed by the participants of the non-formal education settings has two distinctive features: invented 'authentic' culture and culture that is something that exists by itself.

The first one is related to the construction of culture in terms of 'invented tradition', in Hobsbawmian terms (Hobsbawm and Ranger, 1983). The dance group, like many of the State Dance Companies established under the Soviet Union, sought to create a national ballet founded upon the tradition of Georgian folk dance (Shay, 1999). The main idea behind such a transformation was an attempt to create some kind of unique cultural feature in the context of the communist and socialist political system. The development of martial arts in the Georgian context lacks scholarly research; however, there may be parallels with the development of other countries' martial art techniques. For example, the decline and rediscovery of Japanese martial arts is mirrored in the case of Georgia. In both cases, due to social transformation and modernisation martial arts have been re-discovered as a means of character-building, lifestyle and a general codex of behaviour (Hamaguchi, 2005). Taking into consideration these circumstances, young people in both educational settings often attribute historical authenticity and uniqueness to what are often recent inventions.

The second attribute is a very fixed interpretation of culture as something that is taken for granted. It is perceived as having existed long before the individuals and, suggesting that young people's major contribution should be its preservation and advancement. In this light, Georgian culture is something inherited from ancestors, existing independently of individual influences; it is 'embedded and embodied' in shared memories (Batiashvili, 2012). Ethnic identity is one of the most eminent aspects of the construction of Georgian culture. This was displayed in the wording used by young people and their associations with cultural activities. The notion of 'Georgianness' is closely linked to the ethno-linguistic and religious understanding of cultural heritage. One should be Georgian by virtue of birth into an ethnic Georgian family, should speak Georgian, and should preferably adhere to an orthodox Christian faith. The prominent Georgian writer and thinker, Ilia Chavchavadze, summarised this triad in the maxim 'Fatherland, Language, Faith'. Taught from early stages of secondary education, these key features of the Georgian nation were not challenged by the observed young people, like the majority of Georgian society. The ethnic 'Georgianness' of Georgian culture manifested not only in the cultural context but also on a linguistic level. The experimental psychosemantic research has shown that "personal self-realization has necessarily implied the element of being Georgian" (Surmanidze and Tsuladze, 2008: p. 97). This explains why virtually every aspect of the Georgian culture described by young people was implicitly connected to ethnic 'Georgianness', Christianity to Georgian orthodox Christianity, and so on.

The fusion of, at first glance, contradictory notions of static, domestic, familiar and dynamic, and foreign and unfamiliar cultures, as well as the desire to interpret these in a contemporary fashion, is nothing other than a 'bricolage' approach. This refers to the remaking of new culture and identities illustrated by Lévi-Strauss (1966). Though usually utilised from the perspective of mythology or religious beliefs, the existing literature on Georgian youth has already applied the idea of bricolage when observing and interpreting the generation of new Georgian identities among youth (Tsuladze, 2011). Tsuladze (2011) links the bricolage tactics of understanding, recreating and practicing new cultural norms, as employed by Georgian youth, with the 'glocalization' of globalisation trends, and how these are mixed with elements of 'traditional culture'. The concept of glocalisation, which can be described as absorbing global ideas with a local flavour or indigenisation, has been applied to the dynamics of social transformation in the countries of the global south (Khondker, 2004).This is relevant to Georgia in terms of the descriptive and explanatory accounts of the collected data; one of the most repeated theses in the conversations with practitioners and young people was how to rethink Georgian culture. Furthermore, as described by Tsuladze (2011), the "fashionable trend of 'being native" among Georgian youth and subcultures mirrors the idea of "going back to the roots" (Roberts, 2005). At the same time, Georgian culture, perceived by the young people from the non-formal education setting as unique in terms of a blender of different cultures itself, constitutes a sort of 'roadmap' for how to engage in global trends without losing a connection with local traditions and values.

The observed non-formal education settings perfectly fit the described model of cultural participation and its acquisition. On the one hand, association with traditional culture gives legitimacy to the practice of 'Georgian culture' in its mainstream definition without accusations of 'wrong' interpretations or corrupting tradition. This is important in the context of 'bricolage' too. While adapting and mixing elements of traditional Georgian culture with globalisation trends, it is important for practitioners of different cultural activities to remain a part of a universally-acknowledged and accepted 'unique Georgian culture'. In the case of the martial arts group, it is also notable that this particular setting undermines the wildly acceptable claim in Georgia that martial arts are not appropriable for women. On the contrary, the observed community tries to break that stereotype by creating a more engaging and gratifying environment for young women. This is done in the following way: when they (young women) want to engage in activities that are not widely considered to be 'fit' or 'acceptable' for them, they can try to present such activities in the light of "traditional" or "national heritage." The idea of engaging in traditional activities is more acceptable to families and society than being involved in ordinary, sport-oriented martial art groups.

Though they have similarities, dance and martial arts non-formal education settings are also different. The dance group, having a much longer history, is a more mainstream education setting than the martial arts group. As a bigger and more established organisation, the dance group is also more hierarchical in terms of decision-making. Young people, especially those who are involved in the amateur dance groups, have practically no say in organisational development or in creating new dance routines. When it comes to the martial arts group, being a more grassroots and self-organised educational setting, young people can be involved in the daily functions of the community. Their voices and positions are important when it comes to shaping the organisational vision.

Another difference between the two settings is collaboration with other formal and non-formal education institutions. While the martial arts group tries to engage with governmental agencies and expand its activities with schools, for the dance group this is no major priority. This can be linked to the different organisational capacities and strength: the dance academy, an already well-established and known organisation, does not need additional legitimisation and support from state organisations, nor does it need to attract new members. For the martial arts group, this is crucial for its future development and survival.

Compared to the martial arts group, the dance company has a more focused approach to cultural practices and the acquisition of cultural literacy. They are mostly oriented towards dance and related subjects, while the martial arts group members have more diverse interests in and experiences of cultural practices. Besides practicing martial arts, they are often also interested in history, poetry, art, painting, ethnography and folklore. Eventually, this manifests in different levels of cultural literacy. Young people from the dance group have less diverse cultural interests, understanding culture mostly in relation to dance, while martial arts group members think about culture in more general terms (through traditions, values, and art).

Studying those non-formal education settings, besides answering core research questions, also raised a number of issues and queries for future inquiry. The first is the idea of self-reported egalitarianism in the martial arts group. Literature focusing on leadership in martial arts groups suggests that there are two main approaches: transactional and transformational. Transactional leaders give well-defined tasks, which are then monitored, while transformational leaders aim to motivate adherents to excel stated milestones (Rowold, 2006). While the martial arts setting clearly takes the transformational leadership approach, allowing more freedom of action,[6] further investigation is needed to understand whether the leadership style truly results in transformation and whether members are as equal as was reported.

A recurring theme across all interviews was the diversity of members of both non-formal education settings. Often this diversity contradicted the uniformity of other young people outside their friends and peer circles. This raises two

6 If the same approach is applied to the dance group, the leadership style leans more towards transactional leadership, with clear instructions and participants agreeing to "complete the assignments in exchange for commensurate material or psychological compensation (e.g., recognition, awards)" (Rowold, 2006: p. 313).

questions for future research: by what criteria do young people define diversity and which elements are underrepresented in young people's judgments?

In this regard, it is important to remember that, while diversity can be recorded in terms of ideological spectrum, values, interests or tastes, in reality a majority of young people share the same characteristics. Many respondents had moderately conservative values in terms of cultural preservation and stressed the importance of unique Georgian identity to what Giddens calls ontological security: legitimised meaning in life and an ethical guide (Giddens, 1991). Previous research regarding young people's identities in the Georgian context highlighted that there is a clear pattern of how auto- and hetero-stereotypes are formulated based on an in-group/out-group division (Tsuladze, 2011). Membership in the groups is seen as an important factor for constructing these stereotypes (Petkova and Lehtonen, 2005). As the discussed settings represent very close-knit groups of young people, this can contribute to perceptions of being different compared to other groups.

Young people's knowledge about culture in Georgia and Europe is another dimension of the findings that needs additional investigation. Both formal and non-formal education settings in Georgia suggested that their goal is to transfer knowledge about culture to younger generations; however, interviews indicate that their factual knowledge is somewhat superficial and one-dimensional. While the young people's understanding of Georgian culture has been discussed in this chapter, their knowledge of Europe is characterised by the idea that European culture is a set of universally shared values and beliefs.

The findings of this research into these non-formal education settings has many implications for the wider academic field. In the Georgian context, for instance, it brings attention to the importance of further investigation into non-formal education settings and their influence on the cultural acquisition of young people. There are currently few attempts to explore this topic in detail.

Conclusion

This research into Georgian non-formal education settings provided information about how young people and practitioners engage in the production of various forms of cultural knowledge and practice. The major topic related to cultural reproduction and transfer was the simultaneous preservation and modernisation of traditional Georgian culture. This idea is situated in the framework of bricolage techniques, which create new cultural practices and interpretations by taking pieces from local and global contexts. The important caveat in this regard is that traditional, overwhelmingly "ethnic" Georgian elements are the keystone to this process. In contrast, pieces of culture learned from another context only serve as supplementary ways of creating new cultural practices.

For young people, culture is fixed within a framework of universally accepted values, ethical rules, and history. Some elements can be changed or modified, but it is unthinkable for them to witness fundamental changes. This idea is particularly interesting because many of the aspects and traditions of Georgian culture discussed with young people in the context of non-formal education settings are recent innovations or creations. Besides their similarities, the discussed settings vary in their interests and the complexity of their activities. The dance group has a narrower focus regarding the specific dimensions of Georgian culture, especially in the setting of the amateur dance classes. Meanwhile, the martial arts group takes a more holistic approach to the production of cultural practices. This is manifested in their efforts to engage with other aspects of Georgian culture.

Self-reported engagement in cultural practices outside the non-formal education settings was limited for the most part. A lack of free time and the homogeneity of the offered cultural events were mentioned as reasons for the relatively low levels of participation. However, it is important to note that the cultural participation of young people was predominantly identified with established, classical or high culture activities, like going to museums, theatres or art exhibitions.

Non-formal educational settings provide the opportunity to practice culture in ways that are not covered or envisaged by formal education. Formal education institutions are oriented on the theoretical and passive transfer of culture, while the discussed non-formal educational settings enable young people to experience and practice culture actively. Nevertheless, young people and practitioners, for the most part from the martial arts group, claimed that the state agencies and stakeholders that are responsible for the cultural policy usually do not engage or collaborate strategically with non-formal education settings. Future research and policy should focus on the inclusion of non-formal education settings when formulating policy documents regarding youth and their inclusion in cultural activities, in order to facilitate greater cultural acquisition in young people.

References

Batiashvili, Nutsa. 'The 'Myth' of the Self: The Georgian National Narrative and Quest for Georgianness', in Aleida Assmann and Linda Shortt, eds., *Memory and Political Change*, pp. 186–200 (Palgrave Macmillan, London, 2012).

Chincharauli, Mariam. 'Musical art and globalization in the 20th–21st centuries (the case of Georgia)'. *Multidisciplinary views on popular culture: Proceedings of the 5th International SELICUP Conference*, pp. 123–133, (Universidad de Castilla-La Mancha, Toledo, 2014).

DVV international Georgia Country Office. 'Adult Education Centers in Georgia' (2017). http://www.dvv-international.ge/fileadmin/files/caucasus-turkey/Georgia/AECs_in_Georgia_ENG_without_photos.pdf (Accessed on February 6, 2020).

Giddens, Anthony, *Modernity and self-identity: Self and society in the late modern age*. (Stanford University Press, Stanford, 1991).

Hamaguchi, Yoshikazu, 'Innovation in martial arts', in Joseph Maguire & Masayoshi Nakayama, eds., *Japan, Sport and Society: Tradition and Change in a Globalizing World*, pp. 7–18 (Routledge, London, 2005).

Hobsbawm, Eric and Terence Ranger, eds., *The invention of tradition* (Cambridge University Press, Cambridge, 1983).

Kadagidze, Lamara, 'The role of education in the formation of civil society'. *European Scientific Journal* 11/10 (2015), 100–111.

Khondker, Habibul Haque, 'Glocalization as globalization: Evolution of a sociological concept', *Bangladesh e-journal of Sociology*, 1/2 (2004), 1–9.

Khoshtaria, Tamar, Mariam Kobaladze, and Tinatin Zurabishvili. "History in Danger and Youth Civic Engagement: Perceptions and Practice in Telavi, Georgia." In *Understanding Youth Participation Across Europe*, pp. 293–315. (Palgrave Macmillan, London, 2018).

Lévi-Strauss, Claude, *The savage mind*. (University of Chicago Press, Chicago, 1966).

Mindiashvili, Beka, Giorgi Gakheladze, and Irakli Taboridze. "Religious and Ethnic Diversity in School Textbooks." *Tolerance and Diversity Institute* (2016).

Navrozashvili, Natia, '„შავფაროსნები"- საბრძოლო ხელოვნებით გამორჩეული მებრძოლები', Ambioni, (2015). http://www.ambioni.ge/savfarosnebi (Accessed on September 24, 2019).

Networking European Citizenship Education (NECE). 'Recommendations on Citizenship Education in Georgia' (2015). https://www.bpb.de/veranstaltungen/netzwerke/nece/216825/georgia (Accessed on February 6, 2020).

Order of Minister of Georgia, Document number 8/ნ. [Online] https://matsne.gov.ge/ka/document/view/1197912?publication=0 (Accessed on February 6, 2020).

Patton, Michael Quinn, 'Qualitative research and evaluation methods' (3rd edition), *Thousand Oaks: Sage* 5/3 (2002), 299–301.

Petkova, Diana, and Jaakko Lehtonen, eds., *Cultural identity in an intercultural context*. (University of Jyväskylä, Jyväskylä, 2005).

Ranger, Terence, 'The Invention of Tradition in Colonial Africa', in Eric Hobsbawm and Terence Ranger, ed., The Invention of Tradition, pp. 211–262. (Cambridge University Press, Cambridge, 1983).

Ritchie, Jane, Lewis, Jane, Nicholls, Carol M.,, and Rachel Ormston, eds., *Qualitative research practice: A guide for social science students and researchers.* (Sage Publising, London, 2013).

Roberts, Martin, 'Notes on the Global Underground: Subcultures and Globalization', in Ken Gelder, ed., *The Subcultures Reader*, pp. 575–586. (Routledge, London, 2005)

Rowold, Jens, 'Transformational and transactional leadership in martial arts', *Journal of Applied Sport Psychology*, 18/4 (2006), 312–325.

Shay, Anthony, 'Parallel traditions: State folk dance ensembles and folk dance in "The field"'. *Dance Research Journal,* 31/1 (1999), 29–56.

Surmanidze, Lali, and Lia Tsuladze, 'The formation of nation-state and cultural identity: A Georgian perspective', *IBSU Scientific Journal (IBSUSJ), 2/*2 (2008), 86–102.

Tabatadze, Shalva, Natia Gorgadze, Kakha Gabunia, and David Tinikashvili. "Intercultural content and perspectives in school textbooks in Georgia." *Intercultural Education,* 31/4 (2020): 462–481.

'*The Georgian National Youth Policy Document*', The Government of Georgia (2014), http://msy.gov.ge/files/Youth_Policy_(Engl)_Final_July_2014.pdf (Accessed on February 6, 2020).

Tsuladze, Lia, 'Youth Identities through Bricolage in a Changeable Society: The Case of Georgia.' In *Multiculturalism: Critical and Interdisciplinary Perspectives*, pp. 67–76. (Oxford. *Inter-Disciplinary Press,* 2011).

(by Cornelia Sylla)

Chapter 8 From distinction to resonance – outline of a spectrum of youth culture in Germany

Abstract: This chapter presents two case studies of non-formal educational settings in Germany that represent different approaches to how young people conceptualise, practice and experience culture: a performance group focusing on music, dance and literature and a pro-European political group. Both case studies were analysed separately but are also contrasted here to give an impression of the spectrum of diversity in conceptualisations and practices of culture.

Both organisations were quite democratically structured, allowing young people to grow into the role of practitioners. The inner-organisational cultures lay on a spectrum that can be described using two theoretical approaches: the theory of "resonance" by Hartmut Rosa (2019a) for a group of young people creating and performing music and dance together (performance group), and Bourdieu's theory of "distinction" for a pro-European political group (political group). While at the performance group participation and inclusion were dealt with in a "resonant" way, and "performance" seemed to be the main method of cultural education, at the political group we found an educational approach much closer to that of formal educational settings. Specific historical knowledge and a distinguished "democratic culture of discussion" were the main criteria for cultural literacy as practiced within this group.

Formally, both organisations were open to all young people. However, we exposed subtle mechanisms of exclusion, especially in the political group, by exploring the questions of how young people's cultural participation and education were influenced by these settings, and what young people and practitioners in the field consider important to their cultural identities or practices.

Keywords: distinction, resonance, youth-culture, discrimination, othering

Introduction

In this chapter, we present two case studies of different non-formal educational settings that are instrumental to young people's cultural acquisition. Both settings allow young people to participate in the conceptualisation and organisation of cultural activities, but their views on culture are essentially different. We have explored how these settings affect young people's cultural participation and education, and how young people and practitioners in the field define and perform cultural identities and practices. Special attention was paid to educational concepts, as well as informal practices within each organisation, to determine the roles these play in young people's acquisition of cultural literacy and culture generally. Through identifying examples of good practice, as well as the needs expressed within the organisations, this chapter contributes to the development of effective strategies for raising cultural literacy and dialogue.

As can be expected of qualitative research projects, not every CHIEF research activity could be planned in detail. All plans had to be adapted to the situations discovered during fieldwork. The following section will briefly outline the development of the research process as it arose in practice.

An initial list of possible research bases included a wide range of sites for youth education (youth fire brigade, youth centres, theatre and dance groups, youth Red Cross, religious groups, etc.). The sites were contacted via e-mail, phone call or by a personal visit. Some of the projects and institutions, especially those only contacted via e-mail, did not respond at all. Of those who did reply, some did not meet the criteria (e.g. participant age), while those that did often rejected participation for a variety of reasons. These included lack of time, small group size, change in leadership, being busy with other projects, or suspicions of interference with their pedagogical approaches. Only one organisation, which had a conceptual focus on pro-EU politics, was instantly willing to contribute to this research (political group).

The next strategy was to contact organisations where researchers already had some kind of connection. This proved successful in two more cases. One researcher had been in contact with an organisation that offers projects including music, dance and performing arts, writing plays, arranging festivals, and performing on different stages. This group also explores topics like racism and other forms of discrimination (performance group). Many young people who participate in these programmes have experienced discrimination themselves.

Participant observations were carried out at both sites, with the intention of covering the broadest range of activities possible. Therefore, several different activities were observed before choosing two per site to more thoroughly document. For the performance group the chosen activities were a weekly choir practice and performance project that ran intensively for 2–3 months, and for the political group a weekend seminar on relations between Europe and Africa and a monthly round table on varying topics (in this case, the EU elections).

Most observations were carried out by the same researcher. A young student assistant carried out participatory research at the political group's weekend seminar. One fruitful exchange between this assistant and the main CHIEF researcher contributed to a new perspective on the group and new data being collected.

Within the political group, almost all participants were keen to be involved with the CHIEF project, apparently because some of their main topics of interest (Europe and young people) overlapped with those of CHIEF. At the performance group it was more difficult to motivate young people to participate in the interviews. In some cases, it was very difficult to clearly distinguish between young people and practitioners; many non-formal educational sites in Germany are run by volunteers, who grow into practitioner roles after first participating in activities themselves. This seemed to be the case in the performance group: Annika was only 19 years old, but her role in the organisation was mostly a professional one, while practitioner Jack Black, aged 28, was also a participant in one of the activities we observed. The political group is run by young people for young people. Only Tim and Marc could be identified as participants only (not practitioners as well). Another individual was older than the previously defined category of "young people" (26), but did not really have a professional role (Benjamin Müller, male, YP).

We tried to achieve as much diversity within the overall sample of respondents as possible. We managed to interview one male and one female practitioner per site. Additionally, the educational background, interview language and self-described ethnicity of the two performance group practitioners also differed.

As for the young people, we only managed to find one interviewee younger than 18 willing to participate. Ethnic, educational and socio-economic self-descriptions varied greatly between sites. While respondents from the performance group showed a wide range of diversity in all these respects, the political group, according to information given by practitioners, is attended mainly by white middle- to upper-class youth. This was reflected in our interview sample, where only Marc described himself as German of Persian and working-class origin.

Two theoretical approaches were found to be appropriate for analysing the phenomena observed during activities and interviews. The theory of "resonance" by Hartmut Rosa (2019a) appeared suitable to describe the concepts behind cultural practices at the performance group site, while Bourdieu's (2010) theory of "distinction" proved useful for explaining the mechanics of the political group.

For purposes of anonymisation without categorising from the outside, all participants were asked to choose a pseudonym. This practice itself led to some interesting points for analysis, because some commented on their choice in interesting ways (e.g. Friedrich, male, YP, because it is close to the German word for peace (Frieden)), while others chose names associated with a certain concept with gestures or laughs that made clear that the reference was intentional (e.g. Jack Black, male, practitioner). One young person, who described struggles of belonging and encounters with racism, chose a pseudonym that could be considered a "classical German" name (Hans-Heinrich, male, YP) without explanation but with some fervour; this invites the assumption that he wanted to provoke or simply manifest that he is German, whatever others might think.

Participation in general can be seen as a difficult ethical issue, since it is always closely connected with power relations and social barriers that exclude certain people. Although we tried, we did not succeed in raising the interest of non-formal organisations frequented by young people who experience barriers to cultural participation on multiple levels. Some organisations did not want to be studied because they felt it would disturb their everyday work, rather than seeing it as an opportunity to participate in the research. We only reached organisations with concepts that were already close to our goals, whose practitioners spoke a "similar language" to the researchers.

Exploring differences between youth cultures in non-formal settings in Germany

In Germany, non-formal education has undergone some changes in the past decade. These are closely linked to changes in the school system. About 10 years ago, the school system reacted to the growing need for afternoon child-care by converting a majority of schools from a part-time (finishing curricular activities around 1 pm) to a full-time schedule (finishing curricular activities at around 4 pm). Many schools now also offer childcare in the late afternoon. Therefore, non-formal education organisations have had to change either their schedules, their locations or both. Many have started coordinating with schools by offering voluntary classes that can be integrated into the schools' timetables. Some organisations have profited from this new collaboration with the formal educational system, but many criticise this development because they feel that they have become assistants to the schools, losing some of the conceptual freedom they had before (Deinet and Ickling, 2013: p. 399).

However, there are still many different voluntary activities offered by non-formal organisations outside schools. Sport clubs (especially football teams, but also gymnastics, dancing and other team sports) are very popular among German youth. In rural areas, voluntary firefighters and similar organisations are also quite common. Music schools are also frequented by a large number of young people. Most organisations are partly financed by state funding and otherwise rely on membership fees. For young people from families with a very low income, the Federal Ministry of Labour and Social Affairs implemented the so-called "Bildungs- und Teilhabepaket" in 2011. This programme was in part designed to allow young people to participate in activities even if they cannot afford the fees, although an evaluation in 2012 concluded that it was more often used to finance school supplies, lunches and class trips (Apel and Engels, 2012: p. 65). Many smaller programmes offer free or subsidised memberships to young people with few financial resources.

The two sites we selected for this research project are quite well-known in the communities that form their clientele. The performance group is a local organisation developed from a private initiative. It is currently connected quite well with the ministry, foundations, educational networks and artists in the region. The political group, in contrast, is a local branch of an international organisation with separate divisions for young people and adults. This group has always been funded by state initiatives and foundations due to its political initiatives and its close relationship with government organisations.

A 'Transcultural' space of creativity: Music, Dance, and Literature Performance Group

The first case study was carried out in an organisation that offers music, dance, and performance projects for young people of all ages (starting at two years of age). Their music and dance styles are designed to be attractive to young people; whatever interests them can become part of the activities. The programme consists of regular weekly activities like choir practice or dance groups, regular festivals and performances, and annual compact projects that lead to a special performance in a well-known alternative theatre in the city.

This association has grown from a small 'intercultural' initiative in 1999 to a "transcultural encouragement project" that currently reaches about 100 regular participants. The site is supported by several different foundations but most of those funds are connected to specific projects. The continual need to reapply for funding is one of the organisation's greatest challenges. They ask participants for a small monthly fee but waive this if someone claims financial difficulties.

The group's main aim, according to their webpage, flyers and practitioners' interviews, is to encourage young people to be creative in all the ways they want to be. They endeavour to make room for young people's interests, and to create a space where they can feel safe to experiment and express themselves. This key element was stressed by all practitioners, and many young people also confirmed that this is what they like about the organisation:

> *First and foremost, we find it important that everyone can be what they want to be. That's one of the main principles.* (Farida, female, practitioner)

Since this case study's focus is on young people aged 14–25, we observed two different activities mostly frequented by this age group: a choir that practises weekly and a "transcultural" performance project with intensive weekend workshops, which goes from the creation of the script to rehearsing scenes and choreography (sometimes in small groups, sometimes all together, sometimes with an external dance coach or music professional). We observed two choir practices over one month and three workshop days over another. The workshops we observed took place on rehearsal stages, part of the large theatre that hosted the final performance. On some occasions, only a few young people met with the practitioner to plan specific scenes or to intensively rehearse their parts, while on others all 18 performers were present. The project incorporated ideas and biographical contributions by all participants, creating a performance that aimed to redefine the notion of "assimilation" and criticise current social power relations.

Choir practice took place within the headquarters of the organisation. The leader of the choir, as well as some of the participants, also took part in the performance project mentioned above. At the time of the observations, the choir was frequented by 3–5 participants, only two of whom were present on all occasions. This could be explained by the fact that a big festival organised by members of the group was taking place at the same time. The leader assured us that, while they would still like to increase their numbers, around 10 young people usually participate in the choir.

Unique individuals, creative chaos and resonance

When we analysed the observation protocols and interview transcripts gathered at the performance group, the first impression was of creative chaos, with unique individuals coming together to create performances that express who they are and what they want the world to know. This led to the application of Rosa's theory of "resonance" to the analysis. Rosa states that the current paradigm of sovereignty, which is at the base of economic growth and which structures all relations between humans and their environment in "modern" societies, necessarily leads to escalation and aggression. No structural reform can change that fact unless the underlying paradigm is transformed. In order to create new utopias, a general shift in human relations (with space, time, history and politics) towards what he calls "resonance" is necessary (Rosa, 2019b: pp. 35–46). For Rosa, "resonance" means neither owning the environment nor being victimised by it, but instead sending out the vibes that are being reflected, and at the same time "listening" to the vibes being sent out by others: the aim is for these vibes to resonate in harmony.

This theoretical perspective, linked with the research goals stated above, led to the following thematic results. First of all participation and inclusion seemed to be dealt with in a specific "resonant" way within the performance group: giving young people space to express themselves, listening to their needs, sending messages to one another. Secondly, for practitioners and young people alike, "performance" seemed to be not only the goal but the method of cultural education. This understanding was closely linked to their perception of culture as something that is created as we speak and that contains rebellion as well as individually-shaped treasures of experiences, and their idea of identity as something absolutely unique. Neither culture and identity were understood as static, which indicates that cultural education cannot simply mean teaching certain facts and reaching a pre-defined goal of cultural literacy. Culture and identity at this site appeared to be something that is continuously shaped by new experiences, something that is constantly growing in different directions.

Participation is the most prominent element of this organisation's concept. Practitioners wanted to give young people space to create their own content without too much guidance. They claimed to provide leadership only in the form of expertise in order to help young people find their own way. In all activities at this site, young people contribute their own creations; their ideas, wishes and talents are recognised and promoted in performances. Even the observer was swiftly invited to participate in finding ideas for the performance or to sing along with the choir.

The way in which diversity is discussed and practiced in this institution is a good example of the innovative, sensitive atmosphere of the group. While every single person acknowledged the diversity of the group in the interviews, diversity is not officially promoted as a goal of the cultural education offered here. In some activities, setting diversity as a goal was openly criticised as pressuring individuals to be 'different' in some specific ways but not in others. When asked about diversity in the group, most practitioners focused on different interests, talents or personalities rather than nationalities, ethnicities or religion. In this organisation, being diverse is considered a common fact that does not need promotion. What is encouraged instead is a caring, respectful form of freedom and individuality, as will be discussed later in this chapter.

This priority can be observed in the way all participants contribute to the inclusive atmosphere. For example, when one participant was more comfortable with English than with German, nobody needed to be asked to switch languages. Everyone seemed to voluntarily help to ensure that no one missed out on any important information; several different participants acted as translators, and everybody – when addressing the English speaker – tried their best to speak English themselves.

These participants' interactions could be described as "resonance" (Rosa, 2019a), since they hear what their surrounding is sending out and react to it in ways they feel are appropriate based on that information. This resonance was especially apparent in young people's answer to the question of whether there were people in the group they did not like. All answers to this question, as well as some general remarks about friendship, could be understood as "I don't like them if they don't like me", meaning people who are impolite or lacking respect. Although this does happen at times, the general atmosphere within the group seemed to be very accepting and positive.

As Jack Black put it when asked about possible conflict in the group:

> *You know, they find how they approach one another and stuff like that. So, I think it is all in good harmony. Yeah. Just like the music, good harmony.*

To him, in the content of what he teaches the group, it seemed slightly less important that participants fully understand an activity than that they resonate with it:

> *We have done like, an Afro beat song […] in Nigerian Yoruba language, [which] is completely different for them, probably new. They do not understand what it meant […] but they were vibing with it.* (Jack Black, male, P)

Cognitive knowledge was, however, also appreciated by Jack Black. He mentioned that the more he himself has learnt about music in general, the more appreciative he has become of the local music he calls *"hereditary"*. Thus, his musical cultural heritage became more valuable to him after learning more about music that was different from what he considers his own cultural heritage. For Jack Black, the goal of cultural education is *"to let people know about, you know, these other parts of the world. The way they do stuff. Because there are people who have zero clue about how other places are."* However, he himself only spoke about "education" when asked about it. His own perspective was focused more on an individual process of growth.

Growing

In connection with these findings on resonance, Jack Black at first did not speak about cultural education or cultural literacy but about *"cultural development"*, which he saw as the heart of the organisation. This can be taken as an indicator that, in this group, cultural heritage is not so much seen as something from the past that needs to be preserved and taught. Rather, it is something that is developed with young people, where adults are mentors and role models but not leaders. They give guidance, not instructions.

> *When young people want to get involved in these kinds of activities, this is the place where they can go, because there are coaches, there are different kinds of people that can [...] assist them and guide them through the right processes.* (Jack Black, male, P)

He himself wants to set a good example but does not pressure anyone to follow his ways: "*So they have seen me in this kind of behaviour [...]. So I guess they could understand how it goes. And if they learn from it, then they do it. If they do not, then they do not!*"

In all activities, several forms of growth may be experienced. This is 'growing' not in the capitalist sense of 'more and bigger is better', but in a more resonant sense of 'growing together': adjusting to your surroundings, other people, yourself and the world in general by transmitting information and in turn listening to what others say trying to create something harmonious.

This principle was also evident in the process of developing the performance. The observer witnessed the growth of the performance as it shifted from hundreds of singular ideas by very different young people and practitioners into one complex performance by the same young people. The final piece still showed each performer's individuality, as well as their integration into a group that had learned to work, dance, sing and play together. During this process, the young people grew together as a group.

Young people also grow individually by watching and working with diverse practitioners, who each have expertise in their fields of interest. Through this process, the young people are encouraged to develop their individual, unique identities.

Creation of identity

When asked about cultural identity, most young people at first referred to this in natio-ethnic terms. Participants who spoke about their experiences of racist discrimination often talked about their own cultural identities in a specific way. They all identified as German, but had doubts or showed hesitation over this categorisation. Some clearly differentiated between their parents' culture and their own, their parents' culture having influenced their identity significantly without being the same. As Marius, for example, put it:

> *I grew up here. That means in fact, I myself identify as German in a way, more than as someone from Ghana. But since both my parents are from Ghana I cannot really say it like that. Well, I can say it like that, because clearly I am German in a way, but for my parents I am not German, although, okay, partly German anyhow.* (Marius, male, YP)

Lisa (female, YP) considered herself Ghanaian AND German, but even that classification, in her view, could not grasp the complexity that she would like to represent: *"It is really very, very complex."* While she claimed not to know much about Europe, she believed that it is just as heterogeneous as her conception of Africa. In some of her statements, her fluid understanding of belonging can be seen clearly. She described culture in general as different values like respect and acceptance, but also as practices such as writing and dancing. When asked about European culture, she struggled, explaining that in her mind this does not exist; she was sceptical about being European herself because she thought it would be like saying she was African, which she felt was too unspecific. Even though she claimed to be German several times, she also spoke about *"the Germans"* as if that expression did not include her. She mentioned *"their country"* and then, in the same sentence, *"we are one nation, so we should help those in need"*. When she noticed that her statements were somewhat contradictory, she reconfirmed that Germany is her country because it is where she lives: she speaks German and holds German citizenship. Her need to clarify "being German" can be seen as a result of discriminatory experiences, and as a reaction to exclusion.

This becomes clearer when contrasted with another young person whose claim to "being German" is not constantly questioned. Friedrich (male, YP), who is not subject to racist discrimination and declared himself to have grown up in a monolingual white German family, also said that he does not have just one culture, that his personality has been influenced by many different cultures. These included his *"maybe conservative"* family and, in contrast, his *"extremely individualistic and open"* friends. Since his ethno-national identity is not challenged by his surroundings, Friedrich has the freedom to focus on other aspects of culture.

This can be seen as an indicator that cultural identity is always shaped by diverse factors, while ethno-national identification seems to be closely linked to experiences of racism. The latter were much more explicitly taken into consideration than nationalities or ethnicities in general. According to Annika (female, YP), participants share their different experiences and shape their identities through this community and their creative work.

The youngest participant's perspective is particularly interesting. Leo (male, YP) was 15 years old, but, of the whole sample, he was the most aware and critical of his own cultural heritage and of the privilege connected with his German passport. In his view, different aspects contribute to his being European: his origins as well as the fact that he lives in Europe and holds a German passport. Being European, to Leo, is closely connected to being privileged, which is not necessarily a good thing. He mentioned that his mother taught him a lot about Europe's colonial past (for example), but that in school *"only the positive aspects [of Europe] are taught*". He considered it important to know both sides of colonial history, because otherwise "*exploitation and corruption will be considered normality*". He found it "*dangerous*" that his classmates did not question the fact that natural resources in different parts of the world are used by European companies without paying a fair price. Additionally, he was the only participant who clearly stated both aspects of cultural heritage: firstly, the influence of multiple diverse practices and structures from the past, and secondly, a new generation creating something new, which no one can define yet because it has so many diverse influences and original possibilities (use of social media, etc.). Of all the participants we interviewed, Leo had the longest history of participation in the organisation's activities, so maybe in addition to his familial education he has internalised the group's values more than anyone else.

Performance

Farida, a member of the management body, defined cultural education as imparting knowledge about different channels of communication and how to express oneself. She stated that her organisation tries to create an alternative space to schools, where only certain cognitive aspects of identity are valued. Practitioners at the performance group try to convey a sense of the value of all individual aspects of young people's personalities. Everyone is invited to show who they are. Through performances, young people share their very individual perspectives, which creates a sense of self-efficacy. Music can serve here as a key to understanding oneself and others, and to expressing identities.

Individual rebellious culture

Rebellion also is part of the identities being created within the performance group. Young people in this organisation are encouraged to create their own content in activities and performances. They are encouraged to be critical of fashion trends, politics and media discourses. Rebellion in this sense can take many different forms, one of which can be described as "*turning around*" (Lisa, female, YP) experiences of racism. That was also the main topic of the show. Experiences of or insights into racism that young people brought along to the planning sessions were used to criticise racism and discrimination in society (Annika, female, YP). In some cases this was achieved by turning situations around, by presenting practices and experiences of racialised youth, or by provoking the power and discrimination exercised by the white German majority.

Rebellious identities can also be seen on a more individual level regarding very specific practices. Hans-Heinrich (male, YP), for example, described how he tried to rebel against his mother by not attending church anymore, only to find that this was not doing him any good. He decided to go to a different church alone, accepting his mother's influence but still wanting to pursue his own path. This helped him to deal with the issues he had with his family on the one hand and his experiences of racist discrimination on the other. At his current church, he meets other young people with similar experiences, "*who just understand what it is like*" (Hans-Heinrich, male, YP). While he seemed to struggle with his relatively strict upbringing and felt that his parents do not understand his situation, he has still adopted the idea that going to church is something he needs to do. In the interview with this young man – who seemed to the researcher rather quiet, reserved and polite – one could see several aspects of his rebellious identity.

The observed creative chaos can be understood as intentionally leading away from a normative notion of 'high culture', instead making room for criticism of governing regimes, racism, exoticisation, and generally against being defined by others. This criticism may be expressed in rebellious, ironic, creative and authentic ways.

Privileged academic "politics-nerds": The pro-European political organisation

The second case study was carried out at a local youth branch of a wider international pro-European political organisation, which combines the positions of different political parties and promotes the EU, with approximately 17,000 members (of all ages) nationwide. Internationally, the youth organisation has about 30,000 members in more than 30 different countries within and outside the EU. The local branch we observed is located in a major city in Northern Germany.

Activities offered by the political group include both regular (monthly) activities and less frequent bigger events. As with the performance group, we observed one of each category. More active members of the group (Ginny female, P; Klaus, male, P/YP; Vincent, male, YP) mentioned that cooperation with schools is a major part of their work, although we did not observe this.

We participated in a round table that meets monthly at a pub, covering a different topic each time. Since the local ministry of social affairs funds this organisation quite comfortably, they can offer a free non-alcoholic beverage to each participant. Sometimes experts are invited to talk about certain topics, but usually members take turns presenting whichever European topic interests them. One session, for example, consisted of a presentation on a game designed to teach European law; another was about media representation of the EU. The session we observed focused on the EU election, which was to take place only two weeks later.

Additionally, a research assistant participated in a weekend seminar, which is organised annually at a facility that hosts conferences and seminars on a regular basis. This seminar also covers a different topic each year. This year it explored the relationship between the EU and Africa. The researcher observed official activities such as presentations and moderated discussions, as well as several informal activities surrounding the programme. The latter were especially interesting with regards to participants' habitus and cultural practices.

Diversity was limited among the participants. The general impression was quite homogenous: white, German, upper class, mostly university students. In the interviews, some participants described the group as "academic politics-nerds" (Ginny and Klaus). Only one participant in each of the two observed activities used terms in their self-descriptions that indicated identification with migrantised and/or racialised youth. One of these volunteered for an interview (Marc, male, YP). Marc was also the only member of the group with dual nationality, which is generally rare in Germany, as the law only allows dual citizenship in exceptional cases. When asked about diversity in the group, all participants stated that they were politically diverse, which was supported by the fact that the group included members of different political parties. One criticised the fact that it was mostly neoliberal (Tim, male, YP). All agreed that they are generally open to members and positions of any political party except extreme right-wing parties like the AfD.[1]

During the analysis of both the observations and interview transcripts, several references to practices and attitudes that could be explained by Bourdieu's theory of distinction (Bourdieu, 2010 (1984)) were identified. In particular, the

> *denial of lower, coarse, vulgar, venal, servile – in a word, natural – enjoyment, which constitutes the sacred sphere of culture, [which] implies an affirmation of the superiority of those who can be satisfied with the sublimated, refined, disinterested, gratuitous, distinguished pleasures forever closed to the profane* (Bourdieu, 2010: p. 7)

could be seen in the data. Most participants stated their preferences for activities that can be linked to a certain "class taste", and showed a tendency to criticise

---

1 AfD is short for "Alternative für Deutschland" (Alternative for Germany). It is a fairly new far-right political party that gained 12.6 % of the votes in the 2017 federal election. Since March 2021 they have been investigated by the Federal Office for the Protection of the Constitution for right-wing extremist activities.

cultural practices that were considered different from their own without reflecting on the circumstances of their genesis.

In general, participants at the political group seemed to be quite career-oriented. Their stated motivation for engaging in the activities of the organisation, as well as their description of their cultural practices in general, included some aspects of privilege. While the young people did note their fortunate position in society, these statements seem to be rather non-critical: they did not connect their privileges to the disadvantages of other people. In accordance with the pro-European programme of the group, being European appeared to these participants as a normal aspect of being in the world.

Portfolio-oriented distinctive culture

One thing that gave the impression that members of the political group were generally ambitious, career-oriented young people was their overall professional appearance. Their methods of presentation at seminars, their organisational structure, and even their clothing and small talk topics led to the conclusion that social and specific cultural capital seems to play an important role here. The student assistant who observed the weekend seminar noted that researching the organisation online made her iron some blouses because she feared she might be "underdressed"; in the pictures of previous seminars, the participants were all wearing dress shirts or blouses. The location of the seminar in an old, distinguished manor added to this initial impression. Although it was important to the practitioners to clarify that the organisation itself could never afford such a location, they nevertheless found a way through coordination with a high-profile foundation that let them use it for free (Klaus, male, YP/P). This is a good example of the social capital these young people possess. In addition, the first conversations in the car on the way to the manor, during which two participants introduced themselves to the researcher, centred on university and internships at very high-profile organisations.

When Klaus, a member of the management board, described his role in the organisation, one could easily forget that he was only 22 years old. He stated that he has to do lots of paperwork, but felt that his formal bureaucracy skills can really contribute to the success of the group. He spoke very professionally about organising teams, fundraising, shifting funds and finding supportive partners. At one point in the interview, he was almost apologetic about not having finished his bachelor's degree yet (for health reasons), which he was planning to do the following semester. All participants from the political group answered questions carefully, showing their knowledge and academic experience; some started by giving an academic definition of culture (Lilly, female, YP). In terms of social capital, they seemed very supportive of each other and even of the researcher. They offered to do whatever they could to support her in her career within CHIEF, one example being willingly doing interviews with her.

Many participants viewed the activities primarily as an opportunity to broaden their knowledge and their networks, and as closely connected to other opportunities for career development. Marc stated that the content of the seminar was interesting to him because the relationships between African and European countries were an important factor in his field of international trade. He was especially interested in contracts and connections in this arena. The fact that colonialism still influences international trading relations today genuinely surprised him: *"I would never have thought that it is still like that TODAY. I thought it was some time in the past, not nice, but over now"* (Marc, male, YP). Tim's description of his motivation was quite similar. He was especially interested in the topic of the seminar as it was closely connected to his university degree subject. Lilly (female, YP) admitted frankly that her motivation to participate in the activities is *"rather selfish. There are free opportunities [for] further education."*

Even their interest in "different cultures" might be derived from these opportunities. The ways in which Lilly, Vincent, Klaus, Marc and Benjamin Müller talked about travelling can also be read as additions to their career portfolio. They all saw travelling as a self-evident part of education, but also seemed to know in advance what it was they wanted to learn. Most of them travelled in connection with their degree, gathering experience in their respective fields. In some cases, they were even more interested in teaching than in learning. Lilly, for example, went to a village in Israel to volunteer in a project promoting *"dialogue between Arabs and Jews"* that was run by professionals from Germany, Switzerland and the Netherlands. She also leads a project developed by a worldwide international NGO that takes menstrual cups to Bangladesh and Rwanda. This project, from the perspective of postcolonial theory, very much reproduces the global power imbalance in which 'Western' knowledge and practices are seen as universal cultural literacy. All these experiences were valued by the young people for the profit they gain from them.

This leads to a perspective on diversity as modern and interesting but potentially problematic, not as something that constitutes society in general. These young people did not see the "normality" of diversity, and therefore judged things as problematic or interesting from their specific perspective. Likewise, connected to this perspective on the world is the idea that "social engagement" in the sense of "helping people in need" is universally a good thing. This is often believed uncritically, without questioning who is defining what needs of which people and why. Another aspect of cultural literacy shared by the young people from the political group also fits into the mainstream discourse of European culture as superior, democratic, and liberal. The group practices a very professional style of discussion, which several young people called *"their culture"*; this was also an aspect they especially liked about the group. While this could possibly also be read as a "resonant" style of respecting others and listening as well as broadcasting, in this case it appears more to be an acquired frame that is directed by an outer order of things.

Diversity from an ethnocentric perspective

Diversity was explained by group members in a very interesting way. When asked about the diversity of the group, most of them stated that they are politically diverse, meaning that they include members from all political parties except the extreme right (AfD). They obviously wanted to create an image for themselves as very open and democratic. This spectrum of diversity was the one most mentioned in these interviews. Some participants also mentioned gender balance, stating that their group of leaders has achieved parity while in most other activities they have a slight majority of participants identifying as male. Other dimensions of diversity were seen as more or less problematic. Some interviewees wanted to change the fact that all group members are German nationals, all academics, and mostly from families with a relatively high socio-economic background. However, this challenge does not seem to have been followed up by direct actions to create more diversity in these social dimensions.

Based on our findings from policy and curricula reviews (Seukwa, Marmer and Sylla, 2018; Sylla, Marmer and Seukwa, 2019), we were surprised on the one hand about how much knowledge the young people participating in this organisation had about German and European history. On the other hand, we were not at all surprised by what kind of knowledge they had. Their knowledge about history was Eurocentric, and more specifically German-centric: they were familiar with all the well-known discourses on how European history begins with the Roman Empire; how colonialism is mainly part of British, French and Hispanic but not so much German culture; and how German remembrance culture is necessary and already successfully implemented in schools.

Some quotes dealing with historical issues illustrate how this ethnocentric view on global history manifested in these young people: "*World War I does not have any influence on today, but the NS-period indeed has a lot of influence on today*", said Vincent (male, YP), and Marc (male, YP) agreed:

> *I find everything that happened during World War II very interesting, especially the whole Europe discussion, how that came about, what moved people at that time and why and how it still exists. I think that is super-interesting. Everything before that is too abstract for my liking. I will never start talking about 1700 or 1600. It is good to know some cornerstones, but it does not affect me.* (Marc, male, YP)

He further stressed that this specific historical knowledge is important for understanding older people who experienced that time, while colonial history was only interesting to him in the context of international trade.

Vincent, who told us that he went to a concentration camp commemoration site with his exchange student, made similar connections between historical knowledge and cultural literacy. He said it is important

> *as an exchange student to get a feeling of the cultural identity of a country, to understand people a little better. […] The NS time still has a lot of influence on the cultural memory of, erm, Germany. And I mean, that is what shaped us in the end. Not that we need to feel guilty, no, I don't, but it has an influence on many things. And to understand what is happening in Germany, you have to know this.* (Vincent, male, YP)

At another point in the interview, he also told the story of the first instance of European unification, which, according to him, happened when *"the Ottomans"* invaded Europe and got as far as Vienna. European identity, in his mind, has always been associated with separating "us" from "them". This can be connected to Bach's (2019) theory that the persistence of a national habitus is based on a long history of conflict over nation-building (Bach, 2019: p. 425).

Privilege

Most young people at this site described either themselves or the other members of the group as quite privileged, as can already be seen in the site description. This, however, did not necessarily lead to any reflection on how this privilege influences their perspectives on the world and on culture.

From their descriptions of cultural practices, these young people's high level of cultural capital is made visible without them noticing it. This is Bourdieu's theory on habitus and distinction in practice, since the "schemes of the habitus, the primary form of classification, owe their specific efficacy to the fact that they function below the level of consciousness and language, beyond the reach of introspective scrutiny or control by the will" (Bourdieu, 2010: p. 469).

Tim (male, YP) was a very interesting participant. He was by far the most critical of the organisation and the EU in general. When asked about activities he shares with friends, he listed some cultural practices (sports, electronic music festivals, and YouTube) that were not as highbrow as those the others mentioned.

However, while Tim was a participant in one of the activities, he was not yet a member of the organisation, and was not sure if he wanted to become one due to his dislike of its strong neoliberal faction.

Spatial dimensions

During one interview in particular (Lilly, female, YP), several different spatial dimensions (family, region, nation, Europe, Earth and Outer Space) could be identified. These can all be considered spheres of cultural education and require different forms of cultural literacy. Most of these dimensions could also be observed in interviews. According to Castro Varela et al., spatial metaphors and concepts are key elements of postcolonial theory (Castro Varela et al., 2009: p. 308). They consider it especially meaningful to determine the position from which a certain space is constructed (ibid.: p. 310). In the accounts of the young people from the political group, all these spheres appeared as concentric circles around the individual interviewee.

The innermost circle of cultural education surrounding the young person is the family. The most relevant aspect of cultural literacy acquired in families is a basic emotional connection with their tangible and intangible cultural heritage. This emotional aspect seems to be linked more closely to families than any cognitive knowledge is:

> *That is where I got the emotional connection that it is important to know about it. […] Facts and dates I learnt at school.* (Lilly, female, YP)
> *With my parents I talk about attitudes more, not so much about details. Rather […] what do you like? What do you dislike? But we don't have real discussions.* (Tim, male, YP)
> *I would observe that, considering my personal emotions, I have always had positive associations with Europe, but that I did grow up that way.* (Ginny, female, P)

Surrounding the family are regional and then national societies. Several young people mentioned specific regions as being more relevant to their identity than the nation, but none of them elaborated on this from the perspective of their personal identities.

The next circle, which all participants from the political group deemed important to their cultural identity and education, was Europe, which will be analysed further in the next section. Given that the European Union is the main focus of the organisation and that these young people took part in our research because they perceived CHIEF's research interests as being very close to their own, this was not surprising.

In several interviews, young people talked about travelling beyond Europe, which they found especially educational.

A more surprising finding was the dimension of outer space, which was extensively discussed by Lilly. She stated that she is very interested in this topic *"and the activities happening there at the moment, especially judicial regulations"* (Lilly, female, YP). Her interest in the judicial regulations of space makes it clear that she thinks within national boundaries and from a capitalist point of view. The following quote shows that she does not doubt "our" right and responsibility to delineate space law:

> *There is BARELY ANY history. It is all produced now, in a way. That is super exciting. In which direction it could develop. The fact that it can drift into very undesirable directions if we take the wrong decisions. That's why I think it is highly relevant to a learning effect.* (Lilly, female, YP)

Ginny (female, P), who is a little older, also mentioned the dimension of outer space, but from a completely different perspective. For her, space is not so much "ours" to discover and to rule, but is the ultimate "other":

> *I once hypothesised that we will probably only be able to come together as one whole world when there is a different species on a different planet. Because, we humans, I think, always need an outgroup, a different group that we can distinguish ourselves from. Maybe there are other possibilities, who knows.* (Ginny, female, P)

Europe – a geographical, a political, and/or an emotional entity?

As stated above, all participants from the political group adamantly supported the general idea of a European Union. Young people's descriptions of European culture and what Europe means to them, however, varied in each individual account, according to whether they saw Europe as a geographical, a political, or an emotional concept. Sometimes they conflated and sometimes clearly distinguished between these aspects.

Vincent, for example, wanted to *"show that the EU is more than just free trade between partner countries"*. He did not specify what he meant by that, but stated several times that he thinks *"Europe is cool."* Here, political and emotional aspects are connected in one sentence, suggesting that the EU is a political construct but also more than that. Vincent said that one of the reasons for his engagement in political activities, as offered by the organisation, is changes in the social climate that threaten European unity. The rise of nationalism, as evidenced by the Brexit movement, Trump becoming president of the USA and the realistic chance of Le Pen winning the presidential elections in France, encouraged him (as well as some other participants) to actively support the European idea.

In contrast with all other members of the group, Marc admitted to not having a lot of knowledge about Europe. When asked about European culture, he stated that for him European culture and German culture are the same, though when later asked about his knowledge of particular European countries he instantly mentioned the cultural differences between them. For example, he said that a French person will act differently from a German person, without naming specific ways in which they diverge. However, from his experience as a trader, he knew that working with people from France is not the same as working with people from Spain. Vincent had similar difficulties explaining what differences and similarities are crucial to determining what is 'European' and what is not:

> *Of course, one could say, well Poland and Russia, there is not really such a big difference, although politically there are immense controversies, because they don't get along at all. But well, one has to say there are many historical similarities, we have a common history. And many countries in Europe have the same experiences, especially in Western Europe, many countries have a colonial past, many have a history of Antisemitism, many have a history of oppressing certain countries, especially the dominance of, I don't know, Russia, Germany in Eastern Europe. And it gets difficult when you go to these bordering countries where it is not really clear, especially Russia and Turkey, where does the alleged… where does it stop? It is not very clear because one cannot define culture that clearly, because it is dynamic. Nevertheless, I think that a country can slide into it and out of it again. But at the moment I get the feeling that in Hungary something is going wrong, which is obviously the case, still nobody would get the idea to say Hungarians weren't European. While for Turkey […] it is not that distinct, also historically it is a bit unclear; one could see it either way.* (Vincent, male, YP)

In general, the interviewees' descriptions of Europe were complex and sometimes contradictory, and they raised questions about power, perceptions and belonging.

Resonance versus distinction – discussion

When contrasting the case studies, interesting similarities and differences can be identified. Both groups showed contradictions in their concepts of cultural diversity, belonging and national culture. The performance group explicitly challenges the perceived image of national culture, promoting a culture of individualism, of creativity and acceptance, criticising racist social structures, and giving voice and space to marginalised/racialised youth. According to Magatti et al. (2019), individualistic approaches risk becoming instruments of neoliberal "*consumeristic culture*" (ibid.: p. 470). To avoid this, they distinguish between "individuation" and "individualization", the first being "*the long-term, relational, and endless process of personal development*", and the latter "*a social condition that seeks to maximize individual liberty and self-determination*" (ibid.). For Magetti et al.,

> *the challenge is to optimistically look for a new type of prosperity, moving away from societal adolescence (based on quantitative growth and consumerism) toward a more mature social organization based on a distinctive model of self-realization, where creativity and human flourishing may become the qualifying elements of a new development model. This is a task that the notion of social generativity may help accomplish.* (Ibid.: p. 471)

This form of social generativity can be seen in statements and activities at the performance group.

Diversity was also stated as a goal in the political group, and its perceived ethno-national and socioeconomic homogeneity was criticised by its members. They would like to become more diverse, but do not necessarily realise that their habitus is very elite, which means that the organisation feels very highbrow and exclusive to outsiders.

While at both sites some activities are held in the English language, the reasons for this are quite different. At the performance group, English is used as a means of including people who are not fluent in German. Young people usually switch between languages to make sure everyone is included in the conversation, and translate for each other. At the political group, the seminar was also held in English because one of the experts did not speak German, but this was seen as a problem. It was said in the discussion that using English creates a barrier of participation to less privileged young people.

Treasure of experience in creative chaos vs. opportunism in high culture

In the two groups, cultural heritage seems to be seen somewhat differently. The differences are somewhat intangible, but when we look at how "experts" are involved in the activities (and which criteria led to the classification of "expert") it becomes clearer. At the performance group, practitioners stated that everyone who wishes to organise any kind of activity can do so. Practitioners are not valued for their name or their certificates so much as their ability to relate to young people and their motivations for sharing their experience. Cultural heritage can in this sense be seen as any set of experiences valuable to someone. It does not need any official validation, nor does it serve any specific purpose. Any experience that can be of value for any reason is considered a treasure, just because it is experience. Jack Black is a good example of this principle. He has no diploma or certificate for leading a choir, but he loves what he does, is a good, self-taught musician, and his charisma is captivating to many young people. The general concept of culture expressed in some of the interviews matches CHIEF's concept of 'heritage in the making'. These activities are more about creativity and self-expression than about learning traditional content. While traditions and history are seen as important, how they are integrated into new creations is even more important.

At the political group, expertise and competencies are structured more in accordance with formal criteria. The experts invited to speak at the seminar were an official ambassador and a university professor. Cultural heritage was seen either as a certain set of acquired knowledge through history and personal education, or as *"a pair of glasses, through which we see the world, and these glasses are shaped by all our experiences"* (Marc, male, YP). Although this quote could be read differently, cultural literacy in this understanding is based primarily on specific, presumed universal knowledge and practices, which individuals need to know in order to get somewhere in life.

By contrasting the ways in which young people at the two sites conceptualise cultural heritage, another aspect of Rosa's theory becomes pertinent. Rosa (2019b) criticises the idea that the modern way of being in the world is based on cutting the link between the genesis and the validity of values and norms (p. 48). Severing the link to the past in this way also means cutting a link to the future (p. 49). At the two sites, the connection to history was very different. While most interview participants from the performance group did not claim to know much about the historical developments that led to their own or their parents' values, they said that they would like to know more, because they do consider it important. This lack of knowledge shows that most of them (except for Leo) did not actively try to link their future to their past, but when asked about it they felt that they should. In contrast, several young people from the political group explicitly mentioned that modern life should no longer be associated with certain parts of German and European history. Their way of speaking about the past reiterates the behaviour criticised by Rosa. In these interviewees' view, German participation in colonialism, for example, is something that they can ignore; although some of them possessed quite a lot of historical knowledge, they did not always consider this very important. One exception seems to be "what happened in World War II", but even here only specific aspects – those that help to construct an identity of Germans as a freed and purged people (Czollek, 2018: p. 24) – were noted. Other information that could challenge this image was disregarded.

Sharing individual perspectives vs. mission

While at both sites there was an atmosphere of respectful discussion, there were still some differences to be observed. At first glance, they did seem similarly participatory and inclusive, but on a closer look, within the performance group thematic discussions focused on sharing one's individual perspective and growing while listening to others, while in the political group discussions were more abstract debates. Participants argue, trying to convince one another of certain views. They seem keener to teach others than to learn from others. While the performance group created a showcase to display their individual perspectives, enabling the audience to take from it whatever they want, young people from the political group took a different approach. This group generally tries to impact international politics more directly. In some interviews, their opinions and missionary ambitions became quite clear. Even when Ginny mentioned that *"we need to invite people from outside the EU, and listen to their perspective on our actions,"* this did not transcend the binary logic of active us vs. passive them. The EU was still constructed as the active party in this interaction, and the 'others' from outside were seen as informers who make sure *"the right actions"* can be taken. Ginny did not consider learning about and from *"others' actions"*.

Conclusion

Regarding the goal of a more inclusive notion of cultural heritage, the way in which certain activities are valued in the organisations is especially notable. The question of why something should be learned, or why something is interesting, marks an essential difference between the two cases. At the performance group, it seems important to learn new things and to express one's individuality regardless of whether this knowledge will serve some higher purpose or not. This leads to a resonant way of interacting with oneself, each other and with more abstract concepts like music and history. At the political group, however, young people were more focused on what they could gain from a certain activity or how they could learn in a more strategic way. In both groups, young people were supportive of each other, and within both organisations active participation, speaking freely, as well as contributing to group discussions and in developing activities, were equally common. Yet their styles of explicit and implicit communication subtly influence the opportunities to participate. While officially both groups are open to all young people curious about the offered activities, and supposedly allow young people to influence the programme according to their interests, the two attract quite different groups of young people. The performance group's resonant style of communication invites young people from a broad variety of neighbourhoods, with different socio-economic and educational backgrounds, to feel welcome and enables them to develop skills and knowledge without pressure. Meanwhile, the political group cultivates an exclusive culture. In this case, participation and group support are implicitly limited to young people who are comfortable with this style because it has been ingrained in them through their privileged upbringing. The lack of critical reflection on this privilege practically leads to the exclusion of Others, without the group wanting or noticing this. Therefore, exclusion is not only a consequence of deliberate segregation but can also occur unknowingly and unwillingly, just by not reflecting on the mechanisms of distinction.

Another interesting question that arises from these findings concerns the link between ethno-national identities and racism (or maybe even the link between identity and discrimination in more general terms). These case studies suggest that national identity is more important to those young people who are subject to othering and therefore struggle to belong. Young people whose national identity goes unquestioned by others appeared to have little interest in this aspect of their identity. We speculate that this is not to be interpreted as common anti-nationalism; rather, since their Germanness is taken for granted, these young people have no need to construct a national identity that is already normalised by dominant discourses and seemingly obvious. They have had the freedom to focus instead on other aspects like regional or political identities. Similar observations were made in the English study of formal education (see Chapter 3). It would be interesting to compare these findings with case studies from other national contexts, but also to further explore how this relates to official national educational policies and practices.

Acknowledgments

Maria Fahr, Anna Siegl, Elina Marmer, Louis Henri Seukwa

References

Apel, H., Engels, D. 2012; Bildung und Teilhabe von Kindern und Jugendlichen im unteren Einkommensbereich. Untersuchung der Implementationsphase des „Bildungs- und Teilhabepakets" im Auftrag des Bundesministeriums für Arbeit und Soziales. Abschlussbericht, ISG Institut für Sozialforschung und Gesellschaftspolitik GmbH, Köln/Berlin.

Bach, M. 2019; Die Demokratie als Achillesferse der Europäisierung. Zur nationalistischen Transformation Europas, in: Dörre, K. et al. (eds.), Große Transformation? Zur Zukunft moderner Gesellschaften, Springer Fachmedien Wiesbaden, pp. 421–434.

Bourdieu, P. 2010 (1984); Distinction. A Social Critique of the Judgement of Taste, Routledge, London.

Castro Varela, M.d.M., Dhawan, N., & Randeira, S., 2009; Postkoloniale Theorie, in: Günzel, S. (ed.), Raumwissenschaften, Suhrkamp, Frankfurt, pp. 308–323.

Czollek, M., 2018; Desintegriert Euch!, Carl Hanser Verlag, München.

Deinet, U. & Ickling, M. 2013; Offene Jugendarbeit und Ganztagsschule, in: Deinet, U., Sturzenhecker, B. (eds.), Handbuch Offene Kinder- und Jugendarbeit, Springer Fachmedien Wiesbaden, pp. 389–400.

Magatti, M., Giaccardi, C., & Martinelli, M. 2019; Social generativity: A relational paradigm for social change, in: Dörre, K. et al. (eds.), Große Transformation? Zur Zukunft moderner Gesellschaften, Springer Fachmedien Wiesbaden, pp. 469–486.

Rosa, H. 2019a; Resonanz. Eine Soziologie der Weltbeziehung, second edition, Suhrkamp, Berlin.

Rosa, H. 2019b; „Spirituelle Abhängigkeitserklärung". Die Idee des Mediopassiv als Ausgangspunkt einer radikalen Transformation, in: Dörre, K. et al. (eds.), Große Transformation? Zur Zukunft moderner Gesellschaften, Springer Fachmedien Wiesbaden, pp. 35–55.

Seukwa, L. H., Marmer, E., & Sylla, C. 2018; National Cultural/Educational Policy Review (Germany). in: Fooks, G., Stamou, E., & McNie, K. (eds.), *CHIEF-WP1_D1.2_National-Cultural-Educational-Policy-Reviews_v1.1_KM* (74–104). http://chiefprojecteu.com/wp-content/uploads/CHIEF-WP1_D1.2_National-Cultural-Educational-Policy-Reviews_v1.1_KM.pdf (Accessed on January 17, 2022).

Sylla, C., Marmer, E., & Seukwa, L. H. 2019; National Curricula Review (Germany). in: Marmer, E., & Zurabishvili, T. (eds.), *Chief-WP2_D2.1_National-Curriculum-Review-Reports_v1.0_14.01.19* (70–110). http://chiefprojecteu.com/wp-content/uploads/Chief-WP2_D2.1_National-Curriculum-Review-Reports_v1.0_14.01.19.pdf (Accessed on January, 2022).

(by Shailendra Kharat, Anagha Tambe and Priya Gohad)

Chapter 9 Post-coloniality, social capital and difference trumps hierarchy: Non- formal cultural education of youth in India

Abstract: The broad objective of this study is to understand how non-formal education processes shape the cultural identities and perceptions of young people. In order to do this, intensive fieldwork was conducted in two organisations based in a Tier II metro city, an important urban centre in the state of Maharashtra in India. Theoretical frameworks including post-colonialism, interactions between nation, culture and globalisation, diversity within Indian culture, and non-formal education were used to analyse the data.

In India, non-formal education is generally seen as secondary to formal education. However, in the organisations that we studied, the picture seems to be more complex. We found that, while young people viewed non-formal education mainly in the shadow of their formal schooling and planned career paths, the former is not always considered inferior to the latter. There were many instances where non-formal education was seen either to be providing young people with alternative career paths or to be filling important gaps in their formal education. In addition, the institutions we studied impart engaging and hands-on training that enrich not only young people's formal education but their lives as a whole.

This study offers a layered conception of cultural diversity. While participants articulated diversity in terms of social identities like caste, religion and language, they also seemed to stereotype their cultural 'other'. Participants seemed to prefer tolerance to resolving every difference. Amongst some practitioners, we also found a keen awareness of plurality within tradition and a desire to harness alternative traditions to further the cause of cultural diversity. We argue that one needs to have a strong sense of hierarchy and contestation, along with diversity and difference, in horizontal relationships in this country. This is because India is riddled with hierarchies of caste, gender and religion, among others.

Perceptions about Europe were also mixed. There were expressions of admiration for the continent, as well as post-colonial anxiety about cultural invasion by the West and a feeling of lagging behind. Some interviewees articulated concerns about colonialism and racism.

Keywords: non-formal education, youth, diversity, post colonial

Introduction

Non-formal education (NFE) emerged worldwide in the 1970s–80s as a mechanism specifically designed for the 'developing world' to catch up with global educational or literacy goals (Rogers, 2007). In India, 25 years after attaining freedom from colonial rule in 1947, it was realised that the formal education system had limited success in universalising education. Hence, the Indian government launched a non-formal education system during 1979–80, with the aim of guaranteeing the right to education for all by targeting adult and adolescent populations left out of the schooling system (Chandra and Shah, 1987). Some of the major initiatives in this direction have included the Total Literacy Campaign started in 1988–89, the *Sarva Shiksha Abhiyan* ('education to all') campaign started in 2001 as an alternative education source for drop-out kids, and the National Institute of Open Schooling. Several non-governmental associations reached out to underprivileged children by providing education outside a formal organisational structure.

This conventional idea of NFE has been expanded by education activists. In the last two decades and more, NFE has gained a new momentum across the world as a force for the de-formalisation of education, urging greater flexibility in school settings and the active participation of learners. Rather than being merely complementary, supplementary or alternatives to the formal educational system, NFE has become a substantive intervention in it. This has gathered momentum as an independent education approach for all – this is inclusive, both cognitive and non-cognitive learning. With this new idea, NFE is framed as life-long learning, providing life skills, work skills and social cultural development. It has also been situated as education that focuses on the local contexts of its participants, and their active involvement in learning. In India, this new conception of NFE has led to a range of initiatives seeking to redefine the functions, aims, pedagogies and values of learning, depending upon the socio-cultural contexts of children and the initiating organisations. These have included a range of projects, both within and outside the school setting, from nature clubs and environmental societies to training workshops for gender sensitization, sex/health education and *sanskarvarga* (refinement classes) for infusing nationalist, religious and cultural fervour.

Cultural education in India has also evolved through non-formal avenues within and outside the school setting, recognising the inadequacy of the formal education system of cultural enrichment. The state has recognised this need through:the CABE (Central Advisory Board of Education) committee report, which noted the importance of integrating cultural education into the school curriculum; *Rashtriya Madhyamik Shiksha Abhiyan* (National Mission for Secondary Education), which provides study tours, art/ cultural camps and teacher training; NCERT (National Council for Educational Research and Training), which conducted a nation-wide survey on how cultural content in schools foregrounds students' voices; CCRTs (Centre for Cultural Resource and

Training), advocacy and facilitation initiatives that focus on local language and local arts and connect school settings with the local community. These initiatives aim to preserve the cultural diversity and heritage of India by focusing on local arts and customs and by imparting multi-cultural and inter-cultural education. These groups are often limited in reach in the context of India's vast educational sector. Cultural education thus needs to be strengthened by articulating culture as discursive and dynamic rather than fixed, and by enabling young people to see themselves as agents in the continuous making of culture.

The state's vision of cultural education has an explicit agenda of underlining 'unity in diversity' within 'Indian culture'. On the other hand, non-profit organisations such as GyanAdab, Raah, TIFA, INTACH and Arbhaat seek to provide more open cultural and artistic spaces and resources to nurture creativity and talent in largely middle-class youth. These platforms are defined by the middle-class desire for (what they perceive as) healthy and holistic development in their children, and organisations tend to focus on targeted groups of youth with specific artistic interests. The selected case studies in this research represent similar non-formal settings.

This chapter examines the cultural participation and identities of young people in a city in western India through non-formal education. The city in which this research was conducted is a growing software hub and centre of higher education that is popularly known as the cultural capital of the region. We selected two non-formal organisations from the city that work with young people to develop their artistic engagement from an alternative, non-dominant approach. The organisations are also crucial in developing the artistic capacities of young people through training and practice, and in preparing them for work in the creative cultural industry. We focused on the everyday cultural environment of young people in terms of family, friends and digital media to help to understand their cultural participation in these non-formal educational settings. The chapter examines how young people from different socio-economic backgrounds perceive and practice culture and cultural diversity. It further investigates how they understand 'Indian' culture, often in juxtaposition to 'western' culture. We aim to show how young people, as well as the non-formal cultural organisations themselves, navigate cultural practices and perspectives that are 'western' or global as well as local. In other words, how do they take into account diverse linguistic, regional, caste, and rural or urban cultural landscapes? We then demonstrate the need for cultural diversity to be reimagined and for young people to become familiar with this concept.

Film club

The Film Club is based in a Tier II metro city. This site is seen as one of the foremost creative spaces in the city because of its founders and the film fraternity associated with it. Moreover, this club is perceived as the only organisation in the city to provide a platform for short films and a conducive environment for learning about the medium of film non-formally. Activities are directed towards attracting youth to meaningful cinema, and engage with a range of youngsters, film enthusiasts, filmmakers and critics.

The Club was started in 2013 by two film personalities; one is a renowned filmmaker and the other a screenwriter-actor. They are well-known on the international film circuit for their locally-rooted films. The Club aims to showcase the best short films across the globe, as well as to create awareness among young filmmakers about the variety and experimentation of short films. It also seeks to develop film appreciation amongst (new and established) audiences. In short, the objective of this non-formal organisation is to propagate a vibrant culture of short films in the city, provide a platform for young film enthusiasts, and encourage youngsters to learn the craft of short filmmaking.

To achieve this purpose, the organisation regularly arranges showings of short films made by filmmakers from diverse localities, within the country and beyond. It also conducts regular screenings for children through a children's film club. The Club also organises a regular workshop entitled 'Shoot a Short', which teaches technical and non-technical aspects of short filmmaking.

This short film club runs on a subscription basis. On the first Saturday of every month, they conduct screenings of short films for their subscribers, and every four to six months they host a week-long workshop that is attended by more than 100 young people at a time.

The organisation has a non-formal setup that conducts educational and awareness activities in the domain of art and culture. Events are mostly attended by young people between the ages of 14 and 30. Most practitioners and volunteers are from the same age group. Many of the films showcased or discussed during their sessions are by European filmmakers, so there is a strong European connection to be explored.

During an interview with a founding member of the organisation, it became clear that funding issues are a major challenge. The members often have to personally invest, which brings certain limitations. Although the organisation is trying its best to showcase films of all kinds, they believe in enlightening its audience on topics "close to home" and display films about India made by up-and-coming Indian film makers. The Club was started with the intention of focusing on short films that were content-driven, but now they even screen international and regional full-length feature films.

The participants have mainly migrated from small towns to this city with aspirations of pursuing careers in a creative field. They admire the founders of the Club, who themselves migrated from smaller cities in a socially and economically marginalised sub-region of Maharashtra state; these founders are now considered to be significant personalities in the local creative field. We conducted fieldwork in what is considered to be, a relatively economically, socially and culturally advanced city. Young participants in this organisation share their socio-spatial 'origins' with the founders of the organisation, who they consider to have 'achieved' a status in a creative field after coming from 'outside'. This explains these young people's admiration for and connection with the founders.

On average, members of the organising team who execute the club's activities are in the age group of 20–25 years. The organisation creates a passionate interest in technical aspects of film in a non-formal atmosphere, but at the same time intentionally or unintentionally equates culture with cinema.

Openness of the organisational culture

The Film Club has made the conscious decision to encourage new young talent and to pursue a unique perspective on films that is located in its local surroundings. Most of the group's participants/ volunteers do not have formal training, or even much exposure to cinema culture beyond some artistic participation; most importantly, these participants have the desire to do something new, and to develop their career differently. Their motivation for participating in this organisation is overwhelmingly professional, due to the desire to develop a career in filmmaking or at least in the arts. This club provides a rare opportunity to meet eminent international artists, a "*cinematic enlightenment*" (Hemant, male, YP), and also equips the volunteers with skills such as working with small budgets. The young participants, however, were rather anxious about not earning enough through volunteering or not getting adequate hands-on work experience. Hallmarks of this organisation are an informal, open, democratic environment, the perspective that film should be linked to other art forms such as dance or painting, encouragement of deep and free thinking, and strong roots in the local surrounding. However, what is adored the most is the opportunity to spend time with its founder artists, renowned for their new/different perspectives in the Marathi film circles. The participants reiterated that having personal dialogue with their 'idols' is an exciting, nourishing experience that challenges their conventional understanding of film, enabling them not just to 'consume' but to 'appreciate' film, and its craft and aesthetic. These meetings change young people's thought processes and help them to develop a more mature perspective that looks beyond the surface; this teaches them to explore film in a multidimensional way. The organisation also gives them a community with shared interest.

The metaphor of *gurukul*[1] was invoked by many participants to articulate their reverence for the teachers and to emphasise that in this non-formal setting they learn not only filmmaking, but also life lessons. There is a near absence of young women volunteers, which practitioners linked to the overall gender prejudices in the film industry, and to young women's supposed inability to take risks or to pursue filmmaking passionately. Interviewed young women participants were less fervent in describing the organisational culture as open.

The new digital youth culture

The major sites of cultural participation for young people, most of whom are aspiring filmmakers, are over-the-top media services (OTTs),[2] as these are private, convenient and have a wide variety of choices, all without having to watch 'bold' content with parents. The participants accept the violent and sexual content of the OTTs as truthful and as an acknowledgment of the dark realities of the world. They find the negativity around OTTs as hypocritical.[3] Although its availability to young children was a concern, and the loss of 'innocence' in the face of populist and marketable content was lamented, "*Every new generation appreciates the content that is found violent by the earlier generation, like*

1 According to some, this system of education 'dates back to around 5000 BC in the Indian subcontinent during Vedic ages' and imparted 'practical knowledge' and 'holistic education' (Chandwani, 2019). However, others contend that the system was steeped in caste and gender-based exclusion (Jamanadas, n.d.). Contemporarily, some institutions (like Vedpathsalas) try to impart training in Vedas through this system (Chatterjee, 2018), but continue to admit only Brahmin students (ibid), excluding non-Brahmins.

2 An over-the-top (OTT) media service is directly provided to viewers through internet connection, rather than cable, broadcast or satellite television, and can be accessed on diverse digital platforms. Some of the most popular OTT sites include Netflix and Amazon video.

3 OTT content is commonly criticised for having nudity, abusive language, and violent and sexual content due to nascent and lenient regulation. For instance, as of now, India does not have clear regulation of these sites whereas films, plays and TV programmes are subject to 'censorship' under Indian law.

relationships are more hostile due to the colonial politics partitioning the Indian subcontinent and to corresponding religious nationalisms. Meanwhile, Ashar (male, YP) directed attention to Germany's struggle to escape its identification with Hitler and its identity as a war-torn country.

The young people either expressed ambiguity about their cultural identity as Indian or 'western', or accepted this as a mixed identity, or as an Indian, but not 'original' identity (Rohan, male, YP). The Film Club urges them to be more connected to their local cultures. Abhijeet (male, P) was critical of young people for not being proud or serious about their 'roots'. Anil urged the rejection of an inferiority complex about one's own culture: "*cultural education would mean knowing your roots, learning to understand yourself in terms of your surroundings, to relate to different people around you*" (Anil, male, P). The Film Club thus seeks to open diverse cultures to local youth through films from across the world, while emphasising the centrality of one's local cultural surrounding. For this organisation, connecting with local culture enables one to empathise with 'different' people, and to embrace the whole world.

Creativity and Culture Institute

This Institute, located in a Tier II metro city, is a multi-disciplinary platform for Creativity and Culture. It seeks to provide alternative art education through programmes like residencies and workshops. The organisation was founded in 2014 by young people (aged 23–25), who mentioned that one of their important objectives was to give the young English-speaking community in the predominantly Marathi-speaking city greater access to creative activities. The residency offered by the organisation accommodates young people from all parts of India, as well as outside the country, and provides them with a facility in which to conduct research, discussions and experimentation. The Institute was created to innovate within and outside of the existing educational ecosystem in India, with an aim of providing resources, tools and processes to other institutions, art organisations and cultural communities. According to the founders, the vision has always been to impart training in various creative processes. However, they also intend to expand the creative cultures across the city, not restricting themselves to the enrolled students as the formal educational system does. The Institute's core concept is to engage audiences locally. This audience comes from various fields, and hence the Institute takes a multi-disciplinary approach to its activities.

The studio also offers cultural workshops related to various art forms, including music, dance, photography and memes, as well as mentorship programmes.

The latter provides students with an innovative learning experience through a unique pedagogical process. These workshops and projects attract young people between 18 and 25 years of age. Programmes are designed around themes such as Meme Regime, artist presentations, discussions on contemporary art, gender issues, etc. Young people are attracted to the organisation because the team there helps them understand various unknown and complicated aspects of art and culture that interest them.

The site is located at an art deco hotel in the marked centre of the city. It offers an urban landscape that helps to sustain a strong connection with the community. The studios in the building are interlinked, providing easy interaction and association between artists. The organisation has set up its own library, which is equipped with books, e-books, catalogues, journals, magazines, and board games related to cultural heritage. The Institute provides a non-formal atmosphere for young people to explore various elements of art, culture, creativity and heritage.

This site focuses on bringing contemporary and experimental art to the city. However, like the Film Club, the Institute faces a lack of consistent funding, which limits its innovative and experimental ideas.

Participants are mainly English speakers, which is primarily due to the site's specific location. Most of them are from an Arts and Humanities or Social Science background, with strong inclinations towards design, the visual arts or music, while a few of the respondents were also engineering or commerce dropouts. Institute members include natives of the city as well as migrants, who often join the organisation as interns.

Non-Formal Educational Settings

The formal higher education and career plans of young people seem to provide a backdrop for their participation in this organisation. Some young people saw it as an internship opportunity to supplement their formal education and career path. Others felt that their aptitude did not match their formal education and wanted to change their career track. In other words, the young people had become involved not to acquire cultural socialisation in an abstract sense, but to develop some grounding for their future careers post-higher education.

However, when a young person enters this organisation, she seems to be in for a very fruitful experience of cultural training and socialisation. The young participants mentioned several of their noteworthy experiences with the organisation. They reported to have experienced a non-hierarchical work environment wherein practitioners, young participants and more experienced members treated each other equally. Young people also told us that they got a lot of hands-on training in various art practices such as logistics, management, keeping deadlines, and working as a team member, as well as contributing to art production. Thereby, they gained a 'holistic experience' of art practices (according to Ryan (male, YP), among others). The organisation also imparts interdisciplinary training in art. Many participants related that they saw not only how various art forms are intrinsically linked to each other, but how art and social world are connected. According to Akshay (male, YP), this training has helped him bridge some gaps in his formal education. This process must have instilled confidence amongst these young and aspiring art practitioners. The motivations that made the founders establish this institute may help in understanding these achievements. Arya (female, P) and Ishan (male, P) told us that they founded this institution out of a deep dissatisfaction with how art has been perceived in India, especially in the up-and-coming cities. According to Arya, for example, this perception limits art to 'painting or drawing', while in places like the USA, where she did her formal training, the idea of 'art' encompasses all kinds of 'creativity'. The founders of the Institute wanted to introduce this culture to India. Such an approach represents an assumption by people inhabiting the erstwhile colony that their society is backward, which does not take note of the historical conditions (read: colonialism) that created this 'backwardness' in the first place. Such a post-colonial condition might be in danger of seeing the pre-colonial traditions of Indian society as completely regressive. However, Arya had a sense of the richness of pre-colonial Indian traditions, which, according to her, recognised the plurality of gender.

Cultural environment of young people

The interviews portrayed the idea that various forces at play in young people's immediate environment, including family, peer group, and their own cultural activities, go a long way in imparting cultural literacy.

Most of these young people were a part of nuclear families living in a historically small city that is transforming into a metropolis. Many reported that their parents came from outside the city, in some cases hailing from different cities. These parents were often highly educated professionals who took interests in cultural activities like movies, the theatre, dance and paintings. In addition, the young people reported that they have a very lively dialogue with their parents on subjects including art and culture. Some young participants' families have connections with various practices of art and culture. Manvi (female, YP) and Akshay (male, YP) told us that such networks have helped them to participate in various art forms. Other interviewees reported having differences with their parents or extended families on issues like whether to follow traditions and sexual orientation. They noted their uneasiness to talk with family members about these differences. Many also reported religious rituals being a part of their families' culture.

In terms of performing culture with their friends, many young participants identified celebrating religious festivals, especially those of religions different from their own. For some, the latter is more exciting than taking part in the festivals of their own religion (Akshay, male, YP and Atharva, male, YP). One prevalent activity among young people was eating out with their friends. Eating 'burger' was reported by many, and others mentioned eating cuisines from different countries. Some reported to watching and discussing about movies and socio-political issues with their friends. There seemed to be a strong European influence that came through their friends. Ryan (male, YP) said that he talks with friends in English, not Hindi, and Atharva (male, YP) found that he adheres to Western culture with friends and Indian with family. Thus, these young people differentiated between their own and 'other' cultures in terms of religion, food and language. Secondly, they are happy to interact with these 'other' culture/s. In addition, many of them, or their friends and family members, have travelled to European countries or the USA. The exposure and socio-cultural networks furnished by their families and friends seem to have provided these young people with a lot of social and cultural capital. It is in the background of this exposure to different cultures that an argument made by one of the practitioners, Ishan (male, P), should be understood: his perspective was that contemporary Indian youth, unlike earlier generations, are unable to distinguish between 'Indian' and 'Western' cultures. According to Ishan, today's youth consider English as their own and not a foreign language.

The young participants seemed to understand cultural diversity mainly in terms of religious and linguistic diversity. This emphasis on religious diversity can be seen in the background of religious majoritarian politics becoming dominant in the country. Young respondents told us that they come into contact with not only various Indian but also European languages. Another significant theme is that culture was often perceived in terms of the food habits that are supposed to be followed by the members of the Hindu religion. For example, Dipti described her culture as being 'Hindu oriented', in which "*not eating non-veg on Mondays*" (Dipti, female, YP) is considered to be an important part.

Internet culture

The Internet is an important aspect of young people's everyday culture. They seem to using the internet for different forms of communication. Manvi talked about the possibility of sharing with 'a total stranger' "*a tweet about mental illness…that I have gone through*" (Manvi, female, YP) and of finding support in the virtual world. Arush (male, YP) said that, thanks to the internet, he could connect with people interested in memes – an area he is passionate about. Other interviewees felt that the internet has a different, unique language. For Arush, abusive language is used so often and casually in online games that no-one in that space takes it seriously. Aparna (female, YP) felt that the language of websites and internet media is 'Americanised'. Use of social media for debate and discussion was quite widespread amongst the young participants, and they had diverse experiences and opinions of this. Manvi mentioned that the medium allows her a lot of flexibility to "*edit… write…PAUSE for a minute…think what I want to say…then write it properly*" (Manvi, female, YP). Aparna, on the other hand, said that even if she has had social media accounts for a long time and needs to use them for communication, she does not "*enjoy it AT ALL*" (Aparna, female, YP). Instead, she finds using social media 'taxing' and energy-sapping experience. All the respondents said that they had had to face bitter, unpleasant experiences while engaging in social media debates. In such instances, nearly all of them maintained that they only indulge in such debates with people they know personally. Hence, they also ensure that the disagreements are dealt with in person and not online.

Perceptions about culture

Most of the respondents have learned about Europe through the internet, electronic media, formal education, family and travel. Some of them were keenly aware that Europe is a place with diverse culture (Ryan, male, YP and Aparna, female, YP). Many young respondents spoke of 'Indian' and 'European' cultures with reference to each other. For Dipti (female, YP), India has a diverse culture, unlike Europe, which has a more homogeneous culture; in Europe, people celebrate festivals privately within their families, while in India these are celebrated publicly. Atharva (male, YP) presented both cultures using binaries such as being 'practical' (European) vs 'emotional' (Indian); 'contentment' (Indian) vs 'growth' (European). Many also identified themselves as being Indians with European influences. This may be understood in the context of these young people's increasing interaction with Europe through travelling there, media exposure, and learning European languages.[5] Another element of their perception about 'Indian culture' was diversity. Aparna (female, YP) mentioned that Indian culture changes according to a person's surroundings, such as their family, while for Arush (male, YP), due to his upbringing in a multi-lingual environment, 'Indian culture' is simply *"confusion."*

Amongst practitioners, perceptions about cultural education included the necessity of inculcating values such as tolerance and inclusiveness, and qualities such as questioning and assessing everything. Neha, one of the practitioners, explained the principles of tolerance and inclusivity. For her, cultural education implies recognising and accepting that culture is necessarily diverse, creating an institutional ecosystem that welcomes these diverse representations of culture. For the practitioners, cultural heritage can be tangible and intangible; heritage always evolves, and Indian heritage has evolved by integrating various forces (Mughal and British, for instance) at different historical periods. Some of those influences may be foreign ones, but we have to accept them as our own heritage. This position notes the diversity and difference of Indian heritage. However, it shies away from recognising hierarchy and contestation as other important related components of India's heritage and culture. The hierarchy in Indian culture is clear in the structures and identities of caste, for example. Romila Thapar, among others, has pointed out how caste hierarchy evolved in India wherein "*...those that laboured for others had a low status*" (2018: p.xxiii–iv). In modern India, the Dalit movement signifies an attempt to contest this caste hierarchy (Omvedt, 1993 and Zelliot, 2012).

For nearly all of the young participants, while resolving differences was a significant part of culture, many looked at it in a more nuanced manner. Arush believed that not all differences need to be resolved, for that might lead to the "*death of individuality*" (Arush, male, YP). Others mentioned that whether they would be interested in resolving differences would depend upon the context: the issues over which difference have arisen, or the person with whom they differ, for instance. They would want to resolve their arguments only if they value the person they disagreed with. Many also mentioned the possibility of differences coming in the way of friendships, suggesting that they value friendship too much to allow the difference to spoil this.

5 The complexity of this interaction is discussed later in the Discussion section.

Discussion

This study on understanding the relationship between non-formal education and the cultural literacy of young people brings out various interesting findings about non-formal education practices, the cultural environment of young people, and perceptions on cultural diversity, difference and 'European culture'.

Non-formal educational practices

The concept of non-formal education has emerged with thinking that education cannot take place only within the confines of formal structures and that emphasis only on formal education cannot guarantee later employment (Hamadache, 1991: pp. 111–2). In this sense, our study shows that non-formal education provides students with exposure to various real-life situations wherein skills learned during formal education can be applied. Moreover, non-formal education imparts non-cognitive learning and training in various lifeskills for the holistic development of young people. Thus, we found that non-formal education both supplements and supplants formal education, meaning that there is a complicated relationship between the two. Even though non-formal education is seen in the context of formal education, the former is not always seen as secondary to the latter. Some young people reported having found their callings –completely different ones from what they believed formal education would lead to – during their explorations with non-formal education, while others maintained that the non-formal education has filled in various gaps in their training.

The non-formal educational practices that we studied can also be understood as part of 'authentic learning'. Authentic learning, Andersson and Andersson have argued, is a process whereby learners' experiences and perspectives are taken to be genuine ingredients of the learning process instead of abstract knowledge (Andersson and Andersson, 2005: pp. 420–4). The hands-on training imparted at the Creativity Institute and the Film Club's insistence on taking one's own, local surrounding as a significant part of the creative process are examples of 'authentic learning'.

Non-formal educational practices can also be understood in terms of the specific pedagogical ecosystem wherein students and teachers engage in relatively unstructured and intimate interactions: here, students learn through observation and conversation, assistance and practice. Such flexible and informal settings contribute to a spontaneous and reflective pedagogical process that goes beyond predetermined schedules, syllabi and impersonal pedagogy (Lewin, 2014). Some participants from the Film Club invoked what they considered the native model of the educational system, *gurukul,* to refer to this teacher-fronted, free and intimate pedagogical setting. This ancient Indian pedagogical system has been revived in modern times in the learning of the Sanskrit language, yoga, *vedic* traditions and rituals, and spiritual and artistic practices, especially performing arts such as music. This system emphasises the embodied nature of knowledge transmitted orally, and students are moulded to embody the knowledge imparted, albeit partially, by a specific teacher (Lewin, 2014; Sankaran, 2020).However, the teacher-centred, authoritarian nature of the *gurukul* system includes only brahmin men and subjects students to rigid discipline. Submission and obligation to the teacher is recognised as going against modern and democratic decentred approaches to educational practice (Sen, 2002). Krishna (2019) sees *gurukul* as an informal structure of learning that normalises unequal student/teacher relationships, and underlines the need to reimagine this and to recognise students' autonomy.

One of the differences between the two sites is their position on gender. Various participants at the Creativity Institute specifically mentioned that they try to be not only gender-conscious but also queer-sensitive, and aim to be an inclusive space. On the other hand, not only were the practitioners in Film Club unwilling to address the issue of the near absence of young women in their organisation but they linked the issue to the broader prejudice within their field. While male participants emphasised openness in the group's culture, a young woman participant noted the need for it to become more open.

The inclusivity reported at the Institute must be considered alongside the fact that most people we interviewed there came from relatively privileged families. This can be seen in two interrelated aspects. One, many reported exposure to Europe through travelling there and through learning various European languages. This was nearly absent in the case of young people from the Film Club. Secondly, none out of 11 young participants from the Film Club mentioned English as a language spoken in their family, while in the case of the Institute 7 out of 12 participants mentioned English as the only or one of the languages spoken in their families. Even though it is a colonial language, knowing English provides an edge in educational, cultural and employment fields in India (Roy, 1993: p. 57).Their familiarity with the language gives young people at the Creativity Institute a socio-cultural advantage over their counterparts from the Film Club; the cultural capital possessed by the former is valued more highly than the latter. Thus, though members of the Institute claim to be inclusive, in practice they may be less so due to their own structural position of being materially and culturally advantaged. However, a practitioner from this site did realise these limitations and reported having made some efforts to overcome them, including translating their programmes into the Marathi language. However, she also mentioned challenges to making these changes due to budget constraints.

Another related difference is regarding the issue of hierarchy. Many actors at the Institute related various concrete experiences that underline its non-hierarchical and informal nature, especially with regard to relations between the trainers and the trainees; established and novice artists; superiors and subordinates, etc. In the Film Club, however, even though the participants mentioned the democratic environment of the organisation, many seemed to idolise the site's founders, partly because of their expertise in the field and partly due to the glamour around their names. Additionally, a practitioner at the site referred to *gurukul* while describing the hands-on nature of the training available. This further reinforces the hierarchical tendencies, considering that the historic *gurukul* system required students to revere and unquestioningly submit to the teacher.

The two organisations that we studied believed that art should reach the masses. However, they struggled to achieve this. Both groups claimed to be thinking about the various forms of art and culture in an out-of-the-box and experimental manner, and believed that the masses have a very stereotypical understanding of art. In addressing this challenge, both underlined the need to change the conception of art in the masses' minds. Here, a couple of issues seem pertinent. One, there is a gap between the conceptions of culture held by these organisations and the mass audience. Does this make the organisations elitist? Second, these groups seem to be doing precious little to learn about common people's understanding of art and processes of the formation of these ideas. This reinforces elitist ridicule of popular culture, instead of critically engaging with it.

The understanding of art practices held by the practitioners were also influenced by the training that some of them had received in the West. Thus, as underlined in the sections on findings, practitioners from the Creativity Institute wanted to instil 'creativity' culture instead of the established 'painting and drawing' concept of art more common in India –this binary has itself been shaped by their training in the USA. This reflects what post-colonial theory has described as erstwhile colonies' idolisation of the West, in which the West is assumed to be superior to the non-West. This has converted the West's former colonies into "an imaginary waiting room of history" (Chakrabarty, 2008: p. 8).

Young people's cultural environment

Young people from both organisations spoke of their cultural environment, especially their family and friends, in different ways. The participants in the Club described their families with reference to socio-cultural identities like caste, religion, region and language, and in terms of the bonding that those identities can create. However, they were also unhappy that their families tend to adhere to 'traditional' identities. In the case of the Institute, some participants mentioned their differences with family members on issues like following traditions and sexual orientations. Nevertheless, here the family predominantly comes across as a space in which art and cultural forms are appreciated and discussed. Moreover, their family members had various links with the art world, which might make their children's entry into it easier. This implies that these young people possess a lot of what Bourdieu (1986) has called 'social capital' in the form of various "network[s] of connections" (ibid.: p. 22) provided by their families' and acquaintances' socio-cultural networks. These, in turn,[6] might give them better access to the art world. On the other hand, while young people from the Film Club lacked these social networks at the level of their families, their participation in the site itself provides them with similar connections. In terms of having and accessing these networks, young people at the Institute and the Club respectively have a head start and lag behind.

While the Club empowers the young people by making them aware of the concrete socio-cultural realities of the country, and by providing the training to convert this awareness into art forms, the cultural training of young people at the Creativity Institute predates their involvement with the site. Thus, young people and practitioners at the Institute get their formal education at better institutions, are better connected with the West, and have families with greater art-related consciousness, who pass on this sense on to their offspring. This means that they are also better endowed with Bourdieu's 'cultural capital', especially in its 'embodied' and 'institutionalised' forms (O'Brien and Fathaigh, 2005: p. 69). However, alongside possessing social and cultural capital, some participants expressed a feeling of being socially alienated due to being part of nuclear families.

The interviewees' friends were painted mainly in negative (the Club) and positive (the Institute) lights. Youth at the Institute reported participating enthusiastically in various activities like eating out, watching movies, and discussing socio-political issues with their friends. On the other hand, Film Club participants

---

6 Bourdieu defined social capital as "possession of a durable network of more or less institutionalized relationships of mutual acquaintance and recognition—or in other words, to membership in a group—which provides each of its members with the backing of the collectively owned capital, a "credential", which entitles them to credit, in various senses of the word" (1986: p. 21).

were rarely forthcoming about their friends, and whenever they were, they tended to be critical of their involvement with 'superficial' activities like dancing in public, going to the pub and clubbing. This means that similar activities were valued differently by the young people at these two sites. Part of the explanation for this difference lies in the socio-spatial travel of the young people at the Club. For youth at the Institute, there seemed to be a cultural congruence between their friends and their broader social environments, both of which belong to the urban space of the city. Many young people at the Club had migrated from rural Maharashtra to this city. Their lives in the city and with the organisation have made them newly conscious of several 'cultural' aspects. This new consciousness, in turn, seemed to culturally dwarf their previous rural friends.

While the participants in the Film Club are predominantly regional language speakers (Marathi), the Institute participants are either multi-lingual or are more comfortable with English than regional language(s). Thus, it might appear that the Club is closer to local (Marathi) culture than the Institute. However, participants in the two organisations defined 'local' differently. Film Club members equated 'local' with their surroundings and everyday practices. Institute participants pointed out the diversity of the city and the fact that their location has always been multi-lingual and multi-religious, even aside from the fact that lately the proportion of non-Marathi speakers has been increasing in the city. This points out that 'local culture' is not a monolith and can be interpreted differently based on various locations and standpoints.

Perceptions about cultural diversity and difference

Practitioners in both organisations spoke about Indian culture and its diversity when speaking about cultural heritage. However, they emphasised different aspects. Film Club practitioners defined diversity in terms of religion, language and caste, while Creativity Institute practitioners spoke about the evolutionary nature of India's heritage and the need to recognise various diverse influences like the Mughal and British empires, as part of the country's heritage.

Many participants in the Club, particularly while talking about cultural diversity, emphasised drawing from alternative traditions within the Hindu religion, such as Charvaka and Lokayat, which are based on materialism and rationalism. This raises several interesting issues regarding tradition and diversity in India and the world. Often, it is assumed that challenges to cultural diversity lie in the fact that several groups follow different traditions. However, the above-mentioned point about diversity within Hinduism can also speak to diversity within every tradition. Advocates of diversity do not always have to remain outside a tradition. On the contrary, the tradition itself provides them with several unconventional forces that can be used to counter regressive interpretations and propositions of tradition. Here, one is reminded of Asish Nandy's argument about getting the religion out of "the metaphorical closet" that the secular Indian state has put it into; this would enable "a dialogue within and between religions" (Chandhoke, 2010: p. 337). This understanding is based on the assumption of 'difference' within a tradition. What it does not consider, however, is that this difference can turn – and has turned – into hierarchy and contestation between different versions or strands of tradition.

Young women at the Club suggested that Indian and digital cultures are masculine and restrictive for women, but many other young participants mentioned diversity as an important component of Indian culture. This understanding has two limitations, however. First, in some cases this diversity turns into stereotyping religious minorities, such as identifying them essentially as followers of their religious festivals and rituals. Second, at least one young person labelled linguistic diversity in his surroundings as being 'confusion'. Stereotyping and confusion arises mainly because, as Rustom Bharucha (2000) has pointed out, the Indian state and society have attached only a symbolic significance to celebrating diversity, doing very little institutional work to ensure that this diversity turns into a meaningful dialogue between and within different cultures. This 'confusion' also arises amongst young minds due to the widely-held assumption that any culture has to be a consistent and monolithic entity. Indian culture – with its myriad diversities in terms of language, religion, caste, region, etc. – is far from embodying such a neat and well-defined notion. The contradiction between young people's 'ideal' notion of culture and their concrete experiences of diversity creates 'confusion'.

Another related element is young participants' views on difference and resolving disagreements. While participants from both sites maintained that resolving difference is part of culture, they also emphasised that not every difference is and can be settled. They seemed to relate difference with 'individuality' and individual differences, both of which they wanted to preserve rather than threaten. Here, the emphasis seems to be on tolerance rather than on coming to agreement as a way to deal with difference. For young people, resolving disagreements would mean compromising the position of one or both the parties. This would entail changing the specific individualities involved in the process of difference, which might endanger the autonomy of the atomised individual assumed here. Because the emphasis is on maintaining the autonomy of the individual, the interviewees preferred to preserve rather than resolve difference. However, in Indian society, like any other, an individual is often not autonomous in concrete terms. Individuals operate within the context of various structures, like caste, class and gender, which are deeply embedded in hierarchies, inequalities and contestations. Differences are often the products of these structures in the first place. Therefore, even though there might be efforts to adapt and negotiate within them, individuals are often compelled to act within the framework of these structures. This may, on numerous occasions, make tolerance difficult and conflict inevitable.

These young people seemed to be quite mature when it comes to dealing with disagreements in the virtual world. They mentioned engaging in debates and discussion on social media. Participants from the Institute were more enthusiastic about this, while the Film Club participants found social media 'superficial and fake'. However, young participants from both sites were conscious of the divide between the virtual and real, and realised that many differences emerging in the virtual world need to be dealt with in the real world.

Perceptions about European culture

The participants' perceptions about Europe were substantially based on their own or acquaintances' travels to that continent. First, there was a profound understanding of India's colonial links with Europe, especially amongst the Creativity Institute participants. Secondly, the young people's understanding of Europe was primarily linked to its relationship to India. There was a strong sense of India being 'lacking' in comparison with Europe. Here, the interviewees seem to be following the post-colonial condition, which is exemplified in what Dipesh Chakrabarty has called the perception of 'cultural distance…that was assumed to exist between the West and the non-West' (2008: p. 7). Thirdly, there was also a sense of disjunction between European and Indian culture: one young participant talked about his family being a sphere of 'Indian culture' and his friendship circle being a sphere of 'European culture'. Since in the Indian context European influence is often treated as synonymous with globalisation, this finding can be illuminated in the background of debate on the relationship between nation and culture in the process of globalisation. Appadurai (1990) argued that globalisation has given rise to cultural forces that have de-territorialised the nation, wherein the cultural relevance of 'nation' gets assimilated into the global culture. However, Leela Fernandes later showed how '…the production of meanings of the global occurs through the idiom of the nation' (2000: p. 616). Our study shows that young people recognise the difference between local and global, and that they actively try to compartmentalise the two in different spheres of their lives. In the process, they perhaps try to avert any possible conflict between them. Fourthly, there was a lot of appreciation for Europe as a place for great artists, architecture, and modernity. Fifthly, there was a streak of anxiety about 'us' falling prey to westernisation, especially amongst some participants of the Club. This exemplifies what Leela Fernandes calls the 'politics of purity', which arises to manage the disruptions caused by cultural hybridity due to India's integration into the process of globalisation (ibid.: p. 625). However, as Vamsee Juluri (2003) has pointed out, there is also an increasing sense that Indians, instead of being on the receiving end of 'cultural imperialism', are actively shaping the globalisation process through invention, entrepreneurship and more (quoted in Pathak-Shelat and Cathy, 2014). For instance, one of the practitioners at the Institute asserted that Yoga is *"our cultural export."*

Thus, the respondents showed two related types of perceptions about Europe. First, fascination about the continent and thereby a sense of lack in their own society, and second, anxiety at possible losses due to the cultural influence of Europe. Both perceptions are created due to post-colonial conditions: the first comes out of a grand assumption whereby the West is considered to be a harbinger of modernity, and the second is a typical response within post-colonial societies, which is rooted in the anxiety that 'our culture' could be overridden by the Western one. Further, as pointed out by Leela Fernandes (ibid.), anxieties about Western cultural dominance give rise to a 'politics of purity'. This might uphold specific kinds of local cultures that would legitimise hierarchical social structures like gender roles.

Conclusion

This paper tells us many interesting things about cultural diversity and difference. Young people realise the importance of resolving difference, but feel that not every difference needs to be resolved as doing so might endanger individuality and autonomy. They believe in tolerating some differences rather than resolving all of them. Their perspective about differences in the virtual world is also interesting: they do engage in debates and discussions on social media, but remain deeply aware of the difference between the virtual and real worlds. Hence, the interviewed young people asserted that differences on social media often need to be dealt with in the real, not virtual world.

Culture and diversity were articulated in terms of caste, religion and language. Most of the time these forces were expressed in a stereotypical manner like taking pride in one's identity and imagining religious minorities only in terms of their religious identities. However, some practitioners did articulate a nuanced understanding of diversity and tradition. Instead of understanding tradition as a homogeneous and anti-diversity space, the participants stressed plurality and the significance of drawing on pro-diversity voices from within a tradition. This perspective enables the advocates of diversity to place themselves inside and not outside a tradition. This might make the struggle for diversity more socially and politically viable.

Amongst young minds, the conception of Europe seems to be multifaceted. Some young people did understand Europe's role in the post-colonial conditions of India. Diya (female, YP) pointed out how British colonialism has impacted various institutions in post-independent India: *"we are essentially European citizens living in India."* For Ryan, (male, YP) *"eastern side is looked very lowly upon"* by the Europeans. However, along with this image, a strong element of fascination and attraction to various European things was also palpable. Europe was often juxtaposed to India, and there was an anxiety that 'our' culture might be usurped by the European one.

A couple of issues need to be kept in mind when identifying policy interventions into cultural diversity in India. One, cultural diversity must include openness to critique from outside and within. In India, cultural diversity is often articulated in terms of groups and communities. While diversity is seen to regulate relations between these groups, their own internal diversity tends to be overlooked and the groups are often assumed to be monolithic. The critique from outside the groups is about diversity and difference between them, while critique from within refers to closer attention being paid to the diversity and difference within the groups. Two, diversity must include everyday non-standardised versions of cultural articulations instead of relying only on textual and standardised conceptions of culture.

Regarding specific policy interventions, our data points to two issues. One is about funding. Practitioners from both organisations emphasised the need to have better funding to realise the full potential of their activities. One can, therefore, think in terms of encouraging multiple sources of funding, including the government and private players. However, funding provided by these agencies can be a double-edged sword in that this may compromise the autonomy of the institution.

The second issue is about the need to having institutional support for inter- and intracultural dialogue in India. This could go a long way in making diversity a practice instead of only a norm. Socio-cultural heterogeneity could be better sustained if we provide better facilities for transmitting 'other' cultures in various parts of India; for example, imparting training in the Tamil language in the north Indian states. However, here too a caution is in order. The three-language formula that was implemented in the 1960s to tackle the issue of linguistic diversity in the country failed miserably due to various loopholes in the policy (Brass, 1994). Moreover, this institutional mechanism must also be conscious that, as well as difference, hierarchy and contestations are deeply embedded in Indian culture. Thus, one often finds that Indian governments give greater institutional encouragement to the Hindi language than other 'regional' languages. Also, the linguistic reorganisation of the states imparted greater institutional prominence to the historically advantaged regional languages in the states than, say, various so-called 'dialects.' Language is only one example: India is replete with such social and cultural hierarchies based on religion, caste, class and gender, and contestations of those inequalities.

Acknowledgements

Prof. Suhas Palshikar and Dr. Cornelia Sylla had read an earlier draft and provided useful suggestions to improve the quality of the text. An earlier version of this article was presented at the International Conference on Urban Transformations, Youth Aspirations and Education in India that took place at IIT, Gadhinagar in February, 2020. We thank the organisations for graciously providing access for doing fieldwork. Shruti Hussain and Amogh Bhongale assisted us in conducting the fieldwork. We are grateful to all those young people who participated in our fieldwork. The authors, however, are alone responsible for the limitations, if any, in the article.

References

Andersson, S. and Andersson, I. (2005). Authentic Learning in a Sociocultural Framework: A case study on non formal learning, *Scandinavian Journal of Educational Research*, 49 (4), 419–436.

Appadurai, A. (1990). 'Disjuncture and Difference in the Global Cultural Economy', *Theory Culture & Society*, 7, 295–310. London, Newbury Park and New Delhi: Sage Publications.

Bharucha, R. (2000). 'Thinking through culture: A perspective for the millennium', In R. Thapar, *India Another Millennium*, pp. 66–84. Penguin Random House India Private Limited.

Bourdieu, P. (1986). 'The Forms of Capital'. In J. Richardon. *Handbook of Theory and Research for the Sociology of Education*, pp. 241–58. Westport, CT: Greenwood.

Brass, P. (1994). *The Politics of India since Independence*. Cambridge: Cambridge University Press.

Chakrabarty, D. (2008). *Provincializing Europe: Post colonial Thought and Historical Difference*. Princeton: Princeton University Press.

Chandhoke, N. (2010). 'Secularism', In N. Jayal. and B. Mehta. (eds.), *The Oxford Companion to Politics in India*, pp. 333–346. New Delhi: Oxford University Press.

Chandra, A. and Shah, A. (1987). *Non-Formal Education for All*. New Delhi: Sterling Publishers private Limited.

Chandwani, N. (2019). 'The importance of the Gurukul system and why Indian Education needs it', Times of India, March 2019. Available at: https://timesofindia.indiatimes.com/blogs/desires-of-a-modern-indian/the-importance-of-the-gurukul-system-and-why-indian-education-needs-it/ (Accessed on November 10, 2019).

Chatterjee, A. (2018). 'Inside vedpathshalas: A unique mix of the old and the new at Pune's oldest institutions', Times of India (Pune), Nov 2018. Available at: https://timesofindia.indiatimes.com/city/pune/inside-ved-pathshalas-a-unique-mix-of-the-old-and-the-new-at-citys-oldest-institutions/articleshow/66577538.cms (Accessed on November 9, 2019).

Fernandes, L. (2000). 'Nationalizing 'the global': Media images, cultural politics and the middle class in India', *Media, Culture & Society*, 22 (5), 611–628. New Delhi: Sage Publications.

Hamadache, A. (1991). 'Non-formal education: A definition of the concept and some examples', *Prospects: Quarterly Review of Education*, XXI (1), 111–124.

Jamanadas, K. n.d. 'Is Gurukula Education Suitable for India?' Available at: http://www.ambedkar.org/research/Is_Gurukula_Education_Suitable_For_India.htm (Accessed on November 10, 2019).

Juluri, V. (2003). *Becoming a Global Audience: Longing and Belonging in Indian Music Television*. New York: Peter Lang.

Krishna, T. M. (2019). 'The guru-shishya structure is inherently prone to abuse. It needs to be demolished', Indian Express, Sept. 2019. Available at: https://indianexpress.com/article/opinion/columns/gundecha-brothers-sexual-harassment-hindustani-music-tm-krishna-6601666/ (Accessed on November 10, 2019).

Lewin, D. (2014). 'The leap of learning', *Ethics and Education*, 9 (1), 113–126, DOI: 10.1080/17449642.2014.890319.

O'Brien, S. & Fathaigh, M. (2005). 'Bringing in Bourdieu's theory of social capital: Renewing learning partnership approaches to social inclusion', *Irish Educational Studies*, 24 (1), 65–76.

Omvedt, G. (1993). *Reinventing Revolution: New Social Movements and the Socialist Tradition in India*, New York: M.E. Sharp.

Pathak-Shelat, M. & Cathy, D. (2014). 'Digital youth cultures in small town and rural Gujarat, India', *New Media & Society*, 16 (6), 983–1001. New Delhi: Sage Publications.

Rogers, A. (2007). *'Non-formal Education: Flexible Schooling or Participatory Education?'*, New York, NY: Springer Science & Business Media.

Roy, M. (1993). 'The Englishing of India: Class Formation and Social Privilege', *Social Scientist*, 21 (5/6), 36–62. New Delhi: Indian School of Social Sciences.

Sankaran, S. (2020). 'Practices of Music Education in Gurukul and Related Systems' In P. M. Sarangapani and R. Pappu. (eds.) *Handbook of Education Systems in South Asia*. Global Education Systems. Springer, Singapore. https://doi.org/10.1007/978-981-13-3309-5_6-1 (Accessed on November 10, 2019).

Sen, A. (2002). 'Basic Education: India's Backwardness and the Lessons of Kerala.' *New Trends*. Kottayam: D C Books, pp.3–8.

Thapar, R. (2018). *Indian Cultures as Heritage: Contemporary Pasts*. New Delhi: Aleph Book Company.

Zelliot, E. (2012). *Ambedkar's World: The Making of Babasaheb and the Dalit Movement*. New Delhi: Navayana Publishing.

Weblinks

- https://mhrd.gov.in/sites/upload_files/mhrd/files/upload_document/Knowledge%20Exchange%20Heritage%20Education.pdf
- http://ccrtindia.gov.in
- https://www.gyaanadab.org
- https://raah.org.in
- https://tifa.edu.in
- http://www.youngintach.org

Part III Cultural literacy in informal education

The third and final Part is dedicated to findings observed in various non-formal settings, where young people met to pursuit a shared interest, hobby or passion together. The aim is to improve our understanding of how grassroots cultural activities shape and are shaped by young people's perceptions of cultural heritage and identity. These chapters introduce a wide spectrum of cultural practices embedded in local contexts, driven by young people's own perceptions of what is culturally significant to them. The emphasis is on participants' self-produced cultural and heritage understanding. These informal youth groups were usually quite open; they did not follow any strict membership rules and sometimes only existed for a limited time period.

Research questions

The ethnographic studies were guided by the following research questions:

- How do young people gain their cultural competences?
- How diverse is the researched group and/or the fieldwork locality?
- What forms of inter-group interactions and communications are present in youth groups?
- What are the relationships both within the groups and with the 'outside world', and how do young people perceive diversity?
- What are the notions of cultural heritage in both its traditional forms and its alternative interpretations (i.e. cultural practices that could be defined as 'heritage in the making')?

Method

For each case study, researchers joined the groups and conducted participant observations, which involved writing detailed field diaries and carrying out semi-structured interviews with young people. In some cases, researchers joined the groups at public spaces they had (re)claimed, such as streets, cafes or squats. Researchers followed the main principles of ethnographic research and engaged in the routine activities of participants in order to explore and see the world through their eyes. They recorded observations of the groups for several months, sometimes even until the group was dissolved. When researchers gained the trust of the participants, they were able to conduct several semi-structured interviews with those who were interested and willing to do so.

These interviews focused on three areas:

1. The form and content of young people's everyday (face-to-face and digital) interactions with other people and cultures;
2. Practices of 'heritage-in-the-making' that define places, sites and modes of 'heritage production' in the context of young people's social and political activism;
3. Young people's perceptions of power relations, social injustice and prejudice, including how these relate to the spread of racism and the stigmatisation of different social groups in local communities.

In each country, researchers also asked contextual or nation-specific questions during the interviews.

Gaining access to the groups was sometimes not easy, because young people chose a non-formal way of organising precisely because they did not have much trust in formal institutions. Often the researchers used their own contacts and networks to connect to young people and gain their trust.

Despite those difficulties, this part of the project proved to be the most exciting one, since it offered an insight into extremely diverse and under-researched educational and cultural domains outside common institutional frameworks. Young people participating in these groups were often critical of mainstream society, and showed a high level of political and cultural literacy and engagement. It was an enriching experience to get to know their views and visions, and to understand the obstacles they encounter while pursuing their cultural practices.

(by Awista Gardi)

Chapter 10 The significance of discrimination and stigmatisation in cultural practices and identities of young people in Germany

Abstract: In the following text, two ethnographic case studies in informal settings, carried out with an antifascist boxing group and a rap group in an urban city in Germany, will be presented. It aims to analyse the ways in which social power relations structure the cultural practices and identities of the groups' participants. First, how young people experience and perceive different forms of discrimination will be elucidated, alongside the stigmatisation of non-hegemonic political stances. This chapter will then explore how and why young people unintentionally reinforce given social power relations by reproducing forms of discrimination themselves. When analysing the findings, deconstructionist theories about social power structures and their effects on subjects were crucial, linking the unequal distribution of power within German society to the individual, institutional, and structural reproduction of discrimination. These findings suggest that social power relations in Germany form a culture of dominance, as Rommelspacher (2011) calls it, in which every subject holds different amounts of power depending on their gender, race, class, ability, and other social categories. Therefore, the cultural practices, cultural heritages, and identities of young people are closely intertwined with social power relations like racism or sexism.

Keywords: social power relations, discrimination, stigmatization, cultural heritage, cultural identities

Introduction

German discourses about discrimination are defined by various, often conflicting narratives. For many decades, those who face discrimination as a part of their everyday lives and their allies have emphasised its structural and institutional character, as well as its relevance to processes of subjectification (Rommelspacher, 2011). At the same time, naming or criticising discrimination is often delegitimised as oversensitivity and a threat to freedom of speech. Some people have explicitly or implicitly advocated for the perpetuation of given social power relations. The tensions that have evolved from those conflicting stances shape all engagement in the topic of discrimination, whether this be in political, academic, artistic or family contexts (ibid.).

The following two case studies are about two informal youth groups in Germany and the role social power relations, such as discrimination and stigmatisation, play in the formation and articulation of their cultural identities. Therefore, one focus will be on analysing the ways in which young people experience and interpret different forms of discrimination they or others face, as well as the stigmatisation of their non-hegemonic political perspectives of the described social and political tensions. Another focus will be on depicting how and why these young people unintentionally play a part in (re)producing forms of discrimination themselves.

The first case study was carried out in an informal antifascist boxing group that met once a week to practice martial arts. This chapter therefore initially considers the relevance of subcultural discourses to the political stances and identities of the young participants. The second case study was conducted observing weekly rehearsals of a Hip-hop group. This is presented in the second part of the chapter, and is concerned with the young musicians' everyday communications about racism, social justice, and political activism.

Part three will discuss the role played by the articulation of political perspectives in the cultural practices, cultural heritage and identities of the young people in the two case studies. In particular, the meaning of the political struggle for social recognition will be analysed. Furthermore, there is a question of how the formation of political identities and transnational and transgenerational communities can be construed as a goal for a more inclusive society. To gain a more in-depth understanding of how discrimination was unintentionally (re)produced by youth in both case studies, the last part of the discussion will examine the normalisation of discrimination in Germany and its social consequences for people living in this local context.

Case one: The boxing group

The boxing group consisted of 20 participants between the ages of 18 and 25, with a core of 5 to 7 people engaging in the training regularly. In terms of gender, the young people identified as 15 cis males and 5 cis females. The participants predominantly positioned themselves as heterosexual, non-disabled, slim and white. Thereby, they can be said to hold structurally privileged positions in German society, which is organised according to diverse social power relations such as racism, sexism, ableism or heteronormativity (Rommelspacher, 2011). Some of the participants identified themselves as working class and non-academic, while others claimed an academic and/or middle-class background. Some worked in part-time or full-time jobs, while others attended universities.

The group can be categorised as belonging to a left-wing subculture. In this context, they can be seen as a part of what Schneider calls the history of antifascism in Germany, which started with resistance against rising fascism in Europe at the beginning of the 20th century and today consists of many spectra (Schneider, 2014: p. 8). Schneider describes antifascism as a movement that acts against different forms of social exclusion and social injustice and that aims for an equal distribution of democratic and social rights in practical terms (ibid.: p. 9). In their political practices, the participants can be categorised as part of the autonomous spectrum of political activism, which focuses on anti-capitalism and direct action, such as demonstrations, rather than parliamentarism (ibid.: pp. 125–7).

In the following section, the diverse aspects of the participants' attempts to navigate social power relations as members of a left-wing political group will be elucidated. These attempts are, on the one hand, defined by a political analysis of social structures and the quest to deconstruct these relations. On the other hand, they are structured by the unintentional reproduction of discrimination by the young people themselves and how they seek to deal with this phenomenon.

The participant's perspectives on social power relations

The following sections explore the ways in which the boxing group's participants view social power relations by focusing on their articulation of political stances, their perspectives on key moments in Germany's history, and their views on formal education, National Socialism, and German colonialism.

The articulation of political stances

Antifascist was unanimously expressed as a shared political stance in the boxing group. As one participant described it, antifascism is

> *more than just being against fascism. So, for me it refers to togetherness, which in principle does not exclude people. A community, in which no one is being treated hostile or attacked because of their appearance or their physical qualities or their gender. And that is for me quite clearly an anti-fascist attitude. Antifascism is also reflected in the rejection of a totalitarian system. One expresses oneself as a clear anti-fascist for the fact that one attacks any form of suppression strongly and in principle also tries that these forces do not act freely. […] Especially because of the German history but also in today's Europe it is important to position oneself clearly and to normalise it in a sports group like ours.* (Tim)

Due to the current situation in Germany and Europe, where right-wing parties are gaining popularity, taking a leftist political stance is important to Tim. His political stance seems to him to be a moral necessity in German society, which in his view is influenced by National Socialism. He sees himself as a part of that society and therefore as responsible for instigating political change and social justice. His choice of words shows that his definition of antifascism critiques every form of social exclusion, not only fascism. This broader perspective may be a direct result of the participants' shared utopia of a world living together in peace. Antifascism, therefore, can not only define certain political stances, but can represent a focus on community-based living. This can also be seen in the following quote, in which Tim explicitly talks about his utopia:

> *My utopia is a society free from any kind of dominion. There would be equality for all people, all genders, for everybody who is a part of this society. It would have to be self-organised. The economy and all the other domains of life would have to be organised from the bottom up with elements that are exchangeable. So there would be no rigidified structures, that couldn't be deselected. To achieve this, everybody who participates in this society must vouch for this. And the capital goods must be accessible for the general public. Yes, abolition of money (laughing). So, these are the most important elements for me.* (Tim)

As one can see, this utopian perspective has been strongly influenced by the participant's cultural literacy in political theories on economics, such as Marxism. To Tim, a society without inequality would have to be self-organised, so that there would be no fixed hierarchies. This perspective links anti-capitalism to antifascism, and also reflects the cultural practices instilled in participants during training. By thinking about martial arts in a political way, the group tries to reduce the pressure of performance they see in many other sports groups as much as possible. This reduction of pressure to perform can be linked to the anti-capitalist stance of the group, in which pursuing efficiency is viewed as a result of neoliberal capitalist conditions.

> *I see myself as anti-capitalistic. I would say this is the primary basis somehow that you decline the existing economic system, because it is based on competition and exploitation. And one could say that above this, there are the –isms and they all have something to do with capitalism. I mean racism, sexism etc. […] And because of that I think that if you are against fascism, racism, sexism etc. and also see yourself that way, an anti-capitalist stance is fundamental. Because in my understanding, only a systematic change can erase all of this.* (Luca)

An anti-capitalist and antifascist stance was seen in the group as necessary to enable a structural change in society. These stances are defined by a wider understanding of social problems that link capitalism and fascism to phenomena like racism and sexism. As Schwarzmeier (2001: p. 14) states, the collective articulation of a social problem is constitutional for social movements, because political attempts to solve social problems can only be based on shared understanding. Therefore, shared perspectives on antifascism and anti-capitalism can be interpreted as relevant to the group's longer-term sustainability.

The group was positioned outside the hegemonic political consensus thanks to its opposition to dominant social structures. In some informal conversations, it could be observed that the participants were aware of that position and seemed to enjoy their separation from the hegemonic political consensus, since this underlines their self-enforced distinction from dominant discourses. As Hall states, the perception of what is seen as politically acceptable is subject to social processes linked to parliamentarian compositions, which constructs what is seen as politically normal (Hall, 2012a: pp. 143–4). This not only creates political norms, but also delineates which views are perceived as valid opposition and which are considered extremist, hence invalid (ibid.: pp. 144–6). This process of construction is influenced by power structures, which privilege political stances that align with a given social consensus (ibid.: p. 145). The group experienced the marginalisation of stances that oppose this consensus. One participant talked about the criminalisation that comes with the label 'extremist':

> *The concept of criminality was extended. Now they label different groups as criminal, that don't do anything bad, if you want to see it through that perspective. They just want a social togetherness in solidarity, but are labelled as anti-constitutional. So it's always the thing, that the society defines what is okay and what is absolutely not okay. And this is affected by the social swing to the right.* (Finn)

In this quote, Finn refers to recent political changes in Germany, where a right-wing party (AfD) and right-wing movements have gained popularity in the past few years. Although the boxing group is marked as politically radical and therefore anti-constitutional by German legal institutions, it does not position itself in opposition to democratic structures: its political objectives focus on the establishment of a democratic society without discrimination, and on 'togetherness in solidarity'. The group opposes the given political structures, *while* simultaneously pursuing an inclusive society. It should therefore not be marked as anti-democratic. Following Hall (2012a), the criminalisation of the group can be interpreted as a consequence of its opposition to a social consensus and not as a result of anti-democratic practices.

Perspectives on history through a collective antifascist memory

When participants spoke about national history, the deconstruction of what was seen as 'naturally German' stood out as an important aspect:

> *The establishment of the German State was very late in comparison to other nations in Europe. I think that this is relatively important for the further history because it explains a lot about it. And this is also important because I think quite often people talk about*

Germany from back in time. And people assume that there was a Germany back then. But there wasn't. (Lara)

So back in the days people identified themselves as Germans in distinction to France as the enemy on the outside and someday the Russians as enemy in the east. And inside Jewish people were the enemies. And this was the only point that defined a shared identity. So, it didn't develop through a shared language or culture, but in distinction to constructed enemies on the outside and the inside. I think this is a quite interesting point of the German history of origins, which gets swept under the table often. And that antisemitism was crucial in the forming of a German identity. (Dennis)

The participants connected the establishment of the German State with processes of othering that allowed the formation of a distinctive German identity. They articulated that there is no such thing as a natural German essence in language or culture, only what is constructed as German. In this, their perspectives align with theories of Hall and Said, who consider the construction of the Other[1] as crucial to the construction of the We (Hall, 2012a: pp. 138–40; Said, 2017: pp. 11–12). According to Dennis, antisemitic violence was foundational for constructing an enemy 'within', and thereby for constructing the German identity. On that matter, his perspectives again match theories regarding antisemitism and racism in Germany, which stress that these forms of discrimination have been and remain a fundamental aspect of the formation of the German identity (Rommelspacher, 2011: pp. 26–9). While the participants' perspectives align with theories derived from research, they differ strongly from dominant national discourses, in which national identity is constructed as natural and not connected to social power relations (Hall, 2012b: p. 200; Messerschmidt, 2011: pp. 68–9).

Because the participants see antisemitism and racism as important elements of the constitution of what is considered German identity, they deemed National Socialism and German colonialism highly relevant aspects of German history and the present:

The National Socialism structures this country even today and did not develop from nothing. Especially if you look at such shit-speeches of Gauland,[2] it is really important, to think about it. To somehow understand how this could happen. For me it is an elemental

---

1 Following Stuart Hall, the term 'Other' is written with a capital O if it refers to categories constituted in processes of othering (Hall, 1994).

2 Alexander Gauland is a member of the right wing party AfD in Germany and relativised National Socialism in a 2018 speech by comparing the Nazi era with a "birds poo in German history" (for further information, see: https://www.tagesschau.de/inland/gauland-ausspruch-vogelschiss-101.html).

> *epoch or the influencing part of the history of what a German state was in the last 140–150 years.* (Thorsten)
> *If you think about where colonialism is present all around you, you will notice it even more. And then you notice that it is very much present everywhere. Shockingly present.* (Dennis)

The participants stressed that German colonialism and National Socialism still influence German society, and emphasised the relevance of naming these structures as "influential for the present." In recognising these periods as key moments of German history, their views differ from dominant national discourses, which define National Socialism and German colonialism as past events that do not impact current social structures (Messerschmidt, 2011: p. 59).

Considering the statements about German history, one can clearly see the connection between the young people's self-identification as antifascists and what they believe to be historically significant. By marking the role of discrimination in the formation of a national identity as a relevant aspect of German history, the participants could analyse the given social structures in their historical context and develop political perspectives to oppose these social relations. As one participant stated, this process of prioritising certain aspects of Germany's history was not performed individually, but collectively: "*These moments [of German history] are surely the moments that were important for my family somehow and that have been important in my social environment somehow*" (Thorsten).

From this quote one can observe that certain forms of cultural heritage, such as ideas about national history, are passed down in families and social movements. In that way, a transgenerational collective antifascist memory has defined the participants' cultural heritage.

Perspectives on formal education on National Socialism and German colonialism

The participants wish for a critical and structural integration of the topics of 'German colonialism' and 'National Socialism' into formal education, and denounced the lack of critical knowledge production in these contexts. Although National Socialism is often addressed in schools, it is not discussed in a way that focuses on the social structures that led to the establishment of fascism and its lasting effects on German society. According to Dennis,

> *In the end, I have to say that we didn't do much about National Socialism either. We just learned that Hitler got the power somehow in [19]33 and that was it. And then there was the war and maybe a few dead people. But how it came to be, what all these circumstances were and the contexts, and above all what it means for the present has not been discussed.* (Dennis)

The knowledge he gained in formal educational settings did not equip him with a structural understanding of National Socialism or its consequences in the present. As the wording 'in the end' implies, he was only retrospectively able to deconstruct these narratives. Other participants highlighted similar problems with the teaching of German colonialism in formal education:

> *It really opened my eyes when I was in 11th grade and had the lessons about [German colonialism]. And that was such an isolated case. How lucky I was back then that I had this great teacher and not someone else? Because otherwise I wouldn't be bothered about it at all or only much later. I would like Germany to include this into formal education.* (Marisol)

As Marisol stated, German colonialism is often excluded from history classes. Her perspective aligns with theoretical analyses that problematise the exclusion of German colonialism from classes as a form of colonial amnesia, which opposes critical reflection on the consequences colonialism still has for German society today (Ha, 2000). Another participant described how he had only heard heroic and colonial narratives about Christopher Columbus that framed him as the explorer of the Americas:

> *You learn something about Christopher Columbus. How great he was and that he found America, even though he actually – no, he thought he found India. And then found America. This thing like: The great heroes who dare to go to sea somehow and explore the world.* (John)

As John's statement shows, the reception of German colonialism is not only structured by amnesia, but also by revisionism. The reproduction of colonial narratives in schools thereby sustains the colonial violence that was once performed by the colonialising nations, through dehumanising colonised people and romanticising colonial violence (Autor*innenKollektiv, 2015: p. 5). As these findings emphasise, racist narratives shaped the cultural literacy of the members of the boxing group from a very young age, influencing their perceptions of German history and current social structures.

The reproduction of discrimination

The following section will illustrate the ways in which discrimination was reproduced in the boxing group, focusing on articulations of sexism and racism and how the participants tried to act on this.

The group's accessibility as structured by informal lines of exclusion

In forming the boxing group, the participants wanted a way to exercise and play sports together without having to pay a lot of money. The group was also founded to create a space where martial arts could be practiced without prioritising or emphasising maleness in the training. As one participant stated,

> *In this training, we want people that maybe don't fit into the classic image of a martial artist, [which is] a male martial artist, to be accepted.* (Finn)

Since there is no advertising, the group can only be accessed via personal contact, which is mainly made in subcultural contexts. Therefore, most of the participants accessed the group through social contacts formed through political activism. The male, white, heterosexual, cis, and able-bodied dominance of the group can be traced back to its form of accessibility, since social inequalities, such as discrimination, form the ways in which people interact with each other (Rommelspacher, 2011: p. 30). For example, they can form colour lines in peer groups or friend groups, which are often segregated by sexual orientation. One participant described the segregation of their peer group as follows:

> *So, I would say, that we don't have many female friends here in our neighbourhood. So, until now there were no women, except for one, who wanted to join the training and was interested in staying in the group. We had some girls here before, who checked this out for a short time, but they never came back afterwards. I think that was a little sad. I think one reason was that they were living too far away, so the training didn't suit them. But whether that's the real reason – I don't know. But that's what I was told when I was asking why they never came back. So maybe we should be friends with more girls here, I don't know.* (Manuela)

Although the group is officially open to people regardless of their gender, the accessibility is structured differently. Since access to the group is mainly gained by peer groups, the lack of non-cis male friends in the neighbourhood leads to a cis male dominance. As Manuela stated, cis women face barriers in accessing the group, either by having a longer journey than the other participants, or by not having easy access to the group because they are not part of the cis male-dominated peer groups in the neighbourhood.

The reproduction of sexism

One cis female participant talked about her interest in martial arts, which she had not pursued in the past due to the reproduction of sexism in mixed-gender groups:

I wanted to do martial arts for a while, but I was always a little discouraged by the open boxing groups. […] I checked out sports at my university. I think this macho behaviour was very bad. (Luca)

The participants were aware of the barriers cis women face in engaging with martial arts and, as mentioned before, aimed to create a space in which martial arts could be practiced without the reproduction of sexism. Nevertheless, the group consists mostly of cis men, as the female interviewee described:

So this is a boxing group which is open to all genders. But nevertheless, it is always the case that mostly men, or men who identify themselves as men, predominate in training. I think that is a pity. I would wish for more female people or LGBT people having access to this. (Luca)

According to the quote, the group is formally open to all genders, but in reality is predominated by cis men, with LGBTQIA+-people mostly lacking access. This cis male dominance is not only present in the boxing group; the wider social networks of the group also contain hardly any non-cis male people. It could further be observed that the two cis women who participated in the sessions regularly, were in romantic relationships with male participants. McDonald uses football as an example to describe how sports are shaped by gender-constructions, locating cis women only in relation to cis male norms (McDonald, 2017: pp. 111–12). She discusses how

[t]he unequal distribution of opportunities, material resources, and sporting knowledge not only greatly determines who gets to play and administer the sport, but also shapes the ways in which the girls and women experience [it] as spectators and players. (ibid.: p. 111)

The martial arts group seems to be shaped by gender constructions, which does not only influence the practices of the workout sessions but the accessibility of the group. Although the participants were aware of this fact, they had not done anything specific to change it. During the study, there were only a few sessions in which cis female friends or siblings of the participants were present. Most of them only attended the sessions once or twice. As one can see in the case study, the unequal distribution of opportunities to access the group leads to cis women depending on cis male gatekeepers, such as romantic partners or brothers, who allow them access to the group. It also leads to the absolute absence of people openly identifying as trans, gender-fluid, agender and/or non-binary.

The reproduction of racism

As mentioned earlier, the participants are mainly white, with only one Person of Colour taking part in the workouts regularly. Therefore, it can be said that the group is white-dominated. While the participants problematised the lack of (cis) women in the group, the lack of People of Colour was only talked about once, in a conversation the researcher had with a white participant. This exception aside, white dominance was not addressed or problematised. Silence about the reproduction of racism and white dominance can be marked as secondary racism, since it prolongs, normalises and perpetuates structures of discrimination (Melter, 2011: pp. 285–6). Thereby, white people develop strategies to bypass reflection on racism, which can be labelled conscious colour-ignorance (ibid.: p. 284). In this conscious colour-ignorance, the participants disregarded the effects the reproduction of white dominance had on their group.

The perpetuation of normalised racism could also be observed in other forms including jokes, the use of racist words or in the objectification of People of Colour. There was almost no communication between white participants and People of Colour. Furthermore, People of Colour were mostly referred to as political objects rather than as significant subjects. For example, People of Colour were primarily present in the form of T-shirts reading 'Refugees Welcome' instead of actual participants in the group. By focusing on People of Colour as victims of racism, the participants reproduced victimising discourses that imagine People of Colour and/or Refugees solely as victims that need to be saved (Seukwa, 2016: p. 198).

According to Rommelspacher, there should be a distinction between being racist and being entangled in racist discourses, since racism is a normalised phenomenon in Germany (Rommelspacher, 2011: p. 34). When the participants reproduce racism, they oppose their own objective of not acting in a discriminatory manner. They can therefore be identified as being entangled in racist discourses rather than believing in overtly racist ideas. This finding underlines the influence that normalised racism has on the cultural practices of young people in Germany and the difficulties young people face in trying not to reinforce this normalisation.

Dealing with discrimination

The participants implicitly and explicitly articulated that discrimination is structurally and unavoidably implemented in German society and socialisation, and should therefore be criticised. While they dealt with discrimination in different ways, all of their attempts were shaped by the belief that discrimination is something bad that should be contained. While this concept can encourage people to act against discrimination, it also normalises a certain way of talking about discrimination and thereby makes addressing its internalisation somewhat taboo (Rommelspacher, 2011). This could be observed in the young people's behaviour.

In relation to dealing with sexism, one female participant described the insecurity cis male participants showed while exercising with her:

> *I felt a little excluded in the beginning. I had the feeling that people are terribly afraid of contact. […] I think that's because people don't know how to deal with someone like me, where they know: Oh she's a feminist, she has an opinion, maybe I'll do something wrong or something. The guys prefer to not do the training with me, instead of telling me: "Hey, if I am punching too hard, just let me know." Instead of making arrangements, they decide to take the easy way out by avoiding me.* (Luca)

The interviewee explained that she felt excluded while training with the group and assumed that the other (cis male) participants tended to avoid people who identify as feminists for fear of being called out as acting sexist. The fear of acting in an illegitimate way therefore keeps the participants from interacting with marginalised groups in general, especially with individuals who position themselves explicitly as anti-sexist, such as feminists. In this context, one might also notice that the absence of cis women in the group was only ever brought up during interviews and never in the group. Although many participants talked about their desire to include more cis women, these articulations did not manifest into actions. Even when one participant posted a link to a podcast on the topic of sexism in martial arts in the group's chat, there was no reaction from the other participants. While there was hardly any conversation about sexism within the group, the topics of class or racial discrimination were even more marginal. The problematisation of exclusion, therefore, aligns with dominant discourses in Germany (i.e. Diversity Management), in which there is a primary focus on the inclusion of white cis women (Krell, 2011: pp. 5–20).

Since the fear of acting in a discriminatory manner causes the participants to exclude the topic of discrimination from their daily cultural practices, they do not seem able to reflect on the ways in which they unintentionally reproduce social exclusion. This avoidance may not only be caused by the fear of reproducing discrimination, but also by an ambivalence about changing social hierarchies, especially since many of the participants hold privileged social positions as white, middle-class, heterosexual cis males. For example, in several informal conversations, the participants pointed out that they were privileged in German society because of their social position as white males, but did not engage in any specific practices to deconstruct these privileges. Since dealing with discrimination would have to include reflection on and deconstruction of their privileges, the avoidance of this topic can be interpreted as a way to preserve the status quo.

Case two: The Hip-hop group

The second case study focused on an informal rap group with some members that are considered, and consider themselves, Refugees,[3] and other members who consider themselves white Germans. Members were aged 20–27. These participants do not link being a refugee to a certain ethnicity or a specific judicial status, but to being socially labelled and self-identifying as one. They therefore use the word 'refugee' as a political category, enabling them to form bonds of solidarity with other people who are (self-)identified as Refugees and with white people who want to perform allyship. The rap group included 10–15, mostly cis male, members who attended rehearsals regularly.

The founder, a white German man, formed the group because he wanted to play music with some of his friends under an official and public label. Another goal was to form a political Hip-hop community in which the culture of Hip-hop could be practiced, as one participant explained:

> *I always wanted to do something political. Something that is open to everyone that brings along another message. Namely the definition of what Hip-hop is for me. And that is a community, that defies all possible boundaries. Even scene boundaries. I mean my Hip-hop culture is not just music, it´s also a lot more. And I wanted to revive that for myself.* (Alex)

The participants write and perform in different languages including German, Arabic, Dari, Farsi, English, and Spanish. The group splits their songs into different parts, with every participant writing and performing a solo in the language they feel most comfortable with. Their music is influenced by the diverse styles the participants listen to, such as rap, rhythm and blues (R'n'B), soul, and gospel. The main foci of their lyrics are political topics, including critique of structural racism and capitalism in the German society. Their lyrics look towards a more social and just society, and call for solidarity with people marginalised by racism and poverty. They perform at many politically leftist events, but their audience contains a wide spectrum of views as well as many left-wing people.

The following analysis will focus on two main aspects of the participants' cultural practices and identities. First, it will consider the ways in which the participants articulate political perspectives that challenge given social norms

---

3 The process of labelling people as 'Refugees' has political and social dimensions in Germany (Dauer, 2018: pp. 90–2). There is the juridical category of a 'Refugee', which often does not coincide with the social category 'Refugee'. The latter includes all Black people and/or People of Colour, who are discursively marked as 'Refugees' (Seukwa, 2016: pp. 196–9).

and create space for a more inclusive thinking. In the second part, the specific role racism plays in the participants' lives will be analysed, as well as the tactics the participants use to act upon this form of social exclusion.

The formation of a more inclusive heritage-in-the-making

The following sections will analyse the ways in which the participants create social and cultural spaces that enable them to articulate perspectives on social structures that deconstruct given power relations and open up new, more inclusive definitions of belonging. To explore these ideas, the role the Hip-hop community plays in enabling the young people to articulate their political stances, how the participants define their cultural identities, and the significance of utopian stances in their cultural practices will be described.

The Hip-hop community as an enabler for political communication

As their motives for involvement, the participants talked about the recognition and appreciation they receive for their music in and outside the group, the collective identity and interpersonal connections formed by being part of a community, and the personal growth and enjoyment they experience:

> *It gives me recognition and I also feel that I am showing what I have written to other people. People think that's great and applaud. And that is a good feeling. I notice that on the one hand it is super exhausting if you think about yourself: Who am I and what am I doing this for? This self-reflection is hard. But it also gives me a lot. And the group is like a small world.* (Katrin)

Being a part of the group seemed not only to enable an individual process of growth, but also to provide the experience of being a part of 'a small world' in which the participants felt cherished. The group also allowed the members to articulate themselves politically by performing songs with political themes or making political statements to a wider public at events:

> *For me it is a great tool to have the music now because you have a great outreach. Basically, I am a person who likes to work in his own circle. That means, for example, when I ride the train that you draw people's attention to it. It is difficult for me to do public talking if, in the end, it doesn't get anywhere. And I try to start where I notice it and get involved talking. Otherwise through the music.* (Daniel)
> *On the one hand there (at an event the group performs) are not only Hip-hop fans, but also people who are there for the protest and what it is about. And there you can reach a lot of people from all sorts of areas. Whether they're listening to punk or Hip-hop or whatever. They are there together for one thing. And we make music for them and that is an honour and an opportunity.* (Aron)

The participants utilised performing in public spaces to articulate their political stances, which mainly focused on anti-racism and anti-capitalism, to a broader public. By engaging in political discourses, they felt themselves to be political subjects and social actors. Alongside this practice, the group tried to form political alliances with groups/organisations from a diverse political spectrum (for example at events protesting for more environmentally friendly politics, events against the popularity of right-wing parties in Germany, or events organised by autonomous political groups). Meeting people from diverse political groups allowed them to exchange ideas, and to position themselves in harmony with the other groups' political stances during events by, for example, verbally articulating solidarity. Since the group is composed of mostly Black people, People of Colour, and/or people who are socially and/or politically labelled as Refugees and are therefore marginalised in Germany (Dauer, 2018: pp. 88–92; Niedrig & Seukwa, 2010: p. 184), this articulation allows marginalised knowledge archives to be heard. It is thus aimed at undermining hegemonic discourse production. Being part of the Hip-hop group could therefore be understood as way of enabling political communication for marginalised people and the self-determined appropriation of public spaces.

In utilising this form of communication, they continue a cultural heritage in which rap music has internationally functionalised as a means of expressing political perspectives and counter-hegemonic speech, especially by marginalised people (Tijé-Dra, 2015: p. 146; Prause, 2013). In their practices, the participants not only consume rap music, but also produce it and use it to articulate their own perspectives. They intentionally align themselves with other Hip-hop artists they deem idols, such as Lauryn Hill, the Fugees, and, in the German rap context, Samy Deluxe, who has used rap music to criticise social structures for many years. Being part of that political tradition in Hip-hop communities seems to have profoundly shaped the participants' cultural identities, since they repeatedly mentioned the relevance of these political and artistic communities at different points of the research process.

The culturalisation of and disidentification with national identities

The term 'culture' came up a few times during the interviews. It was either used to talk about what was perceived as Hip-hop culture or to articulate an understanding of culture based on national and/or ethnic identities, as one can see in the following quote:

> *I met some young people who did a great performance. I was there and filmed how they danced and I'm going to publish it and show it on TV. […] And that is also part of Somali culture.* (Hawi)

This participant talked about what he identified as 'Somali culture' by linking a national identity to cultural practices like dancing. This culturalisation of national identities implicitly stems from the notion that there is a static essence to nations that determines how people act. The perception that national identities define one's character is intertwined with biological narratives that link natio-ethno-cultural groups to phenotypical features (Mecheril, 2010: p. 14). This entanglement can be observed in the following response:

> *Yes, my roots are an issue of themselves. I'm totally mixed, so it's always a little difficult. But I think it is important for someone to know where they come from. And which blood flows in you. It affects how you think and act.* (Aron)

The participant refers to his (cultural) roots as if they were a part of his body, which he articulated through talking about the "blood [that] flows in you." Even more explicitly, the self-description as 'mixed' alludes to discourses of biological and colonial racism. Since (cultural) roots are (unconsciously) perceived as something biological and therefore essential, they seem to inevitably affect how one thinks and acts. By portraying himself in that way, the participant reproduced dominant German discourses that define the term culture as a biological category. Since in this interview a Person of Colour was talking, the internalisation of dominant discourses also has other consequences for the individual, particularly in the problematisation of what is marked as the Other. According to the participant, his 'roots' are an 'issue of themselves' which is 'always difficult'. It can be assumed that the derogative label of his 'roots' stems from the internalisation of mechanisms of othering, which interpret biographies viewed as deviating from the social norm, such as biographies (transgenerationally) linked to transnational migration, as inadequate. Hence, as a consequence of the dichotomisation of *white and belonging* and *non-white and not belonging*, People of Colour and Black people cannot be a part of the (national and) social We in Germany and Europe (El-Tayeb, 2015: p. 36): a discourse Aron seems to have internalised. However, as Ha states, despite all the problematisation of self-ethnicisation, it should not be forgotten that ethnic identification among racialised and marginalised people also facilitates a sense of togetherness, solidarity and the ability to act, which prove to be irreplaceable in the practical management of everyday life and its conflicts (Ha, 2000). Therefore, the line between internalisation and appropriation of dominant discourses seems to be marginal.

As a reaction to that denial of (national) belonging, People of Colour and Black people in Germany have to reinvent more inclusive concepts of home and homeland (El-Tayeb, 2015: p. 50), as one can see here:

> *Home means to me wherever I feel good. It doesn't matter if it's where I was born or if it's somewhere else. Home is the place where I have peace. That's what home means to me.* (Hawi)

The participants defined the concepts of home and homeland as independent from formal national senses of belonging and as more fluid, since they are based on where a person lives or where they feel at home. In this context, the construction of a homeland is linked to a choice one makes rather than to an official practice or assigned natio-ethno-cultural belonging. The identification of a home or homeland therefore refers to specific local contexts, like a city, or the development of emotions that are not tied to localities. National identities are marked as relevant dimensions of cultural identities in dominant discourses (Hall, 2012b: p. 200), but the participants opened up new possibilities of how to refer to local contexts or where they live, and thereby could define their cultural identities in new ways. This cultural practice may stem from different factors, such as transnational social networks or lifestyles, but needs to be analysed in relation to the specific circumstances racialised people face in Europe. In her analyses of cultural identities of Black People and People of Colour in Europe, El-Tayeb calls this cultural practice 'disidentification' (El-Tayeb, 2015: p. 50). The process of disidentification implies the difficulty of identifying with a national identity, and therefore facilitates irritations and discontent with dominant national norms (ibid.). El-Tayeb further understands disidentification as a survival strategy that Black people and People of Colour practice to cope with experiences of racism (ibid.), which is illustrated by the following quote:

> *For me, homeland is the whole world, no matter where you are. You can't just say one place and the others are shit. I was in many countries because we were deported back and forth – in six countries (France, Spain, Belgium, Sweden, Switzerland and Germany). But I was born here.* (Miguel)

The participants' definitions of home and homeland can therefore be considered a strategy to create discursive spaces for marginalised positionalities (El-Tayeb, 2015: p. 50). The cultural practices in the group can be understood as a form of 'heritage in the making', in which a dynamic and inclusive understanding of cultural identity and social belonging is established.

Utopian stances as guidance for current cultural practices

Asked to conceptualise a society they want to live in, the participants spoke about their ideal worlds, which can be, according to Castro Varela (2007: p. 17), marked as utopias:

> *The ideal world is first of all where everyone meets as equals. And everyone can pursue their path and interests. No matter where they come from. I wish for a non-competitive society where people try to live in harmony. And really to wish for the best for everyone. I think that's the only way that humanity can have a future on this planet in the long term.* (Alex)
>
> *Without borders I would say. And loving.* (Josh)

The participants' political goals included trying to transform the present into a future with more social justice. In this context, the cultural practice of playing rap music is functionalised as a political tool to intervene in social structures and progress them towards their normative goals of freedom, solidarity, equality, and being recognised and respected as individuals and as part of German society.

As Castro Varela states, the articulation of critique on social structures always implies a desire for a different society (Castro Varela, 2007: p. 17). Utopias, as expressed here, can be understood as a form of counter-hegemonic speech within which images of society are designed; these designs are often devalued as unrealistic, but they open up horizons of possibility (ibid.: p. 163). Although asking for recognition and rights against discrimination for Black people and People of Colour does not seem like a big structural change at first glance, these questions are often deemed irrelevant or out-of-date in dominant discourses, since many people in the German society see themselves as free of racism (Messerschmidt, 2011). Utopias form a space to search for what is possible outside of hegemonic systems of thought, like the longing for a society based on equality and freedom of movement. Tales of utopias can therefore represent an antithesis to dominant narratives and create new ways of thinking about reality (ibid.: p. 27). While utopias are mostly disparaged as unrealistic and naïve, the perspectives of these participants show that their utopias do not originate solely from their imaginations, but also from their cultural and political education.

Experiences of social exclusion in the context of racism

Racism as a structural form of discrimination plays a significant role in the everyday experiences of young people in Germany. The following sections will describe the consequences racism has on their lives, the ways in which the

Hip-hop group participants intellectually grasp these structures, and tactics they use to counter them.

Racism as a barrier to participation

The participants had experienced and/or witnessed different forms of racism, such as Hawi's example: "*I remember I was on the train one day and a man just insulted us. There were four of us. [...] There were also other days when I experienced racism.*" Hawi, a Black male, described experiences that can be considered everyday racism, manifesting on the level of individual interactions. Everyday racism articulates social lines of belonging that mark Black people and People of Colour as Others. Due to the regularity with which the participant experiences everyday racism, he is repeatedly reminded that his presence in Germany is not normalised.

However, the participants experience racism not only on a level of personal interaction, but also on an institutional and structural level. For example, one interviewee told the researcher about the deportation of another group participant's family, who had lived in Germany for many years:

> *His sister [...] is mentally disabled. The mother had passed out. The police had nothing better to do but to get more reinforcements because I was shouting a little. And it made me very angry and very depressed. I argued with one of the policemen and he said: 'Yes, that is what people have voted for, that's why we can now act like that'.* (Alex)

Deportation is an institutional and judicial practice that distributes chances of social participation based on nationality. This distribution differs according to passports, with German and other EU countries' passports being privileged and non-EU passports at a disadvantage. These regulations are formalised articulations of structural differentiations, and they have discriminatory effects because they hinder people from participating in German society. This institutionally and judicially legitimised discrimination of individuals based on their nationality, which manifested in the described deportation, can hence be marked as institutional and structural racism. As mentioned before, the participants talk about these forms of racism in their lyrics, including the line 'No borders, no nations, stop deportation'. These phrases are often-used slogans at demonstrations.

Witnessing and experiencing racism has had diverse effects on the participants' lives. In the above statement, the participant felt "very angry and very depressed", a fact that might be reinforced by his knowledge that 'people voted for' German institutions to take these actions. Another participant spoke more about negative feelings resulting from experiences in the context of racism:

> *I think it creates a lot of tension. People feel treated unfairly. They think: "Why can't I live like this, too? Why do we have to live here the way we do?" You can become so filled with bitterness.* (Isaac)

This participant verbalised feelings of being treated unjustly, wondering why he cannot live in a less disadvantaged social position and expressing a sense of bitterness caused by the marginalising social treatment he faces. As Rommelspacher (2011) states, these experiences include interactional racism such as micro-aggressions or insults, discrimination in the labour and housing market, racial profiling, symbolic discrimination by racist representation in media, and structural discrimination in laws that keep Black people and People of Colour from fully participating in social and cultural life. According to Yeboah, the experience of marginalisation and symbolic degradation in the context of racism is an elemental barrier to health, since it causes stress, trauma, and results in the deterioration of physical and psychological health (Yeboah, 2016: pp. 143–5). Hence, the experience of racism not only denies the participants full access to German society, but also compromises their physical and psychological wellbeing.

Perceptions of racism

As a social power structure that affects the majority of the participants, racism could be observed as a relevant topic in the group. Racism can be considered a shared subject and (mostly) shared experience, in which the Black participants and/or participants of Colour are marked as deviating from social norms and therefore as not belonging to the social We (Scharathow, 2014: p. 215). Talking about their experiences and criticising the reproduction of racism was observed as a subject that binds the (Black and of Colour) participants together (ibid.: p. 226). Even though Black people and People of Colour experience varying forms of racism, especially regarding their intersections with other forms of discrimination such as ableism, sexism, or classism, they share the experience of being marked as the Other, as the non-German. Sharing experiences of racism with each other allows them to place the deficit assigned to them on other factors than their individual beings. In the Hip-hop group, the Black participants and participants of Colour can share a space in which their belonging is not questioned, as it is in most contexts in Germany, and in which they form the majority. According to Scharathow, shared experiences of being racialised form a collective social knowledge archive in peer groups (ibid.: p. 225), which could also be observed in the case study. In several empirical studies, this shared knowledge archive was found to promote feelings of belonging to specific social groups (ibid.: p. 225). The collective experience of racism and the collective knowledge archives that arise from reflection on these experiences are therefore significant in the formation of the participants' cultural identities.

Although racism is a shared subject, the perceptions of racism articulated in the group showed diverse blank spaces, which can also be observed in dominant discourses about racism in Germany:

> *I think racism exists because [of] prejudices the society has towards people.* (Daniel)
> *Some of them were real assholes. Also the guy from the immigration office, where you can tell it's bitter people who just don't have so much in their lives that they project it onto other people's lives.* (Alex)

The participants assumed that racism emerges from dominant social prejudices and projections of people's subjective bitterness. Their perspectives align with dominant narratives about racism, in which racial power structures are exclusively connected to individual behaviour and thought, or to prejudices or stereotypes, without including the wider institutional, structural and symbolic dimensions of discrimination (Rommelspacher, 2011: p. 30). While the participants were able to place the blame for racist discrimination on the people that reproduce it in direct interactions, they had difficulty analysing social structures and reacting to them in a suitable way. It needs to be stressed that it is not the young people themselves who should be held accountable for struggling to express structural critique on social conditions. Rather, it is the lack of knowledge production about structural dimensions of racism within dominant discourses in Germany that affects the participants' perspectives.

Dealing with racism

Racism as a part of the participants' everyday life has had different consequences on their cultural practices. This can be observed, for example, in their ways of dealing with it. In the interviews carried out during the study, the participants were asked about their reactions when they experience and/or observe racism. One answer was: "*I don't get angry. I think it's stupid. Many people think only they are the best and I find that strange. I always have to say something against it*" (Omar). This participant described not getting angry, but feeling the need to act against the reproduction of racism by verbalising his critique. Another participant recounted:

> *I used to say: Just ignore it. Don't give a damn about them. You should always stay cool, but sometimes there is this one drop that causes the barrel to overflow. And this feeling has lasted for so long, that I could freak out each time.* (George)

George described his former stance of ignoring racism, which he seemed to have revised. Although he tries to stay calm, this is not possible for him in all situations due to the constant repetition of racism causing him to 'freak out'. Since the reproduction of racism can be marked as a reproduction of (symbolic, institutional, structural, verbal, or physical) violence (Yeboah, 2017 p. 143), the participant's reaction of *"freaking out"* can be interpreted as a sign of stress from the constant violence in his everyday life. Such constant exposure may also lead to the feeling of being unable to act against racism in the long term, as was articulated by another participant's question, "*What are you supposed to do against it?*" (Miguel).

The participants seem to find ways to act against racism by coming together as a group, displaying their critique of social structures, and sharing their perspectives with other people. This could be observed, for example, in the direct actions of solidarity during the deportation of one of the participants' family (Miguel's). During the study, the young people told the researcher that Miguel had called Alex to come to his home, where police had come to deport his family. When Alex arrived at the scene, he started documenting the deportation. He later published the video to inform other people of what happened, and to gain public attention and support for Miguel and his family. This tactic was successful, since there was a public outcry and a local news channel covered the deportation. Alex was charged for publishing the video, but the charges have since been dropped. He himself considered his behaviour a necessary reaction to racism, claiming that he would have become complicit had he not done what he could to support Miguel. Risking judicial consequences for publishing the video to support Miguel, Alex as a white person performed the practice of power sharing. The other participants acknowledged this practice and supported him when he was charged.

Discussion

The political struggle for social recognition as a key moment of cultural practices

The findings of both case studies address the struggle for social recognition in various ways. In both case studies, the participants' views strongly differed from dominant discourses regarding national identities and political norms, discrimination, and other forms of marginalisation. The topic of social distribution of power seems to be a central element of both groups, whether in relation to discrimination or to a hegemonic political consensus. Both groups also base their cultural practices on fighting for social and political recognition. Honneth describes love, rights, and social esteem as the three main forms of recognition; all three are essential for the formation of positive identities (Honneth, 2016: pp. 256–9). Social conflicts occur due to the violation of the rules of mutual recognition in terms of rights and social esteem (ibid.: pp. 258–61). Within both case studies, such conflicts could be observed as affecting participants in the context of social recognition. Social movements are often formed through the collectivisation of individual experiences of degradation and marginalisation, just as the observed young people collectivised their own social experiences. Following this collectivisation, both groups aimed to criticise and change given social structures, working towards a more inclusive society. Since both groups articulated their stances from a standpoint that questioned dominant norms, they were both positioned outside the dominant political consensus, albeit in quite different dimensions and with different effects.

The young people required knowledge and cultural practices to form social movements aimed at creating a more inclusive society; however, knowledge archives addressing the deconstruction of social structures are usually not included in what is perceived by dominant discourses as cultural heritage. Due to this fact, the young people had to acquire alternative forms of cultural heritage. In different contexts of alternative cultural heritage, whether from antiracist Black and of Colour communities or antifascist leftist scenes, the young people were able to access information about political resistance from previous and existing organisations that they could utilise for their own cultural practices. Performing an antifascist and antiracist identity also enabled the participants of both case studies to become more visible. This allowed them to take part in left-wing political actions and discussions, or, as in the case of the Hip-hop group, in subcultural political music production and antiracist discourses. It also helped the participants of both case studies to identify themselves with transnational and transgenerational social movements, such as other subcultural antifascist groups in Germany or the international Hip-hop community, and to base their cultural practices on these contexts. This identification highlights the fact that both groups, but especially the Hip-hop group, tried to link their political ideas to broader social movements, and thereby participated in a larger and more effective process. By identifying themselves with subcultural social movements, they were able to develop a shared semantic field, which was evident in their use of language codes typical within the antifascist scene or the Hip-hop community. According to Honneth, this is essential for social movements to articulate and collectivise their individual experiences (Honneth, 2016: p. 261). A further crucial aspect of the collectivisation of the individual experiences observed in both groups was the formation of collective ideas about normative stances, which were developed by accessing the cultural repertoires and practices of former social movements. In this way, the participants defined political norms that shaped their own struggles for recognition. Hence, the main context in which the participants gained cultural competences was through the collective acquisition of the cultural heritage of political social-left movements.

It is interesting that, according to the findings, the collective distinctions from civil society that were performed by the participants in both groups can be understood as a reaction to witnessed or experienced discrimination. To dismantle these distinctions and include the participants in a broader civil society, discrimination and other forms of marginalisation need to be diminished at discursive, institutional, interactional, and structural levels. To be inclusive to all young people regardless of their racialisation, dominant discourses would have to recognise, respect and display the cultural identities of Black people and People of Colour. Furthermore, dominant discourses also need to disseminate profound knowledge about social power structures, discrimination, and diverse opinions on how to deconstruct them. Only by including these alternative and marginalised knowledge archives in the dominant knowledge production would young people be able to face, understand and deconstruct discrimination successfully.

The formation of political identities as an aim for a more inclusive society

The young people in both case studies formed identities that are linked to the alternative cultural heritage of social movements, connecting their identities to traditions of political resistance. These participants' identities were therefore largely shaped by their political stances and utopias. Since these perspectives were developed by reflecting on experienced and witnessed processes of discrimination and other forms of marginalisation, hegemonic social power structures were a crucial aspect of the formation of the young people's identities. The participants formed their cultural identities by responding to the marginalisation they faced. In the boxing group, this became apparent in the political marginalisation the young people met by being labelled as radical and anti-democratic and, therefore, separate from civil society. In the Hip-hop group, many of the young people experienced racism and therefore formed a community with Black people and People of Colour, as well as white people who acted as allies.

Aligning themselves with the described processes of community building, the participants created a heritage-in-the-making that enabled them to form more inclusive identities and more practices of togetherness. These were not based on nationalities or phenotypical features, but on shared political perspectives and utopias. By doing so, they implicitly stressed the constructedness and fluidity of cultural identities and belonging, contradicting dominant discourses of naturalised national identities. In using the constructedness of belonging as an enabler to build more inclusive communities founded on shared normative values, the young people's actions can be labelled as best practices.

Learning about discrimination

In both case studies, the participants positioned themselves against discrimination. While they marked discrimination as normatively negative, some reproduced it unintentionally by articulating reductionist perspectives on culture or by reproducing implicit structural barriers for non-cis males. In the case of the boxing group, Black people and People of Colour were only able to access the club by moving in predominantly racially segregated peer groups. Furthermore, the interviewees' knowledge of discrimination was often limited to individualistic dimensions. Even in social groups aiming to create a non-discriminatory and inclusive togetherness, discrimination was reproduced on individual, symbolic, and structural levels. This finding can be explained with Rommelspacher's theories. Rommelspacher identifies German society as being structured by different, historically-evolved and intertwined forms of discrimination that are normalised and constantly reproduced on individual, institutional, structural, and symbolic levels (Rommelspacher, 2011: pp. 29–31). These forms of discrimination are engaged to legitimise and naturalise social power structures, and are passed down through each subject's socialisation, forming habits of interpretation and action (ibid.: pp. 25–9). Mecheril and Scherschel further state that, within the framework of racialised social relations, all individuals' lives and ways of thinking are shaped by superordination and subordination in the form of conscious, unintentional, and structural experiences of domination and subjugation (Mecheril & Scherschel, 2011: pp. 53–4). Following these propositions, the sole positioning against discrimination cannot enable subjects to act in a less discriminatory manner. Rather, a broad process of unlearning and deconstructing normalised ways of thinking and acting is of upmost importance. This process can only be successful if it is linked to the reduction of discrimination in dominant social structures.

Such a process would require a fundamental change in how discrimination is dealt with in Germany, as it is predominantly made taboo or scandalous, and/or it is repressed. This enables mainstream German society to distance itself from acts of discrimination, while the actual structures of exclusion remain ignored and unchallenged (Messerschmidt, 2010: pp. 41–3). If discrimination is ever mentioned, it is frequently individualised, naturalised or pathologised (Melter, 2011: p. 285). Therefore, discrimination is mostly considered a problem for 'the others' and not for broader social structures (Messerschmidt, 2010: p. 45). The scandalisation and pathologisation of discrimination were also observed in the boxing group. The participants worried about being called out for discriminatory practices and therefore avoided contact with individuals who might criticise them, such as the participant who identified herself as a feminist. Furthermore, the group members impeded open communication about discrimination by avoiding talking about its reproduction in the group or by evading other participants' attempts at addressing the topic. In both case studies, people who reproduced direct forms of discrimination were marked as 'crazy', 'stupid', and/or 'deviant'. Hence, both groups established a normative way of talking about discrimination: marking it as illegitimate. In this way, the reproduction of discrimination forms a threat to one's own political stance and cultural identity that is linked to the notion of acting in a non-discriminatory manner (Rommelspacher, 2011: p. 34). This conflict between the participants' political aims and their reality may cause resistance against proper analysis of discrimination and the consequences change may have to their self-image.

At this point, it is important to stress that, in both case studies, the participants had not learned about structural discrimination through their formal education or dominant (medial) discourses. Hence, they were not fully able to understand social structures or to deeply reflect on their own reproductions of discrimination. The findings stress that learning opportunities need to be installed in formal education and dominant (media) discourses in which young people can learn to recognise discrimination as a structural element of Germany's society, acknowledge their own entanglements in discrimination without having to deny a positive self-image, and develop ways to respond to discriminatory practices.

Conclusion

This chapter focused on analysing ways in which discrimination and stigmatisation structure the cultural practices and identities of young people in Germany, specifically in two informal groups. In the boxing-group, it became apparent that the articulation of political perspectives regarding antifascist, anti-capitalist and anti-discriminatory stances not only formed most of the participants' cultural practices and was therefore crucial to their communication in a subcultural alternative scene, but that it had shaped their cultural heritage and identities.

Experiencing the normalised reproduction of discrimination in wide social structures and a marginalisation in terms of their political stances, which were different from dominant political norms, the participants distanced themselves from mainstream discourses. Instead, they turned to alternative transgenerational and transnational forms of cultural heritage, especially those of politically leftist social movements. This analysis also showed that the normalisation of discrimination and a lack of structural perspectives on discrimination in German discourse led to its unintentional and unconscious reproduction by and within the group; this was evident, for example, in the group's male and white dominance and in the interpersonal communication between group members.

Since many of the participants in the Hip-hop group experienced racism in their everyday lives in Germany, the consequences these experiences had on their cultural practices, identities and heritage were especially relevant to this analysis. It became apparent that the Hip-hop community was their main source of political discourse; this community also provided a transnational and transgenerational cultural heritage that included knowledge archives of the anti-racist perspectives and practices of Black people and People of Colour. Dealing with everyday experiences of structural, interactional and symbolic exclusion, which could be interpreted as fundamental barriers to cultural participation, the group members disidentified themselves from dominant national identities and formed their own concepts of home and belonging. Utopian stances and political perspectives set out the main guidelines for the young people's cultural practices. However, in this case study the unintentional reproduction of discrimination was also discussed as a result of the socialising effects of dominant discourses in Germany.

Common to both case studies is the political fight for social recognition as a key element of the young people's cultural practices. In both groups, the participants were marginalised due to their social positioning in the context of racism and/or because they articulated political stances that differed from hegemonic political norms. Seeking ways to gain social recognition and shape German society in a more inclusive way, the participants had to acquire an alternative cultural heritage; this enabled them to take part in subcultural and community discourses and to articulate their political perspectives publicly. The formation of their political identities could be understood as an attempt at creating a more inclusive society. In other words, the participants formed their cultural identities by responding to the marginalisation they faced. They created a heritage-in-the-making that allowed them to develop more inclusive identities and more practices of togetherness that did not refer to nationalities or phenotypical features. Instead, they were based on shared political perspectives and utopias. In doing so, they implicitly stressed the constructedness and fluidity of cultural identities and belonging, carrying out best practices that contradicted dominant discourses of naturalised national identities.

Nevertheless, in both case studies, dominant discourses that normalise intersectional forms of discrimination were highlighted as relevant factors that shaped the participants' knowledge archives and that hindered their attempts to articulate structural perspectives on discrimination. Their individual positioning against discrimination did not enable the young people in the boxing group to entirely avoid discriminatory actions; this would require a process of unlearning and deconstructing normalised ways of thinking and acting that these young people could not facilitate on their own. These findings emphasise the need for a broad, nationwide reflection on discrimination that teaches young people to identify its internalised forms and how to deal with this successfully.

Acknowledgments

This research would not have been possible without the consent of the young people in the boxing group and the Hip-hop group. Hence, I want to thank them first and foremost for their trust in our research team in Hamburg. This chapter also could not have been written without the support of my colleagues. Therefore I want to thank Elina Marmer, Cornelia Sylla, Anna van Horn and Louis Henri Seukwa for giving me an insight into their critical perspectives and analyses.

References

Autor*innenKollektiv (2015). *'Rassismuskritischer Leitfaden zur Reflexion bestehender und Erstellung neuer didaktischer Lehr- und Lernmaterialien für die schulische und außerschulische Bildungsarbeit zu Schwarzsein, Afrika und afrikanischer Diaspora'*, In E. Marmer, and LEO Berlin (eds.), https://www.elina-marmer.com/wp-content/uploads/2015/03/IMAFREDU-Rassismuskritischer-Leiftaden_Web_barrierefrei-NEU.pdf (Accessed on February 13, 2021).

Castro Varela, M. d. M. (2007). *Unzeitgemäße Utopien. Migrantinnen zwischen Selbsterfindung und gelehrter Hoffnung.* Bielefeld: Transcript-Verlag.

Dauer, R. (2018). 'Zur medialen Konstruktion des Bildungshintergrundes Geflüchteter', *Standpunkt: sozial. Flucht & Studium*, 2018 (2), 86–93.

El-Tayeb, F. (2015). *Anders Europäisch. Rassismus, Identität und Widerstand im vereinten Europa.* Münster: Unrast-Verlag.

Ha, K. N. (2000). 'Ethnizität, Differenz und Hybridität in der Migration: Eine postkoloniale Perspektive', *PROKLA. Zeitschrift für Kritische Sozialwissenschaft, 30*(120), 377–397.

Hall, S. (1994). 'Der Westen und der Rest: Diskurs und Macht'. In S. Hall (ed.) *Rassismus und kulturelle Identität. Ausgewählte Schriften 2.*, pp. 137–179. Hamburg: Argument-Verlag.

Hall, S. (2012a). 'Die strukturierte Vermittlung von Ereignissen'. In S. Hall (ed.) *Ideologie, Kultur, Rassismus. Ausgewählte Schriften 1.*, pp. 126–149. Hamburg: Argument Verlag.

Hall, S. (2012b). 'Die Frage der kulturellen Identität'. In S. Hall (ed.) *Rassismus und kulturelle Identität. Ausgewählte Schriften 2.*, pp. 180–222. Hamburg: Argument Verlag.

Honneth, A. (2016). *Kampf um Anerkennung. Zur moralischen Grammatik sozialer Konflikte*, 9. Edition. Frankfurt am Main: Suhrkamp Verlag.

Krell, G. (2011). 'Grundlegend. Ecksteine, Gleichstellungscontrolling, Verständnis und Verhältnis von Gender und Diversity'. In G. Krell, and R. Ortlieb, and B. Sieben (eds.), *Chancengleichheit durch Personalpolitik. Gleichstellung von Frauen und Männern in Unternehmen und Verwaltungen. Rechtliche Regelungen – Problemanalysen – Lösungen*, pp. 3–24. Wiesbaden: VS Verlag für Sozialwissenschaften.

McDonald, M. G. (2017). 'Feminist Perspective of Race/Ethnicity and Gender in Sport'. In G. Sobiech, and S. Günter (eds.), *Sport & Gender – (inter)nationale sportsoziologische Geschlechterforschung. Theoretische Ansätze, Praktiken und Perspektiven*, pp. 109–120. Wiesbaden: Springer VS.

Mecheril, P. (2010). 'Migrationspädagogik. Hinführung zu einer Perspektive'. In P. Mecheril, and M. d. M. Castro Varela, and I. Dirim, and A. Kalpaka, ad C. Melter (eds.), *Migrationspädagogik*, pp. 7–22. Weinheim/Basel: Beltz Verlag.

Mecheril, P. and Scherschel, K. (2011). 'Rassismus und „Rasse"'. In C. Melter and P. Mecheril (eds.), *Rassismuskritik. Band 1. Rassismustheorie und -forschung*, pp. 39–58. 2. Edition. Schwalbach/Ts.: Wochenschau Verlag.

Melter, C. (2011). 'Rassismusunkritische Soziale Arbeit? Zur (De-) Thematisierung von Rassismuserfahrungen Schwarzer Deutscher in der Jugendhilfe(forschung)'. In C. Melter and P. Mecheril (eds.), *Rassismuskritik. Band 1. Rassismustheorie und -forschung*, pp. 277–292. 2. Edition. Schwalbach/Ts.: Wochenschau Verlag.

Messerschmidt, A. (2010). 'Distanzierungsmuster. Vier Praktiken im Umgang mit Rassismus'. In A. Broden, and P. Mecheril (eds.), *Rassismus bildet.*

Bildungswissenschaftliche Beiträge zu Normalisierung und Subjektivierung in der Migrationsgesellschaft, pp. 41–57. Bielefeld: Transcript Verlag.

Messerschmidt, A. (2011). 'Rassismusanalyse in einer postnationalsozialistischen Gesellschaft'. In C. Melter, and P. Mecheril (eds.), *Rassismuskritik. Band 1. Rassismustheorie und -forschung*, pp. 59–74. 2. Edition. Schwalbach/Ts.: Wochenschau Verlag.

Niedrig, H. and Seukwa, H. (2010). 'Die Ordnung des Diskurses in der Flüchtlingskonstruktion: eine postkoloniale Re-Lektüre', *Diskurs Kindheits- und Jugendforschung / Discourse. Journal of Childhood and Adolescence Research*, 5(2), 181–193.

Prause, L. (2013). 'Mit Rap zur Revolte. Die Bewegung Yén a marre', *PROKLA. Zeitschrift für kritische Sozialwissenschaft. Soziale Kämpfe in Afrika*, 43(170), 23–41.

Rommelspacher, B. (2011). 'Was ist eigentlich Rassismus?' In C. Melter, and P. Mecheril (eds.), *Rassismuskritik. Band 1. Rassismustheorie und -forschung*, pp. 25–38. 2. Edition. Schwalbach/Ts.: Wochenschau Verlag.

Said, E. W. (2017). *Orientalismus*. Frankfurt/Main: S. Fischer.

Scharathow, W. (2014). *Risiken des Widerstandes. Jugendliche und ihre Rassismuserfahrungen*. Bielefeld: Transcript Verlag.

Schneider, U. (2014). *Antifaschismus*. Köln: PapyRossa Verlag.

Schwarzmeier, J. (2001). '*Die Autonomen zwischen Subkultur und sozialer Bewegung*', https://books.google.de/books?hl=de&lr=&id=e6vvPIbiRcEC&oi=fnd&pg=PA9&dq=Subkultur&ots=l8a4tlG5wY&sig=KLC8nzEk8mTIfMW64YA6UlrOWik&redir_esc=y#v=onepage&q=Subkultur&f=false (Accessed on February 13, 2021).

Seukwa, L. H. (2016). 'Flucht'. In P. Mecheril (ed.), *Handbuch Migrationspädagogik*, pp. 196–210. Weinheim: Beltz.

Tijé-Dra, A. (2015). 'Fraktale Metropolen, Unruhe und Rap'. In F. Weber, and O. Kühne (eds.), *Fraktale Metropolen. Hybride Metropolen*, pp. 145–157. Wiesbaden: Springer VS.

Yeboah, A. (2017). 'Rassismus und psychische Gesundheit in Deutschland'. In K. Fereidooni, and M. El (eds.), *Rassismuskritik und Widerstandsformen*, pp. 143–161. Wiesbaden: Springer VS.

(by Dino Vukušić, Rašeljka Krnić and Vanja Dergić)

Chapter 11 'Undocumented culture': Ethnography on BEK social centre in Zagreb

Abstract: This chapter presents the results of an ethnographic case study of squatting in Zagreb, which is centred on the example of the BEK social centre. BEK was founded in early 2018 as a platform for various social, cultural, and artistic content, with the purpose of generating an innovative socio-cultural climate that could holistically develop the local community. We focused our research on analysing forms of organisation, activities and motivations of actors within squats. There are several different aspects to our ethnographic work, starting with the phenomenon of squatting. This chapter will discuss different types of squats and patterns of motivation for this type of housing. We also consider specific perceptions of culture, interculturality and the attitudes of respondents towards "others". A further focus of the research was related to the term "urban struggle", in the context of the occupation of a certain urban locality and different types of activities that take place in newly constructed spaces. Through such an approach, our goal is to investigate the practices of young people regarding activism and participatory models in urban space, and also contribute to the theoretical research discussion of various forms of organising squats or social centres. We also aim to explore cultural patterns contained within the constituent elements of young people's identities. This ethnographic case study is based on eight months of fieldwork, research diaries, and interviews with 13 respondents.

Keywords: squatting, youth, activism, participation, urban struggle

Introduction

The phenomenon of squatting originated in European countries in the late 1960s, primarily as a result of economic and social turbulence caused by a series of social changes in the post-war period (Guzman-Concha, 2015). After World War II, Western European countries (Italy, Great Britain, Switzerland, Spain, West Germany, Netherlands, Denmark, France) went through a period of intense social change marked by the birth of numerous social movements, which were predominantly organised by young people (Horn, 2007). Very soon, the phenomenon of squatting was no longer exclusively a solution for the housing issue and passed into the domain of political and ideological action based on countercultural values (Polanska and Piotrowski, 2015; Van der Steen, Katzeff, and van Hoogenhuijze, 2014). Squatting as a phenomenon does not have an unambiguous meaning, so there are several different critical approaches to the study of the phenomenon and its definition. Friend (1980) and Johnstone (2000) argue that the fact that widespread squatting occurred shortly after the end of World War II proves that squatting is not directly connected to "countercultural events" (see Pruijt, 2003). According to Corr (1999), squatting expresses a desire for a fairer distribution of goods, while Wates (1980) specifies that squatting is a rebellion against the problem of living space, i.e. the inability to provide everyone with at least basic facilities in which to live. Kallenberg (2001) views squatting as a utopian creation that sees making a better society as its task and desire. By placing life in a squat within "do-it-yourself" culture, it can be given postmodern and post-ideological meaning (McKay, 1998; Englander, 1994) or linked to a movement that acts in the moment (Martinez, 2007). In the mid-1990s, an attempt was made to explain the phenomenon of squatting within political-activist discourse, where we can observe the opposing opinions of various authors. Della Porta and Rucht (1995) write that squatting is a left-libertarian movement, while Katsiaficas (1997) offers a radically different view according to a Leninist model of political activism.

From this review of the academic literature, we can conclude that many authors have attempted to explain the phenomenon of squatting. However, these studies mostly researched squats located in Western European cities; very few studies are interested in squatting in the post-socialist countries of Eastern and Central Europe. Polanska and Piotrowski (2015), referring to Howard (2003), Kotkin (2010) and Sztompka (2004), conclude that the absence of such research is the result of the well-established perception that there is a lack of strong civil society development in post-socialist countries. Accordingly, there are no scientific research projects in Croatia dedicated to this topic, although it is a phenomenon that has existed for the last 20 years within the country's urban context, primarily in the capital Zagreb.

Zagreb, the capital of Croatia, went through a turbulent period of political, economic and social transition after the break-up of Yugoslavia and the war that followed (1991–1995). During the period of Yugoslavia, Zagreb was an important industrial centre, but after the transition period many previous factories decayed, leaving behind a large number of abandoned buildings. Since the mid-1990s, young members of the alternative cultural scene have been trying to occupy some of the aforementioned abandoned spaces in order to organise squats, social centres and "hotspots" of independent alternative culture. In this, they are following the example of similar actions in Western European countries. One of the most famous collectives of the Zagreb independent alternative scene is "Attack!", founded in 1997. Members of the collective connected the anarcho-punk and trance scenes on the basis of a common worldview and an ideological frame of reference based on the idea of opposing the values arising from the process of the re-traditionalisation of society in the late 1990s. Strpić (2010) mentions several attempts of squatting in Zagreb, while the city's first long-term squat was organised in 2008 when members of Attack! took over the former drug factory "Medika". In the next few years, a different group of young people occupied another abandoned industrial facility ("Klaonica"), while the subject of our research – BEK – was created in 2018.

BEK was founded in early 2018 as a platform for various social, cultural, and artistic practices, with the purpose of generating an innovative socio-cultural climate in order to develop the local community. Shortly after our study, the squat ceased to exist for reasons that we will discuss later. It developed out of the anarchist collective "Food Not Bombs", which organised the direct action of sharing free vegan food in public spaces. The initial idea behind BEK was to build a cooperation platform that would be available to everyone regardless of their social or financial status. One of the driving motives was to fill the void caused by the lack of free, widely available subversive content and a space that would host this. The building that was squatted in was the abandoned "Vinko Bek Centre for Education and Rehabilitation" (after which the collective was named) – this was formerly an institution for the upbringing, education, and rehabilitation of blind or visually impaired children, youth, and adults. The institution moved to a new location in 2015 after years of warnings about the poor condition of the structure in which children resided; the building was then abandoned, unused and doomed to fall into disrepair. A few years later, a group of young people moved into the building and decided to turn the abandoned space into a social centre. The idea was that the building should take on the role of a public community centre that would host various alternative sub-cultural activities. This chapter presents the results of ethnographic research into BEK and the group of young people involved in the collective. We focused our research on analysing the forms of organisation, activities and motivations of actors within the squat. Another aim was to investigate how the actors within BEK perceived the concept of culture and the main determinants of their (sub)cultural identity. Through such an approach, our goal was to connect empirical material with theoretical concepts in the field of youth sociology, urban sociology, activism and participation, and urban struggle. Ethnographic research on BEK lasted eight months. Participatory observations were performed at regular intervals multiple times a week, or more often if a specific event was taking place at BEK. Parallel to field research, researchers kept intensive research diaries in which they described each visit to BEK in detail. Researchers participated in the majority of daily activities with BEK's residents (cleaning, constructed work, preparing meals, spending time in shared spaces); they also organised a self-defence course, prepared free meals, and took part in nude drawing workshops.

BEK: Between squat and social centre

As noted in the introduction, BEK was founded in 2018 when a group of young people squatted in the abandoned building of the former Vinko Bek Centre for Education and Rehabilitation. The very beginnings of the social centre's work were marked with various activities. Planned activities focused on art and political action, the exchange of skills, creating a self-sustaining platform and a critically-thinking society, as well as raising awareness of problems faced by autonomous spaces, all with the intent of tackling burning issues including the growing housing crisis in Zagreb and Croatia and the marginalisation of the homeless, migrants and LGBTQ+ people. The organisation and the function of the collective were envisioned based on anarchist principles, ideas and values, which meant that all decisions were made by consensus at weekly meetings, which had an open agenda. In the beginning, BEK declared itself a self-organised group of individuals that was open to the community and that made decisions through direct democracy and enforced them via direct action. The ideology that was supposed to be the foundation for all the collective's actions was based on self-sustainability, anarchism, solidarity, antifascism, feminism, anti-consumerism, personal and collective responsibility, and non-violent treatment of humans and animals.

At the outset of any discussion of BEK, we must clarify two concepts tied to our overall ethnographic research. There is a theoretical difference between what is referred to in the literature as a "squat" and what is recognised as a "social centre". In the context of our research, we must show how these two concepts overlap. The appearance of social centres of this type is tied to 1980s Italy, when youth started to organise centres that undertook activities based on "do-it-yourself" principles. These centres breached the boundaries of individual groups and even the broader sub-cultural scene, setting the goal of including the broader local community in their activities (Mudu, 2004). On the basis of such starting points, people involved in BEK aimed to create a social centre that united a broad range of actors with the goal of creating a framework within which to include marginalised groups in the modern Croatian context. These are mostly migrants and homeless people. By the term 'migrant', we mean the group of people who, over the last six years, have come to Zagreb (and to the European continent in general) from the Middle East and Africa (Jović, 2020).. BEK also embodies the idea of giving the broader local community access to cultural reproduction through various workshops, and the centre attempts to affirm young artists by offering them a space to premiere exhibitions and performances. Very soon after the centre was opened to the public, various initiatives and actions began, including a public kitchen where vegan meals using food collected and recycled from Zagreb's farmers markets were cooked and distributed, as well as various workshops (circus, yoga, composting, creating a fanzine, etc.), DIY concerts, film screenings, discussions, exhibitions, DIY festivals, lectures, ateliers, library services, jam sessions, protest participation, and sharing food in the street. The group squatting in the building decided that a kind of a shelter for people in need should be organised within BEK and that other necessities –such as showers, a laundry room, etc. – should be provided in order to give people access to basic living conditions. One such programme was the BEK "shop", where people could take clothes they needed for free or donate clothes they did not need. In cooperation with the "Students for Refugees"[1] initiative, a drive to collect tents and other necessities for people staying in reception centres in Bosnia and Herzegovina also took place at BEK.

The second theoretical concept applicable to the context of BEK is the phenomenon of squatting. There are various definitions of a squat; the social sciences variously define this as an intervention in the development and renewal of an urban environment (Martinez, 2007; Pruijt, 2013), a form of resistance (Corr, 1999), or even an alternative lifestyle (Reeve and Coward, 2004). Research by Pruijt (2013) on the phenomenon of squatting concluded that it was possible to create a typology of squats, mainly categorised according to the motivations of the squatters. He discusses five types of squats: deprivation-based squatting, squatting as an alternative housing strategy, entrepreneurial squatting, conservational squatting, and political squatting (Pruijt, 2013: p. 22).

Our discussion will begin with the fact that a large number of attempts have been made to organise spaces for alternative culture in Zagreb in the past 30 years. This scene has often sought a place to 'put down roots' and perform various types of activities, from cultural and arts activities to action directed at the broader local community (Cvek et al., 2013). BEK is a recent attempt arising from an idea with two branches: one is squatting, and the other is creating a social centre. The initial motivations of respondents regarding their involvement in BEK were

1 A student organisation that deals with education and connecting volunteers with civil society actors, working with refugees.

exceptionally heterogeneous; however, the majority agreed that they wanted to create a social centre through squatting:

> *This whole idea was revolutionary for Zagreb, for Croatia in general, because we literally had a squat that was open to everyone.* (Kaja)
> *One of the main ideas behind BEK was for it to be a subcultural place, not only for punks, hippies, vegans, or whoever, but to be open to all sorts of people who wanted to engage in activism.* (Sak)

For the majority of respondents, motives for engagement with BEK mainly lay in a sense of belonging, helping others and the desire to revitalise abandoned spaces:

> *I didn't have anywhere else to be.* (Isak)
> *Life in the collective inspired me.* (Kaja)
> *When I realised I had the option of coming here to help people, I literally grabbed it and stopped thinking about anything else.* (Boki)
> *It was a typical building occupation.* (Dana)

What drove most of the first occupiers of BEK was the potential they saw in the building itself: *"Everything was already there we didn't have to bring anything. When you see the space, a lot of ideas come to mind…"* (Dana). In addition to individual motives, we were also interested in interviewees' perceptions about their fellow squatters at BEK:

> *Some wanted a place to live, which was also important for me, to live and work in the same place. Some wanted artistic content […] some wanted alternative medicine, some wanted sport activities. There were all sorts of ideas.* (Dana)

Some respondents mentioned political values that were important for them at the BEK Centre, and how those values were viewed by other members of the collective:

> *Not many people recognised the political values that are important to me. We talked about anarchy, freedom, equality, but everyone had a different understanding of it. There was a discrepancy of ideas…* (Dana)

The combination of these three models shows the specificity of the context in which BEK was formed, which is a modern Croatian society still burdened by the process of transition that began in the 1990s. Analysing the transition process in Croatia, Štulhofer (2000) talks about transition winners and losers, where we can easily find people turning to squatting as a response to poverty. On the other hand, it is also important to emphasise that there is a big housing issue among young people in Zagreb today, because of economic differences and the inability to achieve permanent employment. Our respondents often referred to the problem of housing and unresolved housing issues, especially among young people:

> *We wanted to create more programmes and community and solidarity, but people needed a place to stay. Lots of people would come with their problems and ask us if they could live there. They had stories about losing their homes, they couldn't afford it, and housing became the most important (issue) for us.* (Dana)

Bežovan (2004) writes that, since 1990, housing programmes in Croatia have predominantly dealt with the dismantlement of the inherited housing system, concluding that housing conditions in our country show that many people cannot afford an apartment or a decent standard of living. Some of the young people gathered around BEK decided to squat due to the impossibility of owning their own apartment or paying high rent, while some respondents saw this as an opportunity to turn to alternative forms of housing.

The aforementioned typology of squats shows that there are firm starting points for defining each particular type of squat; however, these are inadequate in our case. We believe the heterogeneity of motivations for squatting, and thus the lack of a shared belief in one system of values and interpersonal relationships, actually led to the failure of the idea of BEK as a squat; once consensus over the way of life in the space was lost, the idea of a social centre was automatically extinguished. Nevertheless, in order to try to theoretically substantiate the BEK squat, we can say that it is a hybrid model constructed through the categories of deprivation-based squatting, squatting as an alternative housing strategy, conservational squatting and political squatting.

Creating urban space

The youth gathered around the idea of BEK have an interesting perspective on the debate over "urban struggle". Urban struggle represents the conflict (either latent or manifest) between privileged and impoverished classes in the city, groups that clash over the concept of visibility in public space (Harvey, 2012). It is important to emphasise that it is not only presence in public space that is the goal of impoverished urban groups, but also participation in the "creation of space", both symbolically and physically. The creation of space implies the implementation of various cultural forms and value systems typical of particular groups within an urban context. The youth involved in BEK saw the potential of the building, such as its location and furnishings, and recognised the need for such abandoned spaces to be used as places of cultural production. Pina summarised this idea: "*The city needs this kind of space, and I am in awe of what it could become*" (Pina). All respondents saw the possibility of making a difference, but from different perspectives:

> *I thought that it would really... make a difference. I saw an opportunity to create something new, something valuable for our community, to create a community, something that was missing. To start collaboration between autonomous spaces and to keep all of that alive.* (Dana)

The work of the actors in our research can be perceived in two ways. On the one hand, they were fighting for a physical place within which to base their actions, while on the other they wished to influence the local community at large by sending a symbolic message (squatting) as a promise to develop a society with greater solidarity. Almost all respondents mentioned being accepted by their neighbours:

> *We never had any problems.* (Isak)
> *We had support.* (Sak)
> *They would help us out with water and things [...] it was a police neighbourhood, there are embassies and SOA*[2] *have their apartments there, but we never had any problems. They even said they were glad that we are here, as a social centre.* (Isak)

Sak talked about how neighbours sometimes attended events, such as public kitchens:

> *We had support from most of the neighbours we met [...] they said they were glad someone was there, that the building wasn't empty, that something was happening, that it was alive, that there were some events... some of them would even come to public kitchens, events, or chill on the rooftop.* (Sak)

Once the young people squatted in the BEK building, they encountered another form of struggle: the conflict between two concepts of the 'urban habitus' (Lefebvre et al., 1996). Writing on the relationship between urban space and the people who live within it, Lefebvre et al. (1996) described a distinction between inhabiting urban space and the rationalistic-commercial logic of the urban habitus. Inhabiting represents a symbolic reproduction of space in accordance with the values and norms of a particular local community, while rationalistic-commercial logic seeks the maximum commercial profit from interventions into space. BEK is an example of youth engagement with the idea of the symbolic reproduction of space and of the inclusion of the local community, which offered them support from the very beginning. This is apparent from the interview quotes above. On the other hand, abandoned buildings are often former

2 The Security and Intelligence Agency – Croatia's national intelligence service.

factories, representing an ideal opportunity to invest and create a profitable location in the city; from the very beginning, the actors within BEK were uncertain as to what would happen with the building in the future. Attempts to evict the squatters by shutting off water and electricity are indicators of the fact that animosity towards the youth at BEK did not come from neighbours and others who lived nearby, but from an institutional level. In September 2018, a few months after the centre was opened to the public, the then Minister of State Property began pressuring the squat, aided by certain media outlets and state institutions. According to the minister's statement (Negovetić and Pandžić, 2018), legal proceedings were initiated in order to evict the squatters; meanwhile, dramatic media headlines attempted (Parežanin, 2018) to depict the squatters at BEK as a sect that had illegally appropriated state-owned property. The building's utilities were shut off and six members of the BEK collective were sued for obstruction of public property. Apart from this kind of external pressure from state institutions and media outlets, problems emerged within the collective itself, which had a hard time functioning according to the principles initially established as its basic method and philosophy of operation. At the beginning of 2019, problems with decision-making, differences in envisioning and conducting projects, and clashing worldviews, values, and motives all led to an escalation of internal conflict. This resulted in certain founding members of the collective deciding to move out; shortly afterwards, the squat closed down completely as a result of an eviction order issued on the basis of a final legal judgement.

Understanding of culture and cultural heritage

In conversation with respondents, a frequent question was how they perceived culture and what it meant to them in the context of BEK. Some respondents considered squatting and other activities that took place at the BEK centre as part of alternative culture. Others saw culture as part of the mainstream, something that happens in museums or national theatres. Dana was one of the respondents who occupied and squatted in the BEK building. As a long-time actor in the punk and squat scene in Croatia, she had a broader understanding of alternative culture in the context of mainstream culture:

> *When you say culture or independent culture, there is always the NGO scene and liberal culture, the culture of resistance. BEK would be that, or at least should have been, as I imagined. Our goal was to preserve culture that wasn't documented as part of underground scene where squats have their resistance network.* (Dana)

Some respondents even viewed this "undocumented culture" as avant-garde: "*I see it more as social than cultural. But one pulls the other. We were the cultural avant-garde*" (Lada). Respondents would often discuss the culture they grew up in, surrounded by their families or neighbourhood, and how that shaped their perspectives on culture and what it means to them.

> *I was culturally conditioned by where I grew up… I grew up in my neighbourhood, so I have certain ideas in my head that are from the culture of my neighbourhood… then the culture of the alternative scene and trance scene where I grew up…* (Niki, 26)

Interviewees also mentioned familial transmission of culture, and ideas like what is "our culture", and sometimes, inevitably, "their culture":

> *They never forced anything in my upbringing, if I belonged to certain nation… in fact, until the war, I didn't even know who was Croatian, and I was 15 then. I didn't know who was a Croat and who was a Serb, which was great, and I think kids should be raised like that today, but the situation is the opposite.* (Mak)

For our respondents, learning about their culture among family was often very liberating: "*…they gave me the freedom to form my own identity*" (Laura).

Talking about culture from the perspective of national identity and what it means to them, respondents would often discuss Croatia's heterogeneity and how there can be no unified national identity for the country as a whole:

> *I am more from Dalmatia than from Zagorje. Croatia is really heterogeneous, different by its regions and way of life… even the culture is different in the south, the east, and the west, and I am more home in Italy […] than in Zagreb.* (Mina)

Mina explained that she does not see herself as someone with a sense of national identity, but rather as someone who has a connection to the place she grew up, to the place she lives, and to traditional way of life, and she discussed how these factors affected her life choices. Again, this led to the conclusion that

> *… national identity […] in the south and west of Croatia are different, and if I want to identify myself, don't get me wrong, but I would rather identify myself as someone from Dalmatia than as someone from Croatia.* (Mina)

When defining cultural heritage and where they saw its presence in their life, respondents concluded that it is "*everything that is of material, physical, or spiritual value that can be connected with a certain culture*" (Boki) or simply "*[…] what we leave behind*" (Isak). Some viewed cultural heritage as "*the diversity we carry with us from our upbringing*" (Kaja), while others believed that "*Everything is more or less cultural heritage*" (Boki). Laura suggested that because culture heritage is "*what is recognised in the community […] it should be left and respected*"

(Laura). Some respondents placed culture heritage in the past as something that shapes us as members of society: "*Cultural heritage is something we learned, something that conditioned us*" (Niki). Mina described this idea further:

> *If you go and stop young people in the street and ask them what cultural heritage is, most of them would mention cathedrals and folk dances […] when they learn about it, they have this idea that it is something old, something our grandmas did, something really boring […] they do not identify it as something that is close to them… that something they could create could be culture.* (Mina)

Trying to contextualise where BEK fit into this idea, some respondents discussed BEK as "*real cultural heritage that society is currently creating*" (Mak). One respondent applied the idea of cultural heritage to their life, describing "echoes" of his cultural heritage:

> *Echoes of my cultural heritage are apparent in my work at BEK, the way I wanted… the way I forced some things to happen, and that is a result of what I had learned in the trance culture and squatter culture. 'Self-sustaining culture'.* (Niki)

The majority of our respondents did not want to talk much about their understanding of European culture(s) or identities. When they answered our questions on this subject, they would usually say that they did not consider national borders necessary. Respondents wanted to talk about regional identity and differences rather than national or European identity. However, Lada mentioned perceiving the existence of a European cultural identity and how others interpret this:

> *Those from other continents see a certain European cultural identity. I experienced that stigma when I was at a residence in one European country, where I represented the typical European avant-garde for them […] when I talked with others, they all used expressions like European beauty, European something… we clearly see that. That is based on mutual political history. Also, political history, philosophical history, humanistic history, social history, you can see that direction where freedom, human rights are being developed, women walk freely, and you can see other aspects where people are fighting, there is war, violence… we colonised the rest of the world.* (Lada)

To the question of whether there is such a thing as European identity, she responded: "*It is relatively possible, but not absolutely. But it can also be matter of perspective*" (Lada).

As concerns culture and its perception amongst the youth in the BEK collective, there are a few levels on which our results can be interpreted. As is apparent from the quotes cited above, the youth action at BEK was built on inclusive foundations from the outset, with a strong feeling of responsibility towards the "underprivileged" and the desire to create a social framework based on greater solidarity. Our results are especially interesting when viewed in the context of sub-cultural theory. Haenfler (2013) defines a subculture as a relatively diffuse social network of shared identities that creates subtle meanings around particular ideas, practices, objects, and feelings of marginalisation by a perceived "conventional society". Cohen (1997) divides the lifestyles created by youth subcultures into four sub-systems (clothing, music, slang, ritual), which can be divided into two more basic groups – clothing and music, and slang and ritual. A typical conception of sub-cultural groups frequently emphasises stylistic differences (Hebdige, 1979). Taking this background into account, we may conclude that youth within BEK primarily define culture as belonging to various sub-cultural styles; this makes them a heterogeneous group in one sense. Their common feature is conflict with what they call the mainstream, to which they see themselves as an alternative. These concepts are vital to our discussion of the understanding of culture held by the youth within BEK. Some actors do not display countercultural elements. According to Hebdige, counter-culture can be interpreted as those actors (movements, initiatives, groups, and individuals) who seek to realise a broader world-view (philosophical, spiritual, social theory, political) and who wish to build alternative institutions. Countercultural actors have created (or endeavour to create) their own media (from fanzines and newspapers to pirate radio stations), as well as "free" schools, hospitals, kindergartens, and food sources (Hebdige, according to Perasović, 2002: p. 488). Thus, actors experience (sub)culture as a defining element of their own identity, and the dominant culture as an oppressive element.

Interaction with other people and "cultures"

As soon as the squatters moved into the BEK building in Nazorova Street in Zagreb, it became a meeting place for many people, mostly youth. They would gather there to find a space to carry out artistic or other work, as well as to help the community by organising workshops, public kitchens, support groups for minorities, events that would include people who migrated to Croatia, and a give-away shop. As already mentioned, when talking about people who migrated to Croatia, we refer to people who have come to Zagreb in the last few years and who are predominantly from the Middle East and Africa. It is important to note that this is often labelled a 'migrant crisis' in the media, which in conversations with our respondents was marked as an inappropriate term due to its stigmatisation of this group of people. That is why the young squatters work to include this population in various activities, from organising meals and accommodation to involving them in cultural and artistic activities. The initial motivation for most actors within BEK was to organise a space that would serve as a meeting point for diverse individuals, regardless of the cultural differences between them: "*One of the most important factors for me was that the space was open and welcoming to everyone*" (Kaja). This same inclusiveness later became problematic, as the permanent residents of BEK encountered issues with visitors who had different political and ideological views from them. Many people would come to BEK simply to find a place to stay for a few days while travelling through Croatia. People from BEK discussed engaging with what they perceived as different national cultures:

> *A lot of new things happened every day, we had guests from France, Brazil, Argentina, Spain, and Portugal, simply coexisting in the space generated spontaneous meetings and spontaneous action from individuals.* (Dana)

Respondents would often discuss their motivations for organising activities directed towards people who migrated to Croatia and how such activities were arranged at BEK: "*squatting and opening social centres is really important in the region because people still think that migrants bring sickness, problems, wars…*" (Kaja). This was particularly important because many people attempting to pass through Croatia on their migrant route ended up staying in Zagreb, and were housed in the former hotel Porin in the neighbourhood of Dugave.[3] The BEK collective organised a clothing collection for migrants, as well as offering to store collected clothes for other: "*[…] we jumped in to help with storing clothes for migrants*" (Isak).

What they considered "intercultural" activities were always mentioned as one of the main motivations for organising the collective and opening a space that is welcoming and free for everyone: "*In the summertime, we would have people from all over the world, literally all over the world*" (Niki). It is important to highlight two things we observed through conversations with our respondents. Often the term national culture of "others" was perceived as a homogeneous culture situated in a particular national context, so it was interpreted as something static and fixed; meanwhile, the domicile culture was often seen as more diverse, characterised by, for example, different local cultures or subcultures. Also, respondents defined interculturality as a term used to describe the interactions

3 Because of changing political relationships with migrants since 2015, a few non-governmental organisations have attempted to organise various events and activities for migrants, as well as meet certain needs (such as collecting clothes, organising Croatian language workshops, helping migrant families assimilate into society, helping children with their new school environment, etc.). One place that attempted this was the BEK Social Centre. All their actions were voluntary.

between different cultures, most often in terms of different national cultures. It is important to note that this type of interaction could be studied in relation to different subcultures within a certain society.

Respondents discussed how BEK's location in the city centre helped them to collect and recycle food, which allowed them to organise public kitchens: "*we were really privileged because almost every day we would go to Dolac*[4] *to recycle (food), and food was never an issue. We had beds, all the basic things… we had water*" (Morana, 25). Respondents assumed that learning about what they perceived as national culture leads to improvements in intercultural communication: "*[…] if people had more space to express themselves, to do so more freely, there would be a free exchange of ideas among cultures*" (Sak). The public kitchen allowed people to "*grow closer through food*" (Kaja); the respondents concluded that

> *you can learn a lot from different people, a lot of useful things. Not only about squatting as a way of life, but about some life lessons. […] when there are more people that live the same way of life as you and you share hardships, you become closer.* (Isak)

In addition to discussions regarding interviewees' relationships with "others", we also asked about their interactions with the residents of the neighbourhood in which BEK was located, with people in public space, and with representatives of the law:

> *We had support from most of the neighbours we met […] they said they were glad someone was there, that the building wasn't empty, that something was happening, that it was alive, that there were some events… some of them would even come to public kitchens, events, or chill on the rooftop.* (Sak)

Representatives of the law (police and communal wardens), who visited occasionally, were not described as supportive: "*[…] they didn't come all the time or bother us… they would come because of the noise, but they were polite*" (Dana). Some respondents mentioned that the first day they held a public event, the police came and asked several people for their identity documents: "*the same day, the police came and asked six of us for our ID[s], and we were written up for not having documents…*" (Dana). Other than this, they did not mention having problems of any kind with neighbours or representatives of the law.

The part of the city in which the BEK centre was located is known for its high property value, as well as the presence of foreign embassies. Respondents often mentioned this when discussing how they felt when communicating with other people in the neighbourhood. Some respondents said that "*I always feel slightly*

4 Zagreb's central farmers' market.

stigmatised" (Boki), while others did not perceive this: "*That didn't bother me*" (Kaja). Even though not all respondents discussed stigmatisation, some would casually mention it: "*There were some people who would say something ugly when they saw us on the street*" (Saki). One respondent, who lived at BEK for several months, said that he noticed stigmatisation, but that he also understood it in the context of this part of the city:

> *Sometimes I would notice more looks, but it was understandable because we lived in conditions without water or electricity, and that interferes with personal hygiene, which affects the way you behave in society, which affects how that society is going to perceive you.* (Boki)

For the most part, related questions resulted in respondents identifying different types of stigmatisation present in society, mainly directed at "migrants":

> *I don't like to call people migrants, because borders are a problem of the entire planet. You rarely have the opportunity to meet migrants [...] This is why squatting and social centres are important for our region, where people still think that migrants bring sickness, problems, wars, and whatnot.* (Kaja)

"What went wrong?"

When the interviews were conducted, respondents had recently moved out of the BEK centre, which resulted in a great deal of conversation about what went wrong with the experience. Almost all of the respondents spoke of constant discussion and conflict based on a lack of agreement as to the aims and values they wished to represent as a collective: "*We didn't have a mutual set of rules. Not rules, but values and a sort of frame, something that was common to all of us, what we stood for, what we agreed upon*" (Mina). However, the greatest issue was the principle of openness, which invited anyone to become a part of the collective; this resulted in the frequent appearance of people with different, often radically so, political and ideological beliefs. This created problems that were at the heart of later communication issues:

> *Being open and welcoming to people that you don't know and you met yesterday and today you start living together [...] what happened is that a few of us wanted it to be an antifascist place with zero tolerance for fascism, but some people didn't want to declare it as such, some of them didn't have an opinion on that.* (Kaja)

As a result, the collective faced trust issues, which Boki refers to as "capitalist paranoia": "*We had this fear that, if we weren't careful, some other group would come in and take over the space, which is, as I see it now, really absurd capitalist paranoia, but what can you do. It happens*" (Boki). Interestingly, although they perceived it as an "*anarchist commune*" (Boki), a few respondents wanted a leader, or saw the value of having

> *one person who would have more responsibility than the rest of us and who would say, we will do it this way, we need to do it that way. Instead, we decided to have meetings where everyone would gather, we would sit down and talk, talk, and talk about a problem, but we would not resolve it.* (Boki)

Along similar lines, Mirna said: "*My mindset is very far from the idea of the existence of rules, dictatorship, and a leader with sole authority, but that's really what we needed*" (Mirna). This was not the most common attitude among respondents, but it indicates the lack of a common political and ideological base among them: "*There should be some rules, of course, anarchy doesn't mean that there aren't any rules, anarchy isn't chaos, anarchy is order, but people don't understand that*" (Keni).

Discussion

The issue of youth participation in social processes has long been an issue for public policymakers in numerous Western countries. The examination of questions regarding the idea of modern citizenship most often emphasises the importance of encouraging youth participation, to the extent that this discourse has nearly become cliché. Improving opportunities for participation and generally creating a space within which youth voices can be heard more clearly– especially in relation to those policies that directly or indirectly affect youth themselves – has become a routinely declared goal for many state administrations. Increasingly, youth participation has been called for as a potential way to resolve a range of social issues (Bessant, 2004). Numerous studies throughout the past two decades point to a general decline in civic participation in social processes; on the basis of a wealth of local and international research, the same conclusion can be drawn as concerns young people's political and social engagement (Putnam, 2000; Ilišin, 2003; Banaji and Buckingham, 2010). Although countless surveys show decreasing youth informedness, lack of interest in politics, and a reduction in youth involvement in organisations that fight for particular goals. Some researchers claim that youth activism is not in decline, but is simply changing form – involvement manifests in a different way than in previous generations, including through volunteer activities (Earl, Maher and Elliott, 2017). Ilišin et al. (2013) emphasise that the majority of young people in Croatia do not trust bodies of representative and executive power, least of all political parties. In another, more recent study, Franc and Međugorac (2015) confirmed this thesis, finding that there is an extremely low level of trust in political institutions among young people. They especially highlighted distrust towards political parties and the Croatian Parliament. In this context, the young people gathered around BEK are an interesting case; they represent a kind of anomaly, acting differently from most of their peers by being involved in different aspects of social participation.

The actors within BEK, as young people wishing to participate in social events, raise another important issue that is often left out of analyses of potential youth participation. As a social centre deeply rooted in do-it-yourself culture, BEK represented the idea of youth participation through what we shall term 'direct action'. Doherty, Plows, and Wall (2003) see direct action as an attempt to directly influence political and social injustices, bypassing conventional, institutionalised political processes as well as the media. In his book *Direct Action: An Ethnography*, Graeber (2009) uses ethnographic methods to study forms of direct action in different social contexts. He concludes:

> *Direct action aims to achieve our goals through our own activity rather than through the actions of others. It is about people taking power for themselves. In this, it is distinguished from most other forms of political action such as voting, lobbying, attempting to exert political pressure through industrial action or through the media. All of these activities concede our power to existing institutions which work to prevent us from acting ourselves to change the status quo. Direct Action repudiates such acceptance of the existing order and suggests that we have both the right and the power to change the world. It demonstrates this by doing it.* (Graeber, 2009: p. 304)

Some of the young people gathered around BEK emphasised how important direct action is for them and their goals, among other things because of their disillusionment with political and other formal institutional forms of action:

> *We didn't want to be part of any governmental or non-governmental association and we felt that anything we wanted to do could be done by a couple of individuals working as one…We refused to be part of the system.* (Boki)
>
> *I don't like meetings and bureaucracy, I avoid it as much as I can, and I go more with concrete actions and concrete things. It may even be related to my childhood when I was a member of the SRP (Radical left party) as a teenager… That's where I got disgusted with politics and all those backstage games, and that's why I'm going with concrete things* (Mak)

During the existence of the BEK social centre, numerous programmes were organised that can be considered (and that the actors themselves consider to be) forms of direct action. These programmes embodied exactly what Doherty, Plows, and Wall (2003) found to be a key determinant of direct action: an attempt to correct social injustices. These programmes worked with various marginalised groups such as people without secure residence, people who migrated to Croatia, who seek asylum, who live in poverty, members of the LGBTQ+ community, and other socially and economically deprived groups. In the squat, a public kitchen was organised twice a week, there was a so-called 'free shop' where people in need could find free donated clothes, and those who did not have a place to sleep were offered temporary accommodation. In addition to direct material assistance, various cultural and artistic programmes were organised with the aim of providing free content to as wide a group of people as possible. The BEK centre offered a library that loaned books for free, art workshops, and a space for band rehearsals or film screenings. Concerts of various musical genres were also held in the squat every week.

BEK's residents displayed almost no identification with a national identity; this was frequently seen as an element of oppression or as the exclusion of differences. Actors experienced (sub)culture as a defining element in their own identity, perceiving the dominant culture as more oppressive. It is important to distinguish several types of oppression that young people found in the dominant culture. First and foremost, having encountering various prejudices within their local environments, they felt that mainstream culture attacked their identities. Our respondents saw the oppression of the dominant culture in the attitude of the social majority towards others, attributing this relationship to established cultural patterns or, in their words, the closed cultural system of the majority in Croatia. It is interesting to note that our respondents still connected 'other cultures' with a particular national identity that individuals possess. Such a situation is often influenced by an established, somewhat banal understanding of national identity as an exclusively descriptive or spoken term, rather than as a constitutive element of the identity of our respondents or people with whom they interact.

Conclusion

Having completed this ethnographic research on the BEK Social Centre, we may draw a few conclusions regarding various aspects of the studied phenomenon. First, it is important to emphasise that BEK cannot be placed precisely within the typology of squats offered earlier in this discussion; instead, it exemplifies a hybrid model in which the majority of residents had several motivations for their involvement. However, there were common starting points, which mostly involved the desire to contribute to increased solidarity in Croatian society, the recognition of "others" and marginalised groups as equally valuable, and increased awareness of problems like homelessness and poverty in modern society. It is interesting to consider the possibility that the position of our respondents, which we may consider marginal, directly affects their engagement with other marginalised and vulnerable groups, yet we will not discuss this issue further as our empirical data cannot confirm the existence of such a connection. Some respondents found themselves unable to find their own housing and decided to turn to squatting, which then resulted in an activist desire to help others and to try to change the society in which they live. By operating within the urban space, these social actors attempted to change the environment both symbolically and physically. Symbolic change here primarily refers to the symbolic reproduction of space filled with inclusive, sympathetic behavioural value frameworks. The physical aspect of influencing space is that of occupying an abandoned building and applying new meaning to a pre-existing structure. BEK's actions also offer a framework for producing cultural content that might otherwise be obscured due to the distinction between "mainstream" and "underground" culture.

Research into BEK has shown how important it is to research the various groups that live within an urban context who frequently bear the stigma of "marginal" phenomena; these are, in fact, interesting social groups whose deviations from aspects of the dominant culture serve to mitigate the lack of inclusive forms of behaviour and solidarity within the local community. Future analysis should include more extensive and detailed research into the phenomenon of squatting and social centres, with the necessary inclusion of comparative analysis in order to build conclusions based on multiple examples within several different social contexts. It is also necessary to analyse housing policy and its role in the phenomenon of squatting, as well as the role of city/state bodies in regulating spaces within the city and defining usage policies for particular spaces.

References

Banaji, S. and Buckingham, D. (2010). 'Young people, the Internet, and civic participation: An overview of key findings from the Civic Web project', *International Journal of Learning and Media* 2(1): 15–24.

Bessant, J. (2004). 'Mixed messages: Youth participation and democratic practice', *Australian Journal of Political Science* 39(2): 387–404.

Bežovan, G. (2004). 'Stambena prava u Hrvatskoj i problemi njihova ostvarenja', *Revija za socijalnu politiku* 11(1): 89–106.

Cohen, P. (1997). 'Subcultural conflict and working-class community'. In P. Cohen (ed.), *Rethinking the Youth Question*, pp. 48–63. London: Palgrave.

Corr, A. (1999). *No trespassing!: Squatting, rent strikes, and land struggles worldwide*. South End Press.

Cvek, S., Koroman, B., Remenar, S., and Burlović, S. (2013). *Naša priča:15 godina ATTACK!-a*. Zagreb: Autonomni kulturni centar.

Della Porta, D. and Rucht, D. (1995). Left-libertarian movements in context: A comparison of Italy and West Germany. In J. Jenkins and B. Klandermans (ed.), *The Politics of Social Protest: Comparative Perspectives on States and Social Movements*, pp. 229–272. University of Minnesota Press.

Doherty, B., Plows, A., and Wall, D. (2003). 'The preferred way of doing things: The British direct action movement,' *Parliamentary Affairs* 56(4), 669–686.

Earl, J., Maher, T. V., and Elliott, T. (2017). 'Youth, activism, and social movements,' *Sociology Compass* 11(4): e12465.

Englander, S. (1994). *Cracking the Movement: Squatting Beyond the Media.* New York: Autonomedia.

Franc, R. and Međugorac, V. (2015). Mladi i (ne) povjerenje u institucije: moguće odrednice i posljedice. In V. Ilišin, A. Gvozdanović and D. Potočnik (ed.). *Demokratski potencijali mladih u* Hrvatskoj, pp. 47–63. Zagreb: Institut za društvena istraživanja u Zagrebu i Centar za demokraciju i pravo Miko Tripalo.

Friend, A. (1980). The post war squatters. In N. Wates and C. Wolmar (ed.), *Squatting: The Real Story*, pp. 110–122. London: Bay Leaf Books.

Graeber, D. (2009). *Direct Action: An Ethnography*. Stirling: AK Press.

Guzman-Concha, C. (2015). 'Radical social movements in Western Europe: A configurational analysis,' *Social Movement Studies* 14(6), 668–691.

Harvey, D. (2012). *Rebel Cities: From the Right to the city to the Urban Revolution.* London: Verso.

Haenfler, R. (2013). *Subcultures: the basics*. London: Routledge.

Hebdige, D. (1979). *Subculture. The meaning of style*. London: Routladge.

Horn, G. R. (2007). *The Spirit of '68: Rebellion in Western Europe and North America, 1956–1976*. Oxford: Oxford University Press.

Howard, M. M. (2003). *The Weakness of Civil Society in Post-Communist Europe.* Cambridge: Cambridge University Press.

Ilišin, V. (2003). 'Politička participacija mladih i politika prema mladima: Hrvatska u europskom kontekstu,' *Politička misao: časopis za politologiju* 40(3): 37–57.

Ilišin, V, Bouillet, D., Gvozdanović, A., and Potočnik, D. (2013). Mladi u vremenu krize, *Prvo istraživanje IDIZ-a i Zaklade Friedrich Ebert o mladima, Institut za društvena istraživanja u Zagrebu*, Zagreb: Friedrich Ebert Stiftung.

Johnstone, C. (2000). Housing and class struggles in post-war Glasgow. In M. Lavalette and G. Mooney (ed.), *Class Struggle and Social Welfare*, pp. 139–154. London: Routledge.

Jović, D. (2020). *Nacionalna sigurnost i migrantska kriza: politika RH prema izbjeglicama s (bliskog) istoka* (Doctoral dissertation, University of Split. University Department for Forensic Sciences).

Kallenberg, F. (2001). Desire is speaking. Utopian rhizomes. In S. Poldervaart, H. Jansen and B. Kesler (ed.), *Contemporary Utopian Struggles. Communities between Modernism and Postmodernism*, pp. 91–116. Amsterdam: Aksant, Amsterdam.

Katsiaficas, G. (1997). *The Subversion of Politics: European Autonomous Social Movements and the Decolonization of Everyday Life*. New Jersey: Humanities Press, Atlantic Highlands.

Kotkin, S. (2010). *Uncivil Society. 1989 and the Implosion of the Communist Establishment.* New York: The Modern Library.

Lefebvre, H., Kofman, E., and Lebas, E. (1996). *Writings on Cities (Vol. 63).* Oxford: Blackwell.

Martínez, M. (2007). 'The squatters' movement: urban counter-culture and alter-globalization dynamics,' *South European Society & Politics* 12(3): 379–398.

McKay, G. (1998). DiY Culture: Notes towards an Intro. In G. McKay (ed.), *Culture. Party & Protest in Nineties* Britain, pp. 1–53. London: Verso.

Mudu, P. (2004). 'Resisting and challenging neoliberalism: The development of Italian social centres,' *Antipode* 36(5): 917–941.

Negovetić, L. and Pandžić, I. (2018). Skvoteri su bez struje i vode: 'U državnoj zgradi živi sekta', *24sata,* 12 September, https://www.24sata.hr/video/u-drza vnu-zgradu-uselila-sekta-skvoteri-zive-bez-struje-i-vode-590062 (Accessed on October 9, 2020).

Parežanin, L. (2018). Pacifističko-vegansko-sektaški teror, *Kulturpunkt.hr,* 14 November, https://www.kulturpunkt.hr/content/pacifisticko-vegansko-sekta ski-teror (Accessed on October 12, 2020).

Polanska, D. V. and Piotrowski, G. (2015). 'The transformative power of cooperation between social movements: Squatting and tenants' movements in Poland,' *City* 19(2–3): 274–296.

Pruijt, H. (2003). Is the institutionalization of urban movements inevitable? A comparison of the opportunities for sustained squatting in New York City and Amsterdam, *International Journal of Urban and Regional Research* 27(1): 133–157.

Pruijt, H. (2013). 'The logic of urban squatting,' *International Journal of Urban and Regional Research* 37(1): 19–45.

Putnam, R. (2000). Bowling alone: America's declining social capital. In L. Crothers and C. Lockhart (ed.), *Culture and Politics*, pp. 223–234. New York: Palgrave Macmillan.

Reeve, K. and Coward, S. (2004). *Life on the Margins: The Experiences of Homeless People Living in Squats*. Crisis. http://www.crisis.org.uk/data/files/publications/LifeMargins_Full.pdf (Accessed March 1, 2021).

Strpić, M. (2010, May 5). Prvo skvotiranje u Zagrebu. *Kulturpunkt*. Retrieved from https://www.kulturpunkt.hr/content/prvo-skvotiranje-u-zagrebu (Accessed April 1, 2021).

Sztompka, P. (2004). The Trauma of Social Change: A Case of Postcommunist Societies. In J. C. Alexander (ed.), *Cultural Trauma and Collective Identity*, pp. 155–195. Berkeley, CA: University of California Press.

Štulhofer, A. (2000). *Nevidljiva ruka tranzicije: ogledi iz ekonomske sociologije*. Zagreb: Hrvatsko sociološko društvo.

Van der Steen, B., Katzeff, A., and van Hoogenhuijze, L. (eds.). (2014). *The City is Ours: Squatting and Autonomous Movements in Europe from the 1970s to the Present*. Oakland, CA: PM Press.

(by Ayça Oral and Ece Esmer)

Chapter 12 The Nightingales: Tactical positioning of young middle-class pious Muslim women in Turkey

Abstract: This chapter presents a case study that explores how young people's cultural practices, participation, and identities are shaped as they establish their own cultural settings within the cultural and political environment in Turkey.

The study presents a detailed account of how the middle-class, pious Muslim youth community reacts, translates, and positions themselves as active participants within a sphere. This chapter considers how these young people adopt contemporary political stances that are authoritative, nationalistic, and conservative in nature and how they envisage their membership in the middle class. By taking a group of young, pious Muslim women as its subject, this case study also aims to explore the frameworks that these young people include in and exclude from their processes of cultural production, which are characterised by interactions with their families, religion, and traditions. The study thereby explores the extent to which the young women embrace these conditions and how they construct their identities in the public sphere through active participation in cultural production processes.

The research also seeks to analyse how the Nightingales reinterpret the politically-charged, critical songs that they perform, and the motivations for deploying these songs within a pious community and audience. The Nightingales' geographically and politically diverse repertoire is also examined to shed more light on the political background of the group.

Keywords: cultural production, cultural participation, youth, muslim women, music performance

Introduction

This chapter presents the key findings and analysis of engagement with young people's cultural practices based on an ethnographic case study of The Nightingales, a concert group comprised of young pious Muslim women. It focuses on young people's active roles as culture makers, presenting the personal and communal lives of young, "pious Muslim women" as they become cultural participants in the current social and political climate in Turkey.

We will try to reveal how pious Muslim women's participation in the public sphere is shifting, whether in the form of a challenge or an anxiety over integration into the current system (power, religion, and family). First, however, it is imperative to understand how the concept of moderate Islam has developed into market-oriented[1] Islamic politics and how this is now enacted through the current conservative Islamic regime under the AKP government in Turkey.

It is necessary to talk briefly about the historical processes behind the increasing participation of religious Muslim women in the cultural domain and public space. There are certain important historical milestones that have determined religious Muslim women's position in culture: the Rearrangement Period (*Tanzimat Dönemi*),[2] the Kemalist modernisation process, and the AKP period. Considering such a background, we can see that the quality of Muslim women's daily life is determined by the relationship between Islam and secularism. It is appropriate to situate the history of these concepts within Turkey's political context, in order to understand the intersectionality between religiousness and secularism and how these forces influence women's lives. Debates and academic productions about the Islamic movement, the concept of conservatism, political Islam and the daily life of pious Muslims can be traced back to the *Tanzimat* Era (from 1839 to 1876), when there was a restructuring process in socio-economic and political life. What *Tanzimat* looks like in practice is a pivotal question, especially when analysing how the current political environment shapes everyday life via the top-down policy of Islamisation through education, media, and law.

The concept of citizenship originated with the institution of taxation in the Tanzimat period, as a matter of representation. In other words, "no taxation without representation" was embedded in the Tanzimat reforms. However, the term 'nation' and its meaning for Muslims related more to a sense of unity. The Ottoman Empire was in turmoil and seeking a cure to revive the old order (this was Abdulhamid's particular intention); as a result, there were many identity

1 The AKP gained strength in the political sphere as an Islamic political party with a distinct political agenda informed by religion. "This party, which was closed down and which re-emerged four times, consecutively took the names Milli Order Party, Milli Salvation Party, Welfare Party, Virtue Party, and Felicity Party for the following four decades" (Tuğal, 2009: p. 42). After establishing itself and coming to power, the AKP in the 2000s first supported a political agenda based on religion but changed to a more economic agenda in conjunction with a more hegemonic perspective. The political hegemony invents or promises relief to newly-conceived social identities disillusioned with ideas of "a just order", "equal distribution of income" and "equalities for everybody", as expressed in the Islamic Conservative Party's political discourse. As Tuğal states, "[h]andled within the hegemonic framework, every day practices are no longer the sites either of the spontaneous self-reproduction of society (as in Bourdieu) or of endless games and resistances" (Scott, 1985 cited by Tuğal, 2009).

2 See Mardin, 2000 and Ahmad, 1969.

construction attempts, such as Ottomanism, Turanism, and Turkishness. These new sets of practices were driven by rulers or elite leaders. For example, the Young Turks[3] promoted Turkishness as a new identity, although only about half of this group were Turks or Muslims. Turkishness was supported as a practical identity to integrate all Muslims under the Sultan's rule as the Caliph. Using Islam as a way to mobilise people can be linked with its politicisation (see Ahmad, 1991), which gave a somewhat formal sense of homogenous unity. Therefore, the synthesis of Islam and Turkishness as a political identity is a product of the Tanzimat era:

> *Following the inception of the Republic in 1923, the early years furnish us with the example of secular ethnic nationalism replacing Islam as the source of state legitimacy, while in the 1970s and the 1980s, ethnic hyper-nationalism has incorporated more and more Islamic themes into its discourse.* (Sakallıoğlu, 1994)

However, during all these periods continued to take Western models as a basis for education, civil and legal codes, and daily life formations such as dress. Many bans and restrictions were introduced with the intention of imposing secular and western lifestyles. These top-down reforms provoked new tactics and responses from Islamic youth, especially during the 90s and in Turkey. Islamists meanwhile gained strength in the political sphere with the Welfare Party (Gülalp, 2001 and Öniş, 1997), whose political agenda was formed by religion.

The Turkish Republic was proclaimed 'secular' in its foundational period (1923–1946). The Kemalist movement proclaimed the European identity of Turkey and celebrated the ancient history of the pre-Islamic Turks. Even before Kemalism, Ziya Gokalp (an eminent political figure who promoted Turkishness) argued that the Turkish people had a distinctive culture, a product of their long pre-Islamic history, their language, territory and stock (in line with the German theories of nationhood so popular with Arab nationalists). Turkish culture was historically linked to the Muslim Ottoman civilization, but this was in decline by the early 20th century. At that historical juncture, Turkish culture was reoriented towards European civilization. Islam remained an element of Turkish cultural heritage, however, as a kind of cement ensuring social solidarity (Zubaida, 2011).

The conflict between the establishment of a rigid secular state and largely conservative Islamic society has defined contemporary Turkey.[4] However, this dichotomy does not inform every segment of the country's dynamic society.

3 See Ahmad, 1969.
4 See Ahmad, 1991.

This case study offers an opportunity to consider nuances of intersectionality in Turkey by focusing on young and religious Muslim women.

Pious Muslim women have been trying to participate in the public sphere as a political counter-voice since the 1980s, but now they have also become more visible in the cultural domain. After having been politically vocal and active since the 1980s, pious Muslim women have proceeded to play a part in the cultural realm, particularly thanks to increased access to education and economic opportunities in the 2000s.

Debates on this subject (Saktanber, 2007; Saktanber and Çorbacıoğlu, 2008; Çınar, 2008) are mainly concerned with Islamic movements or political Islam (with a focus on women) in terms of the AKP government's support for women's visibility and integration within the public sphere. These discussions often rely on adaptable and ambiguous definitions of an idealised "pious Muslim", and are often informed by the practices and everyday lives of actors. These actors ultimately shape interpretations of Islam in everyday life (especially the daily lives of pious Muslims) regardless of whether the approach is from the bottom-up or top-down.

Due to secular and militaristic state policies, which became sharper with the coup d'état (1980), many different social strata and different ideologies developed a common stance against state policies during the 1990s. That Islamist groups, feminists and leftist organisations came together to protest the headscarf ban is the most striking example. During the 1990s, this political union of feminists and Muslim women provided opportunities for the recognition of certain affinities in terms of politics, culture or lifestyle (Göle, 2000). However, religious Muslim women put an ideological distance between themselves and feminist and leftist groups after AKP came to power. They began to relate to a secular lifestyle in their daily lives while building their visibility in the public sphere (Yılmaz, 2015).

This case study addresses young, pious Muslim women's varied experiences of cultural participation and integration, including the stigma and conflict that they encounter. It also explores young people's attitudes, concerns, and perceptions as they develop their identity on a daily basis. Drawing from research on Islam, youth, Muslim women, and secularism, this study considers intergenerational conflict and similarities. The Nightingales concert group provides us with an understanding of how their self-produced cultural literacies are formed, and what is important to its members as they prepare their music repertoire and select concert locations. Further insight can be found by examining their practices before and after each concert, and how these are embedded in local contexts. This case study pushes us to question how pious, young, Muslim women construct culture as active agents and how they can change the stigmatisation of conservative Islamic codes while holding onto the values and heritage of their community.[5] The Nightingales case also raises questions about community is created and disseminated, and whether these young women are able to transform the cultural sphere within which they exist while still preserving their status in the prevailing community. Two further concerns of interest are: to what extent more (and more active) social integration of Islamic actors in society calls for transformation and/or causes change; and the extent to which a secular political system has regulated institutions and the structure of the government since the beginning of Westernisation.

The Nightingales: Who are they?

The Nightingales is an independent music and concert group that gathers to make music by women for women. The group has been performing at different localities such as cafes, concert halls, college congress centres, and other cultural venues since 2018. The core group of participants consists of 10 young and veiled women, in addition to 15 other veiled and non-veiled women in the chorus. They are all aged between 20 and 29, and most of them are university students. The group only sings to women, but audiences are of different ages and come from different localities. They rehearse in the cultural centres of Istanbul's conservative districts and sometimes in the houses of group members. Members rent a luxury house with a pool on the outskirts of Istanbul once a year and retreat there for a few days to revise their song repertoire. The Nightingales strive to interact with a number of people via concerts. They are consistent in announcing their concerts on digital media.

The Nightingales generally organise their concerts and activities in conservative districts of Istanbul. A conservative neighbourhood in this context means districts like Üsküdar and Fatih, where conservative people[6] have been living since the foundation of the Republic, and areas like Başakşehir that were founded after AKP came to rule (Özet, 2019).

The group has 10 singers, 2 pianists (one of whom also designs the stage costumes), 2 violinists, 1 zitherist, 1 trap drummer, 1 drummer, 1 soloist

5 Stigmatisation here refers to both secular and pious communities' positions/attitudes: being conservative within secular circles, and true piety and the qualities of pious Muslim women in Muslim communities.

6 'Conservative' refers to people in Turkey who live traditional lifestyles and have religious and nationalist sensibilities.

(and guitarist as well), and a photographer (who shoots concert videos and photographs). Band members invite other musicians from their own social circles and audience (mostly veiled) for some concerts and performances. These guests, who play the side-blown flute, the clarinet, the violin and the lute, take their places on improvisation nights. A great majority of band members are university students, but there are some high school graduates who now work in various places. All of them have some amateur musical background dating back to university or high school. The soloist is the lead member of the band because she is the only professional musician. She gives musical training to the members and directs the repertoire. All the core members of the band come from religious middle-class families. Their social and familial backgrounds vary, but they are generally middle-class people with educated families. Leyla and Seda,[7] two band members, stated that they were more comfortable in the Nightingales than in their university's jazz clubs, which include both men and women. They said that they decided to form a women-only band to express themselves more confidently. After they called for participants in the band via Instagram, so many people wanted to join that the band formed its final version quickly.

The concert and performance areas (cafes, cultural centres, etc.) are selected from conservative neighbourhoods, where a considerable number of residents are pious Muslims. Places with large capacity, like conference halls and municipal theatres, are generally preferred. Anyone can access concert areas via public transportation. These sites are generally located in life-centres (near places like squares or municipality buildings) so that the evening concerts are easily accessible to women. The concerts are announced on Instagram. Before attending, each person is requested to fill out a personal information form in order to estimate the number of participants. Payment can be made online or at the entrance to the concert hall. Some women (who are not band members) sit in the entry booth and sell tickets. Fees are fixed at an amount affordable to students with middle income (€4–5).

Evening concerts generally start at 8 pm, with a break of 15 minutes. The concerts last for nearly two hours. The audience arrives at the venue half an hour before the concert begins and leaves half an hour after it finishes. Thus, the audience can make some small talk before the concert and have some contact with band members afterwards. The audience is generally made up of women wearing headscarves. There are a few women who do not wear headscarves within the audience. The usual age range is between 18 and 50, And the audience members

7 These names are pseudonyms.

tend to include mothers, young and single women, undergraduates, and friends of the band. Technical work, such as sound and lighting arrangements and food and beverage services, are done by men working at the locations. The core musical team is positioned at the front of the stage, while the choir has its place at the two rear sides. The clothing of the choir is generally black, and the core members wear harmonious pastel colours. At the earliest concerts the members wore darker clothes, but now the designer, a core member of the team, designs more colourful outfits. The soloist's clothes have become especially bright and vivid. During the concert, the soloist and the first violinist (unlike other band members) interact with the audience. These interactions include applause for motivation and rhythm-keeping, encouraging the audience, talking about the stories behind a song and why they are important to the band members, mentioning the repertoire and song choices, stating the reasons for various changes, and voicing momentary emotions during the concert. During the concert, the band members keep communicating, teasing and chatting with each other. Towards the end, more crowd-pleasing and popular songs are played. The audience members and their children stamp their feet, dance, and take videos of the concert's non-vocal moments. (The vocalist cautions people that her voice cannot be shared because listening to female voices is forbidden according to Islamic law.)

Group photographs are taken at the end of the concert. The audience makes small talk with band members face-to-face, often expressing their desire for future concerts. The band members ask the audience to write their emotions and thoughts on post-it notes, which they then attach to a noticeboard. Most of the audience does so, and many of the comments contain positive feedback and advice for songs. There are many post-its saying that the group's music is inspirational. When the concert ends, some women are picked up by a relative or take public transportation, while some go to cafes together. During the concert, the group members announce that they will share the date of the next concert on online platforms.

The group also holds some activities that they call improvisation nights. On such evenings, audiences join in the event as active participants, singing songs, playing instruments and accompanying the group members. There is no set repertoire during these nights; the flow and the set list are generally determined by the demands of the participants, with minor interventions by the group members. The group members do not feel the necessity to anticipate the audience's reactions and choose the songs in accordance with the sensitivities of the audience. For example, one band member might sing a song in a performance with accompaniment from the other members and the audience. Another difference found in these improvisation nights is the more limited number of band members. Also, the audience consists of active participants, who bring their own instruments and accompany the songs and vocals, which increases the intensity of the performance. At the beginning of these performances, the band members are asked to introduce themselves, to talk about how they founded the group, and their momentary emotions and thoughts and relationship with the music. These performances take place in an area booked for the group (e.g. the roof of a café or culture centre's garden). The group members and active participants sit in a circle, and the band members emphasise "the importance of making music together without the necessity for professionalism". In addition to audience members who sought out the event because of social media announcements, the people who happened to be in the venue beforehand can listen to the music. However, the circle is open to women only.[8] The women who hear the music and come to the circle take the social media account information to follow the band; collective photos are taken at the end of the improvisation night, just as in the concerts.

Definitions and receptions of culture

Interviewees stated that their cultural identity has been shaped by their religion/tradition, the media, and the culture of their parents, which is intertwined with their national identity. They saw music as a type of intangible cultural heritage that leaves them open to other cultures. This theme came up, for example, in the context of building up their repertoire. As one interviewee put it:

> *What am I playing? I do not know. This may be our style as our concert group. I tried to find it so hard, tried to figure out to which channel I belong. Is it Eastern or Western music? Do we love rock or classical music? I guess that what we have not decided yet as 'our concert group' is the style. We all think that good music is good music. We do not look for whether it is Eastern or Western. One of the things we like to do is put some Eastern improvisations into something Western, like a piano. I enjoy such things so much. For example, until Nurhan became a part of the group, I had thought that one of the styles I could hardly bear was Turkish classical music.* (Fatma, 24, Student, Pianist)

The Western and local songs that these women perform constitute a means of intercultural dialogue for them. Essentially, music is a bridge to understanding what they perceive as new cultures and to foster intercultural dialogue:

8 The core group consists of ten veiled women; they stated that they are open to non-veiled women as well, but those are implicitly the minority.

> *Yes, it is. The music must stay away from politics. The compositions are used for various purposes in time, but it is different from what we do. We always emphasise this and make our music with care. Someone who knows us a bit can understand that we don't play Bella Ciao as a communist song. We play from a wide variety of nations like the songs of Arabs, English, Armenians or Azerbaijani. Music is music. It is beautiful this way. And the music does not have to have a nationality. We do many pieces without words, instrumental ones and they don't have a language all in all.* (Fatma, 24, Student, Pianist)

The members of The Nightingales had slightly different reasons for why they prefer to tell less political stories through their chosen songs. Mainly they reported that they are not the representatives or bearers of any political movements, and that they are just making music for, and with, women:

> *Let's talk about Bella Ciao. It is an old Italian folk song. One man goes to the field and says to his wife "Bella". We played the song because we love it and its tale. […] We did not behave politically; we do not play it for political representation. Contrarily, this is just a song and it was not composed for a political purpose. This is just a folk song! So, we want to play it because we love it and we want to save it from the political discourse around it. We play it because of its musical value. Of course, you do not have to be making Armenian propaganda to play an Armenian folk song. We play it for the sake of music, and we approach everything from a musical view…* (Fatma, 24, Student, Pianist)

Fatma thus articulated that making music should not be interlinked with political issues because this harms the music.

Constructing identities in the public sphere

The interviewees mostly identified themselves based on religion, but when it came to conservatism and traditionalism their ideas varied. For example, one interviewee described her perspective on this issue as follows:

> *Can I call myself conservative? Not entirely. And you know concepts have meaning in a society and when I call myself conservative, I do not want to accept the conservative identity perceived by society and probably do not call myself conservative. I prefer explaining myself. Being devout might be used but [only] if we talk about having an identity through religion. Of course, I'm building an identity based on my religion.* (Fatma, 24, Student, Pianist)

There was a huge gap between the generations in this respect. They differed from their parents: even if their parents were not political, these women do not have the same historical and political baggage or the memories of Islamist movement in '80s and '90s Turkey.

> *If we are to talk over an identity, I can say that I am a woman, I'm a strong woman. I'm kind of an optimist and a humanist. I'm apolitical. I think politics separates people, but*

this does not mean I'm someone opinionless. I think I have high emotions. I'm trying to be optimistic, do something beautiful and good quality for life. (Zelal, 27, Student and Part-time employee, Singer)

Some of the interviewees preferred not being labelled and did not identify themselves in ideological terms. Sometimes they used '*mutedeyyin*' (pious), Muslim, and veiled as interchangeable terms to identify themselves but some of them still felt that these terms draw boundaries around their modes of existence. One interviewee expressed her concerns about being labelled with these words as follows:

I try not to feel or perceive that way. I do not want to have this kind of label on me. I do not want to be determined. I do not want to have such a perception. If there is such social stigmatisation, I prefer not to take it personally. (Zelal, 27, Student and Part-time employee, Singer)

Some interviewees saw this kind of self-identification as a way of saying "I am different". The following words of an interviewee opened up this discussion:

I want to see myself this way and want to be recognised and known this way. I remember thinking 'I want it known that I am a Muslim'. I mean I am different; I have a different story; I have a different history. I feel sorry or excited about different things, I had this interest in separating myself from the others. (Elif, 30, NGO employee, Ex-guitarist)

Elif implied that her difference is derived from her veiling. In other words, veiling was an identity construction tool for her when she was a teenager. Although some interviewees disagreed, most of them agreed that they avoid identifying themselves using the term 'conservative', which refers to tradition:

I call myself 'mutedeyyin'(pious). Because if I only call myself Muslim, believing in Allah would be enough. If I call myself Muslim, does that mean all the Muslims must behave like this? No, this is not nice. If I say conservative… I think religious people and conservative people are different and this conservative thing is much more a sociological term. It means conserving what has happened without thinking too much on it. (Güneş, 25, Student, Soloist)

Another interviewee added a new dimension to this issue by mentioning feminist discourse:

I'm aware of the relationship between Islam and feminism discussions. But I do not need to define myself as something different from Muslim. No other ideology is necessary. Islam is my religion and my lifestyle, so I do not need any other ideology to define myself. I can think over some specific issues but belonging to any other ideology apart from Islam makes me feel uncomfortable. I don't feel like belonging to any other ideology as a package other than Islam. (Fatma, 24, Student, Pianist)

The researcher observed that different attitudes towards these concepts caused various conflicts and disputes in the group. In the first months of the concert group, one member changed The Nightingales' dynamics with her political views. After some discussion about the motivations of making music for women, she decided to leave the band. She defined herself as a feminist Muslim, as she explained:

> *I used to feel more of a Muslim, in terms of belonging. I mean, I am a feminist. One of the things that affect my daily life the most and determines my decision making the most is feminism. Still, Muslimhood and feminism equally influence my discursive practices, my comments on things in my everyday life. I like talking to these people about how to create answers for things and what to say in which situation. I have found something like myself you know. Now there are tons of people around me who think like me. I talk to them; I feel like I belong together with them. Call it a community, now I feel like having something like that of my own.* (Elif, 30, NGO employee, Ex-guitarist)

Just as the definitions of religiousness or being Muslim differed, stories and motivations of veiling diverged within the group. For example, one interviewee shared the concerns she held when she decided to wear the hijab:

> *I call myself veiled. I hate terms like covered or uncovered. And some people prefer saying hijab. Hijab sounds so assertive. I think hijab is like a higher piousness level. I may be comparing it to my own lifestyle, but it is like extra piousness to me. But as I've said, I am more idealist in my own life, I want it all but may not achieve. So, the headscarf gives me some relief. But hijab puts more weight over my shoulders.* (Güneş, 25, Student, Soloist)

Another interviewee linked her ideas about the headscarf issue with the question of identity:

> *Of course, the headscarf must not be a political issue. It is completely about religion. This is like saying some stupid things about some girl wearing red or yellow shoes. I prefer wearing a headscarf or not. That is just it. I think treating all veiled women like a homogenous community is wrong. I do not think all non-veiled women have the same opinions. If I don't put all of them under the same category, I don't want to be seen in the same category with all veiled women. I cannot know all of them. I want to be seen as a separate person, as Fatma.* (Fatma, 24, Student, Pianist)

Group members frequently communicate with social groups that differ from themselves in terms of environment, such as universities and musician networks, but religion is an important determinant when creating their inner circle. One of the interviewees emphasised religion when she explained her criteria for choosing friends:

> *What I regard as different in the first place is a religious belief. And lifestyle. I love them [her non-religious friends] so much, anyway. We still talk. We have no problem but if we*

talk about being closest friends or allies, they are the ones similar to us. I think this is not conscious and everybody has the same way since you would be closer to someone with whom you can go to the mosque. You talk to the others but the places you are in differ and you begin spending less time [together]. I also made some friends abroad; we are good friends, but I guess my basis is a religious belief. Apart from that, you cannot come close to those with strong ideological perspectives. It is not possible even though we want it so much. It does not matter if the person is Islamist. Yes, I'm religious but I don't like Islamists. (Leyla, 24, Student, Violinist)

It was important for the Nightingales to articulate the feeling that there is a large gap between themselves and major aspects of their parents' culture and parental beliefs. Differences included the interpretation of religion, and changing daily life and dress codes. One interviewee talked about this generation gap as follows:

It is generally weird as our age is changing. But our mothers and fathers saw something else and they have prejudices. They are more vigilant. I will give an example: They are more prudent. For example, previously we had some red lines but now... My life has changed. For example, this boyfriend thing. I mean not boys as lovers but boys as friends, too. (Selma, 26, Insurer, Singer)

Women who came from a more secular way of life reported themselves lucky because their families were more open to change. One interviewee depicted her feelings about her family as follows:

When I wanted to go abroad via Erasmus, I observed the families of my friends and I observed mine. Sometimes, I can act conservatively and think whether I have to be in that environment or not. But my family put their doubt aside and supported me. I guess this is so precious to me. Thanks to them, I was open to new things. I could protect my essence and join in different circles and try to represent myself. (Fatma, 24, Student, Pianist)

Barriers for social interaction inside and outside the community

Increased visibility of the headscarf in the public sphere sometimes raises conflict. This tends to occur when scarves are encountered in the entertainment sector or in public places such as cultural centres, pubs, or universities; as one interviewee said:

I do not have much trouble when I go to the cinema, theatre, seminars, concerts etc. It's not social but I feel the pressure of alcohol. I mean everyone is, of course, free and no one can mess with one another, but I do not feel good when there is alcohol. For example, the latest concert was in a bar in Taksim. And when you enter, everyone begins looking at you. This is a social difficulty. They find it strange with good reason and think: "What do these women do here?" (Zelal, 27, Student and Part-time employee, Singer)

Some women in The Nightingales emphasised the importance of being conscious of aspects of religion and worship such as veiling. One of them stated her concerns about pressure from men on the headscarf issue:

> *You can think what you want to have in your mind. But to me, hijab is something more coherent. There are so many hijabi women around. I mean some of them are forced by their husbands to veil themselves. But when you say hijab, I think knowledge and consciousness are in this. When you worship consciously and reflect this on your appearance, you have hijab. Then, you are a hijabi woman.* (Zelal, 27, Student and Part-time employee, Singer)

It is possible to say that the behaviours and forms of expression expected from a veiled woman were instilled in these young women by their communities, especially their families. Another issue is that veiled women are generally assumed to have less cultural capital than non-veiled peers. The interviewee explained having some trouble forgetting these expectations and assumptions, which do not identify but build barriers for them. An interviewee stated that wearing a headscarf does limit certain expressions and behaviours:

> *Of course, some individual characteristics come from my family. I mean they always say "You wear a headscarf. Be careful about that. Do not laugh that way". My mother always talks like this. But you go out, you see that you have to live in a way, you have to raise your voice while working as a woman etc. You are in mixed-sex environments. And people see you as a woman with a headscarf, which has a social dimension. I've just realised that. People do not expect you to speak about cultural things like art, literature etc. They regard you as someone with a limited world or vision.* (Zelal, 27, Student and Part-time employee, Singer)

In our case study, Muslim young women coming together for concerts as a form of entertainment, in various districts of the city and mostly in the evening, means that they are involved as active actors in a male-dominated and secular-dominated social life. These encounters can cause conflict and reactions between identities, as one interviewee narrated:

> *I studied at a university where Ramadan never arrives. Everyone acts as if nothing is happening. I have never experienced a different atmosphere. I have never seen it and have always had negative thoughts about it and never wanted to be there. When I was considering high school options, thinking of a high school, people were telling me that this was such a [secular] high school and that I could go to another [religious] high school since it is a place in the Anatolian side where more people like me were present. Since I never felt like that myself, since I didn't have that feeling of community, I never wanted to be there. I can imagine the possible pressure there. I also did not have any Muslim friends in college. I knew that I would also be discriminated against in that environment for reasons like, why I fasted that way, why I fasted during my period and so on.* (Elif, 30, NGO employee, Ex-guitarist)

As has been stated in the historical background section, the educational field is also dominated by secularists (or secularism). Elif stated that she prefers to put up a fight in this field by remaining in solidarity with her own community and by building relationships with the secular community. Because she thinks that her own community does not exercise adequate critical thinking and since she cannot explain the sources of the patterns that make up her own identity, Elif finds it useful to establish social relations with the secular community.

Perspective on creating own culture: Women solidarity

Members reported that, although the concerts are at first glance perceived as activities for women, they not only help form separate relations between women and men but also allow women to come together and feel strong, powerful, and courageous.

> *I think the concert group meets a sociological need as a sociological formation. We have seen that there is a very different atmosphere there with only women. Our first concert was in a school, a very interesting energy came out, the school had some jazz orchestra concerts or mixed rock concerts. Their energy was also different. We shared energy there, which fills a sociological gap. Why can't this be a valuable thing in itself? Do we have to make something feminist or ideological? We shared a pleasant, energetic, and sweet atmosphere, which we liked so much. I speak to those who see music as halal when it is among women only. I might not be thinking like that but seeing some light in women's eyes and offering a comfortable environment to those who could not go to concerts, play music, get on the stage or listen to a concert due to restrictions cast by herself or her family. We are providing such an environment where people feel relaxed and enjoy the music.* (Fatma, 24, Student, Pianist)

Their motivation for gathering together is not limited to playing music. The members reported that they feel increased togetherness, describing the events as areas that allow for self-expression. Examples of this self-expression include making friends, performing art, getting on the stage, creating, and improving their sense of belonging. One interviewee stated:

> *So, as you see when women get together, gossiping is not the only thing they can do. I mean they do not just eat some snacks and gossip to death. Or talk about fashion, something that I love very much. I also follow fashion in a way. But when you say "woman", it does not have to be about spending money or gossiping. When women come together, something really strong emerges. I have realised the power of women and this is so satisfying. Emotional satisfaction is really high.* (Zelal, 27, Student and Part-time employee, Singer)

These women are in constant communication with their audience on social media, both before and after concerts and improvisation nights. During Q&A sessions and live broadcasts on social media, they make speeches about the motivations of young Muslim women for making music. Group members, who have thousands of followers on Instagram, explain the importance and methods of young women making music. This concert group is a model for young Muslim people, as one interviewee explained:

> *Many reactions came from the audience. They liked having such an atmosphere, being a part of such a thing, seeing conservative women coming together and playing, sharing this with women only. All these made a model for many conservative young people.* (Sü, 24, Company owner, Ex-drummer)

Some participants saw this mode of cultural production as a necessity for women. One interviewee expressed her thoughts as follows:

> *What we learnt from there is that these environments are necessary. When there are places like this, women feel more self-confident and stronger when they appear in mixed environments thanks to the motivation and power they acquired there [in separated spaces]. That is why it seemed like an interim work like this was necessary.* (Güneş, 25, Student, Soloist)

The starting point of the concert group was the empowering effect of making music for women. Some of the former group members defined themselves as feminists and the group's repertoire was developed from this perspective. After those members left, the group's discourse has turned more moderate. This element has also transformed thanks to The Nightingales' changing relationship with the audience, and to the strengthening desire to make music for women in public spaces yet within the culture of *mahremiyet* (intimacy, privacy) (Sehlikoglu, 2016). One interviewee described this transformation and her reaction as follows:

> *I had always been alone before, so it was quite a powerful feeling, the feeling that I was together on stage with many women who looked like me. It was also really empowering for them too, it was educating, the first concerts etc. However, in time even though group members all had different tendencies, for instance, Güneş is a woman soloist who is closer to feminism. However, the environment that allowed conservative discourse, The Nightingales was tolerating me with things like "that's what Elif believes, let her be". This was beyond my scope of toleration, you know. Once I experienced something and I just said I will not attend the concert group again. At an event in Tarlabaşı, a woman came by me and said that she knew me, that I was playing the guitar, so she wanted to meet me. We met and she asked if I was still playing. I said I was playing at a café in Üsküdar every week. She then said, "you had this thing within the circle of halal[9] what was it called?" I said, "Do you mean the concert group?" "Oh yes, they played for women-only". I flipped there. What I did to a mixed audience where there are men is not halal and the other one is. It hit me hard.*

9 In Arabic, permissible and acceptable according to Islamic law.

The concert group, which is appreciated for being halal and that there is still an opposite somewhere. (Elif, 30, NGO employee, Ex-guitarist)

Elif's primary motivation to join the group was that she found it empowering to make music with and for women. However, the group members believe that this element of their practice should not be sloganised, and do not intend to give a political message to the audiences. Elif felt disturbed by this, and decided to leave the group because of the conservative and apolitical image of the group.

Another interviewee depicted this transformation in the group's motivation as follows:

The motivation at the very beginning was to make music with women instead of making it with conservative ones. Then, this conservative word came from somewhere and the goal was shaped accordingly. (Sü, 24, Company owner, Ex-drummer)

Discussion

Pious Muslim women's visibility in social and cultural domains in the current political environment

According to the findings of this case study, pious Muslim women's everyday lives and their relationships with politics and culture are diverse both within the group and in wider society, which enables a rich discussion.

The establishment and coming to power of the AKP in the 2000s introduced a political agenda based on religion. The party subsequently modified this to a more economics-based agenda in conjunction with a more hegemonic perspective. To further this agenda, this political hegemony invents or promises new social identities estranged from ideas of a "just order", "equal distribution of income" and "equalities for everybody", as these narratives appeared in the Welfare Party political discourse. As Tuğal states,

[h]andled within the hegemonic framework, every day practices are no longer the sites either of the spontaneous self-reproduction of society (as in Bourdieu) or of endless games and resistances (Scott cited in Tuğal, 2009). Everyday life is rather one of the primary grounds of contestation among different hegemonic projects. (Tuğal, 2009)

In 2002, the AKP became the majority controlling power, and Turkey started to go through serious educational, economic, and socio-cultural transformations in favour of pious Muslim communities (Özet, 2019; Akçaoğlu, 2018; Tuğal, 2009). This trend allowed the pious Muslim middle-class to come forward, and increased the visibility of Muslim women in the public sphere.

As can be seen from this historical context, after the visibility of Muslim women in the political sphere (with the help of the public headscarf struggle) the gate to the cultural domain, which was controlled by secular people until the 2000s, opened to Muslim women when the AKP came to power. Struggling to gain a place in the cultural domain, with its opportunities to access educational professional contexts, Muslim women have had the position of determining and representing what is "religiously acceptable" while trying to exist in the cultural domain under the shadow of the AKP's political agenda. Therefore, analysing the self-positioning and interrelations of pious female actors involved in cultural production processes is necessary to understand how conservative youth feels about Turkey's cultural politics. How and where these women are involved in cultural production processes is the focus of the following discussion.

An observation that is significant in the context of certain women becoming more visible in public space is that some women, who are (or call themselves) conservative, pious, veiled/headscarved (hijab-wearing) Muslims, gather around the musical group. These women keep up with their social media activity, and attend the concerts and improvisation nights as participant observers.

Two important policies had a real effect on the visibility of Muslim women. First, graduates of High Schools for Imams and Preachers were allowed to enter regular universities. Second, the headscarf ban – the legacy of the 28 February military memorandum – was removed in 2007 through the resolution of the AKP government. These two important steps started to change Muslim women's everyday social lives (Yılmaz, 2015; Akçaoğlu, 2018; Maritato, 2020). Meanwhile, the biggest supporters of the struggle against the headscarf ban in the public sphere were feminist women and the libertarian wing of the Turkish left (Göle, 2015). The encounter between secular groups (such as feminists and leftists) and pious Muslim people gave way to political common ground. The daily life practices of these groups also started to be look alike in some ways. As pious Muslims in Turkey have increasingly taken advantage of neoliberalism, privatisation and deregulation, and have adapted to bourgeois lifestyles, they have smoothly integrated into both global markets and the secular state (Tuğal, 2009; Turam, 2012). Thus, we can say that the first significant encounter between these groups caused the Muslim political agendas to resemble the leftist agenda. The removal of the headscarf ban, which contributed to another encounter between Muslim and secular groups, resulted in the integration/involvement of Muslims' daily lives with those of secular groups. Interviewees explained this integration process:

My auntie was the victim of it. I was not because I was younger but when you hear the whole story, you say "Oh yes, there is something like this and living it is another thing." I can argue that these experiences made them have a spirit for struggle. Now, we had some flashbacks and if we have to, we can say that women come here and when they see us make music, some of them even cry. And I don't get it but she says, "Oh, you don't know what we

> *went through." I cannot say this because I did not experience anything* like *this. Of course, I was a little bit impressed after seeing those who experienced it. But they come with many different traces.* (Güneş, 25, Student, Soloist)
> *When I first stepped onto the stage, when it was in the news of Hürriyet, those bigwig brothers released a "fatwah" for me and told me that I was a provocateur and not someone to be talked to. People were running like hell from me since they told so. So, I did not feel belonging for a long time until I knew Muslim feminist women, until I knew some women thinking like me. There was victimisation and I was claiming the identity because of it. It was not like belonging in a group.* (Elif, 30, NGO employee, Ex-guitarist)

Thus, pious Muslim women's daily life practices and socio-economic conditions took a new turn. In this way, Muslim women's everyday lives were partly transferred from the private to the public sphere. Having previously gathered at home for religious conversations, and generally being confined in the domestic space of their homes, Muslim women now started to appear in the cultural and social spaces previously dominated by men and secular people. This may be interpreted both as an act of embracing the secular lifestyle as a supra-identity and as an act of speaking to their own communities through the language of the hegemonic. The increased visibility of Muslim women in the social and cultural domains often presents two co-existing concerns: (1) the tension of more elements being borrowed from secular lifestyles, and (2) a transformation of secular people's expectations of what a 'pious Muslim' should be, based on ideas from the previous century. The secular/pious dichotomy, which was crystallised during the 1980s and 1990s, transformed into a social integration process in the 2000s. Issues like the holy family, abortion, the legitimacy of LGBTQI+ communities are still sticking points. Additionally, the Muslim community reacts negatively to the way in which Muslim women now exist in the cultural domain, thus creating a new contradiction. As a result, incorporating many political and social diversities (in terms of mindset, daily life, taste and dress code), the concert group provides a picture of how the aforementioned encounters come about, where conflicts and associations begin, and how the women shape their own lives through these struggles and social associations. People come together in response to transformations in patterns of life, social space, and the economy. However, this togetherness does not occur in a void; political leadership regulates the ways in which people come together. Therefore, regardless of what participants may think, associational activity does not lead to ordinary people's total and self-conscious control over the economy and cultural forces. Rather, associational activity becomes a site of domination and inequality (Tuğal, 2009).

Dichotomies reconstructing identities within a historical framework

As mentioned in the previous chapter, the 28 February memorandum[10] was a milestone in the socio-political history of Turkey, especially for pious Muslim communities. This turning point, and the AKP's subsequent accession to power, changed many things in pious Muslim women's everyday lives. The new government shifted socio-economic policies and allowed women with headscarves to attend universities, thus creating its own middle class (Akçaoğlu, 2018) that was well-educated and had its own tastes. This new middle class started to come together in shisha cafés, fashion and design houses for pious women (Gökarıksel and Secor, 2009), private universities associated with the AKP government, cultural centres, and holiday resorts where women and men swim separately. Most of these spaces are in particular districts, such as Üsküdar, Fatih and Başakşehir (Özet, 2019; Yılmaz, 2019). With the acceleration in access to information through social media and peer-to-peer interaction, the pious middle class developed a broad spectrum of tastes and interests, diversifying its existence in the city by using spaces dominated by secular people and imitating their ways of entertainment while still observing 'religious restrictions'. From feminist Muslim women with political interests, who came together to found the Havle Women's Association,[11] to young Muslims who became part of the secular entertainment culture in districts like Karaköy and Balat, where upper-middle class secular people hang out and drink alcohol, a wide range of political stances, lifestyles and consumption preferences emerged. In this way, middle-class pious and secular groups' strict prejudices and assumptions about each other loosened, and decades-old ideological reflexes weakened.

Although the notion of 'being a victim of the Republic' created during the Kemalist regime among pious Muslims is not a notion that belongs to the current Muslim generation, it still resonates with young Muslims due to the transference of Muslim social memory. This idea of victimhood is not part of a simple

10 On 28 February 1997, Turkish military members in National Security Council decided to close down the Welfare Party, which was led by Islamist politician Necmettin Erbakan, on charges of anti-secular activities and pro-Islamist policies. The 28 February memorandum, sometimes called a "postmodern coup", refers to a new model of university entrance system for students studying at high schools for imams and preachers. Thanks to the model put in place by the memorandum, the students could only gain a university degree in Islamic studies and theology. See Çandar, 1999 and Dinçşahin, 2012.

11 The first feminist Muslim women's foundation, which was legally founded in 2018 in Turkey.

populist ideology, but rather is a constitutive part of Turkish-Islamist ideology and Turkish-Islamist identity formation. Assertion of victimhood is at the very heart of Turkish-Islamist identity, which structures itself as the victim of Western forces and their internal collaborators, who ended Turkey's golden ages by permanently and secretly working together (Yılmaz, 2017).

Within the scope of this case study, we can say that, unlike pious Muslims who had been excluded from the public sphere during the 1980s and 1990s, the current Muslim generation suffers less from this kind of rejection. Their community haunts are not limited to shisha bars. Living near or passing through streets where bars and taverns are located is not seen as a danger anymore. There are two reasons for this. First, pious Muslims have their own places in which they can feel that they belong. Second, their relationship with secular people has transformed so that the probability of being regarded negatively has decreased. However, one of the motivations that brought the concert group together was the shared narrative of being excluded, which had been transferred to the participants from their families. In that sense, the discourse of exclusion played a part in Muslim women's struggle to exist in the public sphere; still, it was generally a source of motivation to participate in cultural life, rather than a political reflex.

To sum up, the secular/pious dichotomy has become less polarising thanks to the increase in encounters and associations between the two groups, which has led to some self-criticism among pious Muslim women. They conduct this self-criticism as a counteraction of their families and communities using secular language and practices. These pious young Muslim women appropriate certain tools from the secular community in order to be able to express themselves and to reflect on their own communities. The diversity in the mindset of the group members on subjects including religion, tradition, and politics shows us that a predefined and generalised Muslim identity is actually imaginary.

The conservative-liberal and secular-religious dichotomies (Göle, 1996) that were addressed in academia throughout the 1990s can no longer provide a full analysis of current subject positions. We argue that there is a constant positioning within these spaces so as to expand and protect social and economic capital. This continual positioning, which manifests itself in social engagements and cultural production processes, also keeps reconstructing identity. The discourse of the authoritative power assumes the existence of an ideal pious woman thanks to religious and secular communities. These pious Muslim women are well aware of this assumption and position themselves accordingly, while, for example, coming up with their own repertoires, ideas and images. This positioning does not present any political risks for them and it opens up a broad space in which they can move. This space allows those positions that are taken through various manoeuvres to be changed in line with the content of encounters in the social domain.

These positionings exist on quite an idealistic liberal and humanistic discursive plane. However, when considered together with socio-political agendas and political actors, it is clear that any potentially political content may present a threat to their capitals or networks. It is for this reason that the Nightingales take a position of quite universal morality, which can be accepted by everyone and does not bother either religious or secular communities. That is to say, the group members seek to position their socio-political mindset and cultural integration patterns in an incoherent way. However, foundational conflicts take place within their own families and social groups.

Social integration conflicts within the light of tradition, religion, and generation: Tactics of pious Muslim subjects

The current government is implementing a strategy of trying to connect with the conservative urban middle-class. Young people who are children of conservative families respond to this in various ways when designing their daily lives. In other words, the government is establishing a dialogue with young conservatives by giving them opportunities to enhance their economic and cultural capital. These citizens are connecting with power by creating networks of cultural and symbolic consumption.

The AKP government determines its educational and cultural policies through a strategy that is based on a vision of 'acceptable youth' (Lüküslü and Yücel, 2013). In these policies, the AKP government chooses to promote certain cultural and educational institutions, such as private universities associated with the government, cultural centres, and high schools for Imams and Preachers. However, a growing number of young people have been proven to have unpredictable reflexes due to varying social interactions and unlimited access to information, which shows that the AKP government's vision of 'acceptable youth' does not correspond to anything substantial in real life. Some of the Nightingales group members rejected the idea of attending high schools for Imams and Preachers on the grounds that these schools do not bring status or prestige and stereotype their students. The AKP's conservative religious ideology and apparent overlap with the way in which the Kemalist legacy has been framed seems to have facilitated the AKP's zero-sum approach. Defining the nation as Muslim first and foremost, the Islamist tradition in Turkey has been projected as an authentic form of nationalism.

These women seek to place their pious Muslim identities among secular people by choosing educational institutions dominated by a secular curriculum and by articulating their differences to their own communities. These are all specific tactics young Muslim women use against the government's vision of youth, secular people's perceptions about pious Muslims, and the expectations from their families to maintain certain traditions.

The concert group uses such tactics in their cultural production process as well. Careful consideration of the Nightingales' repertoire shows that it ranges from Russian and Albanian folk songs and traditional local songs to globally popular ones. This seems to indicate that they are open to other cultures; some of the songs carry far-left meanings and codes, but they tend to reinterpret or bend the meaning of these. By making such songs context-free, they are able to position themselves in a politically safe area. This position makes The Nightingales popular, but means that they do not bring any particular political perspective or standing to their performances. On the other hand, the experiences of the group members abroad, and the fact that they are knowledgeable about the music of various cultures and locales, indicate that their song choices are based on cultural engagement. As mentioned above, when they tell their pious Muslim audience the story of a particular song, they are often showcasing the romantic and 'less dangerous' parts of the song, not its political content. They also perform songs that promote a sense of nationality; they also play European folk protest music pieces with their eastern instruments, stating that they want to bridge the gap between East and the West. (For example, they perform Bella Ciao with the qanun.)[12] The way these binaries are presented can be interpreted as a tactic they utilise to introduce these songs to their own community. Although they may state that they only choose songs because they are beautiful, the fact that the majority of their concert repertoire consists of songs with political backgrounds is another indicator that this is deliberate.

The group's song choices is one of the reasons that their work is so striking, and one of the key points of this research. This is worth further discussion. Why do these pious Muslim women perform songs that have leftist political and historical weight (such as Adanavi Voghperke, which tells of the Armenian genocide, and the communist anthem Ciao Bella) to their own communities? According to interviews, when they perform songs with a political background, this choice is emphasised only in the context how they sound. In addition, pieces with fewer

---

12 For more information, please visit https://www.britannica.com/topic/Islamic-arts/Musical-forms#ref316602.

political connotations are chosen between stories or background about more potentially charged songs. Adanayi Voghperke (Adana Massacre) is a requiem dedicated to the Armenian massacre carried out in 1909; no story related to the piece is told during the concert. If the chosen songs are politically "dangerous", the group prefer to deal with the dangerous situation by not mentioning it. In other words, the leftist discourse is sometimes made more prominent by its studied absence; on the one hand it is popularised, and on the other it becomes devoid of any political view or it is disassociated with its political origin.

The band's repertoire also shows us that, even though the AKP has been in power for the last 20 years, there is political resentment of the fact that it has not been able to create its own cultural capital and that this resentment is socially reflected. The interview data explains how the struggle for existence is maintained in a cultural arena in this scene, which is an area for encounters and allows The Nightingales to take different positions. By defaulting to the universal messages of the songs, the group turns politically and historically charged pieces into aesthetic products that are merely enjoyed. In this way, the songs become part of their own cultural capital.

Conclusion

This study offers new insights into pious young Muslim women's experiences of active participation in cultural production. The group members we focused on were born in the time of the AKP government. In other words, young people who have never experienced a different government in Turkey more readily see the government as stable rather than changeable. It is possible, in this situation, to observe how authoritarianism impacts the daily lives and cultural participation of middle-class pious young Muslim women. The position of these women within the Muslim community is being redefined, and traditional practices in this community are sometimes found insufficient. As young people that have grown up with the AKP's education, culture, and youth policies, they are direct witnesses to the strategic transformation of the AKP agenda from promoting moderate Islam ideology in the early 2000s to market-oriented Islamic politics from 2007 onwards (Tuğal, 2009). In its first period of rule (2002–2007), the AKP followed a policy called moderate Islam, which prioritised civil politics (influenced by the EU's harmonisation process) that had a democratic pattern. After the 2007 elections, the AKP came to sole power and the Constitutional Court was required to close the party in the following year. 2007 was a milestone in terms of the AKP's policies. The rapid transformation between 2007 and 2011 was a period in which the AKP prioritised the economy and strengthened its communication with Arab countries. After 2011, social revolts opposed to the AKP's market-oriented policies were repressed by the party's anti-democratic politics. Thus, this case study also allowed for a discussion of the youth issue in Turkey, which has been shaped by an increasingly authoritative, conservative, and nationalist AKP government since 2007. (Esen and Gumuscu, 2018). Rather than presenting conflict or tension between Islamist and secularist ways of life, this chapter highlights to what extent the active social and cultural integration of Islamic actors in Turkish society have the potential to change the actors themselves (or vice versa). This exploration is contextualised by the fact that the current political system has dominated governmental institutions and structures since the early 2000s, and that these structures were first formed under a weakened secular political system.

A binary distinction between pious and secular is not relevant today. We see that the visibility found through the use of the headscarf in the public sphere (as advocated by radical Islamist groups in the 1990s), and young women's ways of existing in the public sphere today, are not based on the same old dichotomies. New lifestyle opportunities are openly offered to a pious middle-class that is reconstructing the limitations of radical and/or political Islam.

The process developing on the three main lines described above has had direct consequences on the lives of pious young women. We examined the young women's forms of visibility in the public sphere, and their daily routines and cultural practices. These aspects of young women's lives do not constitute a discourse or reflex against authoritarianism. Rather, we saw that their conflicts with previous generations, and debates among their own communities and peer groups regarding religion and tradition, are related to their cultural practices and the opportunities offered by being part of Turkey's pious middle class.

Even though the cultural production practices of these young pious women promise a liberating and empowering transformation in their individual lives, it leads to a positioning process that is always aware of their relationships with the government in power, and both secular and religious communities; these young women are careful not to jeopardise the social and economic capital they have. Without giving up on their families, who pay for their college tuition, on the societies and networks that will shape their careers when they join the workforce, and on what the government in power makes possible, they create certain areas of freedom in their personal lives. They do this by relating to the actors they encounter in their daily lives, and through discourse and imagination.

Some people in the religious community think that it is forbidden by religion for women to sing; this belief includes a fear that Muslim women will transcend the boundaries that Islam draws for them. The government in power manages this anxiety, and thereby sets out a framework for the decent/proper Muslim woman, by taking into consideration the country's political and economic interests. The government in power needs both a cultural capital of its own and representation of Muslim women in the cultural arena. By observing the fear-demand duality present in this community, the women who present cultural productions include political songs in their own cultural space by decontextualising them or by depriving them of their message under the pretence of universalising them. In this way, they somehow circle the boundaries that have been drawn without really transcending them. They also respond to a need for production and visibility. Therefore, the space for cultural capital that the government in power cannot construct is met, in one way or another, through these actors. These pious Muslim women find ways to both make their own social positions more secure and to construct an empowering space for themselves.

References

Ahmad. F. (1969) *The Young Turks: The Committee of Union and Progress in Turkish Politics*. The Clarendon Press, Oxford.

Ahmad, F. (1991) Politics and Islam in Modern Turkey, *Middle Eastern Studies*, vol. 27(1), pp. 3–21.

Çınar, A. (2008) Subversion and Subjugation in the Public Sphere: Secularism and the Islamic Headscarf, *The University of Chicago Press*, vol. 33(4), pp. 891–913.

Esen, B. and Gümüşçü, Ş. (2018) Building a Competitive Authoritarian Regime: State–Business Relations in the AKP's Turkey, *Journal of Balkan and Near Eastern Studies*, vol. 20(4), pp. 349–372.

Gökarıksel, B. and Secor, A.J. (2009) New transnational geographies of Islamism, capitalism and subjectivity: the veiling-fashion industry in Turkey, *Area*, vol. 41 (1), pp. 6–18.

Göle, N. (1996) *The Forbidden Modern: Civilization and Veiling*. University of Michigan Press.

Göle, N. (2015) *Islam and Secularity*, Duke University Press, Durham and London.

Gülalp, H. (2001) "Globalization and Political Islam: The Social Bases of Turkey's Welfare Party," *International Journal of Middle East Studies*. Cambridge University Press, vol. 33(3), pp. 433–448.

Lüküslü, D. and Yücel, H. (2013) *Gençlik Halleri 2000'li Yıllar Türkiye'sinde Genç Olmak*. Ankara, Efil Yayınları.

Mardin, Ş. (2000) *Türkiye'de Din ve Siyaset*, İletişim Yayınları, İstanbul.

Maritato, C. (2020) *Women, Religion, and the State in Contemporary Turkey.* Torino, Cambridge University Press.

Öniş, Z. (1997) The Political Economy of Islamic Resurgence in Turkey: The Rise of The Welfare Party in Perspective, *Third World Quarterly*, vol. 18(4), pp. 743–766.

Özet, İ. (2019) *Fatih-Başakşehir*, İstanbul, İletişim Yayınları.

Sakallıoğlu, Ü. C. (1994), Kemalism, hyper-nationalism and Islam in Turkey, *History of European Ideas*, vol. 18 (2), pp. 255–270.

Saktanber, A. (2007) Cultural Dilemmas of Muslim Youth: Negotiating Muslim Identities and Being Young in Turkey 1, *Turkish Studies*, vol. 8, pp. 417–434.

Saktanber, A. and Çorbacioğlu, G. (2008) Veiling and Headscarf-Skepticism in Turkey Social Politics, Social Politics, *International Studies in Gender, State & Society*, vol. 15 (4), pp. 514–538.

Scott, James C. (1985) *Weapons of the Weak: Everyday Forms of Peasant Resistance.* Yale University Press.

Sehlikoglu, S. (2016) Exercising in Comfort: Islamicate Culture of Mahremiyet in Everyday Istanbul, *Journal of Middle East Women's Studies*, vol. 12 (2), pp. 143–165.

Tuğal, C. (2009), *Passive Revolution; Absorbing the Islamic Challenge to Capitalism.* California, Stanford University Press.

Turam, B. (2012) *Secular State and Religious Society.* New York, Palgrave Macmillan.

Yılmaz, Z. (2015) *Dişil Dindarlık: İslamcı Kadın Hareketinin Dönüşümü,* İstanbul, İletişim Yayınları.

Yılmaz, Z. (2017) The AKP and the Spirit of the 'New' Turkey: Imagined Victim, Reactionary Mood, And Resentful Sovereign, *Turkish Studies*, vol. 18(3), pp. 482–513.

Yılmaz, Z. (2019) *Zarif ve Dinen Makbul.* İstanbul, İletişim Yayınları.

Zubaida, S. (2011) *Beyond Islam: A New Understanding of the Middle East.* London, I. B. Tauris & Co Ltd.

(by Nele Hansen)

Chapter 13 Creating youth-determined contact zones in the public space and through local and global communities: Street dance in Barcelona

Abstract: In this chapter, we present a study of the street dance community in Barcelona carried out between 2019 and 2020. Our research explored cultural heritage in the making and (sub)alternative expressions of youth culture within street dance, focusing on the significance of public space in these expressions. The methodology involved ethnographic fieldwork, including non-participant and participant observations, informal conversations, and semi-structured interviews with young dancers and key referees.

According to our main findings, street dance practices can be understood as a powerful self-organised subcultural expression set against adult-centred and authority-guided spaces. Through street dance practices, young people can create their own meaningful spaces, especially in the public space, as potential *contact zones* for different identities, enabling the generation of new cultural practices and identities. Our findings point to the multifaceted meanings present in the street and to the interconnection of street dance with lifestyle and a broader value system. Crucial cultural aspects include an intergenerational transfer of knowledge, through oral and corporeal/bodily transmission, and horizontal, collective and informal learning processes. Street dance culture is based on both origins/history and evolution/innovation. Young dancers engage in global community-building networks and can demonstrate new hybrid cultural identities. Although the level of inclusion and integration is generally high, equality in terms of gender is still "a work in progress", as we still observed masculine dominance and patriarchal tendencies in the street dance context.

Keywords: youth, street dance, Barcelona, public space, hip-hop, culture

Introduction

During the last few years, we have witnessed an increasing number of young people practicing street dance at particular places in the city centre of Barcelona. Small groups of young people began to dance in the evening to hip hop music, which they played using boom boxes, in a self-absorbed, cheerful and peaceful way. This led us to wonder: Who were these youngsters and why did they engage in this activity? Why in some particular places and not in others? For the purposes of the CHIEF research, it offered an excellent opportunity to study an *informal* and *self-organised* group that was not led by adult institutions and to examine *processes of cultural heritage in the making and (sub)alternative expressions of youth culture.* Our research was guided by the following questions: do participants of street dance consider their activities meaningful for cultural expression and generation? How do young people live, understand and share street dance? What is the role of *public space/the street* for these activities? In what way is participation as a street dancer meaningful to the construction of young people's identity? Finally, in what way does street dance culture generate community building and senses of belonging?

Description of the scene and site

The street dance collective in Barcelona is a fluid and informally constituted group of young people who practice street dance in different places in the city. Practitioners of street dance engage in different dance styles under the "umbrella" culture of *hip hop*: breaking, popping, locking, house, and hip-hop. Hip-hop culture developed in the 1970s in New York (and later in the Los Angeles area) within African-American and Afro-Caribbean communities, marginalised neighbourhoods that were socially, economically and culturally excluded from the *centre* (for more details on the origins of hip-hop culture see, for example, Kitwana, 2002; Rose, 1994; Ross & Rose, 1994).

The street dance community in Barcelona has had various "ups and downs". What we witnessed was the "rising again" of a cultural expression that had experienced a peak before.[1] The beginnings of street dance can be traced back to the 1980s, when hip hop culture arrived in Spain and Barcelona, mostly through rap music and dance movies. The most important dance styles that were "reproduced" in Barcelona were breaking – dancers are "b-boys" or "b-girls" – and, to a lesser extent, popping and locking. At the end of the 80s street dance activity had stopped, but regained strength by the mid-90s. Social dancing and learning took place mainly on the streets and through imitation and sharing. In the 2000s, breaking remained *freestyle* and street-based, whereas popping, locking and hip hop were increasingly "transferred" to the dance academies. An important generational change took place around 2010, as former freestyle

---

1 The information on the development of street dance culture in Barcelona and Spain in this study is based exclusively on the data obtained from participants and informants, since there are only a few studies on this subject (Bachelors, Masters and Doctoral theses), and they concentrate mainly on hip-hop culture in general and rap in particular (see Reyes Sánchez, 2003; Sandín Lillo, 2015). Breaking is mentioned, but further dance styles are largely unrepresented.

pioneers in Barcelona got older and retired from dance activities. Over the last decade, "institutionalised" street dance has gained more and more importance in dance academies, as competitions and the professionalisation of street dance have increased. Historically, there has been a division between *freestyle dancers* (on-the-street and improvising) and *dance-school dancers* (structured learning and choreographed routines in dance academies), and they have different socio-demographic profiles. Our study concentrated exclusively on the *freestyle collective*.

The geographical origin of participants within the collective varies widely: we found a mixture of Spanish and foreign-born participants, with long or short histories in Catalonia. Some participants identified as Spanish and/or Catalan, while others identified with diasporic, mostly Latin American, identities. Other dancers were born in African or Asian countries. Although their sociocultural backgrounds differ, young people often come from low-income families and impoverished/marginalised neighbourhoods. True to the origins of hip hop, the characteristics of street dance favour a relationship between marginalised neighbourhoods and street dance participation.

The majority of participants in Barcelona are aged between 20 and 30 years old.[2] However, the over-30s engage on different levels, such as teaching in workshops and dance academies, organising events; acting as key referees of the scene. The group's gender balance varied depending on the dance style: while breaking is still male-dominated, young women have a stronger presence in other dance styles like house, while hip hop is more or less gender balanced. Over the last few years there has been an important increase in female participation.

Freestyle dancers gather in specific public places in Barcelona: the M. and U. squares at the heart of the city centre. Every day, starting from 7 or 8 pm, dancers meet there. They advertise their meetings and activities through WhatsApp and a public Facebook group. People stay as long as they want; activities usually last until 2 am, with more activity on the weekends.

> *Square M. is a huge public space in front of the X Museum. It features an elevated section, a kind of platform, and broad stairs to the right-hand side of the museum. The place is shared by skaters, breakers, street dancers and all kinds of other people (citizens, tourists) who just sit around on the square to drink, eat, talk, etc. The place itself has a very exciting and lively atmosphere. (…) Some 10–12 people are dancing for their own pleasure in front of the stairs, at first not forming any cypher (a round circle where one dancer at a time steps*

---

2 The collective is an expression of youth culture where age categories are blurred. Previous studies indicate that "youth" is often defined as the age range of 15–29 (Dávila León, 2004).

> *into the middle and "performs"). (…) Many people sit on the stairs, chatting, watching and drinking. (…) There is an atmosphere of camaraderie and good vibes, very relaxed.* (Fieldwork diary, 16/05/2019)

Street dancers also make regular use of the training rooms of community centres; these have an increasingly important role, since more and more dancers prefer to train in closed spaces that guarantee more privacy (and security, as will be discussed later on). The most important training rooms are located in Barcelona city centre, in close proximity to squares M. and U. and public transport. Community or youth centres provide free training rooms on a regular basis, but sometimes demand in exchange that dancers participate at events or workshops organised by these locations. Freestyle dancers also participate in local, national and international competitions and workshops.

"I am who I am because of the street": The public space as a contagious transmission zone

Public space is central to understanding street dance culture. Reasons for using the street are highly diverse. First of all, the street is free for everyone; it involves no entrance fee, unlike dance academies. Young people have free access to the street at any hour of the day, while youth centres usually close at nine in the evening, leaving little time for people who get out of work at around that time. For many of the informants, dance academies are not an option due to economic constraints and the cost of taking classes. This is the main explanation for the power of street culture in the eyes of young people from low-income families and marginalised neighbourhoods. Lucas explained this further:

> *In order to dance street dance, you don't need anything. You don't need to know how to read, how to write, you don't need to have any means. In order to paint you need a canvas and some paint, and maybe you can't afford it. For music you need an instrument. But for dancing you just need your body and what's inside your body: what you've lived, what you feel, what you may not be able to express in words, and then you can transmit it with the body … I think that's the reason it reaches a greater number of underground scenes.* (Lucas, 30, b-boy and dance artist)

Aside from this, young dancers appreciate the power of the street for other reasons. Street culture means, most of all, a space of the *intersection of differences* and of *interculturality*: it is a *contact zone,* by which term Mary Louise Pratt refers to social spaces where different cultures meet, clash and become familiar with each other (Pratt, 1992).[3] In the case of urban dance, the street offers a *contact zone* for people who might be vastly different in origin, social class, age, education, interests, etc. In this space, any kind of interaction is theoretically possible. This was expressed by David:

> *The street has its own culture, its own codes. Many cultures intersect there. Street culture has the most extensive codes. Because there you have the poorest person and the richest person in the same place. (…) Managing these different codes within the culture… for me street culture is always the most important thing. Because I am who I am because of the street. The street taught me, the street gave me the chance and the street brought me to Europe.* (David, 31, hip hop dancer)

Public space can also signify a point of intersection and potential equality: the street offers an opportunity for positive contagion, with some dancers turning into references for other young people, as BD described:

> *Someone may come by, look and say "Hell, I like it!" and then start learning. Because we do things on the street. Otherwise, if we kept indoors, it would be much more complicated for these situations to happen.* (BD, 31, hip-hop dancer)

In fact, most of the informants learned about street dance by encountering other dancers in a public space; the transmission of freestyle street dance culture happens most often and importantly in the street. Lupus spoke about his entry into street dance culture as a teenager, when he was living in a small town and a neighbour told him about "rappers" gathering in a park:

> *There was something dangerous about it, so I liked it. So I spent a few months crouching behind parked cars to watch them dance, but of course I was afraid. Until one day they caught me and said: "Come over here". (…) I sat down and learned – yippee! And from then on, they were like teachers to me and my friends. (…) I used to sit in the park, and I was forbidden to dance while they danced. I could only watch. (…) I would try the steps and then ask them: "Hey, how do you do this step?"* (Lupus, 35, b-boy and founder of street dance crew)

The street dance community uses the street as a way to transmit and promote their culture, not only to other possible dancers but also to a broader public. In this sense, *"dancers use the public space as a showcase for their cultural expression, it is a way of showing to the broader public what they are doing, what they love,*

3 Pratt refers more specifically to contexts of highly asymmetrical relations of power, such as colonialism or slavery, which is not the case here, although public space is not free of asymmetrical power relations or conflicting interests.

how they have fun, what they are passionate about" (Fieldwork diary entry, 16/05/2019).

For some young dancers, the street also has a political dimension, as it allows them to show resistance by publicly carrying out cultural expressions that are not regulated or imposed by an institution:

> *It's that feeling that you're not doing something they're imposing on you, but rather doing it because you want to, in the space that you want to, and it's not regulated by any law, nor by any entity that controls you. (…) And I believe that in all urban cultures it's important not wanting to be part of society but instead generating a culture of one's own, not governed by other institutions. We're doing it our own way.* (Luz, 24, hip-hop dancer)
> *I think the beauty of street dance is that we can "occupy" a public space for a period of time. (…) I believe that public spaces are made to be occupied, to be danced on, to be transgressed … to be a little dissident. (…) We (dancers) offer the possibility of inhabiting sites that are uninhabited, in a different way. It may be a subway entrance; it may be a square… Because if they are public, they are public. In other words, the public space is for everyone.* (Lucas, 30 years, b-boy and dance artist)

We observed how young dancers claimed the street as a space for self-determined being and doing. Here, rules, dynamics and values are set by the young people themselves and not by adult authorities. The street becomes a meaningful vehicle for asserting a right for youthfulness in society (Bayat, 2010).

However, not all aspects of public space were valued positively by participants. One reservation has to do with the fact that the street, much more than indoor spaces, is associated with the consumption of alcohol and drugs, not only by other people in the street but also by the dancers themselves:

> *Of late, I don't like training too long on the street. It's often very dirty, many people bother you, dancers often smoke marijuana and don't take training seriously.* (Arantxa, 24, electrohop dancer)
> *Street dancing gets mixed with drugs & alcohol here; I try to convince young people to come to the training rooms, trying to turn them away from the "dark side", because in the training rooms you're not allowed to consume anything.* (Ben, b-boy)

The street is also potentially open to disturbances and interruptions, as well as being a place where robberies and physical or verbal violence can occur. The issue of security and the risk of physical violence were definitely much more critical for the non-male informants in the observed group. Many female dancers said that they do not feel comfortable training in the street because men harass them:

> S: *It's not easy [being a woman in street dance] because the environment doesn't make it easy for you. (…) And there are many people in square M. (non-dancers) who get drunk or whatever [inaudible], but this is normal. (…) It's mostly men who go there to annoy a woman, tell her (sexist) things… (…) If I believe he is saying nonsense and*

might get violent with me, I do my best to turn a deaf ear, but I'll be the first one to let it out and say "I need you to go, thank you, just go away. Leave us alone", because in the end it gets too annoying. (…) But it's not easy.

INT: *And do you feel that you have support from others, from other dancers, both girls and boys?*

S: *Yes. (…) The fear we suffer always, somehow, no matter what the degree of harassment. But yes, when someone comes who wants to bother us, everyone tries to get him to leave.* (Susana, 27, krump and wacking dancer)

Evidently, real and perceived degrees of security and freedom in public space vary between informants of different gender identities, since patriarchal dynamics and structure still dominate the use of public space.

Young dancers of all gender identities were highly bothered by how they are treated by the public authority in the street: at a given time during the night (10 or 11 pm) the police turns them away, frequently fining them for playing music. Young dancers may attempt to have a dialogue or to negotiate with the police, but sometimes they have no other option than to find a new spot with less of a police presence. Informants talked of a *double moral standard of the public authority*, suggesting that the municipality uses street dance in Barcelona to present a positive image of the city (Barcelona as a young, open and multicultural place), while at the same time penalising such activities:

BD: *It's very ambiguous. (…) The city council promotes it, but then the fact is that the police come in and say "Hey, hey, shove off!" And on Tuesday, for example, we were fined. Every one of us.*

G: *Everyone. Let me tell you, in the last few years the police seized about 10 or 15 loudspeakers… (…) And we're not doing anything wrong. But they treat us like thieves. And we get angry, man. Because there are a thousand things that are going bad here in Barcelona, and yet they come after us. But actually, we're giving the city something good. Are we doing any bad thing? Loud music. I know there are people sleeping…*

BD: *For me the main thing is that they are false people. They promote you in order to sell Barcelona, you know. "Wow, look at this!" Then suddenly, boom!* (BD, 31, and Gonzalo, 26, hip-hop dancers)

The lack of public support for street dance culture was criticised by many of the young participants. In Spain, as in many other countries, street dance is not recognised as an *art*, and even less as an art worth funding. Dancers involved in projects and collaborations with the municipality frequently have the impression that they are treated like children and not taken as seriously as other dance styles/artistic expressions: "*street dance is still seen as a bunch of kids playing around*" (Mateo, 40, b-boy and coordinator for dance projects). In part, this may be due to the fact that information about street dance is often wrong or incomplete, so that the broader public and authorities still have a stereotyped image of this art form. Dancers wish for a change in public support, although many believe that this could be difficult to achieve.

The culture of street dance: Values, lifestyle and the significance of an oral and intergenerational transmission of knowledge

Participants in Barcelona understood street dance in every moment as a *culture* or *subculture* – they had no doubt about this. Even without being asked, young dancers would use phrases like *"the culture of street dance"*, *"in the culture…"* Informants pointed out the multiple layers to hip-hop (sub)culture, which they considered the "mother culture" or "umbrella culture" of street dance. Key elements of hip-hop culture, for these interviewees, included the simultaneous maintenance and transmission of the origins of hip-hop (such as particular moves, etc.), together with the constant evolution of the culture due to diverse personal or collective interpretations and uses:

> *Dance itself is a great culture. And within dance there is hip hop, which is another culture, and commercial hip hop is yet another culture; they are all different subcultures.* (Arantxa, 24, electro-hop dancer)

Informants were highly aware of the fact, that hip hop is built on four elements: graffiti, DJ,[4] MC,[5] and dance. (Originally the latter only referred to breaking, but has now evolved into broader dance styles). Along with these four elements are the particular values of hip-hop culture: "peace", "unity", "love", "having fun" and, as a later addition, "respect". These serve as the moral guidelines that lead participants in hip-hop culture, not only within the collective but also in their private lives:

> *I like the values that hip hop culture promotes. (…) This interested me and I felt even more attracted by the fact that it promotes such values …* (Esperanza, 22, hip-hop dancer)

Today, conflicts and rivalries are not prominent in street dance culture. The informants stressed values like "respect", "love", and very importantly, "having fun": the "*right for free time and uselessness of activities in these times of bills and suchlike*" (Lucas). Street dance culture asserts the right to *play*, in contrast with young people's worries about the future and increasing responsibilities. We can interpret this as reclaiming youthfulness (Bayat, 2010) within an adult-dominated

4 DJ: Disc-jockey, a person who selects and plays music for an audience.
5 MC: Literally "mic-controller", but actually a term for the person who raps.

society. Hip hop and street dance allow young people to disconnect from reality and from capitalist/individualistic society, to *feel free* and have the possibility to converting into a a "*superhero*". Hip-hop dancers assume a sort of *alter ego*, as Lupus pointed out:

> *Our nickname, in hip- hop culture, is our superhero name. So, in normal life we have the name our parents gave us and the way of life that society imposes on us: study, work, behave well, be a good person … (…). We are lucky in the hip-hop world that we can create an alter ego, we can be a superhero and do what we want: our rules, our laws, and I do what I want. (…) In normal life my name is such and such, but when I get into hip hop, my name is Lupus. Here, I behave normally and do what society tells me: I pay my bills, work and so on; but in hip hop I'm going to paint graffiti, which is illegal, I'm going to dance in the city square, I'm going to throw myself on the floor, I'm going to do things that in the normal world would look weird. (…) It's our way of living our life: be free.* (Lupus, 35, b-boy and founder of street dance crew)

By adopting different characters and alter egos, young dancers are able to counterbalance possible feelings of inferiority or failure (for example, those experienced in the formal educational system), and can escape from the impositions of society. These forms of resistance might even imply certain illegal activities, as Lupus explained. We can understand this as cultural participation embedded in youth communities that reclaims the right to *youthfulness*. It is related to the experience of being a young person – that is, being at a certain stage in life and having a determined social role.

Living and behaving according to hip-hop culture constitutes a concrete *lifestyle*, which is crucial to the identity constructions of the interviewed street dancers:

> *Hip hop is a way of life, a lifestyle. (…) And hip hop is to really live this life. And, really, it is a statement. Not saying "I am hip hop because I dance hip hop", but because you are really living it.* (Markus, 27, hip-hop dancer)
>
> *For example, I am co-director of an urban dance festival (…) but I go out to the street to dance and I meet with kids who train. For me, it's part of my way of doing. It's a lifestyle. I'm closing in on 40 years old, but I think: why not…?!* (Mateo, 40, b-boy and coordinator for dance projects)

One of the most important aspects of street dance culture is how knowledge is transmitted, where it is crucial to maintain a fine balance between tradition and innovation. This highlights the cultural dimension of street dance and contrasts with existing stereotypes about hip-hop culture: "*it's not about some kids playing around and not knowing what they're doing!*" (observation notes in field diary). Historically, knowledge has been transmitted orally and face-to-face. This is still true today, although new technologies, especially the Internet, have been transformative. Since its origins in the 70s, hip-hop culture has been transmitted in person, often at social gatherings and parties. Originally, the dancing (breaking) represented a symbolic fight between different gang members; it was a substitution for physical violence that transformed into a playful competition. Knowledge and information were passed on through observation, imitation, and asking knowledgeable elders. Until the rise of the Internet, knowledge was spread *orally* and *corporally*, that is, *through the body*. For this same reason, information spread slowly across geographical space. Information only arrived through the dancers' social exchanges, and through those who had the opportunity to travel and share their knowledge. For this reason, information arriving in Europe was often misinformed or incomplete:

> *A: (In N.Y.) they did not share that information. So the information that has come to us is above all information from Paris, that is, of older generations. (…) And we do not want this to happen, at least I would not like for a generation gap to happen, because that's when disinformation begins. And then you start not knowing "what was that?", "where do I look for it?" You can look it up on the internet but it's not enough…* (Alex, 24, hip-hop dancer)

To preserve traditional hip-hop knowledge, dancers from Europe/Spain's incipient street dance community would travel to the United States in order to gather direct information from the pioneers (often older dancers with more experience and mobility and with higher incomes). Dancers like Lupus still gather such knowledge during their frequent travels in search of the origins and "stories" of a movement or a dance style:

> *L: Especially when I go to the United States, I try to talk to old school people from every city I go to.*
> *INT: Who are the old school people?*
> *L: The pioneers. People who are now 45–50 years and can tell you part of the story [of hip-hop culture], but not because they studied it but because they have lived it. And I love it when they tell me, "Oh, that day this and that happened and that's why we dance like this".* (Lupus, 35, b-boy and founder of street dance crew)

Knowing the origins of street dance culture in the United States was important to most of the informants. The community tries to spread this information among its members. Young dancers agree that this history needs to be known in order to understand one's own place in history and the symbolic meanings one embodies when dancing, as Carme pointed out:

> *For me it's fundamental to understand the basis. (…) Why that outfit? Why that brand of cap? Why this movement, why those codes, and so on? If you don't know, you are not being respectful. (…) So you are representing a culture that is not, really. You are not being aware*

> *of what it is. It's like being a Christian without knowing who Jesus is, you know? Because it's a culture and every culture has a basis, a history that you really have to know. Whether you share it or not is your decision, but you do have to be aware of what you are doing and how you are meant to represent it, respect it, be careful with and, above all, appreciate and care for it, so that it can move forward.* (Carme, 22, hip-hop dancer)

In this sense, dancers connect the original American stories to their own experiences in Barcelona, and transform original material (particular moves, etc.) into their own creations. In street dance culture, origins and history are crucial, but innovations are also celebrated. An intrinsic part of hip hop is change. Because of its social, oral and corporal learning processes and cultural fusion, evolution has always been part of the game:

> *Many things are merged within break (dance), there are steps that come from salsa or capoeira. So, if you take as a starting point that break (dance) is a fusion of everything, you can add more things, it's quite free. (…) I like innovation, so long as you learn the origins and the tradition first. From there you can go ahead and deconstruct. First build, understand the foundation, and from there deconstruct and personalise it. This is important for any culture.* (Paula, 30, afro-house dancer)

Within the community there is widespread awareness of the need to transmit the culture to future generations. Young members of the street dance collective in Barcelona feel a responsibility to transmit the culture's knowledge, experiences and information to the next generations:

> *We are part of this, the education of the next generation, which also benefits us. I mean, we should feel good about it. "We have co-created", as the Old-G's say, "this path for you". In the same way, we will create a path for those who will follow after us.* (BD, 31, hip-hop dancer)

In street dance culture, horizontal and informal learning processes are key. These were highly valued by informants, since they represent a contrast to the learning processes of formal education and *"the things society forces you to learn"*. In hip hop culture, the rule is that *"each one teaches another"*:

> *Since the beginning [hip hop culture] has been transmitted through generational relays, by people teaching other people: "each one teaches another", which is like saying: whatever you learn, you teach it. You integrate it into your body, you develop it, and then you teach it to the next generation.* (Alex, 24, hip-hop dancer)

Knowledge is passed on among friends and acquaintances through observing, asking, and imitating movements; everything is based on social exchange. For many young dancers, the informal learning process – on the street – is one of the main attractions of the culture. This subcultural lifestyle is oriented towards experienced-based learning processes, as Luz explained:

> *I've always liked suburban cultures; cultures that arise in cities. (…) Learning on the street, learning from experience. (…) It is not as structured as studying a career; it's more an experience of living it and feeling it. (…) I felt that learning through experience was more real than studying something that may give me a lot of information but does not interest me. I learn what I want to learn, not what I am forced to learn.* (Luz, 24, hip-hop dancer)

Teaching is conducted in an informal, horizontal and collective way, within a community that accumulates a collective knowledge base:

> *These are horizontal pedagogies. But it's not self-taught; you are always doing it with other people, so it is a community teaching. (…) It's a spectacular value at the artistic language level, because it has been jointly created by millions of people without their knowing it, a sum of the innovations they have come up with… We have created a collective knowledge that does not belong to anyone (…) I have invented some movements of my own, but they are being imitated by other people after their own fashion, and I love it when I see that something that I have invented has been taken and mutated by someone else. (…) The pedagogical aspect is basic in urban dance because of the exchange of knowledge.* (Mateo, 40, b-boy and coordinator of dance projects)

On a collective/communitarian level, street dance was considered by most informants to be a powerful social tool. It was essentially regarded as a positive reference point in marginalised and violent neighbourhoods, where children and young people often come from families that have been disrupted and/or have economic and sociocultural restraints:

> *The fact that (children of marginalised neighbourhoods) watch people dancing is like "Ah! There's something else in the neighbourhood outside the common things, that is, something that doesn't hurt". It's a way of teaching children "Hey, you have a whole range of possibilities if you want". (…) When you grow up in a neighbourhood and you see nothing but violence, you will be violent. (…) It is important for society to contribute a grain of sand to help these marginal people and say "Hey, I know you're wrong, but I'm going to teach you other things, other ways of doing things".* (Ray, 26, hip-hop dancer)

Local and global community building

Although the dance collective in Barcelona is not fixed or formally constituted, the sense of belonging to both a local and global street dance community was very prominent in the young people's self-identifications. First of all, street dance is a great place for socialising and making friends beyond the barriers of origin, nationality, age or social class, even though informants stated in informal conversations that friendships are also built on national or regional affinity (for example, some Moroccan dancers stated that they hang out more with other Moroccan dancers; some participants of Ecuadorian or Peruvian origin feel more comfortable socialising with *"other dancers from Latin America"*). This affinity was explained by the feeling *"of understanding each other's ways of doing"*. Nevertheless, the majority of informants stressed the fact that they make friends and socialise easily within the dance community, thanks to a shared passion for street dance.

> *If I didn't have dance, my socialisation would have been different. Maybe less so at the university, because I studied here, but I never socialised much because the groups were already fixed. It was more difficult to access culturally closed groups. All the Catalans knew each other from school. Here on the street we all fit in: immigrants, students …* (Mateo, 40, b-boy and coordinator of dance projects)

Young dancers valued the feeling of belonging to a globally-connected community that gives one a "home in every part of the world": dancers travel frequently and connect with the local street dance communities at each destination. These communities offer them information, accommodation, friendship and sharing:

> *I moved here like five weeks ago. And on my second week I was able to type in "hip hop Barcelona" and I saw an Instagram story by Markus. So I messaged him and it was like "Yo, I just moved here. Is there any hip-hop training?" (…) I went to the session, and since then we have managed to chill out and we were able to enter together into a competition and I've met so many people already (…) It's a big, big melting pot. But we all love the same thing. It's very easy for us to relate.* (Jonathan, 25, hip-hop dancer)

The street dance community represents a place where young people can feel accepted and recognised among equals: they can be themselves and connect with others who share the same passion.

In keeping with the dynamics of an international community, most informants affirmed street dance as an "open arms community", with no mechanisms of exclusion based on origin, nationality, age, social class or sexual orientation. The intercultural origins of hip hop culture in the United States were always referred to as a *"cultural encounter, enabling adoptions between different cultures"* (Mateo). Informants believed that, because street dance culture is formed by highly heterogeneous groups in terms of national and cultural origin, the culture tends to be intrinsically antiracist and accepts *the other* in its diversity:

> *A: At least here, no matter who you are, no matter if you are queer or trans, if you dance you can come here. Your sexual orientation doesn't matter, it doesn't matter who you feel you are, if you're female or male or transsexual…. You dance, and that's all. We accept everything. And, generally, hip hop culture is very inclusive. (…)*
>
> *BD: And I also think that we are sort of an example in the sense that we have variety. So there's not going to be racism there. It's like an example of what this culture is, unconsciously promoting that there is no racism here. Our culture is against it.* (Alex, 24 and BD, 31, hip hop dancers).

In the case of Barcelona, the idea of a "humanizing culture" is prevalent among street dancers. The majority of participants asserted that, thanks to the 'melting pot' of cultures in hip hop culture, they had learned to tolerate and understand different kinds of people. This idea was very clearly explained by Arantxa, who comes from a middle-class background and found that for her an open mind was one of the most important learning effects of street dance culture:

> *I have always lived inside a bubble, I never lacked anything, I went to a religious school and have been surrounded by white people with money. Everything was fine, I never had parents who were alcoholics or drug addicts. (…) I had also not had contact with people of colour, never had a father who mistreated a mother. (…) Getting to know hip hop has allowed me to disassociate myself from all that and from people who don't match these ideals, the life that I should be leading. My parents say, "Arantxa, you are always socialising with Latinos or immigrants". I understand their fear, but it's cool, because it gives you other things and it opens your mind a lot, and without hip hop I would not have learned all that, had I followed the life I was supposed to follow. I could have said "I am not racist" or "I am multicultural". But I really wouldn't have had a clue, I wouldn't have any friends telling me what their lives have been like, telling me "Two months ago I came from Venezuela without a single dollar…" (…) A reality that makes you much more human…* (Arantxa, 24, electro-hop dancer)

Friction lines within the community: Discrimination tendencies and gender inequality

However, informants pointed out different kind of conflict and friction lines within the community, especially in the local community in Barcelona. Dancers explained that these tensions are usually due to conflicting interests regarding the commercialisation of street dance culture (to what degree should or can we "*sell ourselves to commercial means in order to gain a living?*"), or to competitive "egos". In general, dancers take different positions with regard to these conflicts, from more extreme to more "harmonising positions",– in an attempt to integrate both aspects into their cultural practices.

Some informants – particularly older ones, with more experience – questioned the image of hip hop as 100 % open to and tolerant of all kinds of identities:

> *Sometimes I think there is a somewhat idyllic idea that this is a super open environment, a very international environment where people have no prejudices… Perhaps this is so in 90% of the cases. But there are possibly people in this culture who have a more macho, homophobic, racist and segregating way of thinking.* (Lucas, 30, b-boy and dance artist)

Lucas's observation is very important because it deconstructs possible idealisations and generalisations of hip-hop culture, which can take distinctive forms and ideologies depending on national or local contexts.

Based on the researcher's observations and the discourse of some informants, gender was highlighted as a possible exclusion mechanism and motive for unequal power relations. Opinions about gender equality and relationships in street dance culture varied widely. Many informants said that there is no gender issue at all (including issues related to sexual identity), and claimed that women and men are given the same opportunities and levels of power within the community:[6]

> *I think it is very even, very connected. (…) I think that everyone likes to dance, both boys and girls, there is no such thing as marginalisation against women. At least in our circle, we try to respect women very much and give them importance. I know that in other places there are people who believe themselves to be stronger, more skilful. Not here, a woman comes here and everyone treats her well.* (Benjamin, 31, popping dancer)
> *They (the boys) took great care of me. I never felt like I was being left out. On the contrary, they always empowered me a lot.* (Paula, 30, Afro house dancer)

This discourse was partly contrasted by the fieldwork and observations. At least in the researcher's eyes, it was possible to observe gender inequalities (although the researcher's outsider position, with less knowledge and experience in the field than young people, should be borne in mind):

> *In the cypher there are more male dancers than female (only two female dancers). This fact seems to have an influence on the gender dynamics: I observe a lot more protagonism from male dancers: they show more initiative to step into the middle of the cypher and perform, they encourage each other a lot. The women don't dare to step into the middle. There are even moments when female dancers try, but they are interrupted by another male dancer or another male dancer is faster and takes rapidly the attention away from the female dancer. I observe this in the case of Paula, who is one of the few female dancers participating. (…) She is really supportive and friendly towards the male dancers in the cypher, but many of them seem to ignore her; they don't even look at her: I sense a kind of excluding behaviour here, that contradicts the comments of Paula herself (…): she has never felt any differentiation or discrimination due to the fact of being a woman. (…) At the same time she tells me about the "aggressive cyphers" and that today she and some other female dancers just "played" in the back, just having fun.* (Fieldwork diary, 04/12/2020)

Some informants – more females than males – confirmed that there is masculine dominance in street dance culture and pointed out the patriarchal structures

6 In my observations I got the general impression, that this opinion was believed to a greater extent by men than by women and younger participants.

and machismo behaviour that assign female dancers an inferior role within the community:

> *I feel that there is a lot of machismo in hip hop. (…) During training sessions there are more girls, but then during battles there are always more boys, and it costs them less to gain recognition. Then there is the idea of being macho, of being aggressive when you dance, which gives you points. (…) The mentality of men is that of a macho, thinking that the female dancers are going there to hook up with them. Not always, but they do have that mentality of trying to "see if I can catch this one", and they don't value how they dance as much. (…) Girls are criticised much more than boys. In Barcelona, dancing freestyle means everyone ends up getting involved with everyone. (…) When the boys do it "Oh, with this … what a fucking master", and with the girls "Pshaw, she's a bit of a slut". As in the real world.* (Arantxa, 24, electro-hop dancer)

Patriarchal structures vary depending on the dance style: in breaking, where men form a majority, discrimination against women is much more present than in dance styles with a higher ratio of female dancers, such as house. Overall, in the few last years, activities/events initiated by female dancers for female dancers have increased considerably. Participants of all genders are seeing an opportunity to change gender norms in street dance, as Esperanza, b-girl and rapper, expressed:

> *As regards the subject of gender there is much work to do. Today the boys are much more aware (of) … the values that hip-hop culture promotes: trying to respect each other, equality, fight against racism and inequality. Nowadays we are opening our minds to all of that, because although the boys sometimes continue doing these things, since we are their friends or sisters, they have to understand it. Women have an important role in hip-hop culture. It is a way of sending a message and having people listen to it. To overcome that barrier in hip hop, which is a very masculine culture, we take the female hip-hop artists as an example (…) You need that to help empower yourself. Hip hop helps us to empower ourselves as women.* (Esperanza, 30, b-girl and rapper)

For sure, times are changing. Feminist movements within society are helping to make identities of non-cis-males (women, transgender, etc.) more visible in street dance. Albeit slowly, these identities are gaining more power in the community and are increasingly able to express themselves without boundaries of discrimination or oppression.

Discussion

This study revealed street dance in Barcelona to be a complex, multifaceted and hybrid culture, with the potential to empower young people searching for self-determined spaces. We have seen how this is articulated through central aspects: the use of public space/the street as a *contact zone* and space for resistance, and the appropriation of a specific lifestyle and value system that serves both individual and collective identity constructions. We have also observed that knowledge is transmitted intergenerationally and that both evolution and tradition are key to the culture. Learning processes are horizontal, collective and informal, while the global approach to community-building is oriented towards the creation of an "open-arms community" with no exclusion criteria.

We can understand these cultural expressions as part of *youth culture,* since the underlying driving force of street dance and hip-hop culture is youth, and participants self-identified as "young man or woman" in relation to other groups of people/society at large. Such an identification is not a matter of age but a perspective on life, lifestyle and values; participants feel young because they share a set of experiences, cultural practices, codes and a lifestyle.

We can define youth cultures as collectively-expressed social experiences of young people: *"through the construction of differentiating lifestyles, mainly in their leisure time, or in interstitial spaces in the institutional life"* (Feixa, 1998: p. 84[7]). The aspect of leisure time, which distances the culture from institutional, adult-dominated spaces, is crucial for understanding the dynamics of youth cultures; we are talking about *" 'youth micro-societies' with significant degrees of independence from the 'adult institutions' that provide specific space and time"* (ibid.: p. 84[8]). One of the main appeals of street dance is its character as a micro-society with its own rules, established collectively by the young participants themselves. Although it may not be free from conflicts, it is not dictated by any adult-regulated institution or authority. The way in which this youth micro-society establishes its own rules is the antithesis to how adults implicitly demand young people to accept the "rules of the game" as they come to adulthood. This is what Bourdieu describes when he talks about "social fields", where the dominant powers (here understood as adult society, with its institutions, rules and norms)

> *lean towards conservation strategies (…), while those with less capital are inclined to use subversion strategies (…) Newcomers have to pay an admission fee that consists of recognizing the value of the game (…) and knowing certain operating principles of the game. They are condemned to use subversion strategies, but they must remain within certain limits, if not, they are penalized with exclusion.* (Bourdieu, 1990: p. 206)[9]

7 Quote translated by the author.
8 Quote translated by the author.
9 Quote translated by the author.

In this sense, we can understand street dance culture as an interruption and interrogation of the social field of adult society; the culture creates a proper "street dance field", and within that field the dominant adult rules and powers no longer prevail. With Bourdieu's reflections in mind, the young people's desire to live by their own rules and codes, style and system of values takes on a new significance. The importance of gaining freedom that many young dancers refer to is essentially a freedom from values and norms imposed by society and its "judgement system": it is a liberating act.

In this sense, we can associate street dance culture in Barcelona with subcultural expression. Originally understood by Hall and Jefferson and the Birmingham Centre for Contemporary Cultural Studies (CCCS) as "cohesive and collective cultural resistance to the dominant order" (Hall & Jefferson, 1991 [1976]), Feixa defines subculture not necessarily as explicit resistance but as a "cultural minority in a subaltern position with respect to a hegemonic or parental culture" (Feixa, 1998: p. 271[10]). Since it originated, hip-hop culture has been subversive, though always intertwining commercial and mainstream elements within its subculture. Although some authors consider that these concepts are mutually exclusive, others affirm that this is not necessarily so and that subcultural youth culture has always, at one time or another, been intertwined with mass media and commercialisation (Huq, 2006; Rose, 1994). In other words, expressions of alternative ways of living, lifestyles and even resistance do not necessarily contradict the desire to make money. Although street dance culture in Barcelona is far in terms of time and space from the original hip-hop culture and cannot be understood outside the context of the diversified evolution of hip hop and street dance – as well as the specific place and time of the research – street dance culture shares some of hip hop's original subcultural characteristics. Within broader adult society, it definitely occupies a subaltern position. Some dancers affirmed that they practice resistance by occupying public space and the street, or simply by preserving and transmitting elements of traditional culture. Others do this more unconsciously or as a "side-effect" of their participation. One particular sector of the freestyle dance community in Barcelona shows resistance by criticising the present-day trends of the commercialisation of street dance (mainly by dance academies and organisers of contests). According to this group, commercialisation involves a risk of disinformation and of losing a sense of community and meaning of the street.

---

10 Quote translated by the author.

The resistance against authority and adult society was also manifested by young street dancers giving special importance to leisure time and the right to "have fun": the right to spend free time in a supposedly "useless" way (according to adults' dominant perspectives). Within these parameters, street dance culture builds on "hedonism, fun, irrationality and emotionality", in contraposition to an adult world "based on values such as rationality, responsibility and obligation, (implying) (…) economic and symbolic power through participation in the labour market" (Hansen, 2017: p. 57;[11] see also Alegre i Canosa, 2007). This is also a form of resistance by "not playing by the rules" and establishing priorities in opposition to what adult society and the capitalist system demands from young people. Street dance and hip-hop groups may be considered "communities of resistance" (Rose, 1994: p. 85) that claim their rights to communal and individual pleasure and to *youthfulness* (Bayat, 2010).

It is specifically in *public space*, on the street, that freestyle youth culture appropriates meanings of space and constructs a sense of belonging. We can see how young dancers claim the right for public space to be treated as an authentically *public* place "where everyone has the right to enter or use it without having to pay money or meet any requirements, that is, they are places where the right of admission is not reserved" (Benach, 2008: p. 89[12]). Freestyle dancers claim that they, like many other youth cultures, "rediscover forgotten or marginal urban territories, (…) give new meanings to certain areas of the city, (and) humanize squares and streets" through their dancing practices and gatherings (Feixa, 1998: p. 96[13]). Public spaces are thus transformed into meeting points with both private and public features, turning the "street into their houses", where dancers "share fashions, music, norms and values" (Feixa, 1998: p. 63[14]). The street provides the street dance community with "ways of being together", in which surprise, the unexpected and other situations reign, allowing young people to put in parenthesis the self-control and the order that must necessarily be kept in other areas" (Urteaga, 2011: pp. 191–192[15]). By carrying out practices like gathering, dancing to music, and celebrating jams and competitions on the street, young people cross the border of what is expected by those who build normality in the public space (Benach, 2008: pp. 89–90). Through this

11 Quote translated by the author.
12 Quote translated by the author.
13 Quote translated by the author.
14 Quote translated by the author.
15 Quote translated by the author.

transgression, freestyle dancers strengthen the main feature of public space, a place where people of all kinds, with "different ways of seeing the world and living life come together naturally": they co-create, shape and reinforce the *contact zones* of people, lifestyles, philosophies and cultures (Benach, 2008; Pratt, 1992). The *centrality* of the public places used by the street dance community is key: it is no coincidence that their main hotspots (squares M. and U.) are located in the city centre of Barcelona. It is in this way that young people can claim their cultural centrality, their importance as actors to be seen and taken into account by society: activities are not carried out in the city's outskirts, but are brought to its very core, to the centre of power.

Special attention should also be paid to the lessons we can learn from street dance culture in terms of *knowledge transmission and learning processes*. Hip hop and street dance culture show how *oral and corporal* memory and knowledge transmission interconnect with the use of social media, the Internet and other technological applications and devices: information is passed on and shared, whatever the medium. We may even see in these types of intergenerational transmission a "present-day successor to premodern oral traditions", as Rose and other authors have suggested (Rose, 1994: p. 72). Cultural heritage is orally and corporally preserved, replicated and shown off on social media. The fascinating cultural key to street dance culture is that it gives importance to the cultural heritage, origins and history – "the foundation" – of dance, but, at the same time, it highly values evolution, innovation, and creativity. The development of a unique style is encouraged: if you are like everybody else, you are lost. This has its expression in the street dance *style* of clothing, accessories, and body decoration, which: simultaneously underscores group belonging (see also Feixa, 1998: p. 97) and the uniqueness of an outstanding individual performance or inimitable character. It is the combination of a sense of community and individuality that marks out street dance culture. If we look at the learning processes in street dance culture, we can see how important *informal learning* is for young people; we can define these processes as "forms of learning that are intentional or deliberate but are not institutionalised. It is consequently less organized and structured than either formal or non-formal education" (Glossary, UNESCO, 2011: p. 80). It is not only informal learning that is gratifying and fruitful for those involved in street dance culture, but also *non-intentional learning*. Generally, these processes do not occur, but happen while carrying out activities such as listening to the radio, reading the newspaper or interacting with other people. This is also true – and this is especially relevant to our case – when we engage in cultural or social activities, even if they are not organised for specific learning purposes, but rather just "to have a good time", pursue a common cause, relax, or engage with other people. In street dance, this type of learning is motivated, horizontal, collective and informal/non-intentional. Thus, street dance practices offer new socio-cultural tools for pedagogy.

In street dance culture we can observe the presence of global and interconnected "community-building networks" (Rose, 1994: p. 78). The street dance community is at the same time local (we have a local community in Barcelona, with particularities owing to space, climate, geography, time, policies, etc.) and global. Street dance culture creates both local and global senses of belonging, within which young people highlight the pleasures and benefits of their international connectedness: this enables encounters and exchange between different nationalities, cultures, lifestyles, dance styles, languages, etc. These intercultural relations aim to forge cultural tolerance and "an open mind", as young people claim, and to bring humanity ever closer. Here, after García Canclini (2004), we can observe the *hybridisation of cultures* converging into one "umbrella" culture: street dance culture. This supports the important finding that young dancers primarily identify as "citizens of the world". Other studies about youth cultures confirm this tendency towards youth's national-cultural identifications in cosmopolitan Barcelona: behind the identification as a "citizen of the world", there lies an *important questioning of the hegemonic system of states and nations, which is based on borders and exclusion. (…) In short, young people speak up against the world organized by strong socioeconomic and power inequalities.* (Hansen, 2017: p. 550[16]).

Conclusion

To conclude the above discussion, we can consider street dance a potential intercultural and learning tool that is able (in principle) to counteract discriminatory or racist practices. Certainly, as seen in the findings, street dance culture is not free of friction, conflict, or contradiction. Equality in gender relations and power is still a "work in progress", and we have yet to see how street dance culture will evolve in this respect. Still, it represents a powerful socio-cultural tool, as it empowers the self-esteem and self-awareness (body and mind) of young people and allows them to engage in fruitful, joyful and challenging learning processes. These kinds of education are horizontal (no teacher-pupil hierarchies and power relations), communitarian (knowledge is acquired and shared within a given community), self-motivated ("nobody, above all no adult, is telling me what to

16 Quote translated by the author.

do or learn") and informal/non-intentional. Street dance culture and its learning processes are full of trial and error. There is permission to "try, fail, try again and overcome", to express oneself through one's passion and personality, to "have fun" without further responsibilities and worries, and there is a right to *presentness* in a society that is always looking one step ahead. This makes street dance a liberating cultural experience for young people around the world, especially coupled with the power of a globally interconnected community and practices and meaningsdetermined collaboratively by the young people themselves rather than institutionally imposed. Thereby, young people are reclaiming *youthfulness* in the public space.

Policies should reinforce informal learning processes in all kinds of areas, including formal education. This indicates the necessity of more funding for programmes and initiatives that go in that direction. As the experience of street dance shows, non-formal and informal environments of cultural socialisation are rich sources of cultural literacy, innovation, creativity and inclusion. A good starting point to improve the experiences of youth involved in such activities would be to clearly acknowledge their practices as cultural heritage on the same level as "institutionalised" culture such as theatre, opera, or cinema. This would mean taking them into account in cultural discourse and when planning and funding the promotion of culture. We need to redefine what constitutes culture and cultural heritage, which arises from the "bottom" and the civil society itself. A first step would be official recognition (with real consequences) of activities like street dance, without the necessity of institutionalisation (integrating street dance into official curricula of public dance academies, for example); in fact, street dance should be recognised as a non-institutional, self-organised and "public" form of cultural expression that "is fuelled" from the use of public space. Public policies should enable, permit and fund the use of the street and other public space for street dance activities (and similar cultural expressions), because the restriction and punishment of the use of the street is one of the major restraints in this area. In this context, it is necessary for policymakers and other stakeholders to see culture as an investment rather than an expense, recognising the potential of culture and cultural heritage to drive local and regional development and/or regeneration.

This also involves a new understanding of what public space is and for whom it exists. Local and regional governments should enhance the use of public spaces as "cultural contact zones" for all kinds of actors and be aware that such areas are not necessarily free of conflict or "disturbance", which are natural elements of negotiating, community building and learning processes. Youth involved in street dance activities remind us that it is sometimes positive to be disturbed in our contact zones; it creates awareness and change.

Certain other issues are especially worthwhile exploring further and in more depth. The *gender issue* was addressed briefly above, but warrants more profound analysis in future, including a comparative study between countries: how are gender relations, roles and structures experienced in different countries, and in particular communities? What similarities and differences can we find? Also, *social class* was addressed only very briefly, although it is a constant transversal element in street dance and hip-hop culture (thanks to its origins), especially with respect to marginal neighbourhoods and dynamics that reinforce informal and communitarian practices on the street, in which young people find themselves having only own bodies and a boom box as resources. As Rose points out: "emerging from the intersection of lack and desire in the post-industrial city, hip hop manages the painful contradictions of social alienation and prophetic imagination" (Rose, 1994: p. 71). As commented in the discussion before, different *learning processes* represent an interesting analytical field within cultural heritage issues and informal cultural practices among European youth, especially when we think about how young people can apprehend socio-cultural content and practices in a constructive, self-motivated and critical way. Above all, we should ask ourselves which spaces allow young people empowerment, self-expression and "trial and error processes", and which learning methods (in formal, non-formal and informal contexts) can enhance the acquisition of particular skills that young people themselves consider useful for their lives.

References

Alegre i Canosa, M. À. (2007). *Geografies adolescents a secundària: posicionaments culturals i relacionals dels i les joves d'origen immigrant.* Retrieved from https://treballiaferssocials.gencat.cat/web/.content/JOVENTUT_documents/arxiu/publicacions/col_estudis/ESTUDIS20.pdf (Accessed on February 18, 2021).

Bayat, A. (2010). Life as Politics : How Ordinary People Change the Middle East. In *Life as Politics : How Ordinary People Change the Middle East.* https://doi.org/10.5117/9789053569115 (Accessed on February 18, 2021).

Benach, N. (2008). Espacios urbanos para transgredir las diferencias. In R. Tello, N. Benach, & M. Nash (Eds.), *Intersticios* (pp. 89–97). Barcelona: Edicions Bellaterra.

Bourdieu, P. (1990). *Sociología y cultura.* México Ciudad: Grijalbo.

Dávila León, O. (2004). Adolescencia y juventud: De las nociones a los abordajes. *Ultima Década, 12*(21), 83–104. https://doi.org/10.4067/s0718-2236200400 0200004 (Accessed on February 18, 2021).

Feixa, C. (1998). *De jóvenes, bandas y tribus*. Barcelona: Ariel.

García Canclini, N. (2004). *Diferentes, desiguales y desconectados: mapas de la interculturalidad*. Retrieved from http://cataleg.uab.cat/record=b1624 206~S1*cat (Accessed on February 18, 2021).

Hall, S., & Jefferson, T. (1991). *Resistance Through Rituals: Youth Subcultures in Post-war Britain*. London: Routledge.

Hansen, N. (2017). Abriéndose camino: mundos juveniles de descendientes de familias ecuatorianas, dominicanas y mixtas en Barcelona (Universitat Autònoma de Barcelona). Retrieved from https://www.tesisenred.net/handle/ 10803/456040#page=1 (Accessed on February 18, 2021).

Huq, R. (2006). *Beyond Subculture*. New York: Routledge.

Kitwana, B. (2002). *The Hip Hop Generation. Young Blacks and the Crisis in African-American Culture*. New York: Basic Civitas Books.

Pratt, M. L. (1992). *Imperial Eyes: Travel Writing and Transculturation*. New York: Routledge.

Reyes Sánchez, F. J. (2003). *Graffiti, breakdance y rap: el hip hop en España* (Universidad Complutense de Madrid). Retrieved from https://dialnet.uniri oja.es/servlet/tesis?codigo=196437&info=resumen&idioma=SPA (Accessed on February 18, 2021).

Rose, T. (1994). A Style nobody can deal with: Politics, Style and the Postindustrial City in Hip Hop. In A. Ross & T. Rose (Eds.), *Microphone Fiends. Youth Music & Youth Culture* (pp. 71–88). New York: Routledge.

Ross, A., & Rose, T. (1994). *Microphone Friends. Youth Music & Youth Culture*. New York: Routledge.

Sandín Lillo, J. (2015). *El Hip Hop como movimiento social y reivindicativo (Trabajo final de Grado)* (Universidad Politécnica de Valencia). Retrieved from http://hdl.handle.net/10251/71229 (Accessed on February 18, 2021).

UNESCO (2011). *International Standard Classification of Education*. Retrieved from http://uis.unesco.org/sites/default/files/documents/international-stand ard-classification-of-education-isced-2011-en.pdf (Accessed on February 18, 2021).

Urteaga, M. (2011). *La construcción juvenil de la realidad. Jóvenes mexicanos contemporáneos*. México Ciudad: Universidad Autónoma Metropolitana, Unidad Iztapalapa/División de Ciencias Sociales y Humanidades.

About the Authors

Monika Bagalová

Comenius University, Bratislava, Slovakia

monikabagalova@gmail.com

Monika Bagalová is a graduate of ethnology and non-European studies at Faculty of Arts, Saint Cyril and Methodius University in Trnava. Since 2014, she has been a doctoral student at the Department of Comparative Religion, Faculty of Arts, Comenius University in Bratislava. She works in visual anthropology, with a specific focus on visual culture and photography in South Asia.

Chandrani Chatterjee

Savitribai Phule Pune University, India

ranimelody@gmail.com

Chandrani Chatterjee teaches English Studies at the Department of English, Savitribai Phule Pune University (formerly University of Pune). She was the recipient of the Fulbright fellowship in 2012–2013 to the University of Massachusetts, Amherst, USA. She was selected as an associate in 2014 and invited as Visiting Faculty in 2018 to the Nida School of Translation Studies in Italy. She is part of the Global Shakespeare 2.0 project at the University of Göttingen, Germany (https://www.uni-goettingen.de/en/global+shakespeare+2.0/634041.html). Her research interests include Translation Studies, Comparative Literature, Genre Studies, History of the Book, Early Modern and Shakespeare Studies, Digital Humanities, among others.

Vanja Dergić

Institute of Social Sciences 'Ivo Pilar', Zagreb, Croatia

vanja.dergic@pilar.hr

Vanja Dergić, mag. soc., is Expert Associate in Science at the Institute of Social Sciences Ivo Pilar in Zagreb. She is currently studying for a joint doctorate in the Sociology of regional and local development at the University of Zadar. Her research interests include youth subcultures, social movements, political participation and qualitative research methods. She worked on the projects 'Post-socialist punk: Beyond the double irony of self-abasement' and MYPLACE (Memory, Youth, Political Legacy and Civic Engagement). She has also worked on an ethnographic study about the stigmatisation and political participation of young LGBTQI+ activists.

Swati Dyahadroy

Savitribai Phule Pune University, India

swatidroy@gmail.com

Dr. Swati Dyahadroy is an Assistant Professor at the Women's Studies Centre, Savitribai Phule Pune University. Her research interests include the politics of development and critical understanding of the politics of nation in the post-90s period with reference to the emergence of globalisation and right-wing politics. She has contributed to research projects such as 'Developing Research and Teaching Capacity in Women's/ Gender Studies: Integrating Equality and Quality'. She was also part of the project 'Inclusive Universities: Linking Equity, Diversity and Excellence for the 21st Century' (2013–17), supported under the US-Indo Initiative in collaboration with University of Massachusetts, Amherst.

Ece Esmer

Boğaziçi University, Istanbul, Turkey

ecsmer@gmail.com

Ece Esmer is a graduate student in the Sociology Department of Boğaziçi University in Istanbul. She received her B.A. degree in Sociology from Mimar Sinan Fine Arts University. She is interested in the sociology of religion, gender studies, political sociology, youth studies and qualitative research.

Awista Gardi

University of Applied Sciences (HAW) Hamburg, Germany

awista.gardi@gmx.net

Awista Gardi graduated in Social Work at the University of Applied Sciences Hamburg and worked as a researcher in the EU research project CHIEF from

2019 to 2021. She currently works at the Centre for Migration Research and Integration Practice at the HAW Hamburg. Her work focuses on migration research, cultural studies, postcolonial theory, intersectional discrimination and political education.

Neha Ghatpande

Savitribai Phule Pune University, India

nehaghatpande@gmail.com

Neha Ghatpande is a Project Officer for the CHIEF project. She is an academic and media professional who has contributed to various newspapers and magazines as a journalist. Her research interests are Gender and Development and Gender, Culture and Media. She is a visiting faculty member of the Department of Journalism at Savitribai Phule Pune University. As an academic researcher, she has contributed to various academic articles focusing on formal education settings and young people, cultural socialisation, and young people's voluntary cultural engagement.

Priya Gohad

Savitribai Phule Pune University, India

priks82@gmail.com

Dr. Priya Gohad works as a Research Associate on the CHIEF Project. She holds a PhD in Archaeology. Her research interests are heritage management, ancient Indian history, art, architecture, culture and archaeology. She is a member of the Society of South Asian Archaeologists and a Committee member of the Maharashtra State Bureau of Textbook Production & Curriculum Research. She has been awarded fellowships from the Indian Council of Historical Research (ICHR) and the Department of Science & Technology, Government of India (DST) for her research in Archaeology.

Nele Hansen

Universidad Pompeu Fabra UPF, Barcelona, Spain

nele.hansen@upf.edu

Nele Hansen holds a PhD in Social and Cultural Anthropology (Autonomous University of Barcelona, 2017). In her doctoral thesis she analysed the socio-cultural identities of young people from Ecuadorian and Dominican families in Barcelona, combining different ethnographic and participatory methods. She is a member of the research group jovis.com at the University Pompeu Fabra (Barcelona) and has participated as an anthropologist in numerous investigations run by the group, focusing on issues including youth, gender and ethnographic methodology. Currently, she is the Project Manager of the European project *TRANSGANG* and Researcher in the *RASSIF Project* studying minors migrating between Tangier and Barcelona.

Matej Karásek

Department of Comparative Religion, Faculty of Arts, Comenius University in Bratislava, Slovakia

matkokarasek@gmail.com

Matej Karásek is an anthropologist based at the Department of Comparative Religion in Comenius University in Bratislava, Slovakia. His research interests include new religious movements, religions in India and the anthropology of Balkan states. He has conducted numerous field studies in India, Slovakia and in the countries of the former Yugoslavia. He obtained his PhD degree in Ethnology with a dissertation about the transformation and re-construction of Bengal Vaishnavism tradition and its acculturation amongst Hare Krishna communities. He has taken part in the international research projects Memory, Youths, Political Legacy and Civic engagement (MYPLACE) and Cultural Heritage and Identities of Europe's Future (CHIEF).

Shailendra Kharat

Savitribai Phule Pune University, Pune, India

shailendrakharat@gmail.com

Shailendra Kharat teaches Politics at the Savitribai Phule Pune University. His doctoral research focuses on post-Mandal OBC politics in Indian states. He is a member of the editorial board of reputed Marathi research journal *Samaj Prabodhan Patrika*. He has published on the topics of Indian politics, caste politics, and state elections in India in Marathi and English, and was a recipient of the Indian Council of Social Science Research (ICSSR) National Doctoral Fellowship. His research interests include local politics, elections, caste identity politics, state politics in India and state-society interactions. Since the last few years, he has been doing intensive fieldwork in an urban locality to understand the political mobilisation happening there. He has presented the findings of this research in several seminars and conferences.

Anano Kipiani

CRRC Tbilisi, Georgia

a.kipiani@crrccenters.org

Anano Kipiani was born in Tbilisi, Georgia. Anano holds a Master's Degree in Economics from the International School of Economics at Tbilisi State University (ISET). She also holds a Bachelor's Degree in Informatics from Tbilisi State University. A combination of a more technical background and social science pushed her into policy analytics and qualitative and quantitative data analysis. Her main research interests include the health, religion, social, cultural and educational sectors. She is actively involved in public demonstrations for freedom of speech and expression.

Rašeljka Krnić

Institute of Social Sciences 'Ivo Pilar', Zagreb, Croatia

raseljka.krnic@pilar.hr

Rašeljka Krnić, PhD, is currently working at the Institute of Social Sciences Ivo Pilar in Zagreb, where she holds the position of Scientific Associate. She obtained a PhD in sociology at the Faculty of Humanities and Social Sciences, University of Zagreb and specialises in youth subcultures. Her main research interests are the sociology of subcultures and youth and music, and she has experience in qualitative data analysis.

Ľubomír Lehocký

Comenius University, Bratislava, Slovakia

skladack@gmail.com

Ľubomír Lehocký graduated from the Department of Comparative Religion at the Faculty of Arts of the University Comenius in Bratislava, and is currently pursuing a doctoral degree at the same faculty. He is the editor of the academic magazine Axis Mundi, published by the Slovak Society for the Study of Religions. He has published several studies, articles and reviews and has presented several lectures to the public at scientific conferences. His main research interest is manifestations of folk religiosity and culture in present-day Vietnam, where he has conducted a number of field research studies.

Elina Marmer

University of Applied Sciences (HAW) Hamburg, Germany

elina.marmer@haw-hamburg.de

Dr. Elina Marmer is a researcher and lecturer at the Department of Social Work and at the Centre for Migration Research and Integration Practice at the HAW Hamburg. From 2012 to 2013, she was Marie-Skłodowska-Curie-Fellow, in which role she conducted research on racism in formal education at the University of Hamburg, Department of Education. Elina is interested in migration research, racism and antiracism, critical pedagogy and intersectionality, and postcolonial and decolonial approaches. From 2018 to 2021, she coordinated the HAW Hamburg CHIEF research team.

Ayça Oral

Mimar Sinan Fine Arts University, Istanbul, Turkey

oralayca@gmail.com

Ayça Oral is currently a research coordinator in the Horizon 2020 CHIEF Project. She received her B.A. degree in the Foreign Language Education Department of Marmara University in Istanbul in 2005 and her M.A. degree in Comparative Literature, which was awarded a scholarship, from Istanbul Bilgi University in

2013. She was a private PhD student in the Department of Sociology in Koç University for a year and an exchange student in University of Vienna. She was later a PhD student in Sociology at Mimar Sinan Fine Arts University, Istanbul. Her research interests in sociology are in the areas of popular culture, fandom communities, youth studies and visual sociology.

Anton Popov

Aston University, Birmingham, UK

a.popov@aston.ac.uk

Anton Popov is a Senior Lecturer in Sociology in the School of Languages and Social Sciences at Aston University. He received his PhD from Birmingham University for his study of the cultural production of identity among transnational migrants in Russia. He has also conducted ethnographic research in post-socialist societies and the UK on nativist and ethno-cultural revivalist movements, youth engagement with cultural heritage and collective memories, and migrant and ethnic minority communities. As a PI and project co-ordinator, Dr. Popov has been leading the Horizon 2020 project 'Cultural Heritage and Identities of Europe's Future' (CHIEF), which investigates young people's cultural participation and identities within formal, non-formal and informal educational environments across Europe and beyond.

Yıldırım Şentürk

Mimar Sinan Fine Arts University, Istanbul, Turkey

yildirimsenturk@gmail.com

Yıldırım Şentürk is Professor in the Sociology Department of Mimar Sinan Fine Arts University in Istanbul. He received his M.A. degree in Sociology from the University of Chicago and his PhD degree in Sociology from the University of Illinois at Urbana-Champaign (UIUC) respectively. He is interested in urban and social space studies, neoliberalism, transnational studies, labour, youth studies, and qualitative research.

Louis Henri Seukwa

University of Applied Sciences (HAW) Hamburg, Germany

louishenri.seukwa@haw-hamburg.de

Louis Henri Seukwa, PhD, is Professor of Education at the Department of Social Work and Head of the Centre for Migration Research and Integration Practice at the Hamburg University of Applied Sciences. His main fields of study and interest are educational migration research, postcolonial theories, resilience and educational research under refugee and asylum conditions, intercultural educational research, and educational processes in the non-formal and informal sectors.

Rati Shubladze

Georgian Institute of Public Affairs (GIPA), Tbilisi, Georgia

rati@outlook.com

Rati Shubladze is a professor and head of the Sociology Program at GIPA. He was awarded a PhD in Sociology from the Tbilisi State University in summer 2021. He teaches theoretical and practical research classes in several Georgian universities and participates in independent research projects as a research consultant. His research interests include youth studies, elections, post-Soviet transformation and Europeanisation. He has published academic and peer reviewed publications regarding electoral behaviour, youth culture and political transformation. He previously worked as a policy analyst at CRRC-Georgia. Within this capacity, he was a team member of the EU-funded international project 'Cultural Heritage and Identities of Europe's Future' (CHIEF).

Ebru Soytemel

Aston University, Birmingham, UK

e.soytemel@aston.ac.uk

Ebru Soytemel is a Lecturer in Sociology at the Sociology and Policy Department at Aston University. She received her PhD from the University of Manchester for her study of examining the ways in which urban policies, gentrification and socio-economic policies impact class composition, housing, and the belonging patterns of different social classes in Istanbul, Turkey. Her post-doctoral research at the Oxford Programme for the Future of Cities, School of Anthropology & Museum Ethnography at the University of Oxford examined the impact of big urban transformation projects on the property rights of different groups. Ebru's research interests are social and economic inequality, the relationship between social class and social-symbolic borders, gentrification and social-spatial exclusion, cultural sociology, cultural participation, and the sociology of youth and education.

Eleni Stamou

Aston University, Birmingham, UK

e.stamou@aston.ac.uk

Eleni Stamou is Research Fellow on the Cultural Heritage and Identities of Europe's Future (CHIEF) Project at Aston University. She has carried out research into youth identities and educational pathways, inclusion and the prevention of social exclusion, and education policy in practice. She has previously held research posts at the UCL Institute of Education and at the University of Oxford, Department of Education. She has also worked as policy advisor in the public and charity sectors. She holds an MA and a PhD in the Sociology of Education.

Cornelia Sylla

Universität Rostock, Germany

cornelia.sylla@haw-hamburg.de

Dr. Cornelia Sylla is a postdoctoral researcher in the Faculty of Philosophy at the University of Rostock, Germany. She graduated from the University of Hamburg with a degree in educational sciences. After working in different educational organisations – adventure camps, preschool, environmental education – she returned to the academic field with a doctoral scholarship from the University of Hamburg to study the relationship between social work and the school system and mechanisms of inclusion and exclusion. Her main research interests are marginalisation and intersectionality, especially concerning young people, as well as interdisciplinary co-operation and networking in the field of education.

Anagha Tambe

Savitribai Phule Pune University, India

anaghatambe@gmail.com

Dr. Anagha Tambe is Director and Assistant Professor at KSP Women's Studies Centre, Savitribai Phule Pune University. Her areas of research include gender, sexuality and caste question, disciplinary histories of Women's Studies in India, and diversity and democracy in higher education. She has published on ritual 'prostitution' and debates on sex work in post-colonial India. She was awarded the Fulbright Nehru Academic and Professional Excellence Fellowship for 2018–2019. Anagha has edited, translated and written several teaching and learning resources in women's studies, especially in Indian languages. She has also been the Office-bearer of the Indian Association for Women's Studies since 2014.

Ayşe Berna Uçarol

Mimar Sinan Fine Arts University, Istanbul, Turkey

bernaucarol@gmail.com

Ayşe Berna Uçarol is a PhD candidate in the Sociology at Mimar Sinan Fine Arts University (Istanbul, Turkey). She received her B.A. degree in Sociology from the University of Mimar Sinan Fine Arts and her M.A. degree in International Relations from the University of Istanbul. Her research interests include the labour market, labour rights, neo-liberalism, youth studies and qualitative research methods. She works as a researcher in sociological projects and as a lecturer in private universities in Istanbul.

Dino Vukušić

Institute of Social Sciences Ivo Pilar, Croatia

dino.vukusic@pilar.hr

Dino Vukušić, mag. soc., is an assistant at the Ivo Pilar Institute of Social Sciences in Zagreb and an external associate at the Faculty of Kinesiology, University of Zagreb. He is currently attending a PhD programme at the Faculty of Humanities and Social Sciences, University of Zagreb. His research spheres of interest are the sociology of subculture, youth sociology, the sociology of sports and urban sociology. He has published several papers.

Interkulturelle Pädagogik und postkoloniale Theorie

Herausgegeben von / Edited by Heike Niedrig und / and Louis Henri Seukwa

Band 1 Patricia Baquero Torres: Kultur und Geschlecht in der Interkulturellen Pädagogik. Eine postkoloniale Re-Lektüre. 2009.

Band 2 Heike Niedrig / Christian Ydesen (eds.): Writing Postcolonial Histories of Intercultural Education. 2011.

Band 3 Frauke Meyer: Kompetenzzuschreibungen und Positionierungsprozesse. Eine postkoloniale Dekonstruktion im Kontext von Migration und Arbeitsmarkt. 2012.

Band 4 Susanne Spieker: Die Entstehung des modernen Erziehungsdenkens aus der europäischen Expansion. 2015.

Band 5 Astride Velho: Alltagsrassismus erfahren. Prozesse der Subjektbildung – Potenziale der Transformation. 2016.

Band 6 Mariam Arouna: Positionierungen im Fluchtkontext. Zur Handlungsfähigkeit geflüchteter Jugendlicher vor dem Hintergrund gesellschaftlicher Flüchtlingskonstruktionen. 2018.

Band 7 Mona Massumi: Migration im Schulalter. Systemische Effekte der deutschen Schule und Bewältigungsprozesse migrierter Jugendlicher. 2019.

Band 8 Louis Henri Seukwa / Uta Wagner (Hrsg.): Pädagogik angesichts von Vulnerabilität und Exklusion. Bummeln durch die Landschaft der Randständigkeit. 2021.

Band 9 Sofie Olbers: Theater im Fluchtkontext. Für ein widerspruchssensibles Re-Präsentieren in der Kulturellen Bildung. 2022.

Band 10 Louis Henri Seukwa / Elina Marmer / Cornelia Sylla (eds.): The Challenge of Cultural Heritage and Identity for Inclusive and Open Societies. Young People's Perspectives from European and Asian Countries. 2022.

www.peterlang.com

www.ingramcontent.com/pod-product-compliance
Lightning Source LLC
LaVergne TN
LVHW092009050326
832904LV00002B/28